The Italian Refuge

The Italian Refuge

Rescue of Jews During the Holocaust

Edited by Ivo Herzer

Coedited by Klaus Voigt and
James Burgwyn

The Catholic University
of America Press
Washington, D.C.

This volume is based on papers presented at the
National Italian American Foundation Conference
at Boston University, November 6 and 7, 1986,
under the sponsorship of the National Italian
American Foundation, Dr. Maria Lombardo,
Conference Coordinator. The opinions expressed
herein do not necessarily represent the views of the
National Italian American Foundation nor of its
officers and staff.

Copyright © 1989 Ivo Herzer
All rights reserved
Printed in the United States of America

The paper used in this publication meets the minimum
requirements of American National Standards for
Information Science—Permanence of Paper for Printed
Library Materials, ANSI Z39.48-1984.
∞

LIBRARY OF CONGRESS CATALOGING-IN-PUBLICATION DATA
The Italian refuge : rescue of Jews during the Holocaust /
    edited by Ivo Herzer ; coedited by Klaus Voigt and James
    Burgwyn.
        p. cm.
    "Papers presented at the National Italian American
Foundation Conference at Boston University, November 6
and 7, 1986"—T.p. verso.
    Includes bibliographies and index.
    1. Jews—Italy—History—20th century—
Congresses.   2. Holocaust, Jewish (1939–1945)—Italy—
Congresses.   3. World War, 1939–1945—Jews—Rescue—
Italy—Congresses.   4. Refugees, Jewish—Italy—
History—20th century—Congresses.   5. Italy—Ethnic
relations—Congresses.   I. Herzer, Ivo, 1925–   .
II. Voigt, Klaus.   III. Burgwyn, James.   IV. National
Italian American Foundation Conference (1986 : Boston
University)
DS135.I8I89   1989
945'.004924—dc20   89-7324
ISBN 0-8132-0706-1 (alk. paper)
ISBN 0-8132-0712-6 (pa.)

To the Italian men and women who assisted
and rescued persecuted Jews, 1938–1945

Contents

Foreword

As chairman and president of the National Italian American Foundation and as Italian Americans it is with deep emotion and a feeling of gratitude that we participate in the publishing of these very important papers that came out of our 1986 conference in Boston.

Inspired by the story of Ivo Herzer and following his initiative the foundation decided to conduct this conference aimed at assessing and stressing this virtually ignored chapter in the tragedy of the Holocaust: the story of help given by Italians to the Jewish community in Italy to save many of its members from annihilation or to relieve their suffering.

It was a great honor working on the conference with the American Jewish Committee, Boston University, and the National Endowment for the Humanities in making a most relevant contribution to historic truth; with this book we will also put that truth at the service of the future of an ever more fruitful relationship between Italians and Jews especially in this country. A relationship with diversities should increasingly be bridged by a broader understanding of our human and cultural affinities.

The Italians could not believe that the word "Jew" denoted something different from themselves, and they proved it over and over again. The spontaneous rescue and assistance given by the Italian population to many Jews in the darkest hours of World War II provide a clear record of the true feelings and the moral standards of the Italian people. This record shows that, while repudiating a regime of oppression, Italians have often had the courage to side with the victims of insane ideologies that are alien to our nature and tradition. It is therefore a record of human sympathy and civilization of which we are especially proud.

To those who are even slightly familiar with our history this behavior should come as no surprise. Jewish communities have inhabited Italian cities for twenty centuries. Their relations with the rest of the population could be cited as a model of peaceful, civilized co-existence; in the modern age, Italian Jews melted into Italian society, becoming—in their own feelings as well as in fact— virtually indistinguishable from their fellow Italians. "The Jewish problem," whatever meaning may be attributed to this phrase, has never existed in Italy. Discriminatory policies against the Jewish population were enforced in the last years of the Fascist regime. These policies antagonized the Italian people even more than did any of the other oppressive policies of that regime.

We hope this book—while serving the truth—will help open the way to deeper understanding and esteem between Jewish and Italian people, between two old, noble traditions.

Jeno F. Paulucci, Chairman
Frank D. Stella, President
NATIONAL ITALIAN AMERICAN FOUNDATION

Acknowledgments

The editors wish to express their deep gratitude to the National Italian American Foundation for making publication of this book possible and to the Paulucci Foundation, the National Endowment for the Humanities, Boston University, and the American Jewish Committee's Institute for American Pluralism for their generous support. Special thanks are due to the National Italian American Foundation team: Dr. Alfred Rotondaro, Executive Director, who was a steadfast supporter of the conference; Dr. Maria Lombardo, Education Director, who secured the funding and the conference site at Boston University and dealt efficiently with the myriad administrative and financial details inevitable for an international conference; Larry Vershel, Director of Publications, who provided his expertise in public relations; Geraldine Jones-Roche, whose intelligent and expert work on the word processor smoothed immeasurably the complex job of producing the final copy.

The editors are especially indebted to Susan Zuccotti, Fausta Walsby, and Ruth Feldman, who gave freely and generously of their time to translate from the Italian. Thanks are also due to Joe Tropea and Tom Cardone for their patient and judicious advice, and to Donna Carter, who as copyeditor helped significantly in bringing consistency and order to the book.

On a personal note, the editor gratefully recognizes the full support his wife, Dorothy, and his sons, David and Daniel, always gave him during the long months of labor, frustration, and finally joy, inherent in an undertaking of this kind.

Ivo Herzer

Introduction

The first international conference of historians on the theme *Italians and Jews: Rescue and Aid During the Holocaust* was held at Boston University under the sponsorship of the National Italian American Foundation on November 6 and 7, 1986. This book includes papers presented by the participants, as well as invited papers that the editors believe will help round out the topical coverage offered in this volume. The conference marked the first time ever that the Italian role in rescuing and protecting Italian and foreign Jews had been the central theme of a meeting of historians.

The conference had two main objectives: to establish the first benchmark of the historiography of Italian rescue through the presentation of research results and discussion, and to inform the nonspecialist public of some of the findings that have remained virtually unknown for over forty years since World War II ended.

The question of rescue of Jews by non-Jews, who often risked their and their own families' lives, is receiving scholarly attention today in projects such as the one of the "altruistic personality" by Samuel Oliner. In the Italian case we also have to deal with and recognize the uniquely Italian phenomenon of "institutional" rescue of Jews since the Italian army and the ministry of foreign affairs fought on the diplomatic front against the Nazi demands for the extradition of Jewish refugees under Italian control. The facts in this case raise important questions for students of repressive political systems about the power of national solidarity in the face of state terror and legalized persecution.

The idea to organize a conference grew out of my personal feelings as one who survived thanks to the Italian army in occupied Croatia, 1941 to 1943. In a sense, the conference was born in April 1941, when Germany and Italy invaded and dismembered Yugoslavia. I lived with my parents in Zagreb, the capital of Croatia, which became a puppet state under the rule of the fanatical *Ustaša*.

We were fortunate to have time to escape the deportations of Jews to *Ustaša* death camps; we tried to reach the Italian-occupied zone along the Yugoslav Adriatic coast.

Our train was blocked from continuing the journey at one point and we were stranded in *Ustaša* territory, where the Italian Second Army maintained garrisons. We asked for help from the first Italian soldiers we saw, and their sergeant took it upon himself to escort us and several other fleeing Jews to the railroad station. We then boarded an Italian military train with the sergeant at our side; he managed to bring us across the demarcation line into the Italian zone. Ours was quite a typical story of how the lower ranks of the Italian army spontaneously saved Jews during the *Ustaša* terror of the summer of 1941. Eventually, with full approval of the higher Italian military authorities, about 5,000 Croatian Jews found a haven in the Italian zone. The Italian army, in turn, acted in cooperation with the Italian Ministry of Foreign Affairs, whose policy of protecting Jewish refugees covered all the Italian-occupied territories.

We maintained excellent relations with the Italian military, who showed great sensitivity in trying to ease our fears. In November 1942, under relentless pressure by the Germans to extradite the Jewish refugees in Italian-occupied Croatia to the Germans, the Italians interned all the refugees in occupied Croatia in one relatively large camp and several forced-residence locations. We had considerable autonomy inside the camp, including a synagogue and a secondary school. In July 1943 the army transferred all Jewish refugees to a camp on the island of Rab (Arbe). On September 8, 1943, Italy surrendered to the Allies and the Second Army command planned to provide for our safety by transferring us to Italy, but events leading to the armistice pre-empted any effective action. Nevertheless, most of the former inmates were able to join Tito's partisan forces; a small group of us managed to make our way to Allied-occupied southern Italy.

I came to the United States in 1948 and gradually became aware that the historical facts about the positive role the Italians played in saving Jewish lives remained virtually unknown, even to American Holocaust historians. In 1984 the United States Holocaust

Memorial Council sponsored an international conference, *Faith in Humankind: Rescuers of Jews During the Holocaust,* held at the State Department on September 17–19. Righteous Gentiles from all the countries overrun by the Nazis were invited to participate, as were many of the rescued Jews, but Italy was not initially considered in the program. Rabbi Seymour Siegel, Director of the Holocaust Memorial Commission, and Sister Carol Rittner, R.S.M., conference coordinator, invited me to present the "case" for Italy and, as a result, Italy was included in the program.

The interest generated at the conference by the short discussion of the Italian rescue story clearly indicated that a major public forum, wholly devoted to the Italian rescue, was called for. Despite the persuasive arguments in favor of a meeting of survivors recounting their experiences, I believed that it was first necessary for the facts to be established by historians who have researched not only the rescue, but also the Holocaust tragedy in Italy during the period of the Italian Social Republic (created by Germany after sovereign Italy had surrendered to the Allies). I presented the idea for an international conference to Dr. Alfred Rotondaro, Executive Director of the National Italian American Foundation, who accepted it enthusiastically and provided the necessary support for the conference to come into being.

Why has the role of the Italians in saving and protecting Italian and foreign Jews been left in a dark corner of Holocaust historiography for so long? I can only suggest some plausible reasons, at least for the case of American historians.

First, Fascist Italy was the principal ally of Nazi Germany, and in the early postwar period the sharp distinction between Fascism and Nazism in regard to Jews was better known to the Jews who were the beneficiaries of the Italian rescue activities than to historians. It is now established, based on thorough research, that the Italian army and foreign ministry protected foreign Jews everywhere in Italian-occupied territories. Even though those two institutions were not, strictly speaking, part of the core structure of the Fascist state, it was nevertheless unacceptable during the first decades of the postwar period to point out their positive role in saving Jewish lives.

Second, compared to the persecutions and ultimate murder of

six million Jews—in which the Nazis received often zealous and always indispensable assistance from virtually all the countries under their control—rescue is a small topic. The rescue of Danish Jews by the Danish Resistance and the valiant efforts of Raoul Wallenberg are practically the only two rescue stories that have reached the wider public in the United States. Few were rescued and few were the rescuers.

The above-named reasons might have lost their relevancy after two or three decades, especially in the United States, where the study of the Holocaust developed into a rich field of inquiry with numerous researchers affiliated with universities and other institutions. Unfortunately, there are inter-related obstacles that have stood in the way, directly or indirectly, of giving the Italians due recognition for the positive role they played during the Holocaust.

The first impediment is of a general nature: the study of modern Italian history in the United States has traditionally received low emphasis in comparison with the study of modern English, French, or German history. The same is true, of course, for the countries of southeastern Europe.

The second impediment has to do with the fact that Jewish historiography in the United States, and consequently also Holocaust historiography, emphasizes countries with large prewar Jewish populations that were the centers of Jewish life and culture in Europe. Those were the countries where the tragedy struck most savagely: Germany, Austria, Poland, Hungary, Rumania, the Baltic countries, and the Soviet Union. The family roots of the great majority of American Holocaust historians, as well as their linguistic skills, the *sine qua non* of serious research, have equipped them superbly for the task of historical reconstruction of the great Jewish tragedy. However, the study of Italy's role in the Holocaust requires a combination of linguistic skills that few researchers possess—Italian, German, French, Serbo-Croatian, and Greek—if the actions of the Italian army of occupation are to be analyzed from archival material. It is worthwhile to point out that the linguistic barriers are also operative in another sense: relevant studies in languages other than English remain untranslated, and thus the Anglo-American historians are deprived of much information that is sometimes of crucial importance to a given topic. A good example is the seminal study of Italian Jews under Fascism by the eminent Italian historian Renzo De Felice, first published in 1961.

The authors whose articles appear in this volume were not constrained in terms of how they might treat the topic that falls under their general expertise. Among the topics there are some that are discussed by several authors more or less extensively and from different perspectives.

Several points have to be kept in mind when assessing and analyzing the Italian reactions and attitudes toward the Jews during the period from 1922, when Mussolini came to power, until 1945, when World War II ended. First of all, racism and mass anti-Semitism have been virtually non-existent in modern Italy since the Unification in 1870. *Risorgimento*, the movement for Italian independence (1815–1870) brought complete emancipation to the minuscule Italian Jewish community, numbering less than 50,000 on the eve of World War II. Italian Jews were completely integrated into Italian society and many were on the road to complete assimilation.

Second, Italian Fascism was not anti-Semitic in its goals. In fact, from the time it was founded, Italian Jews joined the Fascist party in relative numbers that were no different from those of the non-Jewish population.

Third, Mussolini's abrupt reversal in his policy toward Jews when he introduced anti-Jewish legislation in 1938 shocked the Italian Jewish community precisely because it was viewed as a betrayal by the nation to which the Jews belonged without any reservations—a situation alien to most European Jews who lived in east Europe. Even though the 1938 legislation did not present any dangers to the physical existence of the Italian Jews, and even though the Italian nation as a whole showed sympathy and solidarity with the Jews, nevertheless the Italian Jews have not completely recovered from the pain of those years.

It is important to note in this connection that 1988 was the half-century mark since the passage of anti-Jewish legislation in Italy. It is a date that the Italian people and the government commemorated with indignation, united in their resolve to defend human rights and democracy.

Fourth, there were two Fascist regimes in Italy. During the first period (1922–1943), Italy was a sovereign country. After Mussolini's fall from power on July 25, 1943, and the Italian armistice on September 8, 1943, which ended Italian participation in the war on Germany's side, Hitler resurrected a puppet Fascist regime, the Italian Social Republic (RSI), headed by Mussolini in Salò in northern Italy. It was during that period (1943–1945) that the Nazis carried out roundups and deportations of Jews from Italy, often with the cooperation of the Fascist authorities.

The papers are grouped under five main thematic headings: I. Jews in the Italian Society from Monarchy to Fascism; II. The Period of the Holocaust: Deportation, Rescue, Resistance; III. Jewish Refugees in Italy; IV. Jewish Refugees Under Italian Occupation; V. The Vatican and the Jews in Italy. A substantial, annotated bibliography organized under topical headings is also included.

Part I presents the fundamental historical framework, which serves as the background for the understanding of specific issues and events discussed in the rest of the book. The two essential notions (already mentioned above) that should be kept in mind are the virtual non-existence of anti-Semitism in Italy after the Unification in 1870 and the sharp differences between Fascism and Nazism in their views of the "Jewish question." The factors that have made the situation of Italian Jews one of *sui generis* are analyzed by Andrew Canepa in a careful overview of the various hypotheses advanced to explain the complete integration of Italian Jews into Italian society, which was possible only because of the way in which Italian masses and leading strata viewed the role of Jews in modern Italy.

The relations and policies of the Fascist state with respect to Jews (in effect Mussolini's attitudes toward Jews) is a subject replete with ambiguities and political expediency. Meir Michaelis presents his thoroughly documented analysis to provide authoritative answers to such questions as: was Mussolini pressured by Hitler to introduce racial legislation in 1938; did Fascism contain the seeds of racism, despite the fact that in the beginning Fascism was not anti-Semitic; in what terms did the Fascist ideologues attempt to create an Italian racist theory; how did the foreign observers of Italy interpret Mussolini's overt pronouncements on the "Jewish question." Some of the questions are still debated today.

Alberto Cavaglion discusses the powerful influence of Benedetto Croce on the political orientation of various Italian Jews who were notable in resisting persecution of the Jews and active in anti-Fascist resistance.

Part II deals with the impact of the Holocaust on the Jews in Italy under German occupation during the period of the puppet Fascist Italian Social Republic. Before delving into the particulars of the persecutions and deportations of Jews from Italian soil, we are given an overall, comparative view of the Holocaust by Paul Bookbinder—not only the contrasts with the rest of Nazi-occupied Europe but also the attitudes and reactions of western democracies when it came to allowing refugees to immigrate.

Liliana Picciotto Fargion, a leading scholar on the Holocaust in Italy, has been conducting a research project to document in detail who was deported, under what circumstances, and how the Fascist state bureaucracy during the Salò regime carried out the orders emanating from the laws passed by the Italian Social Republic. Her article is the most recent and complete summary of her findings, one of which is that the Fascists attempted to retain independence in their anti-Jewish legislation to demonstrate to the Italian people that they were able to act by themselves.

Jewish losses in Italy amount to approximately fifteen percent of the Italian Jewish population, which is among the top survival rates of Jews in German-occupied countries. In the opinion of some historians the central question of the Holocaust tragedy in Italy is why more were not saved, given the positive attitude toward Jews by all strata of the population, including lower and sometimes even high-ranking officials. Attempts to analyze survival rates across Europe in terms of some system of constant criteria have generally had to bow to special conditions in each country, but it is obviously true that the attitude of the population toward Jews was a major factor.

In the next two parts the focus shifts to the history of refugees and immigrants who sought a haven from the Nazi persecution. The problem should be seen in the global perspective, since, long before the "Final Solution" sealed the fate of European Jewry, "rescue" implied opening the national gates to Jews who wanted to emigrate from Germany and later, of course, from the countries that gradually fell under Nazi domination. That Italy under Mussolini, whose ties with Hitler grew progressively closer, would be a haven for refugees was not known or publicized at the time, nor had the topic been studied systematically and thoroughly until Klaus Voigt undertook an exhaustive research project, the summary findings of which are presented in Part III. Voigt deals with the history of refugees in peninsular Italy only, while the story of refugees in Italian-occupied and annexed territories is the subject of Part IV. The methodological problem of researching the fate of the refugees in Italy is to understand how the laws, decrees, and police orders were *in fact* applied, because the civil servants who were in direct contact with specific groups of refugees generally showed great compassion and flexibility in "bending" the rules.

Nowhere was the Italian willingness to interpret the rules in a humane way more evident than in the Ferramonti camp for "civilian internees," but actually meant for Jewish refugees. It was a concentration camp, true enough, but there was no similarity between it and the infamous Nazi camps. The internees were granted considerable autonomy, a secondary school, three synagogues, and cultural activities, and Jewish aid organizations were allowed to send food and other necessities to the internees. Carlo Spartaco Capogreco, to whom we owe the most detailed reconstruction of life in the Ferramonti camp community, points out in his article that the population of the surrounding countryside of Calabria showed strong solidarity with the imprisoned refugees despite the Fascist anti-Jewish propaganda. From the descriptions of the Ferramonti camp, which was under the jurisdiction of the Ministry of the Interior, I gather that conditions were almost identical to those in the two camps where I was interned (Kraljevica [Porto Re] and Rab [Arbe]) even though the competent authorities in those camps were the Italian Second Army and the Ministry of Foreign Affairs.

The third article in Part III is Josef Ithai's memoir of the rescue of about forty Jewish children, most of whose parents had been murdered by the Nazis. The children were in Yugoslavia, on their way to Palestine, when the Axis invasion of Yugoslavia and the subsequent establishment of the Croatian *Ustaša* state forced them to seek safety in the Italian-occupied zone of Slovenia. Their story is a bridge between Parts III and IV, since the children were first rescued by the Italian army and later transferred to Nonantola near Modena. The local population and the priests were successful in hiding all of them after the German occupation in 1943, and the group eventually found safety in Switzerland.

The rescue of Jewish refugees who fled to the territories occupied by the Italian army, which is the subject of Part IV, remained virtually unknown to the American Holocaust historians until the mid-nineteen-seventies. The only reports on this topic were a short article (Roberto Ducci, 1944) and a publication by Poliakov and Sabille of 1946, outlining the events in Italian-occupied Croatia, France, and Greece, largely based on German documents. In 1976 Daniel Carpi published his research on the diplomatic struggle between Italy and Germany for the lives of Jewish refugees in the Italian zone of Croatia, using Italian archival sources for the first time.

We are dealing here with a unique phenomenon in Holocaust annals. Two leading government institutions, the army and the foreign ministry, of Germany's principal ally protected foreign Jews from being seized by the Nazis or their collaborators, as early as the summer of 1941. Menachem Shelah writes about the rescue of Croatian Jews and John Bierman describes how the Italians managed to protect thousands of Jewish refugees in the Italian zone in the south of France until the armistice of September 8, 1943. Why did the Italians do it? Was it just to assert their independence from the Germans, or was it a policy calculated to free Italy from any association with Nazi barbarism? Those historians who have studied this subject agree that the above factors were most probably influential in determining the Italian policy in occupied territories. It should also be noted that as long as Fascist Italy was sovereign, no Italian Jew was handed over to the Germans and the same was true for foreign Jews in Italy, even though it looked as if on a few occasions they were to be expelled to Germany. In the case of occupied territories, historians agree that, first and foremost, the Italians acted for humanitarian reasons.

In Part V, two scholars deal with one of the most controversial questions of the Holocaust: Did Pope Pius XII, in his role as head of the Catholic Church, fail as a moral teacher by maintaining silence in the face of Nazi barbarism? Father Robert Graham offers his exposition on the aid given to Jews in Italy by the Catholic community and the cooperation between Jewish aid organizations and the high Church authorities. Susan Zuccotti analyzes the possible motives for the pope's failure to warn Roman Jews of a probable roundup and concludes that it must be seen as part of the general silence of the Vatican during the Holocaust tragedy. At the same time, it is recognized that the pope approved of the rescue actions of Jews, and until records, still under wraps, become available to future historians the question remains open.

The sponsors of the conference, as well as the participants, see it as an important first step that will lead to further research and widen our knowledge of what happened during those years of terror when few dared to show a human face to the persecuted Jews.

I. Jews in Italian Society
from Monarchy to Fascism

Andrew Canepa

1. Christian-Jewish Relations in Italy from Unification to Fascism

Italian Jewry in the *Postrisorgimento* (Acceptance, Integration, Assimilation)[1]

In the spring of 1932, Mussolini flatly declared to a German-Jewish interviewer: "Anti-Semitism does not exist in Italy."[2] Though the categorical quality of this statement was clearly belied by the Fascist racial laws of just a few years later, it is widely agreed that anti-Semitism has played a far less significant role in the history of Italy than in that of other European countries. It is perhaps superfluous to present evidence in support of a view that is generally taken for granted. I will limit myself to pointing out the nearly total absence in modern Italy of mass violence directed against Jews, as well as the relative unimportance of anti-Semitism in the ideology of the *Associazione Nazionalista Italiana*, which served to distinguish it from other European movements of the right at the turn of the century. Indeed, students of the Fascist period now argue that the racial laws of 1938 marked the first major break between the Italian people and the Duce, ended the so-called "years of consensus," and sounded the death knell of the regime.

Undeniably, emancipation in Italy, extended to the whole of the peninsula in 1870, had been a unique success, in both its positive and its negative aspects: in the security, opportunities, and acceptance accorded Italian Jews, and in the progressive erosion of

1. For overviews of the Italian Jewish community from unification to Fascism, a period referred to as the *Postrisorgimento* or "Liberal Italy," see Cecil Roth, *The History of the Jews of Italy* (Philadelphia, 1946), Ch. X; Attilio Milano, *Storia degli ebrei in Italia* (Turin, 1963), pp. 370–391; Roberto Finzi, "Gli ebrei nella società italiana dall'Unità al fascismo," *Il Ponte*, XXXIV (1978), pp. 1372–1411; Bruno Di Porto, "Dopo il Risorgimento al varco del '900. Gli ebrei e l'ebraismo in Italia," *Rassegna mensile di Israel*, Vol. XLVII, Nos. 7–12 (July/December 1981), pp. 19–41; Arnaldo Momigliano, "The Jews of Italy," *New York Review of Books*, October 24, 1985, pp. 22–26.
2. Emil Ludwig, *Talks with Mussolini* (London, 1932), p. 74.

their Jewish identity. The genuineness of Jewish equality in Italy has been attested to by such informed and not uncritical sources as Cecil Roth, Max Nordau, Chaim Weizmann, and the late Italian Zionist leader Dante Lattes. Jews were fully integrated into Italian society and politics and had access to careers in diplomacy and the military, careers generally closed to them elsewhere in the West. In this light, it is no mere coincidence that both the first Jewish minister of war and the first Jewish prime minister in Europe were Italians: Giuseppe Ottolenghi (1902–03) and Luigi Luzzatti (1910–11). Nor was it simply fortuitous that in Liberal Italy Isacco Artom, personal secretary of Cavour, and later Giacomo Malvano, permanent secretary general at the Foreign Office for over thirty years (1876–1907)—both of them Piedmontese Jews—should have exercised considerable influence over the direction of the foreign policy of the kingdom.

The Jews of Italy, for their part, were more than grateful to the new nation for the equality and opportunities accorded them, and they set about shedding the last vestiges of what a liberal emancipationist had disparagingly called "that particularism which makes them strangers to the rest of society."[3] They succeeded to such an extent that, by the 1890s, informed foreign observers could comment that the Italian community was the most assimilated among European Jewries.[4] Indeed, the history of the Jews in the *Postrisorgimento* is essentially the story of their progressive ethnic and cultural, if not religious, self-extinction. At the advent of Fascism, there were certainly many Italian Jews who could wholeheartedly repeat the sentiments expressed by the noted Islamicist Giorgio Levi Della Vida: "*Appartengo ad un popolo che non mi appartiene.*" ("I belong to a people that I cannot call my own.")[5] The impact of assimilation on the purely religious level after 1870 can be assessed only in reference to sporadic data and scattered,

3. Aurelio Bianchi Giovini, *Storia degli Ebrei* (Milan, 1844), pp. 5–6, "Quel loro particolarismo che gli fa estranei al resto della società."
4. Cf. Anatole Leroy-Beaulieu, *Israel chez les nations* (Paris, 1893), p. 383, and Max Nordau, "Brief an die Juden Italiens" (1898), *Zionistische Schriften* (Cologne-Leipzig, 1909) pp. 371–73.
5. Related to the author by Sergio J. Sierra, a former student of Levi Della Vida and now Chief Rabbi of Turin.

but not isolated, facts. The decline in synagogue attendance and contributions, in Talmud-Torah enrollment, in rabbinical vocations, and in other external indices of religiosity were frequently bemoaned by both rabbis and laymen from various points of the peninsula, while the most insistent warnings were reserved against intermarriage, which was quite widespread. At Mantua, for instance, a Jewish community of medium size counted 117 mixed marriages in the forty years after 1866.[6] The most explicit form of religious assimilation, outright conversion, seems to have been far less frequent. Here we face a complete lack of systematic data and are left with individual, albeit indicative, instances. Conversion often occurred in the case of cultured and wealthy Jews among whom irreligion had already taken its toll and who had much to gain socially, and sometimes politically, from the extreme step (for example, the deputies Giuseppe Weil-Weiss and Emanuele Artom). At times, conversion was based on ideological considerations. The *Risorgimental* patriot and deputy Giuseppe Finzi had his children baptized in the hope of totally fusing them with the Italian people; when Giacomo Venezian, an exiled Triestine Jew and co-founder of the *Società Dante Alighieri*, converted in 1889, he did so in part because he identified Catholicism with *italianità* and considered the Jews as too clannish and cosmopolitan to be truly patriotic.

The Reform movement was weak on the peninsula, perhaps because of the very extent of assimilation: that is, assimilatory pressures were so strong that those Jews who left the orthodox fold chose secularization, irreligion, and apostasy over the compromise solution of a liturgical and doctrinal adaptation that would have preserved their religious affiliation.[7] The search for an alternative secularized religion among assimilated Italian Jews assumed many forms. Some formulated assimilationist interpretations of messianism which equated Judaism with the principles of the French Revolution and announced its imminent disappearance in terms of a higher, universal creed (David Levi). In order to break out from

---

6. Donato Camerini, *Il Vessillo israelitico*, LIII (1905), p. 246.
7. On Reform in Italy, see Milano, op. cit., p. 374 and Elia Richetti, "Tradizione e cultura ebraica tra '800 e '900. La riforma sinagogale in Italia," *Rassegna mensile di Israel*, L (1984), pp. 315–19.

what he called "the narrow sphere of ancestral religion,"[8] Luigi Luzzatti adopted a humanitarian deism close to Unitarianism. A considerable number of other Italian Jews followed the parallel paths of Freemasonry and the Ethical Culture movement in their quest for a secularized faith.

The inroads of assimilation reached beyond religiosity to affect the attitudes of Italian Jews toward their position in the society and politics of the kingdom. Even those Jews who considered themselves constantly as such, and who made positive claims for Judaism and Jewishness, agreed in broad terms that Jews should shed their "particularism" and acculturate to general Italian patterns. These in turn were divided into two schools, which advocated different approaches to integration. The first group sponsored what could be called *la politica dello struzzo* (the politics of the ostrich) and urged Jews not to push, to remain inconspicuous, to keep a low profile so as not to arouse the envy and incite the anger of their Gentile neighbors or to lend credence to their detractors. The second approach was equally assimiliationist but more typical of the Jewish community. It positively encouraged active participation in all aspects of Italian life. The organ of this school of thought was *Il Vessillo Israelitico* (1874–1922), published at Casale Monferrato and later at Turin. Irreligion and apostasy were, of course, roundly condemned time and again by this journal. However, it became so preoccupied with urging assimilation and stressing Jewish contributions to Italy that it was at times ambivalent in its attitude toward religiosity itself. For example, in 1904, while objecting to a comedy that advocated intermarriage, *Il Vessillo* nevertheless congratulated its author, Arturo Foà, on the play's success, since it rewarded the talent of a young and cultured Jewish writer.[9] Like their French and German co-religionists, Italian Jews had developed a theory of the coincidence of their own particular national loyalties with the universal aspirations of Judaism. Accordingly, the periodical supported Italian colonial expansion in Ethiopia (to save the Falashas from barbarity, ignorance, and in-

---

8. "La cerchia angusta della religione avita." *Avanti!*, April 15, 1909.
9. Ferruccio Servi, *Il Vessillo israelitico*, LII (1904), pp. 165–67.

tolerance) and in North Africa (to redeem the Jews of Tripoli from superstition and Ottoman tyranny).

The general impact of assimilation with its erosion of Jewish consciousness, the development of a political philosophy that raised *italianità* to the level of a religious duty, an interpretation of messianism that tied the mission of Judaism to the Diaspora, fear of arousing the accusation of divided loyalties—all of these factors conditioned the response of Italian Jewry to Zionism at the turn of the century. In 1898, a correspondent for the London *Jewish Chronicle* reported that ninety-nine percent of Italian Jews were opposed to the nascent movement.[10] Though no doubt exaggerated, the statement of this English journalist reflected the nearly universal hostility that Zionism as a political and national cause met among the Jews of the peninsula. With few exceptions (notably among the younger generation), those Italian Jews who did call themselves Zionists espoused an attenuated Zionism, limited to a philanthropic humanitarianism in the aid of less fortunate *Ostjuden* and always accompanied by reaffirmations of loyalty to the generous and beloved *patria*.

Jewish assimilation on the peninsula was facilitated by a number of factors particular to Italy (at least in their convergence): the smallness of the Jewish nucleus—truly *rari nantes in gurgite vasto*; the length and stability of Jewish residence, the Roman *kehillah* being the oldest continuous community in the Diaspora; the all but total absence of Jewish immigration from eastern Europe; the contractual nature of emancipation, which demanded fusion as the price of freedom; the laic ideology of the unitary state; the universalistic nature of Italian nationalism itself (which, until 1938, was defined in cultural and not in *völkisch* or racial terms); and, last but not least, a curious blend of general respect for the persons and rights of individual Jews along with a widespread disregard for Judaism as a religion and as an ethical system, a combination that subtly encouraged irreligion and apostasy among Italian Jews.[11]

---

10. L. B., "Zionism in Italy," *The Jewish Chronicle*, August 26, 1898, p. 8.
11. This last ambivalent attitude emerged clearly in the treatment of Jewish char-

The foregoing portrait of Jewish assimilation in Liberal Italy is tempered by two factors that need to be mentioned. The response of Italian Jews to emancipation should be seen in the context of the reality and concreteness of the equality that was being offered, and also as a crucial, but not isolated, point along a centuries-old continuum of Jewish acculturation on the peninsula. The Israeli historian Raphael Mahler has pointed out that as early as the period of *haskalah* (Jewish Enlightenment) and the French Revolution, Jews were better integrated socially and culturally into the surrounding population in Italy than they were anywhere else in Europe.[12] That the gap between the speech, customs, and values of the ordinary Jew and his Christian neighbor was already narrower in Italy than elsewhere, even before enfranchisement, certainly meant that assimilation was easier, less of a shock, and perhaps less of an ignoble betrayal than, for example, in central Europe. The extent of this cultural interpenetration and reciprocal acceptance and familiarity is also adduced by some to explain why, in fact, little need was felt to radically alter liturgical practices in the synagogues of the peninsula, or why a "residual Jewish consciousness," as H. Stuart Hughes puts it, could characterize even the most assimilated of Italian Jews.[13] Finally, we must not forget that countercurrents of Jewish revival did indeed surface in the first two decades of the century, especially in Rome, Tuscany, and Emilia, with the dissenting voices of more orthodox Zionists, the formation of a school of historical studies at the rabbinical college of Florence, the *pro cultura* circles, the proliferation of Jewish periodicals, and the founding of a Jewish youth movement.[14]

---

acters by contemporary Italian novelists. See my essay, "The Image of the Jew in the Folklore and Literature of the Postrisorgimento," *Journal of European Studies*, IX (1979), 260–73.

12. Raphael Mahler, *A History of Modern Jewry, 1780–1815* (New York, 1971), p. xxii and Ch. V.

13. H. Stuart Hughes, *Prisoners of Hope. The Silver Age of Italian Jews, 1924–1974* (Cambridge, Mass.–London, 1983), pp. 1–14.

14. See Elio Toaff, "La rinascita spirituale degli ebrei italiani nei primi decenni del secolo," *Rassegna mensile di Israel*, Vol. XLVII, Nos. 7–12 (July/December 1981), pp. 63–73.

Reflections on the Weakness of Anti-Semitism in Liberal Italy

Given the circumstances outlined above, it has consequently been argued that the very extent of Jewish assimilation in Italy accounts for the weakness of anti-Jewish feeling and its overt manifestations on the peninsula that were noted at the outset of this article. Presumably, since Italian Jews were like everyone else in Italy, they passed unnoticed and unmolested. However, it can be well demonstrated that assimilation and anti-Semitism are largely independent phenomena, in that Jewish integration is no antidote to anti-Jewish prejudice, nor is anti-Semitism on the whole an effective check to assimilation. In this connection, it should suffice to point out the hyper-assimilated state of French Jewry at the time of the Dreyfus Affair or the far more tragic case of the Jews of Germany, who were so steeped in their cultural surroundings as to adopt in many instances the *nationalist* ideology, which fed the racism that ultimately led to their destruction. On the peninsula, clerical anti-Semites were particularly active at the turn of the century at Ancona and Mantua, localities with two of the most highly assimilated Jewish communities in Italy. Moreover, the fusion/rejection antithesis repeats the illusory alternative originally presented to the Jews of Europe by the emancipationists and later taken up by liberals, anti-Semitic and otherwise. At the turn of the century, Jewish nationalists, who rejected this dichotomy, argued in fact that the assimilationism of western Jewry served only to confirm the claims of anti-Semites, to the extent that by rejecting their heritage the Jews seemed to, and in many cases did, accept the negative image of Judaism and Jewishness purveyed by their opponents.[15]

A variant of this first explanation of the weakness of anti-Semitism in modern Italy was put forward by Antonio Gramsci in his writings on the *Risorgimento*.[16] Gramsci argued that the Italian national consciousness of the Jews of the peninsula was formed at

---

15. For example, Ahad Ha'am (Asher Ginzberg), "Slavery in Freedom" (1891), in *Selected Essays* (Philadelphia, 1912), pp. 171–94 and Dante Lattes, "Gli effetti dell'assimilazione," *Il Corriere israelitico*, XL (1901–02), pp. 27–30.

16. Antonio Gramsci, *Il Risorgimento* (Turin, 1949), pp. 166–68.

the same time and in the same way as that of non-Jews, in the sense that both groups had to overcome the anti-national forces of religious cosmopolitanism and local or ethnic particularism in the course of the movement leading up to unification. This shared experience of "parallel nationalization" in turn determined a relative absence of friction between Italian Jews and their Gentile neighbors.

The above line of argument, albeit attractive and widely diffused, is erroneous and misleading. In the first place, it cannot explain the absence of mass anti-Semitism in post-*Risorgimental* Italy, because with few exceptions the masses were not involved in the national movement at issue: the peasantry and orthodox Catholics were indifferent or hostile to unification and were not nationalized until long after the *Risorgimento*. Nor should we forget that, to the extent that it was expressed openly, the popular attitude to Jewish rights during the *Risorgimento* was not unequivocally favorable. Moreover, there is no reason to believe that "parallel nationalization" was unique to Italy and did not occur elsewhere, including countries of later mass anti-Semitism. Jewish participation in the revolutions of 1848, for example, was no greater in Italy than it was in Germany or Hungary. Finally, the basic premise of Gramsci's interpretation is fallacious. It essentially argues that anti-Semitism has not flourished in modern Italy because Jews and non-Jews were alike, that is, they were equally and simultaneously national-minded, during Italy's formative period. As such, this interpretation is a subdivision of the assimilationist one previously expounded and is therefore open to the same criticism.

Another explanation that has received some currency and that has been accepted by the leading historian of Fascism, Renzo De Felice, is that the Italian Jewish community after unification was not prominent in the economic life of the country, either on the national scale or on a local level, and that anti-Semitism was thereby deprived of a corresponding economic motivation.[17] By claiming that Jewish professionals and businessmen in Italy were

---

17. Renzo De Felice, *Storia degli ebrei italiani sotto il fascismo,* 3rd rev. ed. (Turin, 1972), p. 21.

by and large inconspicuous, this interpretation is the economic counterpart to the previous argument regarding the social, cultural, and political assimilation of Italian Jews. The view that a lack of Jewish economic integration, as reflected in an occupational distribution differing sharply from overall national patterns, contributes to Jewish-Gentile friction is essentially correct, and has been supported, for instance, by a study of the cases of Germany and France.[18] However, the contention that Italian Jewry somehow formed an exception to the rule, a case apart, is highly questionable. The occupational distribution of Jews in unified Italy was similar to that of their co-religionists in other parts of western and central Europe, the only distinction being a greater concentration of Italian Jews in the civil service and the professions. In short, Jewish occupational patterns in Italy were just as anomalous as they were elsewhere.[19]

Moreover, though there did not exist an Italian Rothschild or an Italian Bleichröder, the economic position, or impact, of the Jews in Liberal Italy was far from insignificant. To be sure, poor Jews constituted a majority of the community and were particularly numerous in the larger centers and in some of the medium-sized ones, and as late as 1912 fully one-third of Italian Jews were still the object of public and private charity.[20] However, this did not detract from the prominence and conspicuous contributions of Jewish financiers and entrepreneurs. In the last third of the nineteenth century and at the beginning of the twentieth, Jewish capital was important in developing certain key sectors of the infrastructure behind the country's economic take-off (railroad building, internal navigation, rural electrification). It was substantial in the textile industry, in rural land development, and urban construction, and it was particularly considerable in the insurance

18. Robert A. Kann, "Assimilation and Antisemitism in the German-French Orbit," *Leo Baeck Institute Year Book*, XIV (1969), pp. 92–115.

19. See the tables in Arthur Ruppin, *Soziologie der Juden* (Berlin, 1930–31), I, 348 and Livio Livi, *Gli ebrei alla luce della statistica: evoluzione demografica, economica e sociale* (Florence, 1920), p. 121, and the analysis of 1901 census data by E. Raseri, "La popolazione israelitica in Italia," *Atti della Società Romana di Antropologia*, X (1904), pp. 82–93.

20. See, for example, Carlo Levi, "Gl'israeliti poveri nel comune di Modena," *La Riforma sociale*, VII (1897), pp. 962–69 and Ermanno Loewinson, "Die Juden Italiens," *Ost und West*, XII (1912), pp. 1121–22.

business, where the leading company (the Assicurazioni Generali) and several others were in Jewish hands. Much of this capital was channeled through family banking firms (for example, Weil-Weiss and Malvano at Turin, Weil-Schott and Pisa at Milan, Treves at Venice), and through investment banks such as the Banca Italo-Germanica (Rome) or the Banca Italiana di Costruzione (Genoa). On a regional basis, Jewish capitalists were most important in Tuscany, Piedmont, Lombardy, Emilia, and the Veneto, where, for instance, at the turn of the century the Treves de' Bonfili family was considered the wealthiest in the region.

Finally, the prominence of numerous Jews in several professions cannot be underestimated as an element underlining the disparity between Jewish occupational distribution and general Italian patterns. This holds true for government service, the academic world, and the legal profession, and especially in the case of the so-called "cultural service industries"—publishing and journalism—which are particularly in the public eye. During the *Postrisorgimento*, there were five Jewish firms (Treves, Bemporad, Lattes, Formiggini, Voghera) among the major publishing houses of the peninsula. Jews also figured prominently as owners, editors, and journalists in the Italian newspaper industry. A singularly notorious case is that of the Hungarian-born banker and advertising agent, Ernesto Emanuele Oblieght, who in the early 1880s held the controlling interest in six leading papers and caused a national scandal when he attempted to sell his share to a French investment company.[21] Several Italian Jews, among them Giacomo Dina, Edoardo Arbib, Attilio Luzzatto, and Primo Levi, were nationally eminent newspapermen, while the local importance of Jewish journalists was occasionally quite considerable, as in Rome in 1890, when five of sixteen dailies had Jews as managing editors.[22] Thus, in the professions, as in business, Jews were far from insignificant or inconspicuous, and it is incorrect to deny or diminish the economic position and visibility of the Jewish community in Liberal Italy.

21. For this incident, see Emma Parodi, *Roma italiana, 1870–1895* (Rome, 1896), pp. 295–296, and Valerio Castronovo, *La stampa italiana dall'Unità al fascismo* (Bari, 1973), pp. 88–91.
22. Cf. *Guida Monaci*, Anno XXI (1891), p. 510.

Correspondingly, a lack of Jewish economic importance cannot be adduced as an explanation of the relative absence of anti-Semitism in modern Italy, and the search must lead us elsewhere.

A more plausible reason may be found in the lateness of Italy's industrialization, whose take-off in 1896–1908 trailed that of other major continental economies by several decades. It would follow that the damage to the material position and social status of the lower middle classes, occasioned elsewhere by monopolistic concentration in the closing decades of the last century, was considerably delayed on the Italian peninsula. Economic and social anxieties, as well as fear of Jewish competition, characterized the threatened *Mittelstand* and petty bourgeoisie of Germany and France and led them in turn to form the mass base of political anti-Semitism in those countries.[23] As a consequence of retarded economic development, such factors could not have played a significant role in Italy. This explanation is essentially valid. However, it fails to take into account the existence of a substantial intellectual proletariat in Italy at the turn of the century.[24] A widespread humanistic petty bourgeoisie of unemployed and underemployed doctors, lawyers, and teachers constituted a potential recruiting ground for anti-Semitic agitators and indeed contributed to the contemporary anti-Jewish movement in France.[25] In Italy, though the same social element participated in anti-liberalism, it did so in other ways, and this fact indicates that discussion of the fortunes of anti-Semitism on the peninsula cannot be limited to socio-economic considerations alone.

The principal factors that have determined the decidedly secondary importance of anti-Jewish hostility in modern Italian history are demographic, historical, and political. Fundamental to any study of Jewish-Christian relations in the *Postrisorgimento* and beyond is the fact that the Jewish community of Italy was ex-

---

23. This is the thesis of both Paul W. Massing, *Rehearsal for Destruction: A Study of Political Anti-Semitism in Imperial Germany* (New York, 1949) and Robert F. Byrnes, *Antisemitism in Modern France*, Vol. I: *The Prologue to the Dreyfus Affair* (New Brunswick, N.J., 1950).

24. See Marzio Barbagli, *Disoccupazione intellettuale e sistema scolastico in Italia (1859–1973)* (Bologna, 1974), Ch. II.

25. Byrnes, op. cit., pp. 269–79.

tremely small both in absolute numbers and in relation to the general population. Between 1861 and 1911, the Jewish population of Italy grew from roughly 34,000 to nearly 40,000, but its proportion of the total population dropped steadily from 1.38 to 1.15 per thousand inhabitants. The only other areas of Europe with a lower proportion of Jews were Scandinavia and the Iberian peninsula.[26] In contrast to the other major nations of western and central Europe, the demographic insignificance of Italian Jewry served to weaken the mass appeal of anti-Semitism. The relative smallness of the native Jewish nucleus, along with the economic backwardness of the country, also meant that Italian anti-Semitism was in turn deprived of another demographic consideration that contributed to intergroup friction elsewhere. That is, the influx of immigrant Jews from eastern Europe, which the Jewish communities of England and the Continent rightly feared as an unsettling factor,[27] bypassed the Italian peninsula in the period prior to World War I.

The argument that a small and stable Jewish population would discourage anti-Jewish hostility is not meant to deny the existence of historical cases of "anti-Semitism without Jews," explainable in terms of scapegoating and displaced aggression. However, the absence of a substantial Jewish minority tends to diminish anti-Semitism by depriving anti-Jewish agitators of a concrete target and a plausible scapegoat. Thus, in the United States during the present century, anti-Jewish sentiments have been far stronger in the Northeast, where the bulk of the Jewish population is concentrated, than in the South, where racism and nativism would presumably predispose the whites to anti-Semitism.[28]

The Italian case followed a similar pattern. Anti-Semitism during the period 1870–1915 was strongest in those regions and lo-

26. See the statistical overview by Roberto Bachi, "The Demographic Development of Italian Jewry from the 17th Century," *Jewish Journal of Sociology*, IV (1962), pp. 172–91 and the comparative table in Arthur Ruppin, *The Jews of Today* (London, 1913), pp. 38–40.

27. Cf. Zosa Szajkowski, "The European Attitude to East European Jewish Immigration (1881–1893)," *Publications of the American Jewish Historical Society*, XLI (1951), pp. 127–62.

28. Donald S. Strong, *Organized Anti-Semitism in America* (Washington, 1941), pp. 144–45 and *Public Opinion, 1935–1946*, ed. Hadley Cantril (Princeton, 1951), pp. 381–84.

calities where the peninsula's Jewish population was centered. This did not, of course, prevent sporadic attacks against the Jews in religious pronouncements or newspaper articles in such unlikely places as Sardinia, with a Jewish population of ten in 1871. Apart from infrequent and isolated instances, though, anti-Semitism was all but totally absent from the South and the islands, regions that had practically not known Jews since the Spanish expulsions of four centuries earlier. Symbolic of the situation in these parts of Italy is a revealing anecdote. The late historian and jurist Arturo Carlo Jemolo used to recount that a Jewish friend of his, exiled to a southern village for his anti-Fascist activities, aroused the curiosity of his peasant hostess by never attending Mass. When he explained to her that he was a Jew, she exclaimed, quite dumbfounded, "*Macchè ebreo! Lei è bianco come me*" ("Nonsense, you're just as white as I am!").[29] Along these lines, it is indicative that the best-known popular demonstration of humanity toward Jews during the *Postrisorgimento* occurred at the southern port of Brindisi, where in 1891 a shipload of 400 Jewish refugees from Corfu were warmly received, fed, housed, and clothed by the local inhabitants and were even offered land to settle on by the city council.[30]

Another demographic factor that played against the emergence of mass anti-Semitism in Liberal Italy was the ethnically homogenous nature of the population of the kingdom. It has been argued that the strong anti-Semitism in contemporary central Europe was a paranoic reaction to the insecurity of the nation-state in Germany and Austria, faced, as they were, by the existence of large national minorities within their borders.[31] This evidently could not have been the case on the peninsula, where non-Italian ethnic and linguistic groups were exiguous and scattered. Indeed, at the time of unification, citizens speaking as a mother tongue a language other than Italian or one of its dialects comprised less than one percent of the entire population.[32]

29. From a conversation with A. C. Jemolo in Rome on December 4, 1973.

30. Cf. *Il Vessillo israelitico*, XXXIX (1891), pp. 209–11; *The Nation*, July 30, 1891, p. 83; *The American Hebrew*, August 14, 1891, p. 23.

31. P. G. J. Pulzer, *The Rise of Political Anti-Semitism in Germany and Austria* (New York, 1964), pp. 70–71.

32. Tullio De Mauro, *Storia linguistica dell'Italia unita* (Bari, 1965), pp. 14–15.

This last demographic consideration leads into a discussion of the weakness of ethnocentrism and racism as a whole in modern Italy.[33] The vast majority of Italians are characterized not so much by nationalism and ethnic prejudice as by "familism," *campanilismo* (village-mindedness), municipal loyalties, or regionalism. Along these lines, Massimo Salvadori incisively observed that in Italy nationalism and xenophobia were more pronounced as one moved up the educational and socio-economic scale.[34] This is due not only to the retarded nationalization of the Italian masses, or to the essentially cultural and therefore elitist nature of Italian nationalism itself. It also reflects the absence on the peninsula of that patchwork of linguistic groups and ethnic minorities that exacerbated national consciousness in central and eastern Europe from its inception and later contributed to the appeal of anti-Semitism.

Cultural and historical factors also played a role in hindering the emergence of a popular race consciousness in modern Italy. Though the scope of this paper is not diachronic, it should be pointed out that aside from a largely rhetorical anti-barbarism, particularly intense during the invasions of the late 1400s and early 1500s, xenophobia had always been relatively absent from the peninsula. In early modern France (and *mutatis mutandis* in Spain and England), an essentially political conflict between the nobility and the bourgeoisie was articulated in racial terms (the Gallo-Teutonic controversy) and initiated what Hannah Arendt has aptly called "race-thinking before racism."[35] In Italy, while there was no lack of a basis on which to fabricate such a mystification (Lombards in the north, Normans in the south), the noble-bourgeois polemic assumed other forms, a fact that suggests the existence of cultural obstacles to formulations in narrowly ethnic terms.

In this connection, a number of factors involving considerations of cultural heritage and national character suggest themselves.

---

33. Apropos of racism in modern Italy, see the illuminating observations by Renzo De Felice, op. cit., pp. 26–30.

34. Massimo Salvadori, *Italy* (Englewood Cliffs, N.J., 1965), pp. 6–7.

35. Hannah Arendt, *The Origins of Totalitarianism*, 2nd rev. ed. (Cleveland–New York, 1958), pp. 161–65 and Léon Poliakov, *The Aryan Myth: A History of Racist and Nationalist Ideas in Europe* (New York, 1974), Ch. II.

However, it should be pointed out that they are concepts that are not easily amenable to systematic, not to say objective, analysis. I refer to the cosmopolitan influence in Italy of religious syncretism, classical humanism, and Catholicism, or the persistence of the universalistic myth of Rome which, as Léon Poliakov recently maintained, so dominated Italian culture as to exclude rival interpretations of the country's historic destiny in terms of a struggle of races.[36] It has also been argued that the presumed superficiality, kind-heartedness, and sentimental humanitarianism of the Italian people effectively inoculated them against the particularly virulent forms of Judeophobia—a position taken by such noted students of Italian-Jewish history as Cecil Roth, Raphael Mahler, and Bruno Di Porto.[37]

More specific to the period under consideration is the colonial movement. The rise of European racial theories in the late nineteenth century coincided with the scramble for Africa, lent it a rationalization, and was in turn reinforced by it.[38] Italian colonialism arrived late, and it generally failed to evoke popular enthusiasm. Moreover, Italy's mission in Africa was not justified by an appeal to the so-called white man's burden, but rather with the demographic argument of colonies as an outlet for excess population.[39] Finally, the formation of a race consciousness in connection with Italian imperialism was discouraged by the fact that Italy's colonial possessions (Libya, Eritrea, Somalia) were inhabited by peoples whom the leading Italian anthropologists considered members of the white race (Enrico Morselli) or progenitors of a Eurafrican species that supposedly settled the Mediterranean basin in prehistoric times and to which most Italians still belonged (Giuseppe Sergi).[40] Due to these circumstances, imperial expansion did

36. Ibid., Ch. IV.
37. See Roth, op. cit., pp. 156, 388, 533; Mahler, op. cit., p. 114; Di Porto, "L'emancipazione difficile tra i pregiudizi del tempo," La Voce repubblicana, August 17, 1978, p. 3.
38. See V. G. Kiernan, The Lords of Human Kind (Boston, 1969), pp. 230ff.
39. For all these aspects of Italian colonialism, see J.-L. Miège, L'impérialisme colonial italien de 1870 à nos jours (Paris, 1968), pp. 40–45 and Claudio G. Segrè, Fourth Shore: The Italian Colonization of Libya (Chicago, 1974), Ch. I.
40. Enrico Morselli, Antropologia generale (Turin, 1911) and Giuseppe Sergi, The Mediterranean Race (London, 1901).

not feed biological racism or scientific anti-Semitism in Liberal Italy as it did in the larger European colonial powers.

It would be incorrect to suggest that race-thinking was unknown to Italian culture in the *Postrisorgimento*. Indeed, biological determinism was fundamental to the Italian positivist school of physical anthropologists, ethnographers, and sociologists known as "anthroposociology." However, Italian racism was turned inward, so to speak, and directed against the inhabitants of the country's south, or against Mediterranean peoples in general, to explain the supposed decadence of Latin nations.[41] Moreover, race consciousness did not extend to popular culture, nor did it permeate literature or grass-roots organizations as it did, for example, in Germany. Indicative of the scant appeal of race prejudice among the popular masses is the case of Italian immigrants in the United States, who in the early period of settlement generally constituted an obstacle to white solidarity by fraternizing with Negroes until, of course, assimilation and economic competition effectively reversed their sympathies.[42] The absence of a widespread race consciousness contributed to the weakness of anti-Jewish sentiment and, in addition, determined that Italian anti-Semitism itself, until well into the Fascist period, was formulated in terms other than race.

There were, furthermore, two political, or institutional, factors that militated against the spread and effectiveness of anti-Semitism in Liberal Italy, both of which trace their origins to the period of the *Risorgimento*. The first has to do with Jewish emancipation on the peninsula.[43] The contractual nature of emancipation, or Jewish legal parification, in nineteenth-century Europe involved serious implications for the emancipated in that an ill-defined self-

41. See Massimo L. Salvadori, *Il mito del buongoverno. La questione meridionale da Cavour a Gramsci*, 2nd rev. ed. (Turin, 1963), Ch. VI and Emiliana P. Noether, "Latin Decadence: An Intellectual Apologia (Italian Racial Theories in the 1890s)," an unpublished paper read at the meeting of the New England Historical Association, Worcester, Mass., October 5, 1974.

42. George E. Cunningham, "The Italian, a Hindrance to White Solidarity in Louisiana, 1890–1898," *Journal of Negro History*, L (1965), pp. 22–36 and Alexander De Conde, *Half Bitter, Half Sweet: An Excursion into Italian-American History* (New York, 1971), p. 332.

43. For a recent survey of all the aspects of emancipation discussed below, see my study, "Emancipation and Jewish Response in Mid-19th-Century Italy," *European History Quarterly*, XVI (1986), pp. 403–39.

improvement and assimilation were demanded of them, creating a situation in which European Jewry was left open both to charges of incomplete fusion and to self-doubt. The terms of emancipation within Italy were equally severe. However, while Italian emancipationists shared assumptions and expectations regarding the Jews with their counterparts in other lands, there are two significant distinctions to be made between parification in Italy and elsewhere, distinctions that affected the fortunes of Italian Jewry in the post-emancipatory period. They relate to the legal process of the extension of equal rights and to the relative unanimity of views on the Jewish question within the liberal camp. In both cases, the situation on the peninsula was particularly favorable to the solidity and permanence of Jewish equality once it had been attained.

There were three basic patterns of Jewish emancipation in the West. There was, first of all, the Anglo-American model of unconditional equality without a specific emancipatory decree, in conformity therefore with the traditions of Anglo-Saxon common law. In western Europe, the French model prevailed. It provided for a conditional, contractual emancipation, but it granted immediate, full legal parity in an apposite decree, and relied on social forces to transform and assimilate the Jews with the natural passage of time. In central and eastern Europe, the German type predominated. This model involved a gradual, step-by-step extension of economic, civil, and political rights in a lengthy process of "emancipation by installments"; and it depended on the educative effects of the laws themselves for the transformation of the Jews (their "civic improvement") and, at times, on decrees that actually mandated various aspects of acculturation. The danger implicit in the third model was that by protracting the process of emancipation the Jewish question was kept alive and hotly debated in political circles for an extended period of time, thereby calling into question and weakening the final emancipatory installment. It should be no surprise, therefore, that Germany, where emancipation was first proposed in 1781 by an enlightened Prussian public official, was also the country where the issue was debated for the longest period of time (ninety years, to 1871) and where Jewish equality, once achieved, was most seriously questioned.

The Italian case most closely follows the French model. Although until Unity the peninsula remained divided among a number of petty states, each with a different legislation regarding the Jews, emancipation in Italy was achieved in the year 1848, with the royal decrees of March and June establishing full civil and political equality in the Kingdom of Sardinia. After this date, both the emancipationist campaign and the polemics against it ceased, and Jewish legal parity was no longer defended or questioned per se, but rather became a datum of *Risorgimental* liberalism and of its institutionalized form, the Piedmontese state. As such, emancipation was extended to the whole of the peninsula with the geographic expansion of that state. Moreover, as in France, the debate on the Jewish question in Italy was relatively short (at most twenty years, 1828–48). Furthermore, in contrast to both France and Germany, where the liberal camp itself was sharply divided on the issue, Italian liberals during the *Risorgimento*, with the qualified exception of F. D. Guerazzi, were unanimous in their support of Jewish rights. Indeed, the three leading figures of the *Risorgimento*—Cavour, Mazzini, and Garibaldi—were philo-Semites, and Cavour in particular closely collaborated with several Jews and defended them on more than one occasion. Our aim, of course, is not hagiography. What we wish to emphasize is that the juridical form of emancipation (a single act rather than a series of installments), the brevity of the debate on the issue, and the undivided stand of the political camp that made religious equality an integral element of its program determined that after the *Risorgimento* the new legal status of the Jews was more solid and less questioned in Italy than in other parts of western and central Europe.

Finally, the Catholic Church, which had opposed this equality at mid-century, was powerless to do anything about it in the period following the *Risorgimento*. As Eugenio Artom pointed out in the 1940s, Italy has the distinction of being the only European nation "that effected its unification fighting against its own religion and that managed to achieve victory without any religious oppression."[44] The Church, against whose presumed moral interest and

---

44. Eugenio Artom, "Per una storia degli ebrei nel Risorgimento," *Rassegna storica toscana*, XXIV (1978), p. 144: "la sola nazione che la unificazione abbia raggiunto lottando contro la propria religione e la vittoria abbia saputo conquistare senza nessuna oppressione religiosa."

against whose concrete temporal power unity had been achieved, urged Catholics for decades after 1870 to abstain from national politics. Had the clericals been willing and able to coalesce with other interests to form a Church-backed conservative party, the Jews of Italy might have fared much worse. As it was, the heritage of the *Risorgimento* and the continuing church-state conflict meant that Italy at the turn of the century was, on the level of politics, laws, and official culture, a laic country to a greater extent than many other European nations.[45]

Currents of Opposition in Pre-Fascist Italy

In Italy, a number of demographic, historical, and political factors averted the rise of the radical racial anti-Semitism that characterized political life in France, Germany, and Austria from the mid-1880s until the end of the century. However, modern political anti-Semitism was not unknown to Liberal Italy, and its appearance on the peninsula should not be discounted, especially as it provided an indigenous tradition to which the Fascists later made reference. Apart from more or less isolated manifestations in the nationalist and anarcho-syndicalist movement of the early 1900s, Italian anti-Semitism during the *Postrisorgimento* was represented chiefly in two distinct currents: the liberal and the clerical.[46]

In the first two decades after the "breach of Porta Pia" in 1870, various Italian liberals on different occasions employed anti-Semitic arguments, whose leitmotiv was the disturbing specter of an unintegrated "state within the state" and a preoccupation with centrifugal forces of national disunion conceived in terms of Jewish exclusiveness and divided loyalties. The anti-Jewish statements of these liberals can be interpreted in light of their concern over the cohesion of the new Italian state in the 1870s and 1880s, a period

45. See the comments of the contemporary Protestant minister Alexander Robertson, *The Roman Catholic Church in Italy* (London, 1903) pp. 145–52, pp. 273–75, from an anticlerical standpoint, and the memoirs of Giorgio Levi Della Vida, *Fantasmi ritrovati* (Venice, 1966), pp. 75–80.
46. On these two currents, see my essays, "Emancipazione, integrazione e antisemitismo liberale in Italia: il caso Pasqualigo," *Comunità*, No. 174 (June 1975), pp. 166–203 and "Cattolici ed ebrei nell'Itala liberale (1870–1915)," *Comunità*, No. 179 (April 1978), pp. 43–109.

crucial to its consolidation, during which Catholic opposition was particularly serious. The assimilatory claims of emancipation upon the Jews formed the underlying, predisposing determinant of liberal anti-Semitism, while an insecure, exasperated nationalism acted as its proximate cause, transforming expectation of eventual integration into emphatic demands of immediate fusion. Anti-Semites constituted a decided minority within the liberal camp. However, the equivocal legacy of emancipation continued to color the attitude of not a few ostensibly philo-Semitic liberals in the late nineteenth century, who insisted on the rapid assimilation of the Jews, sometimes through a policy of mixed marriages. It also contributed to the formation of Benedetto Croce's ambiguous position on the Jewish question and, as Meir Michaelis has recently pointed out, to Mussolini's own attitude as well.[47]

The other major strain of pre-Fascist anti-Semitism was formed by the journalistic and electoral campaigns of clerical elements, especially from the early 1880s to the turn of the century and again on the eve of World War I. In contrast to the liberal current, Catholic anti-Semites were more significant in numbers, more persistent in time, and more representative of their ideological camp as a whole. It should also be emphasized that while the anti-Jewish assertions of liberals did not arise from their liberalism per se, the anti-Semitism of clericals was intimately tied to both traditional religious anti-Judaism and the Church's opposition to modernity, which continued to mold its attitudes toward the position of Jews in Christian society until it came to terms with secularization. Finally, though liberal anti-Semitism in Italy was limited to what would be called "xenophobia" in Gavin Langmuir's typology of prejudice, clerical anti-Semitism in the *Postrisorgimento* often extended to "*chimeria*," unobservable fantasies that brand a group as subhuman or inhuman (for example, the blood and ritual murder libels adduced by some clerical journalists).[48]

47. Dante Lattes, *Benedetto Croce e l'inutile martirio d'Israele*; Ferruccio Pardo, *L'ebraismo secondo Benedetto Croce e secondo la filosofia crociana* (Florence, 1948); Luigi Russo, "La polemica di Benedetto Croce contro la Massoneria e gli ebrei," *Belfagor*, IX (1954), pp. 95–99; Meir Michaelis, "Riflessioni sulla recente storia dell'ebraismo italiano," *Rassegna mensile di Israel*, XLVIII (1982), pp. 167–78 and "L'ebraismo italiano dallo Statuto albertino alla legislazione razziale," in *Israel. Un decennio, 1974–1984* (Rome, 1984), pp. 251–73.
48. Gavin I. Langmuir, "Prolegomena to Any Present Analysis of Hostility against Jews," *Social Studies Information*, XV (1976), 705ff.

Roughly forty major Catholic newspapers and periodicals participated in the anti-Semitic movement during the liberal period. They were published almost entirely in northern and central Italy, with a particularly high concentration in Piedmont and in Rome. The political geography of clerical anti-Semitism was somewhat less distorted, as the press of all major Catholic currents, except the modernists, was represented. However, while the organs of both "transigent" Catholics, conciliatory on the church-state question, and Christian democrats occasionally printed anti-Jewish invectives, the mainstay of the campaign was formed by the publications of the so-called intransigents, who uncompromisingly opposed the post-unitary liberal state. In spite of some local situation that gave rise to economically motivated anti-Semitism, the anti-Jewish campaign of the clericals was essentially an indirect counterattack on liberalism and secularization, and it abated at the very time that anti-clericalism was subsiding and that clericals and moderate liberals were allying against socialism in defense of common class interests.

However, even at the height of the movement in the 1880s and 1890s, clerical anti-Semitism was a marginal phenomenon, out of the mainstream of Italian life and politics. It never had the opportunity to coalesce with other anti-Semitic and anti-liberal currents to pose a threat to liberal institutions, as in France during the Dreyfus Affair. And, in sharp contrast to the situation in the Wilhelmine Germany, where anti-Semitism was also a vehicle for the integration of the Church-backed Center Party into the German political establishment,[49] the anti-Jewish campaign of Italian Catholics served only to further isolate the Church from the political life of the Kingdom of Italy.

49. Cf. Uriel Tal, *Christians and Jews in Germany: Religion, Politics and Ideology in the Second Reich, 1870–1914* (Ithaca–London, 1975), pp. 95–96, 239–40.

Meir Michaelis

2. Fascist Policy Toward Italian Jews: Tolerance and Persecution

Emancipation of the Jews in Italy, extended to the whole of the peninsula after the capture of Rome in 1870, had been an outstanding success, in both its positive and its negative aspects: in the perfect equality accorded Italian Jews and in the progressive self-extinction of the Italian Jewish community. Until the second half of 1936, anti-Semitism on the peninsula was a phenomenon devoid of political significance, isolated from the mainstream of Italian life. The anti-Semitic campaign of the Catholic press, which lasted from the early 1880s to the turn of the century, did not worry the Jews. Far from threatening their position, it merely served to isolate the Church still further from the politics of the kingdom; as clerical forces finally made their peace with the state after 1900, they concurrently muffled their anti-Jewish polemics.[1] Nor did the happy situation of Italian Jewry change with the Fascist seizure of power. During the first fourteen years of Mussolini's rule—the "honeymoon period"[2]—the official attitude of the Fascist regime to the Jewish minority was summarily expressed in the phrase: "The Jewish problem does not exist in Italy."[3]

True, the Fascist March on Rome, on October 30, 1922, aroused a certain amount of uneasiness in Jewish circles, owing as much to previous Fascist invectives against "English Zionism" and "Jewish Bolshevism" as to the general enthusiasm that the triumph of the Blackshirts aroused among anti-Semitic elements abroad, particularly in Germany.[4] Even so, very few students of

1. A. M. Canepa, "Cattolici ed ebrei nell'Italia liberale (1870–1915)" Comunità XXXII, April 1978, pp. 108–9.
2. M. Michaelis, Mussolini and the Jews. German-Italian Relations and the Jewish Question in Italy, 1922–1945 (Oxford, 1978), p. 48.
3. See, e.g., the interview granted by the then under-secretary of Foreign Affairs, Dino Grandi, to the Wiener Morgenzeitung, reported in Israel, May 24, 1926.
4. See "Männer und Waschweiber," Völkischer Beobachter, November 1, 1922; "Nel nuovo Ministero italiano," Israel, November 3, 1922; "Rom und Jerusalem," Jüdische Rundschau, November 3, 1922. On November 3, 1922, Herman Esser,

Italian Fascism alluded to a Jewish problem in Italy before the birth of the Rome-Berlin Axis. Robert Michels, the noted sociologist, warned of a possible clash between Fascists and Jews as early as December 1922. Bolton King, a leading British authority on the *Risorgimento*, charged the Fascists with "dislike of Protestants and Jews" in a book published nine years later.[5] But these were the exceptions that proved the rule.

Official Fascist spokesmen, echoing their master's "philo-Semitic" and "anti-racialist" pronouncements, emphatically denied the existence of anti-Jewish prejudice in Italy. Even so, the latent tension between Fascist nationalism and Jewish internationalism occasionally found expression in the writings of Fascist scribes. In 1926 Luigi Villari, in a book published in London, frankly admitted that Mussolini's aversion to international finance and his rapprochement with the Vatican had certain untoward implications as far as his relations with religious minorities were concerned. Given Villari's importance (he was the leading Fascist propagandist in the Anglo-Saxon countries until 1939), his observations are worth quoting in some detail:

> Once in power, the Fascist Government neglected no opportunity of showing deference to Catholicism. The prime minister, in his speeches, frequently spoke of it as the national religion of the Italian people and of the Papacy as a valuable asset for the nation. . . . In connection with this Catholic tendency Fascism has also adopted to some extent an attitude of hostility to Judaism and Protestantism, inasmuch as it regards them as essentially foreign to the Italian spirit. Anti-Semitism among Fascists is the result not of any dislike of the Italian Jews who are absolutely absorbed into the nation and are good patriots, but of suspicion of the international activities of foreign Jews, especially of those representing the great financial interests of Paris, London, Berlin, and New York, and of dislike of the Russian Bolsheviks, whose leaders are mostly Jews. The same phenom-

---

one of Hitler's earliest followers, announced amid rousing applause that "Germany's Mussolini" was Adolf Hitler, see W. Maser, *Die Frühgeschichte der NSDAP. Hitler's Weg bis 1924* (Frankfurt/M.-Bonn, 1965), p. 356.

5. R. Michels, "Der Aufstieg des Faschismus," *Neue Zürcher Zeitung,* December 29, 1922; B. King, *Fascism in Italy* (London, 1931), pp. 48–49.

enon has been noticed in several other countries since the war, including Britain.

Villari concluded by affirming that Fascist objections to non-Catholics had nothing whatever to do with religious intolerance: "It is only against the foreign character of certain aspects of Judaism and Protestantism that Fascism protests, and not against religious dogmas. There are indeed many Jews and Protestants among the Fascists, some of them in prominent positions."[6]

After Hitler's success at the *Reichstag* elections of September 1930—he won 107 seats out of 577—Fascist publicists began to display an ever-increasing sympathy for the "German imitation." But while praising the Führer's stand on a variety of issues, they took care to dissociate themselves from his racialist aberration. Corrado Pavolini (brother of a future party secretary) deplored the anti-Jewish mania of the National Socialists, affirming that the correct solution to the problem was assimilation, not expulsion. Franco Ciarlantini, a former chief of Mussolini's Press Bureau, insisted that a gulf separated Fascism from Hitlerism on the racial issue.[7] Mussolini himself was even more emphatic than his henchmen in rejecting Hitler's Nordic heresy. Speaking to Emil Ludwig in 1932, he expressed himself in harsh terms on the racial doctrines of his maladroit disciple:

> Of course there are no pure races left; not even the Jews have kept their blood unmingled. Successful crossings have often promoted the energy and the beauty of a nation. Race! It is a feeling, not a reality; ninety-five percent, at least, is a feeling. Nothing will ever make me believe that biologically pure races can be shown to exist today. Amusingly enough, not one of those who have proclaimed the nobility of the Teutonic race was himself a Teuton. Gobineau was a Frenchman; Houston Stewart Chamberlain, an Englishman; Woltmann, a Jew; Lapouge, another Frenchman. Chamberlain actually declared that Rome was the capital of chaos. No such doctrine will ever find wide acceptance here in Italy. . . . National pride has no need of the delirium of

6. L. Villari, *The Fascist Experiment* (London, 1926), pp. 201–2.
7. C. Pavolini, *Germania svegliati* (Rome, 1931), pp. 76–80; F. Ciarlantini, *Hitler e il fascismo* (Florence, 1933), pp. 45, 54, 58–59.

race. . . . Anti-Semitism does not exist in Italy. . . . Italians of
Jewish birth have shown themselves good citizens, and they
fought bravely in the war. Many of them occupy leading positions in the universities, in the army, in the banks. Quite a few
of them are generals; General Modena is commandant of Sardinia.

As for German anti-Semitism, Mussolini agreed with his interlocutor that it was a side-tracking stunt: having lost the war, the
Germans needed the Jew as a scapegoat to strike at. And when
Ludwig pointed out that the anti-Fascist exiles in Paris had accused
him of barring the admission of Jews to the Italian Academy, the
Duce replied that the accusation was "absurd": "Since my day,
there has been no Jew suitable for admission. Now Della Seta is a
candidate; a man of great learning, the leading authority on prehistoric Italy."[8]

In June 1932 (less than two months after the talks with Ludwig),
Mussolini published his celebrated treatise on Fascist doctrine, in
which the concept of the nation is defined in "anti-racialist"
terms: "Not a razza (race), nor a geographically defined region, but
a people historically perpetuating itself; a multitude unified by an
idea and imbued with a will to live, the will to power, self-con-
sciousness, personality."[9] Not content with rejecting racialism in
theory, the Fascist dictator gave practical proof of his anti-racialism by making a man of Jewish extraction, Guido Jung, his minister of finance in July of the same year. The appointment, like the
statement of Ludwig, was an indirect rebuff to Hitler, by then the
leader of the strongest political party in Germany, who was loudly
proclaiming his ideological solidarity with the "great man south
of the Alps" and his desire for an alliance with him.[10] The Italian
Jews could hardly fail to be impressed by the apparent antithesis
between the Duce and his German imitator; on October 27, *Israel*,

8. E. Ludwig, *Colloqui con Mussolini*, 2nd ed. (Milan, 1950), pp. 71–73. Ugo
Ojetti, a prominent member of the Italian Academy, informs us that Mussolini did
in fact bar the admissions of Jews, his statement to Ludwig notwithstanding (U.
Ojetti, *I taccuini 1914–1943* [Florence, 1954], p. 391).
9. "La dottrina del fascismo," *Opera Omnia di Benito Mussolini*, XXXIV (Florence, 1961), p. 120.
10. See, e.g., Hitler's preface to V. Meletti, *Die faschistische Revolution* (Munich,
1931), p. 7.

the Zionist weekly, in an editorial devoted to the tenth anniversary of the March on Rome, emphasized the "radical difference between the true and authentic Fascism—Italian Fascism, that is—and the pseudo-fascist movements in other countries which . . . are often using the most reactionary phobias, and especially the blind, unbridled hatred of the Jews, as a means of diverting the masses from their real problems, from the real causes of their misery, and from the real culprits."[11]

After Hitler's rise to power on January 30, 1933, Mussolini and his propagandists seized upon the apparent contrast between "philo-Semitic" Fascism and anti-Semitic National Socialism in order to win western (and Jewish) sympathy at a moment when the Duce needed French and British support for his projected African venture. Luigi Villari, in an essay written in late 1933 and published the following year, affirmed that eleven years after the March on Rome relations between Jews and Gentiles were better than ever before: "There was a moment after the outbreak of the Russian revolution, many of whose leaders in the early days of Bolshevism were Jews, when certain expressions of anti-Semitism occurred in Italy as in every other country on both sides of the Atlantic. But they did not last; very few of the Italian subversive leaders were Jews; and in fact the immense majority of Italian Jews had no sympathy of any kind with Bolshevism or Communism. Today it is safe to say that anti-Semitism is non-existent in Italy." As an example of Fascist "philo-Semitism" Villari quoted Mussolini's speech in commemoration of Luigi Luzzatti, the famous Jewish economist, who had been prime minister in 1910–11: "Luigi Luzzatti enters into the ranks of these wise, agile and pure intellects which in all times honor their country; it is just that their country should deplore his disappearance and honor him."[12]

In 1934, very few people thought of challenging Villari's account of Italian (and Fascist) benevolence toward the Jews, despite the fact that the triumph of the brownshirts in Germany had given a fresh impetus to the anti-Semitic currents within the Fascist

11. "Decennale," Israel, October 27, 1932.
12. L. Villari, "Luigi Luzzatti," Twelve Jews, ed. H. Bolitho (London, 1934), pp. 123–25.

movement.[13] Among the exceptions was Villari's most implacable opponent, the anti-Fascist historian Gaetano Salvemini, who pointed out, in an article published in the summer of 1934, that Mussolini's alleged "philo-Semitism" was no more than a characteristic example of his notorious duplicity; while posing as a defender of the Jews in order to gain sympathy abroad, he was stirring up anti-Jewish feeling at home. To be sure, in the past Mussolini's approach to the Jewish issue had been very different from Hitler's:

> Mussolini has never let loose in Italy a wave of anti-Semitism comparable to that which we are witnessing in Germany today. In Germany anti-Semitism had already become widespread during the last decades of the last century when Bebel, the Socialist leader, defined anti-Semitism as "the Socialism of the fool." It had deputies in the Reichstag and enjoyed the support of court circles. In Italy, on the contrary, there has never been any anti-Semitic feeling. . . . The Italian counterpart of German anti-Semitism is the persecution of Masonry. All of Italy's misfortunes are traced by the Fascist doctors to democracy, to Socialism, and to Freemasonry, whereas according to the German Nazis all of Germany's misfortunes are due to democracy, to Socialism, and to the brown-haired non-Aryans who have polluted the blond Germanic race.

An incident showed, however, that Mussolini "would not be averse to stirring up an anti-Semitic movement if he found it convenient." Salvemini then proceeded to describe in detail the recent arrests of real or alleged Jewish anti-Fascists at Ponte Tresa and in Turin, followed by a vicious outburst of anti-Semitism in the controlled Fascist press:

> On March 11, 1934, an automobile containing two young men, Mario Levi and Sion Segre, was stopped at the frontier station at Ponteresa [sic] as it was about to enter Italy from Switzerland. The police asked the two men to get out. One of the young men, Mario Levi, escaping from the police, threw himself suddenly into the river and, assisted by Swiss customs agents, managed to reach Swiss territory. He was carrying on his person a large

13. For details see M. Michaelis, op. cit., pp. 58–62.

quantity of anti-Fascist leaflets, which were to have been secretly distributed in Italy. The other young man, Sion Segre, was arrested, as were the relatives and friends of both of them at Turin, fifteen persons in all. . . . So far, nothing out of the ordinary. Incidents of this sort and mass arrests of suspected persons take place continually in Italy. And the government never fails to vilify the anti-Fascists and call them enemies of Italy, hired by foreign gold, etc. What is striking in this case is that the government had the news printed in the papers under the following headline: "Anti-Fascist Jews in the Pay of the Expatriates." Furthermore, all of the fifteen persons arrested were made to appear as Jews, while in reality six of them are Christians. And, finally, the official announcement failed to indicate that of the nine arrested who were really Jews, one, Professor Giuseppe Levi, of the University of Turin, was the father of the young man who escaped to Switzerland, and two were his brothers; that another was the father and another the sister of the young man arrested at Ponteresa [sic]; that two of the other Jews were arrested because they, too, were related to the one who escaped into Switzerland; and that only two of the Jews were not relatives of either of the young men. There was, then, in the official announcement the deliberate intention of extending the responsibility of the two young men not only to their families—for that is the custom today in Italy—but also to the entire Jewish community. To confirm the anti-Semitic tendency of the announcement of March 31, there was a violent anti-Semitic article in the Roman daily *Il Tevere*, reproduced by all the Italian papers. Anyone familiar with affairs in Italy knows that neither the *Tevere*, in the first place, nor the other papers, subsequently, would have published this article without express orders from Mussolini . . .who, by means of his press bureau, is the real editor of all the papers in Italy.

The object of this anti-Jewish campaign, according to Salvemini, "was to let the Italian Jews know that if other Jews were discovered taking part in anti-Fascist activities, all the Italian Jews would have to pay for it. Either all the Jews prove themselves one hundred percent in favor of Fascism both in Italy and abroad, or the whole Jewish community in Italy will be persecuted as it is in Germany." Mussolini's threat was not slow in producing tangible results:

The newspapers of May 3, 1934, report that two Jewish news-papermen have started a weekly entitled *La Nostra Bandiera* in Turin, that is, in the city where the arrests of the previous month had been made. The program of the paper is "to defend the religious traditions of the Jews," which in Italy have never been threatened by anyone, and "at the same time to combat energetically the work of those coreligionists whose activities are not in accord with the objectives of the regime."

The Italian Jews would have done well to realize, however, that an excess of Fascist zeal on their part would do more harm than good:

If these two journalists should succeed in convincing the Italian people that a Jew cannot be other than a Fascist, they will have laid the foundation for a wave of anti-Semitism that will break out and sweep Italy the day the Fascist regime collapses, be that day near at hand or in the far distant future.

Salvemini was certain that Mussolini's blackmail would "not be successful in proselytizing those Jews now hostile to Fascism. They will continue to fight the regime just as the Protestant, Catholic and free-thinking anti-Fascists are fighting it, regardless of their creed and social class. What will Mussolini then do against the Jews? Will the thunder follow the lightning? The future alone can answer this question."[14]

Not content with harassing the Jews in his newspapers, the Duce also encouraged "moderate" anti-Semitic tendencies beyond the borders of Italy. In December 1934, the following anti-Jewish resolution was submitted to the international Fascist Congress at Montreux and unanimously approved:

Considering that certain Jewish groups in certain places have installed themselves as in a conquered country, openly or secretly exercising an injurious influence on the material and moral interests of the homeland which gives them hospitality, constituting a kind of state within a state, profiting from all the rights and exempting themselves from all the duties; and con-

14. G. Salvemini, "Will the Lightning Follow?," *Neither Liberty nor Bread: The Meaning and Tragedy of Fascism*, ed. F. Keene (New York, 1940), pp. 290–92.

sidering that the said Jews have furnished or are furnishing by their conduct elements useful to international revolution destructive of the ideas of country and Christian civilization [this Congress] denounces the nefarious activity of these elements and pledges itself to fight against them.

This resolution, which was signed by the Italian delegate, Eugenio Coselschi, in order to please the numerous Jew-baiters among the non-Italian participants, may be described as an attempt to strike a balance between explicit condemnation of "certain Jews" and implicit condemnation of Hitler's racial persecutions. While calling for resistance to the activities of "subversive" Jewish elements, it unequivocally rejected the idea of a "universal hate-campaign" against Jews as such, maintaining a careful distinction (incompatible with racial anti-Semitism) between good and bad Jews and leaving each signatory free to deal with the "Jewish problem" as he saw fit.[15] Even so, the signing of an explicitly anti-Semitic document by an official spokesman of the Fascist regime was a new departure in Italian politics that could not but cause dismay among the Jews and their friends.[16]

Oddly enough, Mussolini's first anti-Jewish campaign was passed over in silence by practically all contemporary students of Fascism; even Jewish writers gave it little publicity. There were several reasons for this. For one thing, the threats of Mussolini's underlings were not translated into action; no anti-Jewish measures of any kind were adopted during the period under review. For another, the anti-Jewish polemics were strictly unofficial and their significance was obscured, as Mussolini presumably intended that they should be, by both the official condemnation of German racialism and the official manifestations of Fascist benevolence towards the Jews in general and the Zionists in particular; speaking to Nahum Goldmann in November 1934, the Duce went so far as to describe

15. "Il Convegno di Montreux e la questione ebraica," *La Nostra Bandiera*, May 1935. The Germans did not attend, having no interest in a Fascist International, which they could not control (A. del Boca and M. Giovana, *I 'figli del sole'* [Milan, 1965], pp. 62–75).

16. One of those friends was Ezio Garibaldi, nephew of the *Risorgimento* hero, who denounced the resolution in the columns of *La Nostra Bandiera* (May 1935); Garibaldi was particularly incensed at the fact that the signatories had put the "material interests" of their respective countries before the "moral" ones.

himself as a "Zionist."[17] Last but not least, the friction between Fascists and Jews was overshadowed, if not eclipsed altogether, by the increasingly violent clash between Rome and Berlin over Austria. After the assassination of Dollfuss on July 25, 1934, the "Jewish question" on the peninsula inevitably receded into the background, and by the end of the year, Italian Jewry had reason to feel that the storm had definitely blown over. The rapprochement between Italy and the western democracies, culminating in the anti-German coalition known as the "Stresa front" (April 11–14, 1935), gave a fresh impetus to the "philo-Semitic" tendencies, Mussolini being more than ever anxious to dissociate Fascism from anti-Semitic National Socialism.[18]

Even after the Fascist aggression against Ethiopia had led to the collapse of his alliance with Paris and London, the Duce continued to play the Jewish card for all it was worth. In October 1935, he sent an extravagantly philo-Semitic message, the last of the series, to Jewish students in the United States. It is worth quoting in full:

Fascism does not desire that Jewry should renounce its religious traditions, its ritual usages, its national memories, or its racial peculiarities. Fascism desires only that the Jews should recognize the national ideals of Italy, accepting the discipline of national unity. In Italy no difference exists between Jews and non-Jews either in the political or in the social spheres. For many years the Italian Jews have taken an active part in the political, scientific and artistic life of Italy. In a word, a Jewish question does not exist in Italy. I, at least do not know of one. Wherever I have detected the faintest trace of anti-Semitic discrimination in the life of the State, I have at once suppressed it. Whatever the foes of Fascism may say, we are tolerant to all. Neither I nor any other exponent of the [Fascist] regime has ever expressed anti-Jewish views. In these great days of the Italian nation I declare that Italian and Jewish ideals are fully merged into one.[19]

17. Mussolini-Goldmann conversation of November 13, 1934 (English translation in Memories. The Autobiography of Nahum Goldmann [London, 1970], pp. 153–63).
18. M. Michaelis, op. cit., pp. 80–81
19. Message to Jewish students in the U.S., quoted in La Nostra Bandiera, December 1935. The message was followed by yet another attempt to harness "world Jewry" to the Fascist chariot. On December 20, 1935, the Palazzo Chigi commissioned

Coming at such a moment, this attempt to identify Judaism with Fascism predictably failed to produce the desired effect. The organ of the German Zionists roundly denounced it as "Italian propaganda," pointing out that the absence of a Jewish problem in Italy—which could not be ascribed to any merit of Fascism— was irrelevant to the question of Italian aggression in Africa. To be sure, the Duce had a perfect right to demand loyalty from his Jewish subjects; he would have done well to realize, however, that Palestine Jewry had an equal duty of loyalty to the Mandatory Power.[20] Western Jewish spokesmen were equally unimpressed by Mussolini's philo-Semitic rhetoric. The prevailing reaction was aptly expressed by Professor Selig Brodetzky of the Jewish Agency Executive in a talk with two eminent Italian Jews, Dante Lattes and Angiolo Orvieto, whom Mussolini had sent to London with the aim of mobilizing Anglo-Jewish opinion against the sanctionist policy: the leaders of Anglo-Jewry, while appreciating Italy's splendid pro-Jewish record, "had no desire to be dragged into international disputes."[21] Attempts to win over Palestine Jewry were equally unsuccessful; nor were western Jewish financiers prepared to support Mussolini's African venture.[22]

Undeterred by these rebuffs, the Duce and his advisers continued to woo "international Jewry" until the eve of the Spanish civil war. In May 1936 Corrado Tedeschi, a Jewish Fascist, was permitted to publish a pro-Zionist article in Mussolini's review, *Gerarchia*;[23] and as late as the beginning of July, Ugo Dadone, head of the Fascist propaganda organization in Egypt, in a talk with the Jewish Agency representative in Cairo, Nahum Wilenski, called for the establishment of a strong Jewish state. From a note of the

Eli Rubin, an Austrian Jewish publicist, to write a pamphlet on "The Jews in Italy," a panegyric on the liberal treatment of Italian Jewry, which was to be distributed throughout the world but especially in English-speaking countries. Its object was to influence western opinion in favor of Mussolini's African war and to secure Jewish support in London and New York for a loan of which the Duce was in urgent need (E. Rubin, *Mussolini: Raciste et antisémite* [Paris, 1938], pp. 3–16).

20. "Italienische Propaganda," *Jüdische Rundschau*, October 18, 1935, p. 1.

21. Quoted in R. De Felice, *Storia degli ebrei italiani sotto il fascismo*, 3rd ed. (Turin, 1972), p. 208.

22. M. Michaelis, op. cit., pp. 85–89; on the hostility of Jewish bankers cf. L. Villari, *Italian Foreign Policy under Mussolini* (New York, 1956), pp. 199–200.

23. C. Tedeschi, "La soluzione integrale della questione ebraica," *Gerarchia XIV*, May 1936, pp. 328–35.

conversation, written by Wilenski on July 15, we learn that Dadone put the following three points to his interlocutor:

(1) The Jews would never get Palestine by relying on the British. A parliamentary regime was too weak and too ready to give way to opposition. The Jews should work in association with the Italians, who would not be afraid of the Arabs and who would aim at creating a Jewish state in Palestine, while taking Iraq and Syria for themselves.

(2) There were 500,000 Italian soldiers in Abyssinia, none of whom would return to Italy; to these would be added in due course 500,000 Abyssinians, who would make excellent military material. In addition to this potential army of one million men, there would be some 150,000 Italian troops in Tripoli. It was Italy's object to dominate the Mediterranean, and with these troops available, and Abyssinia as a center, Italy would be in a position to take Egypt and expand still further. It would take a few years to consolidate the present position, but these were the lines of Italian policy, and Britain would not be able to stop it.

(3) In the meantime, the Italians wanted the Jews to settle in the Gojjam area of Abyssinia; the object of this would be, on the one hand to help the Italians consolidate their position in Abyssinia, and on the other hand to foster Jewish sympathy for Italy. Dadone realized that Jewish settlement in Abyssinia could not be an ultimate aim as far as the Jews were concerned. But Italy would be prepared to undertake, in return for Jewish assistance in this matter, the creation of a real Jewish state in Palestine. When the Italians had wanted land for their own purposes in Tripoli, they had not hesitated to push out the existing Arab inhabitants, and the Jews need not fear that the interest of the Arabs in Palestine would be over-scrupulously protected.[24]

For their part, the Zionist leaders had every reason to worry about their dependence on British friendship at a moment when Britain was preparing to appease the Arabs at the expense of the Jews. With the collapse of the anti-Hitler front, however, the Italian card had lost its political value to the Zionist movement. Re-

24. London, Public Record Office/FO 371/19983/6948/106–7.

alizing the futility of a further meeting with Mussolini, Weizmann reacted to the latter's advances by confidentially warning the British of Italian designs in the Middle East;[25] nor was Jewish opinion in Palestine at all responsive to the "pro-Zionist" intrigues of Fascist agents. Jewish hostility to the Fascist regime was further increased by three other factors during the period under review: Italy's support for the Arab rebellion in Palestine; the resumption of Fascist press polemics against "international Jewry," accused of being behind the sanctions; and the growing intimacy between Italy and the Third Reich.[26]

With the outbreak of the Spanish civil war and the beginning of German-Italian cooperation in Spain, relations between the Duce and his Jewish subjects took a marked, if strictly unofficial, turn for the worse. The overtures to the Zionists ceased. The attacks on "Jewish Bolshevism" were stepped up, and a Fascist deputy, Alfredo Romanini, published a pamphlet on the common bond between Fascism and Roman Catholicism and the danger Judaism held for them both.[27] Finally, on September 12, 1936—six weeks before the birth of the Rome-Berlin Axis—Roberto Farinacci, a former party secretary and a member of the Fascist Grand Council, launched a fresh campaign against the Jews. Taking his cue from Göbbels' "terrible indictment" of world Jewry at the Nuremberg rally of the National Socialist Party, he called upon his Jewish compatriots to break their ties with their anti-Fascist co-religionists abroad and to demonstrate their loyalty by supporting Italy's rapprochement with the Jew-baiter Hitler. The link between anti-Semitism and foreign policy was therefore plain from the start.[28]

Although these polemics evoked alarm in Jewish circles, students of Fascism continued to emphasize the profound difference between the German and Italian approaches to the Jewish issue. Commenting on Farinacci's attack, Ernst Basch, an American scholar, insisted that it was wrong to identify anti-Semitism with Fascism as such:

25. Weizmann to Ormsby Gore, July 19, 1936 (Public Record Office/FO 371/19983/101–3).
26. M. Michaelis, op. cit., pp. 90–100.
27. A Romanini, *Ebrei-Cristianesimo-Fascismo* (Empoli, 1936), 2nd ed., 1939.
28. "Una tremenda requisitoria," *Il Regime Fascista*, September 12, 1936.

Since 1933, anti-Semitism has often been described as a Fascist characteristic—which is an altogether erroneous idea. In a religious sense, Fascism is anti-Semitic just as much as it is anti-Catholic or anti-Protestant—that is to say, it opposes the tendency of the Jewish faith, as well as of any other, to establish a separate group consciousness within the nation. In a racial sense, Fascism is anti-Semitic, if—and only if—its basic collective concept happens to be not purely nationally but racially determined as is the case with National Socialism which, unlike Italian Fascism, does not embrace all citizens of Fascist mentality but embraces Germans regardless of citizenship, provided only they are of "Aryan" stock. . . . In Italy proper, such a difference was never felt. . . . Fascism, when it came to power, had neither need nor reason to conjure up something which had not been there before. On the contrary, it would have been an extremely dangerous precedent to demonstrate the fact that a gap *could* be made artificially into the dogmatically indivisible whole of the Fascist nation. Therefore, for twelve years, Italy gave an exhibition of a totalitarian state without anti-Semitism; the roster of Jews important in the Mussolinian hierarchy is impressive and has often been read by others.

As for Farinacci's anti-Semitic outburst, Basch thought that its importance should not be exaggerated:

At the time of this writing, a scare has been thrown into the public by the official party organ, *Regime Fascista*, which published a call to Italian Jews for loyalty, in tones that could well be interpreted as indicating a swing toward anti-Semitism. In the opinion of the writer, this suspicion is unfounded. It seems improbable that Mussolini—who has never yet rejected any nominal Italian willing to come into the Fascist fold, not even the war-subjected Tyrolese and Istrians—would start such a thing now, even as a gesture to bind his new anti-Bolshevik alliance with the Nazis. It is more probable that, aware of the strong leanings of Jews all over the world toward either Liberalism or Socialism, both of which he abhors, he became suddenly suspicious of the sincerity of the professed Fascism of his own Italian Jews. It is most probable, however, that the call for loyalty was entirely sincere, that it was occasioned by the imminence of a close understanding with Germany—a country which, for obvious reasons, is anathema to all Jews—and was meant to remind them, in this special situation of conflicting allegiances, that they are required to be Fascists, and nothing but Fascists, and that it would mean failure in their professed loyalty as Fascists if they permitted any feeling whatever *as Jews* to come to the fore. It is very natural that Italian Jews were not overly enthusiastic at the prospect of having to devote their affection and fidelity to the friendship with a nation that lost no chance to humiliate their name . . . and accordingly it is very natural for *Regime Fascista* to remind them sharply that their Fascist duty is not to make policies but to carry them out, and particularly, not to let another group feeling (treason in itself!) interfere with their performance of this duty. Again, as so often in Fascism, no explanation jibes as well with facts as the literal one.

Basch concluded by reaffirming his conviction that there was no need whatever to worry about the anti-Jewish polemics in the Fascist press:

> In general, it seems to be reasonably well-established by now that a Fascist regime will feature anti-Semitism only if anti-Semitism is also a pre-Fascist characteristic of the respective nation. If so, Fascism will quite probably exaggerate this characteristic into monstrous forms. Otherwise, however, it will be content with enforcing against Jews as against all others the totalitarian concept—which, of course, means the breaking up of the self-conscious community which Jews, under the influence of historical pressure, have formed and preserved in every part of the world for nineteen centuries.[29]

The above was written in the second half of September 1936. A month later, Mussolini's foreign minister, Count Galeazzo Ciano (who was also his son-in-law) went to Germany to conclude an agreement with the rulers of the Third Reich, thus setting the stage for his master's conversion to racial anti-Semitism on the German model.

The anti-Jewish agitation initiated by Farinacci, followed by the formation of the Rome-Berlin Axis, created a market for books on

---

29. E. B. Ashton (pseudonym of Ernst Basch), *The Fascist. His State and His Mind* (New York, 1937), pp. 160–63.

the "Jewish question." For the moment, however, Fascist writers continued to stress the differences between the German and the Italian approaches to the issue. In the autumn of 1936, Giulio Cogni, a twenty-eight-year-old publicist and composer resident in Hamburg, published a monograph on racialism which was a rehash, in Italian form, of Rosenberg's Nordic mythology. But while extolling Fascism and National Socialism as two kindred manifestations of the Nordic spirit, Cogni strongly objected to the identification of "Nordic" with "Germanic blood": "Nordic, Aryan, in the true sense, is not confined to this or that racial particularity: it is not defined within the confines of flesh and intellect. . . . Aryan is equivalent to genius, profound mystery of the spirit." Cogni also took care to dissociate himself from the German brand of anti-Semitism, stressing the superiority of the Italian Sephardi Jew over the German Ashkenazi Jew and denying the existence of a Jewish problem on the peninsula: "The hatred and expulsion of the Jews in the North originated chiefly from the fact that the two races, all too different, not only never merged but remained facing each other in a warlike attitude. . . . This has never happened among us."[30] Ironically, Cogni's defense of his Jewish compatriots was based on the writings of two of his German masters, Houston Stewart Chamberlain and Hans F. K. Günther, who had extolled the Sephardi Jews as a "racial aristocracy."[31] In the spring of 1937, Cogni repeated his objections to racial anti-Semitism in his second book on the subject which contained an appendix by Günther, then the leading German apostle of the Nordic gospel.[32]

The spring of 1937 also saw the publication of the first explicitly anti-Semitic Fascist work on the "Jewish question," written by one of Mussolini's biographers, Paolo Orano, and inspired by the Duce himself.[33] It is symptomatic that Orano's book was entitled *The Jews in Italy*, meaning that the current anti-Jewish drive, as

30. G. Cogni, *Il razzismo*, 2nd ed. (Milan, 1937).
31. G. Cogni, *I valori della stirpe italiana* (Milan, 1937), pp. 133–36.
32. H. S. Chamberlain, *Die Grundlagen des 19. Jahrhunderts* (Munich, 1899), p. 275; H. F. K. Günther, *Rassenkunde des jüdischen Volkes* (Munich, 1931), pp. 324–25.
33. P. Orano, *Gli ebrei in Italia* (Rome, 1937). In a subsequent book *Inchiesta sulla razza* (Rome, 1939), p. 280, Orano made it clear that his attack on the Jews had been inspired by Mussolini himself.

distinct from its two predecessors, was directed against the loyal Italian Jews rather than against the abstractions known as "world Jewry," "Jewish high finance," "Jewish Bolshevism," and the "Judaeo-Masonic clique." Like Farinacci, Orano (who was rector of the University of Perugia and a Fascist deputy in 1937) rejected the German racial theories, affirming that the Jews of Italy were "Italians of the Jewish faith." Like Farinacci, he called upon his Jewish fellow citizens to abstain from manifestations of "separatism" (with particular reference to Zionism and anti-Hitlerism) and to dissociate themselves from their anti-Fascist co-religionists abroad, lest the regime be compelled to reconsider its attitude to the Jewish minority. Unlike Farinacci, however, he made a special point of attacking the Jewish Fascists, claiming that Ettore Ovazza (the Fascist editor of La Nostra Bandiera) was no less afflicted with a chosen-people complex than the Zionist Dante Lattes.[34]

While Orano confined himself to elaborating the social, political, and religious arguments against Italian Jewry, Julius C. Evola, a friend and collaborator of Farinacci's, tried to evolve an original "Roman" version of racial philosophy, in striking contrast with Alfred Rosenberg's Nordic aberration, that would constitute an independent ideological platform and spare the regime the humiliating charge of plagiarism should it decide to turn against the Jews on "racial" grounds. Race, according to Evola, revealed itself in basic behavior that was rooted in a community's desire to be unique. The concept of race was essential because it dealt a death-blow to the abhorred idea of "abstract and levelling universalism." The biological racialism of the National Socialists could not simply be rejected; it had to be transcended. In other words, Rosenberg's notion of bodily race had to be complemented by the notion of the race of soul and spirit. Physical race might be corrupted and distorted by the environment, but in the superior races the spirit remains pure; and the superior races are not those who preserve their physiognomic and somatic features, but rather those who are conscious of the uniqueness of their traditions. Having thus disposed of Rosenberg's claim to Nordic superiority over the Latin

34. Orano, Gli ebrei in Italia, pp. 109–43.

peoples, Evola proceeded to develop a theory of racial hierarchy based on the concept of an Aryan super-race that included the dark-haired Italians as well as the fair-haired Teutons.[35]

Foreign observers were at first inclined to dismiss the proliferation of anti-Jewish writings as a minor matter, attributing it to the Duce's desire to keep the recently forged Rome-Berlin Axis well greased. On May 11, 1937, Sir William Kidston McClure, an acute student of Italian affairs and a former press attaché at the British Embassy in Rome, affirmed in a memorandum to the Foreign Office (May 11, 1937) that Italy was still "a long way from being anti-Semitic," and that such anti-Jewish feeling as existed in certain Fascist circles was "purely political, not racial," racial anti-Semitism being totally out of step with Italian history and traditions.[36] The anti-Fascist exiles, on the other hand, generally took a more pessimistic view, most particularly Giuseppe Antonio Borgese, the outstanding poet and literary historian, who insisted that there was little to choose between Mussolini and Hitler as far as their approaches to the racial issue were concerned. To be sure, the Duce's treatment of his Jewish subjects had so far been "incomparably milder" than the Führer's. But this difference was "merely casual and due to external factors":

> Hitler, in his personal Bible, *Mein Kampf*, has included a penetrating remark about the implicit anti-Semitism of Mussolini's policy, and has praised him on that account. Whenever Italian Fascism was confronted with a positive racial issue, its racialism was at least as ruthless as Hitler's; the extermination of the Arabs in Libya under the governorship of General Graziani makes a more impressive page of history than many pogroms or concentration camps; and as soon as Ethiopia was conquered, terrifying legislation stifled as a criminal offence any intercourse of white conquerors with native women.

Originally the Fascist brand of racialism, as practiced in Ethiopia, had nothing whatever to do with the "Jewish question." By the summer of 1937, however, there were signs that it was about

---

35. J. C. Evola, *Il Mito del sangue* (Milan, 1937); also, Evola, *Sintesi della dottrina della razza* (Milan, 1941).
36. Public Record Office/FO 371/21182/R3585/2476/22.

to assume an anti-Jewish character: "A rumbling of anti-Semitism grows increasingly audible in the controlled press, and while racial dogmas are now frankly floated by juvenile sociologists of the regime, a couple of Jewish merchants who did not substitute the Sunday for their Sabbath were legally flogged in the market of Tripoli." Unfortunately, the Jews and their friends in the democratic countries had so far preferred to play down these manifestations of Fascist hostility, "fathering the regrettable episodes upon minor officials and scribes and leaving unsuspected the magnanimity of the Duce." In a postscript, written on March 1, 1938, Borgese noted that some western observers were beginning to have second thoughts about "philo-Semitic" Fascism.[37]

Mussolini himself, while keeping a discreet silence in public, contributed two anonymous articles to the anti-Jewish campaign. On the last day of 1936, in a short diatribe entitled "Too Much Is Too Much," he justified anti-Semitism as an inevitable reaction to the aggressiveness and exclusiveness of the Jews:

Absent-minded people, or those who pretend to be such, ask themselves how anti-Semitism is born, how and why people become anti-Semitic without any prompting from nature. The answer is very simple: anti-Semitism is inevitable wherever Semitism becomes too obtrusive, too aggressive, and hence too powerful. The excessive Jew begets the anti-Jew. Do you want an explanation for the revival of anti-Semitism in France? Let us read the article by Beraud in the latest issue of *Gringoire*, which shows, mentioning names, that under the government headed by the Jew Blum, a Jewish cell has grown up in every ministry of the republic from where they rule France undisturbed. . . . This list of names speaks for itself. Do you wish to know what proportion of the French people is Jewish? Two percent. No one can deny that there is a more than striking disproportion between the number of Jews and the positions they occupy. Now invert the percentages. Imagine a France in which two percent of the people were Christian and 98 percent Jewish. Clearly, given the ferocious exclusiveness of the tribe, Christians

37. G. A. Borgese, *Goliath. The March of Fascism* (London, 1938), pp. 342, 369–70, 494.

would be banished from public life. At the very most, they would be permitted to work like slaves in order to let the Jews rest on the Sabbath. The originator and justifier of anti-Semitism is always and everywhere the same: the Jew when he exaggerates, as he so often does.[38]

About half a year later, the Duce's conversion to racialism found expression in a fresh journalistic outburst against the Jews. Taking his cue from an article in *Davar*, a Milanese Jewish periodical, he denounced as hypocrites those Jews who denied the existence of a Jewish nation. The Jew who openly avowed his race, he now averred, was more worthy of respect than the assimilationist who pretended to differ from the Gentiles only in the matter of religion. It was racial exclusiveness, rooted in religious contempt for the rest of mankind, that had enabled Israel to preserve its identity throughout the centuries of the dispersion; the late Rabbi Margulies of Florence had put the point well when he said that the Jew "rises on top of the other peoples like oil on water." Judaism was "an outstanding example of racialism which has lasted for thousands of years and . . . which arouses profound admiration." That being so, the Jews had no right whatever to complain if other peoples likewise adopted racialism.[39]

Being resolved to go on with the Axis alliance, Mussolini felt compelled to demonstrate his solidarity with Hitler on the racial issue. But being equally resolved not to make irreversible decisions in advance of events, he was anxious to put off the final rupture with Jewry as long as possible. It was not until July 15, 1938, that he finally threw off the mask: on that day he had the press publish a statement, called the "Manifesto of the Race," in which the Italian Jews were referred to as unassimilable aliens.[40] The manifesto was followed by a spate of anti-Jewish laws and regulations that, in the words of Cecil Roth, the foremost British authority on Italian Jewry, "reduced the position of the Italian Jews to that of pariahs."[41] With that, the debate on the "Jewish question" in Fascist Italy entered a new phase.

38. *Opera Omnia di Benito Mussolini* XXVIII, p. 98.
39. Ibid., pp. 202–3.
40. Full text in R. De Felice, op. cit., pp. 541–42.
41. C. Roth, *The History of the Jews of Italy* (Philadelphia, 1946), p. 528.

A month after the publication of the race manifesto, Martin Agronsky, a noted American-Jewish journalist, went to Italy to find out what impact Mussolini's sudden switch to official anti-Semitism was having on Italian Jewry. To his surprise, most of the Jews he met were still hugging the fond delusion that the racial campaign would stop with journalistic polemics:

> During the last two weeks of August, I spoke with Jewish leaders in Rome, Milan, Florence, Trieste and Turin, the centers of Jewish population. Each assured me that they were confident that the Government's actions were the product of diplomatic expediency. Italian anti-Semitism, they insisted, was merely Mussolini's way of showing his solidarity with Berlin. . . . Neither the August 3 decree excluding all foreign Jews from Italian schools nor the census taken of the Jewish population on August 23 [sic] shook them in this belief.

On September 2 it was the turn of the native-born Italian Jews who had hoped against hope that something would happen to save them:

> The September 2 decree excluded all Jewish teachers and students from every university and school in Italy after October 16, 1938. A single exception was made in favor of native-born Jewish university students, who were permitted to finish their studies. . . . All Jewish-written textbooks, even those "influenced by a Jewish trend of thought," have been banned from Italian schools. The work of educating Italian children to a hatred of the Jew will undoubtedly be the next step. Within the next few years a generation to whom the Jew is a "parasitic growth" and a "human toad" will grow up in Italy, as it already has in Germany.

It was not until September 12 that the Italian Jewish community was finally jolted out of its complacent attitude:

> According to a decree published on that date all persons whose fathers and mothers were Jewish and who had settled in Italy or the Italian colonies (except Ethiopia) since 1919, must leave the country within six months or become subject to expulsion. Profession of Christianity or any other non-Jewish religion was no ground for exception.

On October 6, the Fascist Grand Council decided on further anti-Jewish measures, including a ban on intermarriage between "Italians" and "non-Aryans."[42]

As might be expected, the enactment of the Fascist race laws gave a fresh impetus to the study of the "Jewish question" in Italy. Scholars now began to wonder whether there was not a strong element of continuity in Mussolini's attitude towards his Jewish subjects, his apparent change of heart notwithstanding. Among the first to raise the question was the late Joshua Starr who, in an article written in October 1938 and published in the following January, pointed out that the Fascist movement had been tinged with anti-Semitism from its very inception:

In the early twenties some of Mussolini's highly placed [sic] allies indiscriminately condemned the opposition to Fascism both at home and abroad as Jewish and Marxist. . . . During the tempestuous months before the March on Rome in November [sic] 1922 . . . anti-Semitism was a useful tool in the hands of the *fascisti*. This was not because the 50,000 Italian Jews distinguished themselves in the opposition to the blackshirts but because, like reactionary opponents of Bolshevism everywhere, the *fascisti* resorted to appealing to anti-Jewish prejudice in their efforts to discredit all revolutionary movements.

Starr then proceeded to analyze the anti-Jewish campaign conducted since 1920 by the "dean of Italian Jew-baiters," Giovanni Preziosi (1881–1945), editor of *La Vita Italiana*, whom he wrongly described as a "prominent comrade-in-arms of Mussolini and a member of the Fascist Grand Council." He concluded by affirming that there seemed to be "no reason to suppose that this trickle of (anti-Jewish) propaganda was having any effect upon official circles during those years. Occasionally Mussolini made statements repudiating racism and anti-Semitism, notably in his brief but unequivocal allusion to the subject in the course of an address before the Chamber of Deputies on May 14, 1929, and his attitude is reflected in an editorial discussion of intermarriage in the Milan

42. M. Agronsky, "Racism in Italy," *Foreign Affairs* XVII, January 1939, pp. 391–401.

Il Popolo d'Italia." However, having thus absolved the Duce from responsibility for the anti-Jewish crusade conducted by Preziosi and other Fascist scribes prior to the March on Rome, Starr hastened to correct himself in a postscript, pointing out that Mussolini himself had written a blatantly anti-Jewish article in *Il Popolo d'Italia* as early as June 4, 1919, less than three months after the founding of the Fascist movement.

As for the outbreak of journalistic anti-Semitism in the second half of 1936, Starr agreed with the Rome correspondent of the *Jüdische Rundschau,* Kurt Kornicker, that it was partly a spontaneous reaction to "English Zionism" and "Jewish Bolshevism":

> In the late summer of 1936 . . . the various objectives of the Italian foreign policy were seen to have for once a common denominator in the Jewish issue. Particularly in the Mediterranean, with both extremities, Palestine and Spain, in flames, the recourse to anti-Jewish propaganda appeared inevitable from the standpoint of Italian imperialism. To the Islamic world the Duce was preparing to pose as defender of the faith against Great Britain and her ally, the Jewish Agency for Palestine, while in Spain, on the other hand, it was undeniably true that thousands of Jews were enrolling in the Loyalist ranks.

As for Mussolini's subsequent conversion to anti-Semitic racialism, it was obviously the result of his alliance with Hitler. While the Rome-Berlin Axis "would undoubtedly have developed without the aid of the defamation campaign, the journalists' accompaniment to the diplomatic negotiations was soothing music in the ears of the Nazi rulers. . . . In carrying out the measures for which the press has agitated, the Italian government has undeniably assured itself of an even more cordial alliance with the Third Reich."[43]

The Italian anti-Fascists generally held that Mussolini's sudden jump from "philo-Semitism" and anti-racialism to racial anti-Semitism was exclusively due to his ill-starred alliance with the Jew-baiter Hitler:

---

43. J. Starr, "Italy's Antisemites," *Jewish Social Studies* I, January 1939, pp. 105–24.

The most obvious and the most scandalous example of German intervention in Italian internal affairs was the anti-Semitic campaign and legislation. . . . No one had any doubts of the origin of this campaign and these laws. The will of Hitler was evident, not only in its principles, but also in some details of the regulations themselves; for exceptions were made in some of the general orders so as to put Jews of German nationality in an even worse position than those of other nationalities.[44]

Foreign observers of the Italian scene, while differing on the issue of "German intervention," generally agreed with the anti-Fascist exiles that Mussolini had borrowed his racial theories from Hitler. Daniel A. Binchy, a noted Irish Catholic scholar, wrote in November 1939:

The only problem for Fascism . . . was to bring its policy more closely into line with that of National Socialism, and the sacrifice of 40,000 Jews was considered but a small price to pay for a satisfactory solution. . . . Hitler's visit to Italy in May 1938 represented, not merely the consolidation of the Axis, but the beginning of an intimate collaboration between the two dictators in their domestic policies also. Just two months after it . . . appeared the famous report on "Fascism and Racial Problems," compiled by an anonymous group of "Fascist scholars working under the auspices of the Ministry for Popular Culture." It consisted of ten major propositions (promptly christened by the man in the street "the Ten Commandments of the Axis"). . . . Despite the inevitable assurance of their "essentially Italian" nature, they were for the most part a tepid re-hash of the Nazi racial "philosophy." . . . The practical corollary was, of course, that "the Jews do not belong to the Italian race."

The main reason for the unpopularity of the anti-Jewish measures, according to Binchy, was their obvious foreign origin:

I happened to be in Italy when the new racialist decalogue was issued, and thus had occasion to mark the vivid contrast between the strident welcome given to it in the Fascist press and the resentful shame with which the ordinary people received it.

44. Pentad (five anonymous authors), *The Remaking of Italy* (Harmondsworth, 1941), pp. 103–4.

They were certainly not so philo-Semitic as their Duce had been in the past; indeed they had not the least tenderness for individual Jews as such. What embarrassed and humiliated them chiefly, I think, was that the Government of the nation that had contributed so much to the building of a civilized Europe should have stooped to copy the example of German neo-barbarism.[45]

For their part, the Fascists, who in the past had emphatically denied the existence of a Jewish problem in Italy, now emphatically rejected the charge of imitation, insisting that their leader had been a consistent racialist since 1919.[46] They also insisted that anti-Semitism was implicit in the Fascist creed from the very outset. Camillo Pellizzi, a Fascist propagandist in London, wrote in 1939:

It is often suggested in certain quarters that Mussolini's racial edicts of the autumn of 1938 were inspired or even forced upon him by his German associates. Actually, Mussolini's "racialism" does not tally with the main lines of German racialism. In the case of the colored races it is mainly inspired by political and biological preoccupations; in the case of the Jewish problem it is not so much a blood discrimination as by an acute consciousness of the historical, cultural, and religious differences between the Jewish community and the Italian nation. No claim is made to an Italian superiority as against the Jews, and it is constantly repeated that the policy of Fascism in this field is not inspired by religious or moral considerations but only by political and cultural ones: the basic notion is that the Jews are peculiarly unfit to contribute to the social revolution which Fascism pursues, and that the international character of their community conceals a further danger. Although he had always refrained from legislation in this matter, it was commonly known that Mussolini held these views, and that he usually prevented Jews from achieving any prominent position in the regime.

According to the special Jewish census of August 22, 1938, which included others besides professing Jews, there were no more

45. D. A. Binchy, *Church and State in Fascist Italy* (Oxford, 1941 and 1970), pp. 612, 614.
46. "Assoluta continuità della concezione mussoliniana," *Il Popolo d'Italia*, August 6, 1938; G. Bottai, *Diario 1935–1944*, ed. G. B. Guerri (Milan, 1982), pp. 136–37.

than 10,173 "non-Aryans" of foreign nationality, 1,424 of whom were born in Italy.[47] Pellizzi, however, claimed that over 200,000 foreign Jews had crowded into the Italian kingdom "in recent years, and especially since the beginning of the Nazi regime in Germany." He further complained that the Italian Jews, despite the unofficial discrimination allegedly practiced by the Duce, had become too rich and influential:

> It is calculated that their aggregate wealth amounts to more than 30 billion lira, which means that the inherited wealth of the average Italian Jew is forty or fifty times larger than the average of non-Jewish Italians. Fascists claim that, in addition to their powerful financial position, the Jews had become too important in the cultural and administrative spheres, thus exercising a marked influence on the general conduct of the country and on the upbringing of the younger generations, and that this influence was not the one desired by Fascism. At the same time they continued to show their respect for the individual merits of many Jews in several walks of life.

Pellizzi made no attempt to defend Mussolini's ban on mixed marriages, confining himself to expressing the hope that it would not lead to a rupture between Church and State. He concluded by expressing his sympathy for the Jewish Fascists who were understandably bitter about the treatment meted out to them by their erstwhile comrades:

> Every Italian is willing to recognize that whatever the merits of the present legislation from a general point of view, individual cases of law-abiding and patriotic Jews who feel very hurt by the present anti-Jewish laws are not infrequent and deserve sympathy; Italy is not and never will be a country for pogroms.[48]

Pellizzi was undoubtedly right in claiming that Mussolini had never been a philo-Semite, his frequent pro-Jewish statements notwithstanding; even so, his analysis of Fascist racial policy is un-

---

47. Ministero dell'Interno Archivio Centrale dello Stato/Dir. Gen. Demografia e Razza (1938–1943)/cart. 14/fasc. 47, Rivelazione sugli ebrei del 22 agosto 1938.
48. C. Pellizi, *Italy* (London, 1939), pp. 192–94.

convincing. If the Duce was always opposed to Jewish influence, why did he allow the Jews to become so rich and influential? If his declaration of war on the Jews was not the result of his rapprochement with Berlin, why did he enact the racial laws at the very moment when he was proclaiming his "total" solidarity with Hitler? Moreover, if Fascist racial doctrine did not conform with the main lines of German racial theory, why did he give an "Aryan-Nordic" direction to his racial thinking?

The prevailing unhappiness about the importation of the "Aryan-Nordic" gospel into Italy was also reflected in the writings of Fascist apologists. Given Mussolini's determination to march with Hitler to the end, they were compelled to play down their objections to the latter's "zoological" racialism; even so, they continued to engage in polemics with the German apostles of "Nordic superiority" throughout the period under review. Guido Landra, the author of the "Manifesto of the Race," openly attacked the Nordic heresy in 1939, affirming that the dark-haired Italian was as much a *Herrenmensch* (member of the "master race") as the fair-haired German. Leone Franzi, one of Landra's collaborators, pointed out in the same year that only twelve percent of the Swedish population, the most Germanic of populations, could pass muster as "Nordics." Aldo Capasso recalled as late as 1942 that Mussolini had always condemned the racialist aberrations of Hitler's mentor, Houston Stewart Chamberlain. About the same time Vincenzo Mazzei published a thinly veiled attack on the Fascist imitation of National Socialist anti-Semitism, insisting that the anti-Jewish measures could not be justified on racial grounds and would have to be reconsidered in due course.[49] And while Fascist apologists continued to refer to the "Jewish race," most Italian scholars continued to maintain that such a race had never existed.

The most scathing critique of German racialism to appear in Italy before the fall of Fascism was Giacomo Acerbo's *Foundations of Fascist Racial Doctrine,* a diatribe against the "Nordic barbar-

49. G. Landra, "Die wissenschaftliche und politische Bergründung der Rassenfrage in Italien," *Nationalsozialistische Monatshefte* X, April 1939, pp. 296–306; L. Franzi, *Fase attuale del razzismo tedesco* (Rome, 1939), p. 15; A. Capasso, *Idee chiare sul razzismo* (Rome, 1942), p. 27; V. Mazzei, *Razza e Nazione* (Rome, 1942).

ians" and the concept of the "Aryan" race, which aroused indignation among Hitler's "racial experts." It was followed by Julius Evola's *Synthesis of Racial Doctrine*, a counterblast to the "materialistic" German doctrine of blood and soil, which likewise provoked a hostile reaction in Berlin.[50] While Fascist scholars and publicists tried hard to evolve an original Italian race theory, Fascist propagandists made a vain effort to divert attention from the German origin of Mussolini's anti-Jewish crusade. Some, like Farinacci, affirmed that the racial measures were no more than a logical application of Catholic principles and a logical continuation of the anti-Jewish policy pursued by former popes; others, like Interlandi (the Duce's unofficial mouthpiece) claimed that they were a logical extension of the ban on miscegenation in Ethiopia; yet others pointed to the earlier manifestations of nationalist and Fascist prejudice against the Jews in order to demonstrate the priority of Italian anti-Semitism over its German counterpart. There were, however, a few Fascist scribes who frankly admitted what their colleagues tried to conceal—that the Jews had been sacrificed on the altar of the German-Italian alliance.[51]

Mussolini himself has given us a series of contradictory answers to this question. In 1938, he repeatedly affirmed that it was the conquest of an empire in Africa rather than the alliance with Hitler that had prompted him to introduce racial measures in Italy. About the same time he claimed that his anti-Semitic policy was a defensive reaction to Jewish anti-Fascism at home and abroad. In April 1943, on the other hand, he told Miklós Kállay, then prime minister of Hungary, that he had been compelled to enact certain anti-Jewish laws "because the Germans, who were incredibly intolerant and inflexible in this matter, had insisted." In July 1944,

50. G. Acerbo, *I fondamenti della dottrina fascista della razza* (Rome, 1940); J. C. Evola, op. cit. See also G. Acerbo, *Fra due plotoni di esecuzione. Avvenimenti e problemi dell'epoca fascista* (Bologna, 1968), p. 199; Bonn, *Politisches Archiv des Auswärtigen Amts/Partei/Italien Baron Julius Evola/1941–1942;* M. Michaelis, "La politica razziale fascista vista da Berlino. L'antisemitismo italiano alla luce di documenti inediti tedeschi," *Storia Contemporanea* XI, December 1980, pp. 1003–45.

51. T. Interlandi, "Il meticciato dissidente," *Il Tevere;* G. Preziosi, "Fra coloro che son sospesi. Gli Ebrei in Italia e il vero problema ebraico," *La Vita Italiana* XLIX, June 1937, pp. 659–68; N. Quilici, "La difesa della razza," *Nuova Antologia* LXXIII, September 16, 1938, pp. 133–35.

he went further, claiming in a conversation with a Fascist journalist that the adoption of an anti-Jewish policy in 1938 had been
due to an explicit request from the Führer.[52] It goes without saying
that neither of these conflicting versions can be taken at face value.
In 1938, Mussolini, stung to the quick by the pope's taunt that he
was imitating Germany, had been anxious to demonstrate the orig-
inality of his racial legislation. Five years later, however, faced
with the utter bankruptcy of his pro-German policy, he found it
expedient to place the blame for his racialist folly on his ally; and
in 1944, with defeat and ruin staring him in the face, he repeated
the charge against Hitler in a more explicit manner. In neither case
had he been actuated by a desire to tell the truth for its own sake.[53]

The fall of Fascism on July 25, 1943, did not put an end to the
racial legislation, since Mussolini's successor, Marshal Pietro Badoglio, was anxious to avoid a premature conflict with Hitler.[54] It
did, however, result in a temporary suspension of the anti-Jewish
press polemics. Both the polemics and the racial persecutions were
resumed and stepped up after the Italian surrender to the Allies on
September 8, 1943, and the setting up of a Fascist puppet republic,
when Hitler decided to treat the part of Italy under German control
as conquered, as well as occupied territory and to extend the "Final
Solution" of the Jewish problem to Mussolini's "non-Aryan" subjects.

After World War II, the former Fascist hierarchs generally maintained an embarrassed silence about their late master's racialist
aberrations, except those who, like Giacomo Acerbo and Luigi Fed-
erzoni, had opposed the racial laws in 1938. The neo-Fascist apologists generally admitted that the persecution of loyal Italians of
Jewish extraction (as distinct from the campaign against "international Jewry") had been a deplorable error. According to Attilio
Tamaro, a Fascist publicist and diplomat who remained faithful to

52. *Opera Omnia di Benito Mussolini* XXIX, pp. 125–26, 146; N. (M.) Kállay,
*Hungarian Premier. A Personal Account of a Nation's Struggle in the Second
World War* (London and New York, 1954), p. 159; I. Fossani, "Diario di Salò," *La
Gazzetta di Livorno,* September 25, 1947.
53. On Mussolini's real motives see M. Michaelis, *Mussolini and the Jews,* pp.
84–89.
54. P. Badoglio, *L'Italia nella seconda guerra mondiale* (Milan, 1946), p. 92; for
a critical analysis of Badoglio's account cf. R. De Felice, op. cit., pp. 428–30.

Mussolini after his downfall, the Duce's conversion to the racial gospel marked "the beginning of the crisis of Fascism." According to Giorgio Pini, chief editor of Mussolini's paper from 1936 to 1943 and under-secretary of the Interior in 1944–45, the race laws were "repugnant to the Italian temperament"; worse still, they undermined the respect for law and order, with unfortunate results. According to Edoardo Susmel, co-editor of Mussolini's *Opera Omnia* after World War II, Mussolini had been wrong to punish loyal Italians of Jewish "race" for the sins of their anti-Fascist co-religionists in other countries. According to Luigi Villari, the Fascist propagandist quoted earlier, the anti-Jewish measures had antagonized Mussolini's friends as well as his enemies:

> While the existence of a Jewish problem demanding some solution was generally admitted, the measures enacted by the Italian government did not help to solve it, but they brought much odium on Mussolini and on Italy in general. They undoubtedly constituted one of the chief mistakes of the Duce, inasmuch as they were unnecessary and aroused a wide measure of disapproval even among loyal Fascists. Their effect abroad was equally deplorable, even among persons who were not prejudicially hostile to Italy, to Fascism or to Mussolini personally.

Even those few who still defended the Duce's anti-Jewish policy, such as Julius C. Evola, Giorgio Pisanò, Rino Rauti, and Rutilio Sermonti, did so rather half-heartedly, stressing the profound difference between the German and Italian approaches to the Jewish problem.[55]

Meanwhile the debate over Mussolini's switch from "philo-Semitism" to racial anti-Semitism was being resumed by the scholars. Most of the explanations offered revolved either around the disastrous Axis alliance or around the ill-starred conquest of the "Empire" in East Africa. At least two writers —the Americans Dante L.

---

55. A. Tamaro, *Due anni di storia* III (Rome, 1950), p. 306; G. Pini and D. Susmel, *Mussolini. L'uomo e l'opera* IV (Florence, 1958), pp. 1–2; E. Susmel, *Mussolini e il suo tempo* (Milan, 1950), pp. 209–10; L. Villari, *Italian Foreign Policy under Mussolini*, p. 202; J. C. Evola, *Il cammino del cinabro*, 2nd ed. (Milan, 1972), pp. 158–59; Evola, *Gli uomini e le rovine*, 3rd ed. (Rome, 1972), pp. 185–207; G. Pisanò, *Mussolini e gli ebrei* (Milan, 1967), *passim*; P. Rauti and R. Sermonti, *Storia del fascismo V: L'espansione e l'Asse* (Rome, 1977), pp. 305, 320–21.

Germino and Michael A. Ledeen—thought that racial anti-Semitism was a logical development of the Fascist creed, while a third, the Israeli Martin van Creveld, reached the somewhat startling conclusion that the "Manifesto of the Race" was not an imitation of German racial doctrine but rather "a refutation thereof," i.e., a counterblast to Hitler's Nordic heresy with its blatantly anti-Italian implications.[56]

Forty-two years after the fall of Fascism, it is generally recognized that the decision to import racial anti-Semitism into Italy was Mussolini's, not Hitler's—the Duce's above-quoted statements to the contrary notwithstanding.[57] But the motive or combination of motives that prompted the Fascist dictator to persecute his Jewish subjects is still the subject of controversy. Was racial anti-Semitism inherent in Fascist doctrine from the outset? Or was it simply a tactical move caused by a shift in the European balance of power? Was it the conquest of Ethiopia that made Mussolini "Jew-conscious" as well as race-conscious? Or was it only after the forging of the Rome-Berlin Axis that he felt the need to place the Jewish problem "squarely on the racial plane" in order to demonstrate his "total solidarity" with Hitler?

Another subject of controversy was the strident contrast between the German and Italian approaches to the Jewish issue in the Axis-occupied territories. While Jews were being rounded up and deported all over Europe, those of Italian citizenship continued to enjoy complete immunity; furthermore, the Italian-occupied territories in France, Yugoslavia, and Greece became havens of refuge for the Jews of those countries until the Italian surrender to the Allied Powers. In 1938, Mussolini had launched an anti-Jewish campaign in order to strengthen his tie with his Axis partner. Why, then, did he permit his underlings to pursue policies that were bound to arouse indignation in Berlin?

The first of the open questions—Mussolini's motive or motives for reversing his stand on the "Jewish question" in 1938—has been

56. D. L. Germino, *The Italian Fascist Party in Power* (Minneapolis, 1959), pp. 28, 85; M. A. Ledeen, "The Evolution of Italian Fascist Antisemitism," *Jewish Social Studies* XXXVII, January 1975, pp. 3–17; M. Van Creveld, "Beyond the Finzi-Contini Garden. Mussolini's 'Fascist Racism,'" *Encounter* XLII, February 1974, pp. 42–47.
57. M. Michaelis, op. cit., pp. 118–82.

examined in detail by Renzo De Felice, whose *Storia degli ebrei italiani sotto il fascismo* (*History of the Italian Jews under Fascism*) is in a sense the beginning of the scientific study of Fascism. His basic assumption is that prior to his alliance with Hitler the Fascist dictator could not be considered an enemy of the Jews, his vulgar prejudices against "international Jewry" notwithstanding: "Until 1937 the idea of an official anti-Semitism was completely alien to him. The Jews of Italy enjoyed under Fascism neither more nor less 'liberty' than other Italians; persecuted Jews from abroad found in him, if not a protector, at any rate a political leader who frequently rendered assistance and opened the doors of Italy to them, unlike—it should be honestly recognized—many other heads of state." Even the racial policy practiced in Africa had no anti-Jewish implications—it affected the Duce's Jewish subjects only as Italians, not as Jews. What, then, were Mussolini's motives for reversing a policy that he had pursued for fourteen years to his presumed advantage? According to De Felice, his main motive was the presumed need to strengthen the Rome-Berlin Axis: "There is no doubt that Mussolini's decision to introduce official anti-Semitism into Italy was chiefly determined by his conviction that it was necessary to eliminate any marked difference in the policy of the two regimes." In addition, there were secondary motives, such as Mussolini's resentment at the opposition of international Jewish financiers to his policy of autarchy, pressure from his own pro-German extremists and—last but not least—his belief that the soft-hearted Italians—and in particular the "defeatist" bourgeoisie—needed "punches in the stomach." Despite its German origin, however, Fascist racialism "had its own special characteristics and could absolutely not be put on the same plane as the German brand, nor that of Germany's other satellites, including Vichy France." Even after his break with the Jews, he continued to deplore the racialist aberrations of the National Socialists, with special reference to Rosenberg's Nordic mythology; nor did he ever approve of Hitler's "Final Solution" to the Jewish problem.[58]

As for "German interference," De Felice agreed with the writer

58. Ibid., pp. 396–99, 411.

that Hitler had made no attempt whatever to impose his anti-Semitic obsession on his Axis partner, and that right up to the Italian surrender there was no evidence of open German intervention in Fascist racial policy.[59]

Was anti-Semitism implicit in the Fascist creed? De Felice thought that in a sense it was, despite the non-existence of a Jewish question in Italy. The sporadic manifestations of Fascist anti-Semitism prior to the rise of Hitler, he argued, had little bearing on Mussolini's subsequent conversion to the "Aryan-Nordic" gospel; what really prompted the Duce to throw in his lot with the Jew-baiter Hitler and declare war on his Jewish compatriots was the Fascist movement's "presumption to represent the sole truth."[60] Twenty years later, in the fifth volume of his biography of Mussolini, De Felice became more explicit: after the conquest of Ethiopia, he now maintained, the Fascist dictator unleashed a "process of totalitarization," designed to prevent a return to normality, which rendered both the Axis alliance and the persecution of the Jews inevitable. The anti-Jewish legislation of 1938 was a slap in the face for the conservative Italian establishment, which had acquiesced in Mussolini's March on Rome, not in order to promote "totalitarian" rule, but in order to prevent it.[61]

The term "totalitarian" was coined by Mussolini's opponents in 1923 in order to expose the true face of Fascism at a time when Mussolini himself was still anxious to conceal it. It was only two years later, after the consolidation of his dictatorship, that the Duce finally decided to usurp the anti-Fascist term of abuse and turn it into a Fascist term of praise. Being the true faith, he now declared, Fascism could not co-exist with any other faith, nor could it tolerate neutrality, let alone opposition. Its aim was to create "the new Italian," in other words, "To fascistize the nation until Italian and Fascist, almost like Italian and Catholic, were one and the same thing."[62] Mussolini made no mention of the Jews in this

59. R. De Felice, op. cit., pp. 242–47.
60. Ibid., p. 450.
61. R. De Felice, *Mussolini il duce. II: Lo Stato totalitario 1936–1940* (Turin, 1981), pp. 3–155, 489.
62. *Opera Omnia di Benito Mussolini* XXI, p. 362. On the genesis of the term "totalitarian" see M. Michaelis, "Giovanni Amendola interprete del fenomeno fascista," *Nuova Antologia* CXXI, April–June 1986, pp. 180–209.

connection; even so, it was clear that there would be no room for minorities in the "monolithic" society that was being planned. Hitler understood the anti-Jewish implications of Mussolini's "totalitarianism" long before the formation of the Rome-Berlin Axis;[63] so did a few others who approached the issue from an entirely different angle, such as the above-mentioned Robert Michels and Bolton King.

Prior to the Italian-German rapprochement, the "totalitarian" solution of the Jewish question envisaged by Mussolini was assimilation and intermarriage, culminating in total fusion: "The frequency of mixed marriages in Italy must be greeted with satisfaction by all who consider themselves good, sincere, and loyal Italians, as it constitutes proof of the perfect civic, political, and above all 'moral' equality between all Italians, whatever their remote descent."[64] Once he decided to march with Hitler "to the end," however, his "totalitarian" intolerance of minorities was bound to assume an explicitly anti-Jewish character, whatever his private feelings about Hitler's Nordic heresy.

The second open question—the reasons for Italian opposition to Hitler's policy of genocide—has occupied publicists and scholars ever since the collapse of Fascism. As early as 1955, Léon Poliakov and Jacques Sabille published a detailed and well-documented account of the way in which the Italian authorities systematically and successfully opposed the anti-Jewish mania of their allies in all areas under their jurisdiction, despite the official anti-Semitism of the Fascist Government.[65] How did this square with Mussolini's determination to demonstrate his "total" solidarity with Hitler in the racial sphere?

Part of the answer is that the community of destiny between the two regimes could not and did not eliminate the profound conflict of interest between the two countries. Though side by side, the two Axis partners never marched in step, and this was reflected in the field of Fascist Jewish policy. Given Italian military depen-

63. A. Hitler, *Mein Kampf*, 15th ed. (Munich, 1932), pp. 720–21.

64. "Matrimoni misti e malinconie inattuali," *Il Popolo d'Italia*, May 29, 1932. Mussolini's authorship of the anonymous article was disclosed by Paolo Orano in 1937 (*Gli ebrei in Italia*, p. 123).

65. L. Poliakov and J. Sabille, *Jews under the Italian Occupation* (Paris, 1955).

dence on the Germans and Mussolini's determination to follow Hitler to the bitter end, the Duce could not mitigate his racialist ideology. On the other hand, the Jewish issue in the Axis-occupied territories served the Fascist authorities as a means of asserting what little freedom of action from their German masters they were able to maintain. This eminently political consideration helps to explain why the zones of Italian military occupation in France and the Balkans became havens of refuge for persecuted Jews: "From an index of abject servility to the Reich in 1938—all the more abject because unsolicited—the *Judenpolitik* of Fascist Italy had become in the course of World War II a test of the regime's remaining autonomy."[66]

It would be wrong to conclude, however, that the rescue of Jews in the Italian-occupied territories was simply a manifestation of Fascist resistance to German encroachments on Italian sovereignty. The truth is that it was also a genuine expression of spontaneous humanitarianism. In the words of Daniel Carpi, a leading authority on the subject:

> The logical and natural question is not, "Why did so and so refuse to participate in cold-blooded murder or even try somehow to stop it?" but rather "How was it that so many people, and even entire nations, directly or indirectly sanctioned such deeds?" It is true that one cannot understand the history of a period without comprehending its internal logic and specific nature, but the criteria by which one measures human behavior cannot be arbitrarily changed to suit the character of this or that period, and it certainly cannot be made to suit the value system which governed the actions of the Nazis. Basic and universal moral norms are always binding, even in times of crisis, even when the majority of mankind ignores them, and the devotion to these norms requires no explanation.

Commenting on the situation in Axis-occupied Croatia, Carpi pointed out that

> the initial steps taken to save the Jews were part of the general responsibility of the Italian Army in the region and a continu-

---

66. A. M. Canepa, "Half-hearted Cynicism. Mussolini's Racial Politics," *Patterns of Prejudice* XIII, November–December 1979, p. 26.

ation of its activities to save the Serbian population. There is no doubt, however, that the Italians eventually devoted special attention to the rescue of the Jews, and for them it assumed political and moral significance far beyond their general interest in maintaining order in the region.[67]

The political aspect of the "Jewish problem" in Croatia was brought home to the Italians in the spring of 1942 when the Croatian-German agreement to deport all Jews in Croatia became known:

> The fact that the agreement had been signed without their knowledge, by a state which, it had been previously agreed, would be under their exclusive sphere of influence, was a severe blow to the status and prestige of the Italian Army. Moreover, according to the terms of the agreement, it was to include the Jews living in the area of the Italian occupation as well. From that time on, the opinion became widespread among various Italian political and military officials that the extradition of the Jews to the Croatians would be tantamount to a surrender to German orders and would for all the peoples of the region constitute a public admission of the weakness of the Italian Army. . . . At the same time, whoever thinks that the episode of the rescue of the Jewish refugees of Croatia can be explained solely on the basis of diplomatic interest errs. Soldiers and civilians on all levels participated in the rescue work and almost everyone regarded the issue first and foremost as a humanitarian problem, which had to be solved for reasons of conscience, which were beyond political considerations.[68]

What was true of Croatia was equally true of France and Greece: wherever the German army marched in, the Jews were rounded up and deported to Hitler's death camps; wherever the Italian army appeared, they remained unmolested. "In Greece, as in France and Croatia, the Italian civilian and military authorities during the occupation years developed extensive activity aimed at protecting

67. D. Carpi, "The Rescue of Jews in the Italian Zone of Occupied Croatia," *Rescue Attempts During the Holocaust. Proceedings of the Second Yad Vashem International Conference—April 1974* (Jerusalem, 1977), pp. 504–5.

68. Ibid., pp. 505–6.

the Jews living there from the German racial persecutions and from deportation to the extermination camps in Poland."[69]

Italian opposition to Hitler's policy of genocide was in part a spontaneous reaction to German barbarism, in part a symptom of the widespread dissatisfaction with the Duce's Axis policy, and in part a manifestation of Fascist resistance to German meddling in the Italian sphere of influence. Some of the credit for this resistance must go to Mussolini, despite his notorious servility toward his German master.[70] Hitler, for his part, was determined to impose his anti-Jewish obsession on the whole of Europe, including Italy. Until Mussolini's downfall, however, he was not prepared to stake relations with Rome on a question of extending the "Final Solution" to the peninsula and to the Italian-occupied territories.[71]

To sum up, from the published and unpublished sources available to us, the following conclusions would appear to emerge:

(1) Although there was friction between Fascists and Jews from the outset, mainly due to Fascist suspicions of Jewish "internationalism," there was no attempt on the part of the Fascist regime to create a "Jewish problem" in Italy until Mussolini decided to throw in his lot with Hitler.

(2) Until 1937, Mussolini's approach to the "racial" issue was not merely different from Hitler's but diametrically opposed to it; according to Fascist doctrine, all persons born in Italy were Italians, provided they belonged to the white race. Intermarriage between Jews and Gentiles was not only permitted but encouraged. Even the few Italian anti-Semites called for the complete assimilation of the Jews, not for their elimination from Italian life, until the growing exigencies of the Rome-Berlin Axis forced them to change their minds.

(3) There was a strong element of continuity in Mussolini's

69. D. Carpi, "Notes on the History of the Jews in Greece during the Holocaust Period. The Attitude of the Italians (1941–1943)," *Festschrift in Honor of Dr. George S. Wise* (Tel Aviv, 1981), p. 25.

70. On Mussolini's complex and contradictory attitude towards Hitler's "Final Solution" see the observations of Roberto Ducci, former Italian Ambassador in London, in N. Caracciolo, *Gli ebrei e l'Italia durante la guerra 1940–45* (Rome, 1986), p. 121.

71. For a detailed analysis of Hitler's attitude see M. Michaelis, "La politica razziale fascista vista da Berlino," loc. cit., *passim.*

thought on the Jewish issue, despite his sudden change of front. Through his career he both attacked and defended the Jews. As early as 1917, he identified the Bolshevik revolution with the "synagogue"; but as late as 1944, he insisted that he was "not an anti-Semite."

(4) Prior to the alliance between Fascism and National Socialism the term "race" was synonymous with "people" and "nation" in Italy; Mussolini's earlier references to the *razza italiana*, therefore, had no anti-Jewish implications.

(5) Racial anti-Semitism was neither a logical development of Fascist "doctrine" nor a logical extension of the ban on miscegenation in Africa. It was, however, a logical consequence of Mussolini's Axis policy. It was inherent in Fascism because and in so far as the "Pact of Steel" was inherent in the Fascist pursuit of empire.

(6) Fascist racialism was neither an original Italian creation, as Mussolini asserted, nor a slavish imitation of the German model, as his opponents claimed, but an unsuccessful attempt to adapt the German racial theories to Italian conditions. The subsequent evolution of the racial question in Italy reflected the conflicting pressures to which Mussolini was subject. On the one hand, he wanted to convince the Germans of his loyalty; on the other hand, he wanted to impress Italian and western opinion with his "magnanimity" and avoid a clash with the Church. As a result, he fell between two chairs. His watered-down version of Hitler's Nuremberg laws displeased the Germans, antagonized Italian and western opinion, and alienated the Church. Far from strengthening the Axis alliance, it merely added a new dimension to the conflict of interest between the two countries. Worse still, it marked the beginning of a rupture between the Fascist regime and the Italian people, as well as the end of the idyll between Italy and the Holy See.

(7) Hitler was determined to impose his racial obsession on the whole of Europe, including Italy. Until Mussolini's downfall, however, he was not prepared to stake relations with Rome on a question of extending the "Final Solution" of the Jewish question to the Italian sphere of influence.

(8) After the Italian armistice of September 1943, the part of Italy under German control was treated as conquered, as well as occu-

pied, territory. Mussolini's attempts to remove the Jewish question from German hands were therefore doomed to failure from the start. And while it is true that the Duce was too much of an Italian to approve of the "Final Solution," it is equally true that he and his henchmen helped to create the conditions that made the Holocaust possible. In the words of Piero Caleffi, a veteran Italian-Jewish anti-Fascist: "Consciously or not, the Fascists had been the *anticipatori* (originators) of the extermination camps."[72]

72. P. Caleffi, *Si fa presto a dire fame* (Milan-Rome, 1955), p. 135.

Alberto Cavaglion
(translated by Fausta S. Walsby)

3. The Legacy of the *Risorgimento*: Jewish Participation in Anti-Fascism and the Resistance

Confronted with the emergence of the racial laws, Benedetto Croce, from the tranquility of Palazzo Filomarino in Naples, reacted to the final collapse of liberal principles by writing an essay on Tullo Massarani (1826–1905), an almost-forgotten nineteenth-century figure of liberal-democratic Judaism. A Cavourian reformer and a friend of Giosuè Carducci, Massarani, at the end of a long life, had become the model and example for a substantial group of radicals and socialists, not necessarily Jewish in origin. In his essay, later included in *Letteratura della nuova Italia*, Croce surveyed the major phases of Massarani's adventurous life, reviewing the intellectual merits of this writer and critic. Croce even slightly overvalued the political achievements of this strange Jewish personality who was the first translator of Heine in Italy. In his conclusion, spurred by the dramatic news of those gloomy days of September 1938, Croce could not refrain from remarking, "No one could have suspected and imagined what we have seen to our astonishment in our times."[1]

This was not just the indignation of the man of letters, stunned by the shabbiness and vulgarity of those dark hours. That essay on Massarani brought to light the disillusionment of the old liberal, the melancholy of the author of *Storia d'Italia dal 1871 al 1915* and *Storia d'Europa nel secolo XIX*, the disappointment of one who had continued to hope for a return of the values of *Risorgimento* liberalism in Italy, believing they would offer a firm

---

1. B. Croce, "Aggiunte alla letteratura della nuova Italia: Tullo Massarani," *La Critica*, XXXVI (1938), pp. 328–336 and in B. Croce, *Letteratura della nuova Italia* (Bari: Laterza, 1939), vol. 5, pp. 395–405. For Massarani see at least the correspondence *Una nobile vita*, ed. R. Barbiera (Florence, Le Monnier, 1909).

guarantee against modern totalitarianism. In his work of cultural anti-Fascism, Croce referred constantly to these values and to the golden age of Giolitti. Croce wanted to rediscover the merits of a ruling class that had been unjustly reviled and rehabilitate an era to whose development Jews such as Tullo Massarani, Alessandro D'Ancona, and Luigi Luzzatti had contributed.

Thus, Croce's moving pages on Massarani have a double meaning for our theme: Jewish participation in anti-Fascism and in the Resistance. First of all, Croce's 1938 essay sheds greater light on the relationship between the Neapolitan philosopher and Judaism, a relationship that should be put in its historical context and not simply studied in an impressionistic way. Second, in those pages and in so many other Crocean writings of the same period was an implicit warning to Jewish readers. This was not the first time that Croce had suggested to which past one should relate and toward which "religion"—"the religion of liberty"—they should channel their own need for faith and desire for redemption. It is superfluous to add that between 1938 and 1943 Croce transformed his abstract "astonishment" into concrete acts of solidarity for the victims of racial discrimination. More than one Jewish professor banished from Italian universities found the doors of many foreign academies open to him thanks to Croce's providential letters of introduction. These deeds have not yet received the appreciation they deserve since they were carried out quietly and modestly and never widely publicized.

Thus, starting with the Massarani essay, we grasp immediately the two fundamental axes around which the whole discussion on Jewish participation in the Resistance revolves. The legacy of the *Risorgimento* in men like Massarani, linked to Croce's "religion of liberty," is at the root of the choices made by almost all the exponents of the Resistance. In the Rosselli brothers, Carlo and Nello—founders of the movement known as *Giustizia e Libertà* (Justice and Liberty), in whose ranks so many Jewish partisans fought—there is evidence that the lessons of Croce's ethical-civil historiography were applied to the realm of politics. From 1925 onward, the figure of the Neapolitan philosopher and former minister of education became a symbol for young Jews. Crocean influence emanates from the pages of the Jewish journals of those years. The reports to meetings made by the most recent recruits from Jewish organizations are all inspired by a vision of the world that is Crocean in every sense. The counter-manifesto of the anti-Fascist intellectuals, edited by Croce and published on May 1, 1925, in *Il Mondo*, was signed by men like Riccardo Bachi, Guido Castelnuovo, Mario Falco, Tullio Levi-Civita, Gino Luzzatto, and Rodolfo Mondolfo. Furthermore, according to the late Guido Calogero, another famous supporter of the Justice and Liberty Movement, Enzo Sereni, the Zionist and Jew, first recommended that Calogero read Croce when he attended the Liceo Mamiani in Rome.[2] We should also recall that the late Arnaldo Momigliano was one of those professors who was dismissed from the university after 1938 and for whom the road to London exile was opened thanks to Croce's intervention. We hardly need say that one of the most obvious characteristics of Momigliano's historiography is precisely the historicist and Crocean need to search in oneself— thus in one's Jewish origins—for the most valid justifications behind each historical problem.[3]

The cultural itinerary of three victims of the Nazi-Fascist savagery, Emanuele Artom, Leone Ginzburg, and Eugenio Colorni, confirms what we stated above regarding the spread of Croce's philosophy. In an autobiographical work, *La malattia filosofica*, written in 1939 on the island of Ventotene, Eugenio Colorni recounts having experienced, during his adolescence, the Zionist and Jewish influence of his cousin Enzo Sereni. Colorni withdrew from these influences in the early 1920s in Milan when, as a student at the Liceo Manzoni, he was thunderstruck (hence the "philosophical illness" that gives the book its title) when reading Croce's *Breviario di Estetica*. Colorni experienced an infatuation with idealism that lasted until 1932, a kind of fever that subsided only

2. G. Calogero, "Compagni di liceo e di università," *Per non morire* (Writings of E. Sereni), ed. U. Nahon (Milan, Federazione Sionistica Italiana, 1973), pp. 68–73 (but Calogero's article had already been published in Hebrew in *Niv Hakevuzà*, December 1954).

3. A. Momigliano, "Historicism Revisited," *Sesto contributo alla storia degli studi classici e del mondo antico*, vol. 1 (Rome: Edizione Storia e Letteratura, 1980), pp. 23–32.

when, through the Milanese publishers "La Cultura," Colorni published his first monograph *L'estetica di Benedetto Croce. Studio Critico*, a work that earned praise from Croce himself. The year before, following a chance meeting in Germany with the idol of his youth, Colorni had noted in his diary: "[Croce is] the greatest teacher of my life and of our generation." In the mid-1930s and on the eve of the racial laws, Colorni distanced himself from idealism and also left the clandestine Justice and Liberty Movement to join Lelio Basso's socialist group in Milan. For some time he associated with the Jewish communist Eugenio Curiel in Trieste. Later Colorni was arrested and sent into internal exile, but he never gave up his respect for, and devotion to, Croce's teachings. Following his escape from Ventotene, Colorni fought in the name of the "religion of liberty" until his dying day, May 30, 1944, when he was mortally wounded in Via Livorno in Florence by a Nazi-Fascist patrol.[4]

We find the same feelings of admiration, respect, and reverence for Croce if we move from Colorni's Lombardy to Emanuele Artom's Turin. Born in 1915 into a cultured family that was faithful to Jewish traditions, Emanuele Artom was first educated at Liceo d'Azeglio, where his literature teacher was Augusto Monti,[5] the anti-Fascist follower of Croce, and later in the Arts Faculty of the University of Turin, where a large proportion of the teaching staff held idealistic views. Right up to the days before he joined the Monte Bracco partisan group above Barge (Turin), all young Emanuele's readings were Crocean. I shall mention only one quotation in his *Diari*, notable because of its date, September 6, 1943. Artom writes, "I started to reread Croce's *Storia d'Italia*. For my research on the history of patriotism, I note the ideas on pages 3 and 4 on the missions of the peoples and on the mission that the new Italy should establish for herself."[6]

4. E. Colorni, *Scritti*, ed. Norberto Bobbio (Florence: La Nuova Italia, 1975); cf. also under "Colorni" in *Dizionario Biografico degli Italiani* (ed. E. Garin) and E. Tagliacozzo, "L'uomo Colorni," *Tempo presente*, December 1980, pp. 46–55.

5. See Augusto Monti's comment to E. Artom, "Proposta di riforma scolastica," *Quaderni del CDEC*, 1, 1961, pp. 93–102. It should be noted that, three years before the racial laws, Prof. Monti had published a book (*L'iniqua mercede* [Milan: Ceschina, 1935]), containing a short story "Un savio Nathano monferrino," pp. 301–62, replete with affectionate comments on the Jewish community of Acqui.

6. E. Artom, *Diari (gennaio 1940-febbraio 1944)*, ed. E. Ravenna and P. Debe-

Only because of local civic pride did Artom fail to include Massarani among the precursors of his Jewish patriotism, among the prophets of what he habitually called the "mission of the Jewish people." Before referring to the Mantuan Massarani, Artom turned to David Levi, the well-known Piedmontese exponent of liberal Judaism, who was a contemporary of Massarani. Levi, however, was a scholar of Giordano Bruno and not of Heine; he was an exponent of a religious Mazzinianism and Saint-Simonianism, as well as favoring a humanitarian and ecumenical religion free from dogma. Throughout the period before the 1944 tragedy, Artom became a passionate admirer and scholar of David Levi. Artom spent entire days transcribing Levi's unpublished autobiographical memoirs and his personal correspondence with Mazzini and with Rabbi Margulies.[7]

For young men in their early twenties like Emanuele Artom or Eugenio Colorni, the historical works of Croce and the issues of *La Critica* showed them the lost and broken thread of nineteenth-century liberty. In particular, the *Storia d'Italia dal 1871 al 1915,* published in 1928, helped them find the truest vein of *Risorgimento* patriotism, helped them rediscover the dawn of the "new Italy," helped them learn the lesson taught by those teachers, including Jewish ones, who had tried to reconcile the legacy of the fathers with the needs of modernity. True, in that imposing fresco, such an expert on the history of Italian Judaism as Emanuele Artom will notice minor mistakes or inexactitudes regarding particular events in the community. Nevertheless, that was not enough to make him change his view.

Having joined the *Italia libera* group in Val Pellice and Val Germanasca in the Waldensian Valleys, (the "Israel of the Alps," his companions used to say) Artom was arrested on March 25, 1944. Two weeks later, following beatings and torture, he died in the

---

neddeti (Milan: CDEC, 1966), p. 72; see also the volume *Tre vite dall'ultimo '800 alla metà del '900* (Studi e memorie di Emilio, Emanuele, Ennio Artom), ed. B. Treves (Florence: Casa Editrice Israel, 1954); a book that not by chance was reviewed in *La Stampa* of Turin by a partisan of the Crocean mold, Franco Antonicelli. The review is in F. Antonicelli, *Scritti letterari (1934–1974),* ed. F. Contorbia, preface by N. Bobbio (Pisa: Giardini, 1985), p. 175.

7. On D. Levi, "Jewish utopian," and Artom, his disciple, cf. L. Bulferetti, *Socialismo risorgimentale* (Turin: Einaudi, 1949), pp. 81–103; E. Artom, *Diari,* pp. 8–9.

Nuove prison in Turin. He was buried near Stupinigi and at the end of the war not even the site of his grave could be found.[8]

As for the third person we mentioned, Leone Ginzburg, scholar of Russian literature and pioneering collaborator in the Einaudi publishing firm—our argument might seem different, in view of Ginzburg's east-European origins, but it is not. Norberto Bobbio recalls that in the anti-Fascist circles of Turin, Ginzburg was known as "the most Crocean of us all."[9] Purely by reasons of birth Leone Ginzburg lacked the component of the *Risorgimento* dear to Colorni or Artom, but his fervent Crocean philosophy gives food for thought. A supporter of the Justice and Liberty Movement, Leone Ginzburg was arrested in November 1943 in Rome at the press, where he was printing propaganda material. He died in Regina Coeli prison after being tortured in an unsuccessful effort to force him to give information useful to the enemy.

Crocean philosophy and *Risorgimento* liberalism are thus the two most recurring common denominators in the choices that young Jews made before and after 1938. The very name of the partisan group that Emanuele Artom joined, *Italia Libera* shows the clear Mazzinian mark of guerrilla war and conspiracy against the invader. Yet Crocean philosophy and *Risorgimento* liberalism (Massarani, David Levi) obviously were not the only motivating factors. Other causes, which we shall consider later, were determining factors in the aims of the armed revolt. These ideal causes, these ideological motives, were restricted in scope, but they served as a stimulus for the very many who, rather than protecting their lives by going into hiding, preferred to go to the mountains and join the Justice and Liberty groups, or the Garibaldi or Matteotti groups, or even the so-called Autonomous groups. Preserved in the archives of the Centro di Documentazione Ebraica Contemporanea (CDEC) in Milan are the records of about four hundred anti-Fascist and partisan Jews from all over Italy. Compiled by those involved or by their relatives, and supplemented with various types of doc-

---

8. E. Artom, *Diari*, pp. 177–180.
9. N. Bobbio, "Ebrei di ieri e ebrei di oggi di fronte al fascismo," in *La difesa della razza*, special issue of *Il Ponte*, November–December 1978, p. 1315. L. Ginzburg, *Scritti*, ed. N. Bobbio (Turin: Einaudi, 1964).

uments, those records reflect only a fraction of the true number of Jews who contributed to the partisan struggle. According to the experts, they represent perhaps only a fifth. That amounts to at least two thousand men and women out of a Jewish population of about 44,500 at that time.[10] These and other data available to us do not allow us to draw many conclusions on the Jewish contribution to the Italian Resistance. Paradoxical though it may seem, this topic, although it was discussed at length, was not studied much after the war.[11]

First, we must clear the ground of some recurring misunderstandings. We must recognize that in Italy, there never existed a form of collective Jewish adherence to the Resistance comparable to that in France, or to the Jewish brigade of the Isle of Rab. Any interpretative effort thus inevitably becomes complex. It is necessary to follow the movements of individuals who, after the Nazi invasion, fled their respective cities, enlisting in partisan groups whose headquarters were close to where their relatives were hidden. Different was the case of the many foreign Jews who had already arrived in Italy after 1933 or who fled to Italy after April 1941 from Croatia and after September 1943 from the South of France, previously occupied by Italian troops. In this case, too, however, foreign Jews made their decisions individually.

The question has been raised whether it is justified to speak of a "Jewish" contribution to the struggle for liberation. In a situation

10. L. P. Fargion, "Sul contributo di ebrei alla Resistenza Italiana," in *Rassegna mensile di Israel*, March–April 1980, pp. 132–46.
11. Cf. at least G. Formiggini, *Stella d'Italia Stella di David. Gli ebrei dal Risorgimento alla Resistenza* (Milan: Mursia, 1970); G. Valabrega, "Aspetti della partecipazione di ebrei alla seconda guerra mondiale," in G. Valabrega, *Ebraismo, fascismo, sionismo* (Urbino: Argalia, 1974), pp. 139–55; *Ebrei in Italia: deportazione, Resistenza,* ed. G. Donati (Florence: CDEC, 1975); L. P. Fargion, "Sul contributo di ebrei alla Resistenza italiana"; S. Sorani, *La partecipazione ebraica alla Resistenza in Toscana e il contributo ebraico nella Seconda Guerra Mondiale* (Florence: Giuntina, 1981); G. Arbib, *Partecipazione di ebrei alla Resistenza nell regione Piemonte,* degree thesis, Univ. of Milano, Department of Political Science, 1980–81; M. Sarfatti, "Ebrei nella Resistenza ligure," in the proceedings of the meeting *La resistenza in Liguria e gli Alleati (1943–1945)* organized by the Istituto Storico della Resistenza in Liguria (proceedings in press). For a general background one must always refer to R. De Felice, *Storia degli ebrei italiani sotto il fascismo,* 3rd edition (Turin: Einaudi, 1972); M. Michaelis, *Mussolini and the Jews: German-Italian Relations and the Jewish question in Italy* (Oxford: Clarendon Press, 1978); C. Delzell, *Mussolini's Enemies: The Italian Anti-Fascist Resistance* (Princeton: Princeton University Press, 1961).

as described above, the risks of trying to define and categorize the behavior of such different personalities as, for example, Eugenio Calò, Mario Jacchia, and Ildebrando Vivanti, are understandable. The first of these was born in Pisa in 1906 to a family of modest means. In October 1943, he moved from the machine shop where he worked in Arezzo to the mountains with the partisans and joined the founders of the 2nd Favalto Battalion of the 23rd Pio Borri Brigade. Taken by surprise by the Germans on July 12, 1944, and then tortured, Calò never revealed the location of his command and was shot. Mario Jacchia, a lawyer from Bologna, nine years senior to Calò, had already been a volunteer in World War I. In the winter of 1943, he was one of the commanders of the partisan forces in northern Emilia. He was arrested while trying to destroy material that compromised his group and was murdered on August 20, 1944, following lengthy torture. The Brescian Ildebrando Vivanti was wounded in action and condemned to death in Valle Gesso above Cuneo.[12]

If we shift from the early anti-Fascists with idealistic motives to those who made decisions during the German occupation, we can see how the discussion becomes complex. There have been efforts, for example, to trace elements common to the spirit of Judaism and the spirit of the Resistance. Norberto Bobbio has identified in "radicalism" a probable common ground for understanding.[13] Others have spoken of a predisposition to democracy and justice. This is all true to a certain extent. There is no question that, particularly in Piedmont, given the connections with *Risorgimento* traditions, there was a high percentage of anti-Fascist Jews. Bobbio himself is ironic about his "honorary Jewishness," particularly because in the mid-1930s in Turin, he shared in anti-Fascist activities promoted mainly by individuals from Jewish families. The high point of this activism in Turin came in 1934 with the famous roundup at Ponte Tresa when Jewish intellectuals such as Sion Segre Amar and Mario Levi were arrested.[14]

12. See the relevant biographical records in *Ebrei in Italia: deportazione, Resistenza*, pp. 49–53.
13. N. Bobbio, *Ebrei di ieri ebrei di oggi*, p. 1316.
14. G. L. Luzzatto, "La partecipazione all'antifascismo in Italia e all'estero dal

However, this is still a long way from arguing that there is a natural inclination towards anti-Fascism, unless we accept and give posthumous historical validity to one of the paradoxes dearest to the scientist Cesare Lombroso. According to him, the Semitic race is *by nature* revolutionary because it was always forced to emigrate. To propose the equation that Jewishness equals anti-Fascism undoubtedly means stretching reality and falling into a kind of second-rate sociological theorizing. Viewing the matter dispassionately and considering the percentages, we find that the behavior of the Jewish minority, first in dealing with Fascism and later in the Resistance, is no different from the behavior of Italians in general. There are no substantial positive or negative differences.

First, we must state that the Jewish community, on the eve of World War II, was one of the most assimilated in Europe. Thus it would have been unlikely that those who became partisans of the anti-Nazi cause did so out of a sense of Jewishness. In the best of cases, Judaism was a matter of faint recollection linked to a tradition that had been dormant for at least a generation and a half. In several cases we can confirm that, if anything, the true prime mover was Crocean philosophy. As we have tried to show, Croce's "religion of liberty" was sometimes confused with, or even preceded, the ancestral religion. But that is not enough. For greater clarity we must enter the heart of the Crocean system. In doing this, we feel we are acting correctly and loyally towards those who placed the utmost faith in Croce's philosophy. On closer inspection, the issue of the existence of a Jewish anti-Fascism verges on becoming an incorrectly formulated question. Perhaps it is a false problem. To speak of Jewish anti-Fascism (or for that matter, of Jewish Fascism) means admitting the concreteness of two abstractions and thus following a logically erroneous and historiographi-

---

1918," in *Quaderni del CDEC*, 2, 1962, pp. 32–44; G. L. Luzzatto, "Eli ebrei e l'opposizione al fascismo," in *Rassegna mensile di Israel*, April 1965, pp. 151–59; S. Segre Amar, "Sopra alcune inesattezze storiche intorno alle passate vicende degli ebrei d'Italia," in *Rassegna mensile di Israel*, May 1961, pp. 236–38; S. Segre Amar, "Sui fatti di Torino," in *Quaderni del CDEC*, 2, 1962, pp. 125–34; S. Segre Amar, "Testimonianza," in *Carlo Levi*, (drawings from prison, 1934) (Rome: De Luca, 1983), pp. 43–47.

cally unproductive nominalistic line. A meaningless concern, Croce would have commented sarcastically. And his disciples Artom, Ginzburg, and Colorni would have concurred.

If writing history means always and only the history of unique and individual people who operate in a given reality, it follows that abstract categories do not help at all. To work correctly one must consider each case, investigate various biographies with increasing precision, acquire new data, ban the use of misleading terms, enter the concrete reality that Italian Jews shared with their non-Jewish fellow citizens.[15]

Naturally, in each individual investigation we will find various and multiple combinations of different factors: Judaism, Crocean philosophy, Mazzinianism (for example in Fernando Schiavetti, the exiled republican Jew from Leghorn) and Carlo Cattaneo's legacy, and so on. Whether Judaism acted as a prime mover or later motivator is a matter that must be considered case by case. Only by analyzing Emanuele Artom's formative years can we conclude that Judaism had a stronger effect on him than on Leone Ginzburg, whereas Crocean philosophy gave them both decisive impetus for rebellion. "L'assiette de leur être n'était que partiellement juive" wrote Richard Marienstras appropriately about European Jews, and it is a pertinent observation in our case, too.[16]

Judaism was certainly the element that triggered a rebel instinct in Augusto Segre, whose life as a partisan is described vividly in the central part of his *Memorie*. Augusto Segre was a member of an orthodox family from Casale Monferrato, the son and grandson of rabbis. When he returned to his city on the eve of World War II, he already had behind him considerable experience as a militant in Roman Jewish organizations. The makeup of his personality was

15. Here I am using some points from the essay by Piero Treves, "Antifascisti ebrei od antifascismo ebraico?" *Rassegna mensile di Israel*, January–June 1981, pp. 138–49. The fact that Piero Treves, son of the socialist leader Claudio Treves, begins his essay with this homage to Croce's ideas seems to me further evidence in support of my thesis. I wish to express my gratitude to Professor Piero Treves, with whom I discussed this matter at length.

16. R. Marienstras, *Être un peuple en diaspora*, pref. by P. Vidal Naquet (Paris: Maspero, 1982), p. 25; on F. Schiavetti cf. *M. Tesoro, E. Signori, Antifascisti in esilio fra repubblicanesimo e socialismo*, pref. by A. Garosci (Florence: Le Monnier, 1987); Alessandro Levi's autobiographical notes "Ricordi di giorni penosi" are in A. Levi's *Scritti minori storici e politici* (Padova: Cedam, 1957), III, pp. 393–418.

entirely Jewish, to the point that we can show, in support of our general premises, a certain kind of justified and very understandable aversion to Mazzinianism, to Crocean philosophy, and to Croce himself. Segre rightly reports a few of Croce's inopportune comments on the "barbaric and primitive" character of Judaism and reproaches Croce for his excessively bitter preface (written, one regrets to say, in 1947, right after the Holocaust) to Cesare Merzagora's book *I pavidi*.[17]

Here we clearly find ourselves poles apart from Ginzburg's ideology and also far from Artom's studies on the *Risorgimento*. Segre's is another point of view that induces caution before offering any general or systematic theories.

Augusto Segre follows the ups and downs of Commander "Poli's" partisan division without ever violating any *mitzvah* (Divine commandment). In his autobiography he recalls the blessing his parents gave him before his departure and he describes in detail the metal box containing the *mahzor* (prayer book) and the *tallit* (prayer shawl), a box that he buried and that for the "kippur of the Resistance" he calmly and joyfully dug up.[18]

But Segre's memoirs are unique. They are the exception that proves the rule regarding an endemic assimilation. Along with Augusto Segre, one need remember only one other religious Piedmontese Jew, a great scholar of Jewish ritual and music, a man whose makeup was entirely Jewish—Leo Levi. As a witness to the 1934 roundup in which a number of Turin Jews were involved, Levi recounts how he survived the dangers of an interrogation thanks to his ability to read from right to left, an ability derived from reading Hebrew characters. Sitting facing his inquisitor, using his well-trained eyes, it was not difficult for him to take advantage of his interrogator's few moments of distraction to read "backwards" the statements already made by his fellow prisoners.[19]

If we exclude these few isolated cases in which Marienstras's

---

17. A. Segre, *Memorie di vita ebraica (Casale Monferrato-Roma-Gerusalemme)* (Rome: Bonacci, 1979), pp. 107 and ff. (for Raffaele Vita Foà), pp. 370–71 (for Croce and Merzagora).

18. A. Segre, *Memorie*, p. 330.

19. L. Levi, "Antifascismo e sionismo: convergenze e contrasti," in *Quaderni del CDEC*, 1, 1961, p. 59.

axiom loses its validity and if we follow the line of "each individual case," all our expectations may be disappointed or denied. In most cases a certain "lack of political awareness" prevailed, an indifference to the major events of those years and to Judaism itself. The candor with which the writer Primo Levi, born in 1919, evokes that period is striking. He describes the esthetics and d'Annunzian fashion that attracted and seduced many young Jews, his contemporaries, though they did not adhere to Fascism. Certain pages of *The Periodic Table* are very eloquent in this matter. And one should not laugh if Primo Levi defines himself and his companions in the Valle d'Aosta as "the most disarmed partisans in the Piedmont." "Disarmed" has a double meaning, both literal and figurative: disarmed in the cultural sense but also disarmed in the strict sense of the word. The revolver that Primo Levi had under his pillow on the night of his arrest, December 13, 1943, was very small, perhaps broken, but elegantly inlaid with mother of pearl, "like those used by women in films."[20]

September 8, 1943, the day when Italy surrendered to the Allies, upset everything and resolved any doubts or uncertainties that had remained after 1938. It was a psychological trauma that triggered reflexes that had been inoperative until then; it was a trauma that brought about, even if belatedly, the rediscovery of Jewish identity. One found oneself literally and metaphorically "disarmed" in facing those enormous responsibilities. Only then did the decision that had been made by a few isolated individuals become the practicable and practiced path. It was then that the equally valid axiom of Hannah Arendt, "One does not escape Jewishness," replaced Marienstras's principle.

In investigating the formative years of each individual, one can make various and sometimes surprising discoveries. For example, let us look at Enzo Sereni, born in 1905 from a well-to-do Roman family. Of the three Sereni brothers, Enzo undoubtedly had the closest ties to Judaism and to the history of the Jewish people. His older brother, Enrico, a volunteer in World War I, died quite young. His younger brother, Emilio, adhered to Marxism and Communist

20. P. Levi, *Il sistema periodico* (Turin: Einaudi, 1979), p. 155.

anti-Fascism and after World War II became a Communist deputy in Parliament. Enzo's Zionist choice was rather precocious. We can trace it to Weizmann's visit to Rome in August 1923. "I listened to Weizmann's speech until two o'clock yesterday. It moved me greatly and I felt uplifted spiritually," Sereni wrote in his diary. For Sereni, Zionism meant a decline in his anti-Fascism, *extrema ratio* when facing the impending dictatorship. The year 1927 brought him to Israel with his young wife Ada and his little daughter Hanna, where he contributed to the creation and development of Kibbutz Givat Brenner. In his theoretical writings, he mixed the influence of the Jewish prophetic tradition with elements of Italian reformist socialism. After Italy's entry into the war, Sereni was faced with a decision that could not be put off. He chose not to isolate himself, but to act, and he enlisted in the British army. He was engaged in liaison missions with the Intelligence Service first in Crete, then in Egypt and Iraq. In the decisive phase of the Allied liberation of southern Italy, Sereni was posted in Puglia. From there on June 15, 1944, he left on his last mission. He was accidentally parachuted into the middle of German positions in Pratomagno, was arrested and deported first to Bolzano, then to Dachau.[21]

What has not been sufficiently emphasized until now is the role played by the professor under whom Sereni studied in his university years. This was Ernesto Buonaiuti, the priest suspended *a divinis*, author of *Pellegrino di Roma*, the most unfortunate victim of the "modernist" battle. Buonaiuti was one of the creators of the innovative movement, declared heretical in 1907 in the papal encyclical *Pascendi*. A brilliant journalist, a stirring orator, a great teacher with a critical awareness of religious reformism, Buonaiuti became a professor of the history of Christianity at the University of Rome after World War I. His charismatic influence went beyond the circle of catechumens, as we see in the biographies of two Jews who had interests in modernism, Arturo Carlo Jemolo and Giorgio

21. On Sereni see R. Bondy, *The Emissary. A Life of Enzo Sereni* (Boston/Toronto: Little Brown, 1977), and *Per non morire*; also, C. L. Ottino, "Cenni sull'esperienza sionista e antifascista di E. Sereni," *Quaderni del CDEC*, 2, 1962, pp. 67–85.

Levi Della Vida.[22] Particularly in the latter's autobiography, we notice a unique form of friendship and sympathy. In 1931, Della Vida, along with Buonaiuti and three Jews, Fabio Luzzatto, Vito Volterra, and Giorgio Errera, was among the twelve Italian professors who refused to swear an oath of allegiance to Fascism.[23]

In the period 1922–1924, between Mussolini's coming to power and the Matteotti murder, numerous Roman Jewish figures in addition to Della Vida followed Buonaiuti. To support Buonaiuti and Zionism at the same time was not at all a contradiction. One did not exclude the other, and both ideas suggested the existence of an anti-Fascist germ. In the list of these Roman friends one should include Max Ascoli, Felice Momigliano, Alberto Pincherle, Tullio Levi-Civita, and naturally, Enzo Sereni. Sereni, along with Buonaiuti, not only engaged in lively discussions on the political effects of the recent Balfour Declaration, but also found time to discuss a degree thesis on the book by Tobia. The thesis was later published thanks to Buonaiuti's interests. Thus, paradoxical though it may seem, the excommunicated priest, Buonaiuti, was remembered in the founding of Kibbutz Givat Brenner.

As we can see, not everything can be summarized in terms of Crocean historicism or Judaism or Zionism. Around 1907, Croce and Gentile had taken a firm stand against the "hybrid" modernist position of Bonaiuti and his friends in the name of a reasoning that was philosophically correct (philosophy going beyond religion and giving it life) but was politically a harbinger of struggles and disturbances to come.

That did not prevent the generation that grew up after those divisions from observing and making judgments with proper detachment outside the restraints of any theoretical scheme. Years later, when those men took up arms against Nazism and Fascism, it happened that three figures who in real life at best had ignored each other (that is, Croce, Weizmann, and Buonaiuti) found themselves in harmonious agreement.

The continuity between the threads of the Italian *Risorgimento*

22. A. C. Jemolo, *Anni di prova* (Vicenza: Neri Pozza, 1969), pp. 168–77; G. Levi Della Vida, *Fantasmi ritrovati* (Vincenza: Neri, Pozza, 1966), pp. 132–33.
23. G. Levi Della Vida, *Fantasmi ritrovati*, pp. 147 and ff.

and anti-Fascism was represented for Sereni in Vittorio Alfieri's *Autobiografia*. This book is almost obsessively recalled in Sereni's diary ("a notebook with a picture of Vittorio Alfieri because his personality is the one that suits me most").[24] The *Risorgimento*, prophetic Judaism, Crocean philosophy, modernism: these are the elements that make up the spectrum of the Jewish Resistance.

Naturally, among Jewish intellectuals, socialism occupies a major position and, after the 1921 schism, so does communism. One cannot say that the Marxist world represents a separate world, detached from the rest. We have already seen Colorni adhere to socialism at the peak of a strongly Crocean phase. We can give an analogous example with Eugenio Curiel, who approached the Italian Communist party in 1936 while his philosophical thoughts were still revolving around the great problems of Italian idealism.

A nephew of Ludovico Limentani, another Jewish signatory of the manifesto edited by Croce, Curiel was born in 1912 in Trieste. He studied engineering and physics and associated with the youth groups of the Justice and Liberty Movement. Like Colorni, he was arrested in 1939, and he too was sent to Ventotene but never ceased writing and thinking. His articles on trade unionism and corporatism provoked the reaction of the authorities. By luck, he succeeded in escaping from internal exile and went underground, but he was surprised by a German patrol shortly before the Liberation and on February 24, 1945, was shot.[25]

A mathematician and philosopher, or rather a philosopher because he was a mathematician, Curiel was among the Jewish intellectuals who, in the second half of the 1930s, had first begun to investigate areas that were outside the realm of Croce's idealism. Following the traditions of his city (the first to discover Freud's psychoanalysis, with Italo Svevo) Curiel had entered the world of the exact sciences, the world of those "pseudo-concepts" unknown to Croce. Bruno Pincherle, a pediatrician also of Jewish origins, took a path similar to that of Curiel. Arrested twice by the police,

24. E. Sereni, "Dai diari giovanili," *Per non morire*, p. 37.
25. N. Briamonte, *La vita e il pensiero di E. Curiel* (Milan: Feltrinelli, 1979); E. Curiel, *Scritti (1935–1945)*, F. Frassati, ed., preface by G. Amendola (Rome: Ed. Riuniti, 1973).

once in 1925 and again in 1928, Pincherle was a follower of the Rosselli brothers, and along with Leone Ginzburg became director of the newspaper of the Partito d'Azione, *L'Italia Libera* in Rome. After World War II and until his death in 1968, Pincherle was involved in left-wing parties. Already with the dawning of Salvemini's anti-Fascism, Pincherle's rigor had attracted the attention of the major anti-Fascist leaders. Pincherle did not have the philosophical mentality of Colorni or the mathematical training of Curiel. All his life he had a boundless passion for Stendhal, whom he studied zealously and whose rare editions he collected. Like many others from his city, all his life he maintained a taste for irony and a sense of the rational. Anti-Fascism was one category in his existence.[26]

From its origins, socialism had regarded and continued to regard with admiration Croce's teachings even after 1921. There was a vivid recollection of the youthful sympathy with which Croce had watched the birth of the Italian Socialist party, his association with Labriola, his collaboration on *Critica Sociale*, Turati and Treves's review.

On the socialist side, too, we would do well to treat each case individually. We have an almost exemplary text that can serve as a motto for our discussion. It is an article written by Antonello Gerbi, the Jewish Americanist, born in Florence in 1904, who was a contributor of the socialist periodical *La Giustizia*. Gerbi was a

26. "Lo stendhalesco dottor Pincherle," ed. G. Chiesa, *Quaderni di Palazzo Sormani* (Milan), 8, 1984 (including Pincherle's "Note Autobiografiche," writings by Apih, Guagnini, Scheiwiller, Crise, Grechi). Sergio Forti was also born in Trieste on March 20, 1920, and died near Norcia on June 14, 1944. He was a naval engineer in the Viareggio shipyards. Speaking of Trieste, we should not forget twenty-four-year-old Rita Rosani, formerly a teacher in the Jewish school on Via del Monte, the famous street immortalized in Saba's poem. Rosani is the only woman partisan who died in combat. Her profession also requires a comment. In fact, if a linking factor must be found, then it must be said that after the institution of the family, the institution of the school brought unity among those who were persecuted. In almost all the major Italian cities, the cream of the academic teaching staff found refuge in the Jewish schools. Those classrooms became little factories of anti-Fascism. Milan is a memorable example; cf. C. Cases, *Il testimone secondario* (Turin: Einaudi, 1986), pp. 5–23. University teachers who had lost their jobs and students who did not want to remain idle met in these schools. Milan could not have the same experience as Trieste, but Rosani was nevertheless an "indomitable leader" according to the posthumous medal awarded her after the Liberation. When in September 1944, near Verona, Rosani's unit was entirely surrounded, the little teacher from Trieste was the last to withdraw and fought to the end of her strength.

democratic interventionist and then an early anti-Fascist and was a noteworthy essayist and scholar (*La Disputa del Nuovo Mondo* is his best-known book). In the realm of Gerbi's reading, Croce occupies a very important place. In Gerbi's review of Croce's edition of *Cunto de li Cunti* by G. Battisti Basile, we find perfectly expressed and synthesized the unanimous and ecstatic reaction of so very many fellow Jews to Croce's writings.

In that review, Gerbi explains how Croce's tireless work brought to mind the ancient Jewish *dayenu* refrain, the "very ancient blessing" from the Passover evening. According to Gerbi, Croce, "an amazing worker," continues to create "new claims for the gratitude of his readers among the Chosen People." Already this Semitic metaphor for Croce's readership stands out, but then we read what Gerbi adds in a half-serious, half-facetious tone: "If [Croce] had recognized the autonomy of the economic form and not intuition, it would have sufficed; if he had recognized lyrical intuition and not the identity of history and philosophy, *dayenu;* if he had written *Filosofia dello Spirito* and not the twenty-five volumes of historical, literary, and political writings, *dayenu;* and I shall stop because my tedious refrain might end up longer than that of Rabbi Hachiba."[27]

Gerbi was wrong to be so cautious. That refrain was destined to become increasingly popular, as Gerbi himself later saw. If in 1928 Croce had written *Storia d'Italia,* it would have sufficed, the anti-Fascist Jews repeated aloud. Instead, in 1932 came *Storia d'Europa.* The refrain became an unstoppable allegorical chorus of a renewed Passover ceremony for those young slaves, subjects of a new pharaoh.

Naturally, Croce's influence was not equally strong or ritualistic in all socialists. For example, in Gustavo Sacerdote (1867–1948) it must be said that his Judaism occupied a very notable or perhaps preponderant position. Trained to become a rabbi at Moncalvo, where he was born, Sacerdote in 1892 opted for socialism. His

27. Don Ferrante (Antonello Gerbi), "Croce e Basile," in *La giustizia,* 19 July, 1925. This excerpt mentioned in P. Treves, "Profilo d. A. Gerbi," in *A. Gerbi, La disputa del Nuovo Mondo* (Milan-Naples: Ricciardi), 1983 pp. XLI-XLII. Here also (p. XXXII) some important considerations on Enzo Sereni's Roman Zionism.

decision broke off a promising career, and it was a choice made not only by him but also by many of his contemporaries who, without an inclination toward business, and, in fact, showing humanistic tendencies, had been directed toward becoming rabbis. A new faith was replacing the old. There is continuity between the articles that Sacerdote wrote in the *Vessillo israelitico* about the nature of the Hebrew language and his first reports for *Il Grido del Popolo* and later for the daily paper of the Italian Socialist Party *Avanti!* The power of utopia expressed by the prophets in the Old Testament strengthened when in contact with the Marxist classics and became totally identified with the spiritual regeneration hoped for by Turati. Sacerdote's career within the Socialist Party advanced with lightning speed. He quickly became the only Berlin correspondent for *Avanti!* and he was the leading figure who united the destinies of Italian socialism and German social democracy up to the outbreak of the First World War. On returning to Milan, Sacerdote continued to write and study. Assyriology and linguistic philology were his two preferred fields of interest. But his love for the *Risorgimento* was no less important. At the end of his life, Sacerdote also became a biographer of Garibaldi. Before the tragic outbreak of the persecutions, Sacerdote managed to reap the benefits of his former rabbinical vocation by producing an excellent translation, published by Mondadori, of Thomas Mann's *Joseph and His Brothers* (1933).[28]

That need for an absolute, that desire for a total renewal of society, was thus nurtured not only by Croce's idealism. These feelings and sensations were also found among those who followed the path of communist anti-Fascism. We have seen this in Curiel and also in Emilio Sereni, Enzo's brother. But here we should at least recall the name of Umberto Terracini, who became a deputy in the Constituent Assembly and who in the 1950s took a critical position in the Italian Communist party. From Genoa, where he lived before the war, Terracini had at first taken refuge in Swit-

---

28. There is no study on this unique figure of Piedmontese anti-Fascism. See at least the entry edited by E. Collotti for the *Dizionario Biografico del Movimento Operaio Italiano*, edited by F. Andreucci and T. Dotti (Rome: Ed. Riuniti, 1975).

zerland. In the summer of 1944, he retraced his steps and joined Communist partisan bands.

Nevertheless, only one book exerted an influence comparable to that of Croce's works. This book was *Socialismo Liberale* by Carlo Rosselli. Many people had read it when it first came out in Paris in 1930. Almost everyone reread it after the author, along with his brother Nello, was killed in France in 1937, by the French *cagoulards* in collaboration with the Duce's secret service. Gobetti's and Salvemini's influence on that text tended to tip the balance against Croce's influence, but at the same time provided the Jewish reader with new suggestions and emotions. From the first page, from the first line, *Socialismo Liberale* attracted the attention of those partisans whom, in our too rapid review, we have remembered and those who unfortunately we can only mention by name (Carlo Levi, Ugo della Seta, Franco Momigliano, Giorgio Diena, Giulio Bolaffi, Vittorio Foà, and Silvio Jona).

Rosselli's opening, so bright and clear, succeeded in stirring its readers in a way that no volume of Croce's managed to do. What was implicit in Croce's *Storia d'Europa* became explicit in Rosselli.

At the end of World War II, Croce commented ironically on the idea of liberal socialism, spitefully calling it a chimera. The political choices of many former Jewish members of the Action Party reflected the effects of that fierce opposition. Some people remained faithful to the demands of Croce's clarity; some remained forever tied to Rosselli's original ideal of reunification. Liberalism and socialism, according to Carlo Rosselli, "are two very elevated but unilateral visions of life that tend to blend with each other and complete each other." Greek rationalism corresponds with the former and Israel's messianism corresponds with the latter. According to Rosselli, Greek rationalism is dominated by "love for liberty" and "respect for autonomy," and by a "detached and harmonious" concept of life. In mentioning Renan's *Histoire du peuple d'Israel*, Rosselli explained immediately afterward that socialism owed some of its special characteristics to the messianism of Israel: the "entirely earthly" idea of justice, "the myth of equality," "a spiritual torment that forbids all indulgence."

A spiritual torment that forbids all indulgence. This is the most eloquent formula, whose fascination not even the Jewish Communist partisans could escape. It was no longer a time for resignation. In homage to that "spiritual torment," the readers of *Socialismo Liberale* wanted to show themselves that Judaism was not synonymous with passivity and inertia. The heirs of Massarani and David Levi, the pupils of Buonaiuti or Croce, all who took up arms and did not lay them down again until after April 25, 1945, translated into the practical terms of political and military struggle the desire for justice of the prophets of Israel.

II. The Period of the Holocaust

Paul Bookbinder

4. Italy in the Overall Context of the Holocaust

The minutely planned and highly organized roundup and murder of millions marks the Holocaust as one of the most monstrous occurrences in human history. Today's interest in the Holocaust springs from the recognition that this phenomenon was not a Jewish problem but a problem for all western civilization. Although the idea for the general overall operation of the extermination of the Jews was in German hands, the magnitude of the task required the cooperation of large numbers of non-Germans as well. While the German people, and the Nazis in particular, have a reputation for efficiency, detailed historical research has revealed that the Nazi regime was, in fact, generally characterized by duplication, inefficiency, interdepartmental and personal conflicts, and indecisiveness. Sad to note that the smoothest-running, best-organized, and least strife-ridden program that the Nazis carried out was their extermination program.[1]

It ran well even though it spanned thousands of miles and required the cooperation and coordination of large numbers of people of many different national groups. The high level of cooperation that the Nazis received from their own population and from the Poles, the Lithuanians, the Hungarians, the Rumanians, and the French, among others, stands in striking contrast to the general reaction and specific actions of the Italians. The Italians, along with the Danes and the Bulgarians, were not overwhelmed by anti-Jewish prejudice, who did not significantly cooperate with Nazi plans for Jewish extermination, and, most importantly, worked actively to save Jews. What makes the Italian experience particularly impressive is that while the government and majority of people in Denmark and Bulgaria acted as one, the large number of

1. Raul Hilberg, *The Destruction of the European Jews.* Revised and definitive edition; 3 vols. (New York, 1985).

Italians who worked to save Jews had to do so in the face of government policy and the will of a leader who, while sometimes ambivalent, was generally trying to please the Germans and maintain a close alliance with them.

Such historians of the Holocaust as Lucy Dawidowicz and Helen Fein, who look at the Holocaust in statistical terms, point out that fewer than twenty percent of Italian Jews were killed by the Nazis, about the same percentage as the Bulgarian Jews and at the bottom of all the statistical tables.[2] This figure might have been even lower had the plan to move many Jews from the Italian-occupied zone of France to areas of liberated North Africa in September 1943 succeeded. Those plans were thwarted by a premature announcement by General Eisenhower of Italy's armistice agreement, which brought about German military action that prevented the evacuation.[3] It is easy to attribute the difference of the Italian response to such factors as geography or population size. However, as Lucy Dawidowicz stated,

> Denmark's dramatic rescue of its Jews and the overwhelming cooperation that the Italians gave their Jewish compatriots cannot be attributed merely to geography or population size, though these factors helped the undertakings to succeed, but are rather the consequences of the repudiation of anti-Semitism and the commitment to unconditional equality.[4]

The factors conditioning these responses in Italians, so different from those of most Europeans, may give clues to dealing with and preventing prejudice, hatred, and genocide.

The history of the Jewish community in Italy began in the days of the Roman Empire. In spite of oppression, persecution, and expulsions, this history of two thousand years made the Jews an integral part of the Italian experience in a way that was unique among the western nations. Thus, with emancipation during the middle of the nineteenth century, Jews in Italy could become part of Italian civil and political society more easily than their co-

---

2. Lucy Dawidowicz, *The War Against the Jews* (New York: Bantam Books, 1976), p. 544; Helen Fein, *Accounting for Genocide* (New York: Free Press), pp. 350–57.
3. Fein, *Accounting for Genocide*, p. 57.
4. Dawidowicz, *The War Against the Jews*, p. 484.

religionists could in other western societies. This radical improvement in the conditions of Italian Jews and the change in attitude on the part of their Christian countrymen was truly startling. As Cecil Roth describes it:

> In 1848, there was no European country (except Spain from which they were entirely excluded) where the restrictions placed upon them were more galling and more humiliating. After 1870, there was no land in either hemisphere where conditions were or could be better. It was not only that disabilities were removed, as happened elsewhere during these momentous years, but that the Jews were accepted freely, naturally and spontaneously as members of the Italian people on a perfect footing of equality with their neighbors.[5]

A comparison with the German experience is useful here, since German Jewish legal emancipation was completed by 1870 as well. No one would describe the relationship between Jewish and Christian Germans in the last years of the nineteenth century as "free acceptance on a perfect footing of equality." While Italian Jews were gaining prominent positions in the government and the army, political anti-Semitism in the German-speaking countries, Germany and Austria, was on the rise.[6] Racial doctrine made its appearance in Germany, thus adding an additional component to traditional religious and economic anti-Semitism. This racial doctrine, which became stronger in the twentieth century, contributed to the success of National Socialism. Racial doctrine played no role in the comparable period in Italian history and was even resisted by Mussolini and the Fascists. In the German-speaking countries, the prerequisites for anti-Semitic violence existed in popular bitterness and resentment. The violence remained temporarily in check because the Wilhelmine government officials, particularly the police and the judges, had an overriding commitment to law and order and the protection of life and property at all cost, even if that property or life belonged to a despised alien.

---

5. Cecil Roth, *The History of the Jews of Italy* (Philadelphia: The Jewish Publication Society of America, 1946), p. 474.
6. Peter G. J. Pulzer, *The Rise of Political Anti-Semitism in Germany and Austria* (New York: Wiley, 1964).

In Italy, widespread anti-Semitic hatred did not exist, thereby precluding the potential for violence.

In eastern Europe, particularly in Tsarist Russia, popular anti-Semitic violence with substantial government encouragement burst forth periodically. In Russia, the years immediately preceding World War I were characterized by anti-Jewish pogroms and a government-sponsored ritual murder trial.[7] Large numbers of Italians, both Jews and Christians, protested against the anti-Jewish violence in Russia.

The substantial hostility toward Jews held in check in Germany and occasionally flaring up in Russia was not confined to central and eastern Europe, but was in evidence in the Latin West as well. France, the main force in Jewish emancipation during the enlightenment and revolutionary periods of the eighteenth century, was convulsed by popular anti-Semitism, which showed itself most clearly in the Dreyfus case. Yet, the severity of anti-Semitism and the relative positions of Jews in Germany, Russia, and France varied significantly. It was possible for a Jew to be a captain in the French army although not a member of the military establishment. It was inconceivable for a Jew to be an officer in the German or Russian armies.

In the Italian army, in sharp contrast to France, Germany, or Russia, Jews could be and were generals. The fact that Jews could rise to the highest ranks of the Italian army is a clear indication of the degree of acceptance that they had attained within Italian society. Furthermore, the experience that Italian Christians had of serving under and with Jews in the army contributed to the generally positive role that the Italian army played in helping Jews during the Holocaust. This sympathetic and supportive role stands in marked contrast to the general hostility manifested by the German, most eastern European, and Vichy French armies. The Jews in all European nations were extremely patriotic during World War I. Tragically, their high volunteer and casualty rates were unrecognized by their fellow citizens in most countries. In Germany, for example, Jews enlisted, fought, and suffered casualties far be-

7. Maurice Samuels, *Blood Libel* (New York: Schocken Books, 1962).

yond their percentage of the population. Yet, most Germans associated them with draft dodging, desk jobs, and profiteering. Italy was one of the very few nations in which Jewish participation in, and contribution to, the war effort was realistically assessed.

During the 1920s, anti-Semitism was rampant in Europe. It was most obvious in Germany, where the Nazi party grew to be the largest and most successful political party in that nation's post-World War I history. The National Socialists' anti-Jewish appeal was the cornerstone of their ideology. Adolf Hitler and the National Socialists looked to Mussolini and the Italian Fascists as their models, and indeed the leaders and the movements shared much. However, Mussolini and the Italian Fascists were not anti-Semitic in their appeal or program in the 1920s. While Hitler repeatedly declared, "The Jews are our misfortune," Mussolini declared to Emil Ludwig, "The Jewish problem does not exist in Italy."[8]

In the 1930s, as the forces and ideas leading to the Holocaust coalesced, the contrast between Italy and the rest of continental Europe became particularly striking. In Germany, Hitler and the Nazis came to power, and within two months the first restrictive law against the Jews was on the books. A popular mood of hostility toward Jews dominated the streets, the schools, and the churches. In all eastern European countries, with the exception of Bulgaria and Soviet Russia, popular anti-Semitism, fascist anti-Semitic movements, and institutional hostility toward Jews boded ill for their future. Bulgaria was free of all these factors.[9] While Russia had a strong tradition of popular and governmental anti-Semitism, the Bolsheviks, beginning with a vigorous personal effort by Lenin, battled against widespread anti-Jewish sentiment and removed all traces of institutional and governmental anti-Semitism. In France, popular anti-Semitism, expressed by nationalist groups such as *Action Française* and fascist groups such as the *Croix de Feu*, threatened the place of Jews within French society. When a leftist

8. Emil Ludwig, *Talks with Mussolini*, trans. Eden and Cedar Paul (Boston: Little Brown, 1933), p. 84.

9. Frederick Barry Chary, *The Bulgarian Jews and the Final Solution, 1940–1944* (Pittsburgh: University of Pittsburgh Press, 1972).

coalition in the National Assembly chose the Jewish socialist leader Léon Blum as premier, many Frenchmen voiced the slogan, "Better Hitler than Blum." Once again, important differences were manifested from one country to another. Léon Blum did become premier of France. No Jew could have been Chancellor of Germany, and the Jewish cabinet minister of the 1920s, Walter Rathenau, was viciously slandered and assassinated in 1922. Before World War I, Italy had already chosen a Jewish premier and a number of Jewish cabinet ministers without the violence or vicious public opposition that the French demonstrated toward Léon Blum and the Germans toward Walter Rathenau.

Until 1933, the year when the National Socialists came to power, neither the Italian government nor the Fascist party evidenced anti-Semitism, and the popular variant was not a significant factor in Italian life. While the Fascist party adopted anti-Semitism as part of its program under the influence of the German model in 1938 and passed restrictive laws aimed at Jews, Italian Fascism never pursued its anti-Jewish program with the fanaticism of other fascist movements. When Italy's Fascists are compared with the Nazis, the Rumanian Iron Guard, or the Hungarian Arrow Cross, the relative lack of fanaticism on the part of most Italian Fascists and even the resistance of some of them to anti-Semitism distinguishes them from their European comrades.[10]

Italian Fascists were different from other Fascists not only in their attitudes and actions, but also in their ideology. A basic component of fascist ideology was the division of all peoples into two categories: friends and foes. A community of friends unified itself in opposition to the foe. The ideal foe was a category of people living both inside and outside the country where the community of friends resided. For ideologues in all but the Italian Fascist movement, that foe was the Jew. Thus German, Rumanian, Hungarian, Croatian, and even French fascism was unified against the Jew as enemy. For the major Italian fascist thinkers, including Mussolini himself, Alfredo Rocco, and Giovanni Gentile, the foe

---

10. S. J. Woolf (ed.), *Fascism In Europe* (London: Methuen, 1981); Stein Ugelvik Larsen (ed.), *Who Were the Fascists: Social Roots of European Fascism* (Bergen: Universtetsforlaget, 1980).

was the Bolshevik, who was not seen, as in eastern Europe, as synonymous with the Jew. While there may have been a strong undercurrent and sometimes overcurrent of anti-Semitism in Italian popular literature, it did not condition popular attitudes or mold the political ideology of a significant number of Italian political thinkers, not even those who were Fascists.[11]

By the early 1940s, Europe was at war, and the Germans and their allies had overrun much of Europe. Following the advancing and occupying German armies were special troops who had as their overriding goal the "Final Solution," the monstrous extermination solution of the "Jewish problem." On the heels of the invasion of the Soviet Union in 1941, these *Einsatzgruppen* (extermination squads) moved into Polish and Russian territory, and the extermination process began. Spreading from east to west, the roundup and the extermination process engulfed most of Europe. The Nazis expected their allies and puppet states to support their policies and to turn over to the SS authorities all Jews under their control, both their fellow countrymen and foreign Jews living in countries they occupied. Rumanians, Latvians, Lithuanians, and Croatians did so enthusiastically. The Hungarian authorities willingly turned over the non-Hungarian Jews in their occupied territory. Admiral Horthy, the longtime Hungarian leader, hesitated to surrender Hungarian Jews, mainly because he was uncertain about the final outcome of the war. Thus, under Horthy's direction, the Hungarians delayed the surrender of Hungarian Jews. However, the Hungarian Fascists, most of the military, many in the church, and large numbers of citizens clamored for the elimination of the Jews. Ultimately, Horthy was removed and replaced by a more cooperative leader and the destruction of half of Hungary's Jewish population was ensured.

The Bulgarians refused to turn over their Jews to the Germans. In Bulgaria, the government leaders, the army leadership, churchmen, and the general population stood together. Although there had been examples of anti-Semitism in Bulgarian history, the

---

11. Andrew Canepa, "The Image of the Jew in the Folklore and Literature of the Postrisorgimento," *Journal of European Studies*, IX (1979), p. 260–73.

Bulgarians viewed themselves and their history as being free of anti-Semitism, and that perception conditioned their attitudes and actions in the 1940s.[12] The Bulgarians did, however, round up non-Bulgarian Jews in areas they occupied militarily and turned them over to the Germans. The Vichy French authorities occasionally vacillated about surrendering French Jews to the Germans, but usually cooperated with the SS. They were, however, unequivocal and zealous in their efforts to round up non-French Jews in areas they militarily controlled.

In relation to other Europeans, the Italian response during the 1940s stands out. Until September 1943, the Italians never actively cooperated with German "Final Solution" policies. During German occupation, in almost every area, whether it involved Italian Jews, for whom feelings were strongest, or even non-Italian Jews under their control, large numbers of Italians impeded and obstructed SS efforts to round up Jews and send them to death camps. The extent of Italian resistance in various areas was determined by the particular military commanders and civilian officials who had authority, but the level of this resistance was high. For example, Italians intervened to provide sanctuary and prevent exterminations in Croatia.[13] They actively interfered with Nazi efforts in southern Greece and the Maritime Alps in France.[14] After 1938, when he had endorsed anti-Jewish policies, Mussolini was often frustrated by the extent of Italian resistance to his racial policies. Yet, even during his public anti-Jewish period, Mussolini never supported the extermination program. While he may have harbored private bitterness toward individual Jews such as Claudio Treves, the socialist leader whom he regarded as his archenemy, he never became a hater on the order of Josef Goebbels or Adolf Hitler.[15]

Vichy French and Italian documents concerning Jews under Ital-

12. Chary, *The Bulgarian Jews.*

13. Ivo Herzer, "How Italians Rescued Jews," *Midstream* (June/July 1983), pp. 35–38.

14. Léon Poliakov, *Jews Under the Italian Occupation* (Paris: Editions Du Centre, 1955). Daniel Carpi, "Nuovi documenti per la Storia dell'olocausto in Grecia. L'atteggiamento degli italiani, 1941–1943," in *Michael, The Diaspora Research Institute, Tel-Aviv University*, 7 (1981), pp. 119–20.

15. Arnoldo Momigliano, "Review," *Journal of Modern History* (June 1980), pp. 282–84.

ian occupation affirm the uniqueness of Italian attitudes toward
Jews. The statements and actions of Italian authorities demonstrated sympathy and humanity totally lacking among an over-
whelming number of German and French officials.[16] The effectiveness of Angelo Donati and other Italian Jews working with the
cooperation of the Italian army to save their fellow Jews angered
German officials. The Gestapo planned to kidnap Donati so that
he could no longer work with the Italian occupation authorities
who were protecting him and supporting his efforts. Even though
Jews had been purged from the Italian military by the racial laws
in 1938, the fact that Jews had gained general acceptance and significant positions in the Italian military made the Italian army a
vehicle for resistance to anti-Jewish manifestations. As a result of
their positive attitude toward Jews, the army leaders often resisted
German pressure to round up Jews and even blocked German efforts to do so.

Sympathy toward Jews on the part of the Italian military reflected a generally held attitude of Italians toward Jews and blunted
the entire thrust of the anti-Jewish program of the Fascists. Whatever the pre-1848 history of Italian Jewry might have been, the
Italians did not view themselves or their society as anti-Semitic,
and that perception conditioned their actions. As Meir Michaelis
declares,

> The severity of racial laws was tempered by corruption and inef-
> ficiency, by the philo-Semitism of the Italian masses, by the
> Italian capacity for compromise and *combinazioni* (flexible ar-
> rangements) and—last but not least—by the growing anti-Axis
> feeling within the Italian ruling classes.[17]

Philo-Semitism is not an expression that could be used to describe
the attitude of any other national group toward Jews between 1938
and 1945.

The accounts of individual Italian Jews who survived the Holocaust confirm the substantial differences between the Italian ex-

16. Poliakov, *Jews Under the Italian Occupation.*
17. Meir Michaelis, *Mussolini and the Jews: German-Italian Relations and the
Jewish Question in Italy 1922–1945* (London: The Clarendon Press, 1978), p. 413.
In *Michael,* 7 (1981), pp. 119–20.

perience and that of any other group of Jews. These accounts give substance to the generalizations concerning the Italians and the rescue of Jews.[18] In Rothchild's *Voices from the Holocaust*, Ora Kohn, a Jew from Turin, attests the uniqueness of the Italian experience when she discusses both the warnings she received from her Christian Italian neighbors and the help in finding temporary refuge. She managed to escape to Switzerland in the face of a German roundup of Jews.[19] In that final escape, she relied on the factor of corruption and dealt with smugglers. In the end, however, the cooperation of a young Italian army officer in charge of a border patrol was decisive in facilitating her escape. Kohn was moved to learn that this young army officer had refused to take money for his part in the escape of a group of Jews. Unfortunately, although Switzerland is often perceived as a place of refuge, many Jews were stopped at the Swiss border and turned back.[20]

The special attitude toward Jews did not reflect a general acceptance of all non-Italians or other ethnic and national groups. The Italians demonstrated their share of racism when dealing with the Ethiopians they conquered. Luigi Preti compares Italian colonial legislation with that of other European powers and declares, "colonial legislation of fascist Italy was the most backward."[21] Thus, the Italian attitude toward Jews, which conditioned so much of their activity during the Holocaust, was a direct reflection of their perception of Jews and their historical place within Italian society. Gaston Orefice, a Jew from Livorno who survived with considerable help from fellow Italians, declares, "Even in those hard times Jews were in the Italian milieu. We were different but we were not outsiders."[22]

While Italian Jewish beliefs and practices had always been characterized by variety, after emancipation Jewishness was self-

18. Susan Zuccotti, *The Italians and the Holocaust: Persecution, Rescue, Survival.* (New York: Basic Books, 1987); Sylvia Rothchild, *Voices from the Holocaust* (New York: New American Library, 1981).

19. Rothchild, *Voices from the Holocaust*, p. 205–9.

20. Alfred A. Hasler, *The Lifeboat is Full*, trans. Charles Lam Markman (New York: Funk and Wagnalls, 1969).

21. Luigi Preti, "Fascist Imperialism and Racism," in *The Ax Within: Italian Fascism in Action*, ed. Roland Sarti (New York: Franklin Watts, 1974), p. 196.

22. Rothchild, *Voices from the Holocaust*, p. 212.

defined rather than defined by the greater community. Jews who were assimilated or had even converted could retain as much Jewishness as they desired. In his study of six significant Italian writers who were of Jewish origin, H. Stuart Hughes describes this situation: "My Italian experience suggested that the residual sense of Jewishness was a very 'private' matter—that is, it was far more perceptible to Italian Jews themselves than to outsiders who encountered them—a situation just the reverse of the German in 1933."[23] An Italian Jew could be a practicing Jew if he wanted to be one or he could totally assimilate or convert and lose his Jewishness as far as the perceptions and reactions of his Italian Christian neighbors were concerned.

Italian, German, and eastern European Jews contrasted markedly in terms of their psychology of escape and resistance. Bruno Bettelheim has observed that many Jews gave up their struggle to escape or resist because they believed that their fellow countrymen were either hostile to them or indifferent to their fate.[24] This feeling led to the conclusion that they would get no support if they were able to elude the Nazis temporarily. The result was an attitude of fatalistic resignation. In eastern Europe, most partisan groups would not take Jews, and some would turn them over to the Nazis or shoot them. Thus the epic tragedy of Leibl Fehlhandler, leader of the heroic Sobibor death camp revolt.[25] Fehlhandler, who helped organize and lead the revolt of 3,000 prisoners at the Sobibor extermination camp in Poland, was among the 300 prisoners who survived the uprising and escaped from the camp. After surviving the escape and a period of fighting in the forests, he met his death at the hands of the right-wing anti-Semitic Polish Home Army. Italian Jews and other European Jews who could get to Italy were given a spiritual lift and found it possible to maintain the drive to resist and escape because of the support of the vast number of Italians whom they encountered. No Jew making contact with an Italian partisan group had to fear being turned over to the Ger-

23. H. Stuart Hughes, *Prisoners of Hope* (Cambridge: Harvard University Press, 1983), p. 2.
24. Bruno Bettelheim, "The Effect of Hopelessness on the Will to Resist," a lecture presented at Milton Academy, Milton, Massachusetts, April 1985.
25. Yuri Suhl (ed.), *They Fought Back* (New York: Schocken, 1975), pp. 7–51.

mans or being shot in the back. The paralyzing effects of the belief that one's fellow countrymen are hostile or indifferent were not factors in Italy.

Certainly the deep roots of the Jews in Italy contributed to the response of Italian Christians to their Jewish fellow citizens. Rome had the oldest Jewish community in the western world. As Cecil Roth states, "The only city in the western world in which Jewish settlement remained uninterrupted throughout the Middle Ages, from remotest times down to the present day, was that for the rule of which the popes were themselves immediately responsible— Rome."[26] While there is considerable debate about the role of the pope and his Vatican administrators in relation to the Holocaust, there is clear evidence that, from the lower levels at least through that of bishop, there were substantial church efforts to help the Jews. Whatever the criticism of Pope Pius XII, it is clear that the Italian rank and file clergy made a valiant effort to help Jews.[27]

Decisive differences characterized the attitudes and actions of the Austrian and German clergy and the Italian clergy. Both the Austrian and the German churches failed to mount any substantial resistance to the anti-Jewish teachings and actions of the National Socialists.[28] Many of the Italian clergy were able to overcome the deep anti-Judaism in church teaching in a way that their central and eastern European brethren could not. Thus, they were able to reach out with charity and sympathy to help Jews.

A comparison of England and the United States at the onset of the Holocaust serves to place the Italian experience in as broad a context as possible and to bring it closer to home. While both England and the United States provided a haven for numbers of Jews, restrictive British colonial policies and American immigration policies sharply limited the numbers of Jews who could take advantage of these places of refuge. England closed the doors to

---

26. Roth, *The History of the Jews in Italy*, p. 42.

27. See the contribution of Robert Graham in this volume. On a personal note, the one surviving member of my wife's large eastern European family was a second cousin who was able to get from Poland to Italy and found sanctuary in a monastery.

28. Gordon Zahn, *German Catholics and Hitler's Wars: A Study in Social Control* (New York: Sheed and Ward, 1962); Gunter Lewy, *The Catholic Church and Nazi Germany* (New York: McGraw-Hill, 1964).

Palestine, the desired haven for Zionist Jews. Those Holocaust writers who are among her harshest critics accuse the British of secretly seeing the Nazi extermination process as a convenient solution, saving Britain from an aggravated colonial problem in the Middle East which might be brought on by increased Jewish settlement in Palestine.[29] It is not necessary to be quite so damning to realize that substantial numbers of Englishmen, both in the foreign service and the army, did not do all that they could to rescue Jews.

The United States refused to make exceptions to its restrictive quota system, and the debate in the United States in 1938 about the Wagner-Rogers Bill demonstrated a deep well of domestic American anti-Semitism. The Wagner-Rogers Bill proposed to take in 10,000 Jewish refugee children in excess of their national quotas. The bill was fiercely opposed by a range of groups from the Daughters of the American Revolution to the American Legion. These groups vented their nativist sentiments and anti-Jewish feelings, and, in spite of the efforts of Senator Wagner of New York and Congresswoman Rogers of Massachusetts and the more open-minded and humane Americans they represented, the bill was defeated. Its defeat typified a pattern of resistance to rescue efforts and military action to effect rescue, a pattern that characterized American policy throughout the Holocaust period.[30] Motivations ranged from the political indifference of President Franklin Roosevelt, to Secretary of State Cordell Hull's mild opposition to action, to active anti-Semitic hostility and clear resistance to rescue efforts on the part of Breckenridge Long and many other officials in the State Department. In light of the relative security and lack of direct German military pressure on the United States, American indifference and hostility toward the Jews of Europe appears all the more inexcusable, and the openness and tolerance displayed by such a large number of Italian officials becomes even more striking.

29. Richard Rubenstein, *The Cunning of History: The Holocaust and the American Future* (New York: Harper & Row, 1987).

30. Henry Feingold, *The Politics of Rescue: The Roosevelt Administration and the Holocaust* (New Brunswick, N.J.: Rutgers University Press, 1970).

Clearly, there were anti-Semitic Italians, and Italian history and culture were not free of prejudice toward Jews. Mussolini and his Fascist party contained elements with strong anti-Jewish attitudes. They assaulted the Italian Jewish community and wounded it deeply. Meir Michaelis states:

> Although over four-fifths of the Jews of Italy survived the war, Italian Jewry suffered a blow from which it is unlikely to recover in the foreseeable future. Thousands had abandoned the community, and some 6,000 had emigrated; many of those who remained were physically and spiritually broken. The habit of Jewish life had been interrupted, and in many places its setting had disappeared.[31]

Yet, the Italian survivors had a more positive feeling about their countrymen than did most European Jews, and those who wanted to go home again knew they would be assured a joyous welcome. Many owed their lives and debts of gratitude to Italians.

The Holocaust is to a considerable extent a study in the potentialities of human evil and inhumanity. However, within all the horror, there were still sparks of good and hope. These should be recognized, studied, and communicated to our children. Italy was one of these sparks which illuminated human good, compassion, and tolerance. For too long, the Italian experience has been overshadowed by the need to reveal to the world the scope of Nazi crimes and the complicity or indifference of so much of the western world. While the evil cannot be forgotten, its darkness all the more serves to contrast with the light of the Italian response.

31. Michaelis, *Mussolini and the Jews*, p. 414.

Liliana Picciotto Fargion
(translated by Susan Zuccotti)

5. The Jews During the German Occupation and the Italian Social Republic

To understand the fate of Jews in the various western European countries, four factors should be considered:

(1) the Nazi intention to destroy local Jewish communities, more or less evident in every occupied nation;
(2) the autonomous power retained by each invaded country, or, the degree of political subordination;
(3) the attitude of local public administrations; and
(4) the attitude of the local population.

I shall not linger on the first point, which has been amply treated elsewhere. For a general analysis of the Holocaust, country by country, I recommend two of the most significant historical contributions of recent years: the expanded edition of Raul Hilberg's *The Destruction of the European Jews* (1985) and *L'Allemagne nazie et le génocide juif*, edited by the École des Hautes Études en sciences sociales (1985).[1] As for the second point, as is known, the history of Italy in the Fascist period can be clearly divided into two parts: the period of the equal alliance with Germany (March 1939–September 1943) and the period of the subordinate alliance (September 1943–April 1945) with a brief interregnum of barely forty-five days.

Anti-Semitism was expressed by the Italian state in both periods, but with the important qualitative difference that in the first period, it was intended to discriminate, humiliate, and persecute the Jews, while in the second, in connection with the German presence, it was intended to separate the Jews from the rest of the

---

1. R. Hilberg, *The Destruction of the European Jews*, New York-London 1985; *L'Allemagne nazie et le génocide juif*, Colloque de l'École des Hautes Études en sciences sociales (Paris, 1985).

nation and imprison them. It should be remembered that, with a few isolated exceptions, anti-Semitism in Italy did not have a popular base or a real and distinct tradition; it was simply the product of an alignment of Italian Fascism with one of the central currents of the Nazi ideology. This policy was implemented in September 1938 with the appearance of the anti-Jewish laws.

Scholars agree in excluding any explicit German request for an Italian anti-Semitic policy. In fact, looking at Italian-German relations in 1938, it appears clear that Mussolini had no need to make concessions to Hitler. At the end of March, the climate of friendship between the two nations was still rather cold. The *Anschluss* with Austria had constituted a powerful reversal for Italy at a time when the latter was, among other things, still wavering between an accord with France and Great Britain and an alliance with Germany. Thus, the more Hitler made advances leading toward a military pact, the more Italy objected, fearful that public opinion was not prepared, and fearful also of an aggressive action in Alto Adige. It seems clear, then, that Mussolini had chosen to endorse an anti-Jewish policy well before deciding in favor of the Pact of Steel, signed on March 22, 1939. The first official anti-Semitic step, in fact, went back to February 1938, with the publication of the *Informazione Diplomatica number 14*, an ambiguous government declaration that denied rumors of pending anti-Jewish legislation while at the same time making obscure allegations about the disproportion between the slight number of Jews and the role they played in the life of the nation.[2] In addition, according to the diary of the well-known Fascist leader Giuseppe Bottai, the preparation of the text of the so-called "Law for the Defense of the Race" was assigned to Guido Landra as early as the end of October, 1937. These factors illustrate the absolute Italian autonomy and independence in the field of anti-Jewish policy. The Italians emphasized that same independence later when the alliance had become effective, and they acted upon it especially after 1942 in their occupied territories in France, Yugoslavia, and Greece,

2. The complete text is cited in Renzo De Felice, *Storia degli ebrei italiani sotto il fascismo* (Turin, 1972), p. 272.

when the diverse anti-Semitic concepts of Germany and Italy conflicted in the area not of abstract politics but of daily practice.

The rather extraordinary fact is that even in the second period, when Fascism—having collapsed with the *coup d'état* of July 25, 1943, and having been restored with German support of the following September 8—again adopted anti-Semitism, it did not seem merely to have followed the German lead.[3] Certainly the climate differed, and we cannot fail to consider the political context in which the Repubblica Sociale Italiana (RSI) was operating, heavily influenced in every field by Germans determined to make Italy a satellite state. Nevertheless, in the present state of research, no surviving document indicates that the Germans directly pressured the RSI for the arrests and internments of Jews, or for the confiscation of their property. On the contrary, it seems that one can detect in the neo-Fascist anti-Semitic policies a certain rivalry and competition, an anxiety to affirm sovereignty and independence. This can be seen in the continual diatribes on the categories of Jews to be arrested, and in the Italian insistence that the internees in concentration camps be left in Italy and not deported elsewhere.

As for the third point listed above—the attitude of public administrations—it is useful to remember the fundamental role such administrations can play in the more or less strict interpretation of the law. This is particularly true of anti-Jewish measures, which tended to transfer jurisdiction from the judiciary to the executive power. All decisions in racial matters were referred exclusively to the Ministry of the Interior and could not be appealed. They were equally binding on the public administration and on the judiciary.[4]

In this regard, it is difficult not to be astonished today at the manner in which the laws, discriminatory at first and destructive of all freedom later, were accepted by the agencies charged with executing them. Government officials remained neutral and indifferent, as if the matters were merely routine. We have, for example, no evidence of resignations in protest. The new laws were accepted

3. For the problem of anti-Semitism during the Italian Social Republic, see L. Picciotto Fargion, "The Anti-Jewish Policy of the Italian Social Republic (1943–1945)," in *Yad Vashem Studies*, Jerusalem, vol. XVII, 1986, pp. 17–49.
4. M. R. Lo Giudice, "Razza e giustizia nell'Italia fascista," in *Rivista di storia contemporanea*, n. 1, 1983, p. 73.

as legitimate, and responsibility for their application was similar to that for any other law of the period.

However, beneath an apparent general conformity, there was a great diversity of attitudes. In contrast to the Nazi state machinery, the Italian machinery was not inclined toward militant anti-Semitism by tradition or by direct physical experience with Jews, little known because they were so few in number. The Fascist law itself, especially in the first five years, provided exceptions that were broadly applied. The harshness of the laws was tempered sometimes by the generosity of government officials and sometimes by corruption. This is clearly evident in the stories of the persecuted, whose individual experiences ranged from extreme harshness to extreme gentleness. In fact, there is a need for a detailed study of substantive and local variations in the application of the anti-Semitic laws. What we can say with certainty is that contrasting tendencies toward harshness and gentleness existed within the same public administration. The education and the cultural inclinations of each government official, therefore, played a fundamental role.

During the second anti-Semitic period, when the real physical danger began, that role grew enormously. It was not by chance that the major part of the help extended to Jews came from low-level civil servants who had not been affected by the central government's anti-Semitic propaganda and who perhaps had never seen a Jew in their lives. These were good-hearted men who only saw terrorized people in need of help. Scores of communal employees provided official seals for false identity cards and false ration cards. Policemen warned victims of their imminent arrests. There were even *podestà* (mayors) who hid Jews in their homes or destroyed lists of names.

Having honored those government officials who did not betray their own humanity, however, we must emphasize that no individual examples of generosity should or can detract from the monstrous state machinery that was placed at the service of injustice. *Prefettura* (provincial government) and police documents clearly testify that examples of generosity were the exception; perfunctory, if not actually zealous, execution of orders was the norm.

The bureaucratic machinery of the persecution, especially in the period of the RSI, was perfectly oiled and functioned almost automatically. The Council of Ministers decided; the Ministry of the Interior ordered; the chief of police circulated instructions; the prefects of the various provinces passed along their orders; the local police executed them. Everyone could consider himself innocent and refer responsibility to his superiors. The truth is that everyone was involved, for otherwise the machinery would have been obstructed. The RSI, as we will see later, provided the legal cover for the arrests and, to some extent, furnished the Nazis with a quota for deportation.

As for the fourth point, perhaps the most significant for Italy, it is evident that the attitude of the local population is fundamental to the safety of a persecuted minority: The more intense the popular ill will, the stronger the inclination to intolerance and endemic envy, and the more, at the moment of the outbreak of the crisis, the masses line up on the side of the persecutor, whose objectives in the last analysis they share. This was not the case in Italy, where the entire population (especially the most humble, who regarded the period of the RSI as something strange and distant) was disposed to help. We are speaking here especially of barely educated country people, endowed with an ancient sense of the family and of affection, incapable of wronging Jews, who usually knocked on their doors seeking hospitality in family groups. We also include lower-middle-class people in urban areas in difficult economic straits—anti-Fascists by natural inclination rather than by rational conviction, on whom Fascist propaganda had little impact. Also disposed to help were enlightened middle-class individuals, anti-Fascists through political education and for that reason inclined to help those persecuted by Fascism. These were joined by humble priests, accustomed to spreading words of charity, who felt obligated to practice their preaching by saving poor persecuted human beings. Around the Jews and against the blind Fascist bureaucracy and the Nazi brutality, a wall of solidarity arose which extended from complete protection at the risk of personal safety to the obstruction of the rules of the authorities. How many times the survivors, emerging from hiding after the war, heard people say, "But everyone in the village knew you were Jews!"

Having made this introduction, let us now discuss how the actual events unfolded.

After September 8, 1943, and the German occupation, Italy was automatically included in the project of extermination of the Jews of Europe which, as is known, had been communicated by Reinhard Heydrich, chief of SIPO-SD [*Sicherheitspolizei-Sicherheitsdienst*] to Nazi leaders at the Wannsee conference in January 1942.[5] On that occasion it was noted that the "Final Solution" was to be applied to eleven million people in thirty-one different countries mentioned on a two-part list. Under the letter "A" were listed invaded countries; under the letter "B" were those under German influence, whether allied or neutral. Italy was under the letter "B." Statistics were included for every country. In Italy the "Final Solution" was expected to apply to 58,000 Jews. That statistic was not far from the reality, and had evidently been provided to the Germans by the Italian Ministry of the Interior since, although the situation had altered by 1942, Italy had 58,412 people of "Jewish race," including foreigners, according to the "racial" census of 1938.[6] The foreign Jews included refugees in transit trapped in Italy by the war, as well as Italians deprived of their nationality.

After signing the armistice with the Allies, Italy became a country where the methods and structure of the Nazi persecution could be applied. That extension was grafted onto the Fascist persecution already in operation in the form of discriminatory legislation making anti-Semitism the official policy of the state.[7] That legislation had been in effect since September 1938, or for about five years.

5. Verbal transcript of the conference presented at the Nuremberg trial (NG 2586) reproduced, among others, also in United Restitution Organization, *Judenverfolgung in Italien, den italienisch besetzten Gebieten und in Nordafrika* (Frankfurt am Main, 1962), pp. 43–45.

6. S. Della Pergola, *Anatomia dell'ebraismo italiano* (Rome, 1976), p. 54.

7. For the story of the Jews in Italy under Fascism, the most complete study is R. De Felice, *Storia degli ebrei italiani sotto il fascismo* (Milan, 1972) (latest edition); well-documented also in M. Michaelis, *Mussolini e la questione ebraica, Le relazioni italo-tedesche e la politica razziale in Italia* (Milan, 1982) (original edition: *Mussolini and the Jews: German-Italian Relations and the Jewish Question in Italy 1922–1945* [Oxford, 1978]); a good synthesis is: S. Zuccotti, *The Italians and*

Without entering into a discussion of the origins of anti-Semitism in Italy, or of the reasons that led Mussolini to endorse it, we will say only that anti-Semitism was not part of the Italian cultural tradition. In contrast to Germany where, in a certain sense, one can speak of pervasive anti-Semitism throughout the society and the Nazi bureaucracy, the government in Italy had to convince public opinion of the justice of its position by means of a thorough propaganda, and create a specific agency, the Direzione Generale per la Demografia e Razza, to manage its anti-Semitic policy. That policy was, in a sense, more cold-hearted and rational than the Nazi version, and perhaps even more monstrous, but certainly less efficient. Italian anti-Semitism, not finding its roots in the deepest political and social history of the country, was a strategic choice adopted after 1936 by Fascist leaders to eliminate causes of friction with Germany. It was state anti-Semitism introduced artificially, rather than popular anti-Semitism. With this premise, and preceded by an anti-Semitic propaganda campaign and a special Jewish census (typical measures of every repressive regime), a series of laws was issued, one after another, which placed the Jewish community on the margin of the life of the nation and deprived the Jews of elemental political and civil rights, making them in fact second-class citizens. From then on, the Jews lived in a humiliating, uncomfortable, and hopeless situation. This was particularly true of those who lost the possibility of working, exercising their professions, retaining property over a certain value, or serving in

---

the Holocaust (New York, 1987). For the experiences both of the different Jewish communities and of individual Jews under the Italian Social Republic, see G. Mayda, *Ebrei sotto Salò. La persecuzione antisemita 1943–1945* (Milan, 1978). The most precise estimate of the number of victims of the deportations, although it too needs to be updated by now, is that presented by the Centro di Documentazione Ebraica Contemporeanea (hereinafter cited as CDEC) of Milan in G. Donati, *Ebrei in Italia. Deportazione, resistenza,* ed. CDEC (Florence, 1975). In addition, see: "Gli ebrei in Italia durante il fascismo," *Quaderni del CDEC,* n. 1 (Milan, 1961) (reprinted Bologna, 1981): n. 2, Milan 1962: n. 3, Milan 1963; A. Spinosa, "La persecuzione razziale in Italia," in *Il Ponte,* July 1952, pp. 964–978; August 1952, pp. 1,078–1,096; November 1952, pp. 1,604–1,622; July 1953, pp. 950–968; G. Valabrega, *Ebrei, fascismo, sionismo* (Urbino, 1974); *La difesa della razza,* special issue of *Il Ponte* ed. U. Caffaz, November 30–December 21, 1978; L. Picciotto Fargion, *L'occupazione tedesca e gli ebrei di Roma* (Rome-Milan, 1979); *Spostamenti di popolazioni e deportazioni in Europa, 1933–1945* (Bologna, 1987). The many other more specific studies of local incidents or particular aspects of the problem would be too numerous to list here. Interested readers should consult the excellent bibliography by Sarfatti in this volume and at the end of Michaelis, *Mussolini and the Jews,* cited above.

the military, and who lived in a climate of material and moral deprivation.

The outbreak of the war in June 1940 caused no major changes in the life of the native Jewish community which, though stricken, had succeeded in again carving out a niche within Italian society. However, thousands of foreign Jews who found themselves in Italy as refugees or in transit during this period were arrested and interned. Mussolini's fall on July 25, 1943, was naturally greeted as a liberating event. Jewish leaders immediately asked the new government, headed by Marshal Pietro Badoglio, to abolish the racial laws, but they received only limited attention. The prime minister was afraid to confirm the already aroused suspicions of the Germans,[8] who were watching the new Italian situation with apprehension, ready to intervene in the event of any sign of defection from the alliance (and some say that they would have intervened even without a defection). Strangely enough, no one at the time thought of the possible tragic consequences of the existence in Italian government offices of lists of Jews in every province, complete with addresses, which was the product of the census conducted by the Ministry of the Interior in August 1938 and updated in 1942.

After the announcement of the signing of the armistice between Badoglio's government and the Allied powers, events unfolded in rapid succession.[9] In a commando-style operation, the Nazis liberated Mussolini, a prisoner of the king on the Gran Sasso. German troops stationed in Italy as allies were directly transformed into an occupying force. A new Fascist government, no longer monarchic but republican, was constituted from elements remaining loyal to Mussolini. Italy was divided into two distinct parts: one in the South under an Allied administration and headed by the king and Badoglio (Regno del Sud), and one in the North under German control and headed by Mussolini (Repubblica Sociale Italiana, also called Repubblica di Salò). Rome was no longer the

8. P. Badoglio, *L'Italia nella seconda guerra mondiale* (Milan, 1946), p. 92.
9. For events linked to the fall of Fascism on July 25, 1943, and to its restoration the following September 8, see especially: F. Deakin, *Storia della Repubblica di Salò* (Turin, 1963) (original edition: *The Brutal Friendship. Mussolini, Hitler and the Fall of Italian Fascism* [London 1962]).

seat of the government. The capital of the RSI was transferred to the shores of Lake Garda.

Horrifying incidents occurred from the very onset of the occupation. Between September 15 and 22, 1943, a company of the SS passing near Lago Maggiore conducted roundups and massacres of Jews.[10] On September 16, Jews in Merano, near Bolzano, were arrested and deported in the direction of Austria. On October 9, there was a German roundup in Trieste.[11] But the incident that most clearly announced the onset in Italy of anti-Jewish persecution in the Nazi style was the roundup in the Jewish quarter in Rome on October 16, 1943.

To understand the structure of the persecution introduced in Italy by the Germans, it is useful to compare it with that of other occupied western European countries, particularly with France, a neighbor not only geographically but also politically. For the Republic of Vichy and the Republic of Salò had more than a few elements in common.[12] In this regard, the French defendant Edgar Faure introduced a document of great interest to us at the Nuremberg trials (1945–46). It was a voluminous German report entitled "The Jewish Question in France and Its Treatment," dated July 1, 1941, and edited by *SS-Hauptsturmführer* Theodor Dannecker, charged with the "Final Solution" in France.[13] Divided into chapters with graphs, prints, and samples of census forms, it described the various phases of preparation for the deportations.

From the document, applicable also to Italy, two elements are clear: the coordinated and premeditated character of the persecutions in occupied western Europe; and the Nazi realization of the necessity to work gradually in the West. (In the East extermination was rapid, radical, and, in many cases, performed on the spot.)

10. *Procedimento penale contro Krüger Hans ed altri*, Tribunale di Osnabrück. Cfr. trial documents and sentence pronounced on July 6, 1968, in Milan, Archivio Centro di Documentazione Ebraica Contemporanea (hereinafter ACDEC), AG, Denuncie e processi—10B; See also G. Mayda, op. cit., pp. 79–85.

11. G. Donati, op. cit., pp. 29–30.

12. For the anti-Jewish policies of Vichy France, see: M. Marrus and R. Paxton, *Vichy France and the Jews* (New York, 1981); S. Klarsfeld, *Vichy-Auschwitz* (Paris, 1984–1985).

13. Report from Dannecker to the RSHA, office IV J., Paris, 1 July 1941. Document presented by France at the Nuremberg trial (RF-1207) and reproduced in H. Monneray, *La persécution des Juifs en France et dans les autres pays de l'ouest, document presenté par la France à Nuremberg* (Paris, 1947), pp. 84–116.

The first element is demonstrated by the weekly meetings of the German military, diplomatic, and political administrations at the Paris headquarters of the SIPO-SD, and the periodic meetings at Adolf Eichmann's Office of Jewish Affairs (B4) at Gestapo headquarters in Berlin. At these meetings, national experts on the Jewish question from France, Belgium, and Holland defined anti-Jewish principles and actions according to various local conditions.

But the second element, gradualism, is the one that most readily prompts considerations that we can apply to the Italian case. For Dannecker in France, gradualism meant having time to condition public opinion through anti-Jewish propaganda, conduct a general census of the Jews, seize their property, and impose (or have imposed, through Vichy) anti-Jewish legislation. Then, to coordinate the anti-Jewish measures better and to give them a French flavor, a special agency was created within the Ministry of the Interior at Vichy called the General Commissariat of Jewish Questions. Only after completing this phase could Dannecker proceed without too much difficulty to arrests, internments, and deportations.

If we analyze the Italian Fascist policy toward the Jews after 1936, we will note an extraordinary similarity with some of the later French provisions regarding the Jewish question. Anti-Jewish propaganda was initiated at the end of 1936 in Italy by means of the press and, somewhat later, the universities, the cinema, and the radio. In June 1938 a special agency called Demografia e Razza was created within the Ministry of the Interior and charged with the coordinated execution of the official anti-Jewish policy, which had just been announced. The special census of pure and mixed-blooded Jews, conducted with great zeal between July and August 1938, reached an objective similar to the one directed by Dannecker in France: it identified the Jews and determined their addresses, their family groupings, and the nature of their employment; after 1943, it facilitated raids on Jewish homes. Finally, the Italian anti-Jewish legislation shared many points in common with the laws imposed in France—for example, the definition of a Jew, the prohibition of the professions, and the naming of Aryan administrators for Jewish businesses.

We can confirm that in Italy during the German occupation, the preparatory phase was omitted because of the rush of events, but also and especially because it was not needed, since it had already been completed. In fact when Dannecker arrived in Italy at the beginning of October 1943, charged with the same tasks that he had already completed in France the year before, there was no need to apply the same gradualism used in other western European countries before proceeding to the deportations.

According to the current state of research on the Jewish experience in Italy between 1943 and 1945, we can clearly divide events into three distinct periods. Following the first period of autonomous lightning raids conducted by Germans profiting from the Italian power vacuum (October–November 1943), there emerged a period of Italian management of the "Jewish question," both in legislation and in the carrying out of arrests (December 1943–mid-February 1944). This passed finally to a period (mid-February 1944–February 1945) in which the occupier imposed himself upon the directives and policies of the RSI, by now noticeably without autonomy and with its hands tied in this as in other spheres of activity. The power clashes between Italian and German police, both charged with often-conflicting orders from their superiors, can be traced back to this period.

Dannecker directed operations during the first period. He was the special envoy of Adolf Eichmann, chief of the B4 office of the Gestapo in Berlin; Dannecker was charged with organizing the arrests with the help of a special squad of from six to eight men, which he had at his complete disposal. He acted with complete autonomy even with respect to the Gestapo stationed in Italy, and he was tied to no fixed headquarters. In fact, he had to move from city to city to organize raids.

Dannecker was ordered to open his Italian operation with action against the Jews of Rome.[14] This marks a fundamental difference from other western European countries, where initial arrests generally focused exclusively on foreign Jews—that is, on those with no diplomatic protection. In Italy, the first targets of the German

---

14. *Procedimento penale contro Friedrich Bosshammer per la deportazione degli ebrei dall'Italia*, Public Prosecutor, Berlin 1971, *Indictment*, p. 255. In ACDEC, AG, Denuncie e processi—10B.

raids were the Roman Jews, perhaps the most purely Italian Jews of the peninsula, who traced their roots in that city to ancient times. It is difficult to interpret this action. It may have represented an expression of disdain toward the authority of the newly born Italian Social Republic, an expression of defiance of the pope, whose residence certainly was not far from the scene of the roundup, or simply a gesture to weaken the government of Mussolini and thwart any possibility of future negotiations on anti-Jewish matters.

For several days, Dannecker, shut up in his hotel room with the list that supposedly was furnished by the Ministry of the Interior, studied the topography of the former ghetto and the necessary organization for the roundup. Although the Roman incident was not the first anti-Jewish action, the general population, not informed of events elsewhere, was nevertheless caught completely by surprise. Furthermore, no echo of the raids and deportations in other European countries had reached Italy. The frontiers were closed and communications were difficult. Testimony of Nazi brutality had arrived only through the accounts of refugees from eastern European countries—diverse and faraway places.

In Italy the only example of anti-Semitism clearly visible to all, and beyond which no one dreamed it possible to go, was that of the Fascist state, bloodless although tormenting and shamefully discriminatory. In a sense, legalized Italian anti-Semitism served to disorient most people, who did not see soon enough the need to flee. The Vatican presence, believed by many to be a guarantee against increasing barbarism in the conduct of the war in general and in the treatment of the Jews in particular, also relieved popular apprehension.

Then, on October 16, the great roundup occurred in Rome's Jewish quarter, the former ghetto, the very heart of the Jewish community.[15] About 5:30 Saturday morning, soldiers and trucks blocked

15. The roundup in the ghetto quarters of Rome is treated briefly here because many accounts already exist. See for example: M. Tagliacozzo, "La comunità di Roma sotto l'incubo della svastica. La grande razzia del 16 ottobre 1943," in *Gli ebrei in Italia durante il fascismo, Quaderni del CDEC,* n. 3, cit. pp. 8–37; L. Picciotto Fargion, *L'occupazione tedesca.* op. cit.; G. Debenedetti, *16 ottobre 1943* (Rome, 1945); R. Katz, *Black Sabbath. A Journey through Crime Against Humanity* (Toronto, 1969); S. Waagenar, *Il ghetto sul Tevere* (Milan, 1972).

all entrances to the district. German police (a total of 365 men from two police units, the ORPO [*Ordnungspolizei*], and the SIPO [*Sicherheitspolizei*]) went from apartment to apartment, breaking down any doors that were not opened for them. People were forced to leave as they were: women in night gowns, babies half nude. As they burst into the homes, police waved a paper with instructions for the "voyage."

After they were seized in their homes, the arrested Jews were concentrated near the Teatro Marcello. From there, they were taken to the Italian Military College in the Via della Lungara and crowded into the entrance hall, the corridors, and the gymnasium. They totaled 1,259, mostly women and children. After the examination of identity cards, couples in mixed marriages, the children of such marriages, and non-Jews were released the following day at dawn. On October 19, the prisoners were transported in vans to a secondary railroad station in Rome and loaded on a convoy of eighteen freight cars headed for the extermination camp of Auschwitz in Poland. Of the 1,030 who left on the train, only seventeen returned.[16] After the roundup, arrests in Rome continued, but in a less systematic and unexpected manner.

Dannecker's "operational unit" shifted then to other cities in the north. By the end of November, Milan, Florence, and other cities had experienced a *Judenaktion* (roundup of Jews).[17] During the entire period in which Dannecker was occupied with the Jews, the prisons in the large cities functioned as transit stations for deportees. For the convoy that left November 9, 1943, Jews were taken from local prisons to the railroad stations of Florence and Bologna. The loading for the convoy of December 6, 1943, occurred at Milan, Verona, and Trieste.[18] At the end of December, Dannecker gathered with his men at Verona, where his role as expert organizer of the anti-Jewish persecution ended. He later resumed that role by continuing his homicidal career in Hungary.

How did the population react to the roundups and the immediate

16. L. Picciotto Fargion, *L'occupazione*, p. 42.
17. *Procedimento penale contro Friedrich Bosshammer*, p. 263.
18. G. Donati, op. cit., pp. 29–31 and the attached chronological table of the convoys.

deportations? And how did the Italian authorities react? The direct testimony of some who fled from the Rome roundup reveals signs of extreme popular solidarity. Some Jews found refuge in the homes of non-Jewish neighbors. Others jumped from windows while the Nazis were breaking down the doors to the apartments. Some individuals, already arrested, were surrounded spontaneously by the crowds that helped them sneak away through the circle of people. Other Jews, walking in the streets in the desperate search for a refuge, were approached by taxis (whose very presence was absolutely extraordinary for the time) and made to enter.[19] Dozens of Jews found momentary refuge in the numerous churches of Rome. Shopkeepers offered the backs of their stores, and neighbors their cellars. The attics and rooftops of the ghetto area were secure refuges for the Jews who managed to reach them.[20] The attitude of the Roman population was recorded, not without disappointment, by Herbert Kappler, head of the Security Police Command in Rome, who, for bureaucratic reasons even though he had not been the principal director of the roundup, had to draw up the report on the *Judenaktion* for his superiors:

> The attitude of the Italian population has been characterized by clear symptoms of resistance which in many cases has even developed into active aid. In one case, for example, the police force ran into a Fascist in a black shirt carrying an identification card which without doubt had been used a little earlier in a Jewish home by someone who claimed it as his own. Even in the moments when the German police forces were breaking into homes, clear and in many cases successful attempts to hide Jews in adjacent apartments were noted. The anti-Semitic part of the population was not noticed during the action, while, on the contrary, an amorphous mass which, in individual cases even tried to separate the police from the Jews, was observed. In no case was it necessary to resort to arms.[21]

19. An excellent presentation of the individual episodes which occurred in Rome during those hours exists in the documentary film: *Memoria presente. Gli ebrei a Roma* (Rome, 1984) in Rome, Archivio storico audiovisivo dell'Istituto per il Movimento Operaio.

20. M. Tagliacozzo, op. cit., p. 25.

21. Telegraphic report from Kappler to Wolff, October 17, 1943, document in the series "Reichsführer delle SS Himmler" in Washington, D.C., National Archives, microcopy T175, roll 53, frames 2567133–2567134.

After learning where the victims had been taken, spouses, relatives, and Christian friends undertook a pilgrimage, sometimes successful and sometimes not, to the Italian Military College to bring comfort and seek news.

As for the authorities, documents remain in which police officials informed their chiefs that arrests of Jews were occurring in their particular Roman neighborhoods.[22] There is nothing more—no official reaction at the highest levels, neither public nor private. The central police headquarters in Rome seemed unaware of what had happened, as did the same headquarters in other cities where similar horrors occurred. No document indicates that the new Minister of the Interior, Guido Buffarini-Guidi, was preventatively informed of the roundup, or that he reacted to it in any way with the Germans to whom he was devoted and with whom he was in close contact. His contacts ranged from the Chief of Police and SS, Karl Wolff, to the Chief of Security Police, Wilhelm Harster, and the Reich Ambassador to the Italian Social Republic, Rudolf Rahn. These three were key people, as we shall see, in the occupation structure assigned to the search and arrest of Jews, and all three were perfectly up to date with what Dannecker and his unit were doing.[23]

At the highest levels in Berlin, the Nazis decided upon a special squad removed from any local responsibility and directed toward the organization of arrests and deportations. This decision guaranteed freedom of action and absolute mobility, a necessity in a country like Italy, which fluctuated between the status of ally and that of subject. In the autumn of 1943, the political situation was still extremely fluid. It was clear that Mussolini was not secure in his position, that a Fascist internal opposition existed, and that the occupiers were hated by the majority of the population. It was

22. *Elenco degli ebrei arrestati ieri da elementi della Polizia tedesca,* without date, in Rome, Archivio dello Stato (hereinafter referred to as AdS) Questura-Ebrei, B 15, Fasc. "Ebrei della giurisdizione-vigilanza." *Elenco ebrei di questo distretto arrestati in data 16.10.1943* dalla Polizia Germanica (without date) in AdS Roma, Questura-Ebrei, B 18, Fasc. "Ebrei del distretto arrestati dalla Polizia Germanica e Italiana; *Elenco di ebrei arrestati in Via Flaminia,* 19.10.1943 in AdS Roma Questura-Ebrei, B 18, Fasc. "Levi Gaio fu Giustiniano," Cat. A4a.

23. On the organizational structure of the police involved with the arrest of Jews, see: L. Picciotto, "Polizia tedesca ed ebrei nell'Italia occupata," in *Rivista di storia contemporanea,* n. 3, pp. 456–473.

not certain that the police and the government bureaucracy in general would remain loyal. For this reason, the Nazis conducted a rapid anti-Jewish action that would not injure the sensibilities of Italian leaders or make their positions still more vacillating. The Nazis thus acted "outside the law," so to speak, warning no one, and, in contrast with their actions in other countries, as recorded above, without applying the ritual preparatory phase.

In effect, during the first two months of the occupation and the Fascist restoration, we can speak of a real Italian power vacuum. The government of the Republic of Salò was painstakingly assembled only at the end of September 1943, and the first meeting of the Council of Ministers occurred on the twenty-seventh. It was soon apparent that its margin of maneuverability was very narrow in the areas of the progressive exploitation of Italy, of the requisition of Italian manpower for German military fortifications, of the internment in Germany of young soldiers who refused allegiance to the RSI, of continual disputes about the creation of a Republican army, and of the hardships caused by a war that had gone on for well over three years. The government of the RSI was squeezed between popular discontent and its distrust of the Germans, whom it nevertheless needed to assure its continuity.

E. Friedrich Moellhausen, representative in Rome of German Ambassador Rahn, described the situation thus:

> The government [today] is formed of men who, whether they like it or not, are tied to Germany and above all, if necessary, we have the ability to intervene. Moreover we have representatives in every ministry whose role is precisely to present our desires to the ministers and to see that they are met. In this way the groundwork is laid for an effective collaboration. We will save ourselves a lot of trouble if we make use of the Italian government which is at our disposal.[24]

In the climate of tension and lack of clarity about the respective limits of power of the Italians and the Germans, a party congress was arranged to debate and approve the new ideology and political orientation of restored Fascism. It would take the place of the

24. F. Deakin, op. cit., pp. 774–75.

earlier idea of a constituent assembly. The congress was convened on November 14 in the principal hall of the Castelvecchio in Verona. The manifesto presented at the congress was prepared at the headquarters of the Ministry of the Interior by Alessandro Pavolini, with the help and under the control of Rudolf Rahn.[25] The text included eighteen points regarding various subjects. Point 7 addressed the Jews, and constituted the first official position of the RSI toward a question that the old Fascist state, which had fallen on the preceding July 25, had treated in a broad fashion. The point read thus: "All those belonging to the Jewish race are foreigners; during this war they belong to an enemy nationality."[26] The formulation suggested nothing good for the future. In one stroke, all Jews, even Italians, became foreigners and enemies in war, and could thus be treated as such. An anti-Semitism qualitatively different from that in effect between September 1938 and July 1943 had become a part of the government program.

The state on this occasion had in fact two choices: to permit envoys from a police agency in Berlin to arrive and illegally arrest and deport its Jewish citizens without the slightest restraint, or to save the appearance of its sovereignty and intervene by decreeing on its own initiative Italian laws intended to find and arrest Jews and confiscate their goods—laws that could only operate in the way the Germans intended. It would be idle at this point to ask whether there was a formal German imposition. Collaboration in Italy developed automatically, according to a logic by which it seemed better to please the enemy-ally than to become completely subservient to him.

In the policy toward the Jews in particular, anti-Semitism can be seen as an affirmation of autonomy rather than as a helpless application of German orders. This concept emerges also from an examination of the documents, which provide no hint of the existence of an outside imposition on the Fascist government with regard to the Jewish question. Neither Ambassador Rahn in his

25. Telegram from Rahn to Ribbentrop, November 16, 1943, reported in F. Deakin, op. cit., p. 837.
26. R. De Felice, *Storia degli ebrei italiani sotto il fascismo* (Turin, 1972), p. 433.

memoirs,[27] nor the son of Buffarini-Guidi in his book about his father,[28] nor any of the Fascist leaders in the numerous memoirs published in the last forty years mention the issue.

At the meeting of the Council of Ministers on November 24, the Minister of National Education, Carlo Alberto Biggini, was charged with drafting a constitutional program based on the "Manifesto di Verona" to present to a future constituent assembly.[29] In the text, presented at the next meeting on December 18 but never used because the constituent assembly was never called, the difference between citizen and subject was sanctioned. The Jews were in the latter category, and they were denied political and civil rights.[30] The resulting application of what had been determined at the political level was not long in coming.

On November 30, Minister of the Interior Buffarini-Guidi announced a police decree that signaled the beginning of a new direction in the anti-Jewish policy of the RSI, quite different from that of Fascism under the monarchy, which was oppressive and degrading in the field of civil rights but not persecutive on the physical level. The new policy in fact legalized Jewish manhunts, and Fascist police, not to mention the autonomous and unauthorized police who emerged in 1944 and became as dangerous to Jews as their Nazi counterparts. It became a problem to live even in hiding, and if it had not been for the humane and benevolent conduct of a greater part of the population, a much larger number of Jews would have been victims of the deportations.

The text of the police order read thus:[31]

(1) All Jews, even if (formerly) exempt (from the racial laws of 1938), despite their nationality, residing in the national territory must be sent to the appropriate concentration camps. All their

27. R. Rahn, *Ambasciatore di Hitler a Vichy e a Salò* (Milan, 1950) (original edition: *Ruheloses Leben. Aufzeichnungen und Erinnerungen* [Düsseldorf, 1949]).

28. G. Buffarini Guidi, *La vera verità* (Milan, 1970).

29. L. Garibaldi, *Mussolini e il professore* (Milan, 1983), pp. 107–8.

30. Cf. Carta Costituzionale della Repubblica Sociale Italiana, in L. Garibaldi, op. cit., pp. 365, 368, 371–72.

31. Telegram from the Ministry of the Interior to all the Capi delle Provincie, Ordine di polizia n. 5, in Rome Archivio Centrale dello Stato, (hereinafter ACS), R.S.I., Presidenza del Consiglio dei Ministri, Gabinetto, busta 33, fasc. 3/2–2, sottofasc. 13. The text was announced in the newspapers and on the radio on December 1, 1943.

goods and property must be immediately seized to await confiscation in the interest of the RSI, which will direct them to benefit those made indigent by enemy air raids.

(2) All those who, born of mixed marriages, have Aryan status as a result of the existing racial laws must be placed under special vigilance by the police.

(3) The Jews must be assembled in provincial concentration camps to await being sent to special concentration camps set up for that purpose.

This last very serious provision meant that after December 1, 1943, no Jew could remain in circulation, because he was liable to arrest even by the Italian authorities. In the months that followed, in fact, arrests were effected directly by the central police headquarters of the RSI, either by thorough visits to all Jewish households or by real roundups in the style of those lightning raids already carried out by the Nazi mobile units. Recent research has enabled us to determine that the roundup in Venice on December 5–6, 1943, which led to the arrest of 150 Jews in a single night,[32] was coordinated, conducted, and concluded by Italian authorities. All the commissariats of public security had been advised by the police chief of the province on December 1, 1943, to provide "a verbal warning to all Jews, requiring them not to leave their residences and to present themselves every day to the Office of Public Security."[33] The action occurred four days later: "Please proceed immediately to detain elements belonging to the Jewish race. . . . Men should be taken to the local jails of S. Maria Maggiore, women to the Penale Giudecca, and minors to the Centro Minorenni."[34] Police units, divided by zone, went to the homes of families who, caught in their sleep, opened their doors and were brutally arrested. Toward midnight, the Fascists arrived at the Casa di Riposo, an old-age home, broke the lock, and forced their way inside. The

32. Record of Jews deported from Italy, in ACDEC (survey by the author).
33. Telegram from Questore Cordova to all the Commissariati di Pubblica Sicurezza, December 1, 1943, in Venice, Archivio dello Stato, Fondo Questura, Gabinetto, Cat A4a.
34. Telephone message from Questore Cordova to all the Commissariati di Pubblica Sicurezza, Comando Carabinieri and 49th Legione Milizia Volontaria per la Sicurezza Nazionale, in AdS, ibid.

elderly, terrified and dazed, were pulled from their beds, and the kitchen of the institution was robbed of all its provisions.[35] The unfortunate victims of the raid were taken first to the Collegio Mario Foscarini, where they were required to sleep on benches and left without food, and then to the prison of S. Maria Maggiore,[36] where they were formally registered[37] to await transport to an internment camp.[38] This was but one of the many examples of the involvement of the Italian police headquarters. The phenomenon was repeated in Ferrara, Florence, Siena, and Piedmont.

With the order of November 30, a procedure was introduced in the police system that was not new for Italy, but had never before been applied to single Jews or to the entire Jewish population. The Fascist government had, in fact, made wide use of confinement as a system of punishment for opponents of the regime for many years. In 1940, after Italy's entry into the war and as a result of a measure strictly connected with the war, many foreign Jews had been interned as enemy nationals, along with a few hundred Italian Jews who either were or were considered to be anti-Fascists. However, the internment measure had never involved such serious consequences: a concentration camp for everyone, Italians and foreigners, former exemptees or not, now meant preparation for deportation. It will be seen later how preliminary passage through a transit camp, one for every country in western Europe, fit into the precise Nazi design of collecting all arrestees into an enclosed and isolated spot, so they would eventually be deported to the East without problems.

If the RSI did not act with direct responsibility in the deportation and assassination of its Jews, it was nevertheless involved after November 30, 1943, in all preliminary operations intended to trace, arrest, and hand them over to the Germans. The police order

35. L. Fano Jacchia, *Storia degli ebrei rinchiusi nella casa israelitica di riposo e da lì deportati in massa (5 dicembre 1943–17 agosto 1944)*, typed testimony, 1951, in ACDEC, AG, Vicissitudini delle singole Comunità, 13B—Venezia.

36. For more detailed information about these events, see: P. Sereni, "Gli anni della persecuzione razziale a Venezia. Appunti per una storia," in *Venezia Ebraica* (Rome, 1982), pp. 140–41.

37. From a survey of prisoners registered from 1943 to 1945 of the Venice prison performed by Paolo Sereni on behalf of the CDEC.

38. Among the many "minors" arrested, one was eight days old at the time of his arrest, while another was born in prison in Venice, see note 31.

mentioned provincial concentration camps, where Jews were to be held temporarily until more appropriate camps could be set up. Barracks (Borgo San Dalmazzo near Cuneo), villas (Vò Vecchio near Padua), prisons (Regina Coeli in Rome and San Vittore in Milan), Jewish community buildings (Mantua, Ferrara, Venice), and former internment camps for foreigners (Servigliano near Ancona, Civitella del Tronto and Nereto near Teramo) served as temporary camps.[39] Their management was the responsibility of the Ministry of the Interior, specifically the Divisione Affari Generali e Riservati, which in turn delegated it to the prefectures. The latter administered the funds supplied by the central accounting office of the Ministry of the Interior, under the direction of the ministry itself.

Public security agents, the *podestà* of the towns where the camps were located, or delegates from the prefectures were also assigned to the management of the different camps.[40] Fossoli, located six kilometers from Carpi (Modena), became the RSI's choice of the permanent concentration camp established specifically for Jews, in compliance with the orders of Buffarini-Guidi.[41] There were probably two reasons for the choice. First, Fossoli had a pre-existing camp structure for prisoners of war, particularly British and Maltese. Second, it was located on a convenient railroad junction for trains originating in both the North and the South.[42]

The order to prepare the camp, which came from the prefecture of Modena on December 2, asked the *podestà* of the commune of Carpi "to arrange with the police headquarters that the installation work be done and that the functioning of the camp suffer no im-

39. Some of these temporary concentration camps survived the creation of the large camp of Fossoli and were subsequently evacuated by the Germans between the winter and the spring of 1944.

40. *Appunto per capo della polizia Maderno, Valdagno, 16 maggio 1944*, in ACS, Ministero degli Interni, Direzione Generale Pubblica Sicurezza, Divisione Affari Generali e Riservati, Campi Internamento e Concentramento, busta 35. For Fossoli, see Luciano Casali, "La deportazione dall'Italia, Fossoli di Carpi," in *Spostamenti di popolazione e deportazioni in Europa*, pp. 382–406.

41. Fossoli, initially set up for the internment of the Jews, was used by the Germans after the end of February 1944 as a transit camp for prisoners awaiting deportation—the Jews to Auschwitz, the political prisoners to other camps within the territory of the Reich.

42. *Procedimento penale contro Friedrich Bosshammer*, op.cit. and *Perizia storica presentata dal CDEC*, ed. Eloisa Ravenna.

pediment."[43] On December 29, ninety-eight Jews were already interned there.[44] Thirty-seven *carabinieri* were charged with guard duty, as revealed by a letter from an agent who requested wood for the kitchen and for heating.[45] On December 29, the police chief of the province of Modena communicated to the director of the camp that the Minister of the Interior had announced the arrival of 827 Jews from different provinces, asking camp authorities to arrange their placement in barracks of the old camp while waiting for the completion of work in the new camp.[46] He also gave instructions for the registration of the inmates: the recording of general data, the compilation of a list of families with an indication of the paternal heads of family and the inter-family relationships, and so forth. The letter closed thus: "It is necessary . . . to exercise appropriate surveillance for avoiding possible escapes of inmates, watching even their behavior in their barracks and holding at least two roll calls a day."[47]

From the numerous orders found in the local archives of police headquarters and from research in the prison archives of various cities, it is clear that, after November 30, the Italian police were charged with: arrests; temporary custody of places of local internment (mostly jails and security cells, since the provincial concentration camps had been reduced to a small group);[48] transfers to the concentration camp of Fossoli; management of Fossoli for a certain number of months.

In mid-December, perhaps out of fear of disturbing the population too much with the spectacle of the elderly and the sick brutally forced out of their homes, a directive was announced that

43. Letter from the prefecture of Modena to the *podestà* of the Comune di Carpi, December 2, 1943, in Carpi Archivio Comune di Carpi 1943–1949, Campo di concentramento Ebrei, fasc. 2.

44. *Procedimento penale*, op. cit.; *Perizia storica*, op. cit.

45. Letter from Capitano Giuseppe Laudani, Comandante of the Tenenza di Carpi to Commissariato Prefettizio, December 29, 1943, in Archivio Comune di Carpi 1943–1949, Campo di Concentramento Ebrei, fasc. 2.

46. Letters from Questore Magrini to the director of the concentration camp Fossoli at Carpi, December 29, 1943, in Carpi, Archivio Comune di Carpi 1943–1949, Campo di Concentramento Ebrei, fascicolo 2, sottofasc. 4/2.

47. Ibid.

48. *Campi di concentramento attualmente funzionanti*, 5 December 1943, in ACS, Ministero degli Interni, Direzione Generale Pubblica Sicurezza Divisione Affari Generali e Riservati—sez. 2a.

attenuated that problem by exempting from internment and thus from arrest all individuals over seventy years of age and the gravely ill; it also confirmed that the children of mixed marriages belonged to the category of the "protected."[49] The exemption clause for the gravely ill provided agents and simple police guards with the possibility of avoiding numerous arrests.

While many documents convey the cold verbal accounts of arrests, many others reveal, between the lines, the compassion of those charged with so sad a task, if not their complicity in allowing victims to flee with the excuse of advanced age or imaginary or exaggerated illnesses. It is here, perhaps, better than anywhere else, that the dichotomy can be distinguished between the organized powers and the common people who could not understand how entire defenseless families could be dangerous enemies of the state.

Because they are truly extraordinary, some individual cases should be recorded here. They represent only a few among many that often cannot even be mentioned because they have never been reported. Felice Sena, the *vicebrigadiere* (sergeant) of the central police headquarters of Verona, when charged with arrests, went to homes and warned victims of the danger, or found other reasons for being unable to carry out his orders.[50] Eugenio Rami, the *sottotenente* (second lieutenant) of police, and Michele Canosa, the *maresciallo* (highest non-commissioned rank in the police) of public security, both of the central police headquarters of Modena, hid Jewish religious objects and a Jewish fugitive in a convalescent home.[51] Also in Modena, Dr. Tedesco, an employee of the police headquarters, warned several interested parties by telephone of an imminent arrest.[52] The *comune* (town hall) went so far as to deliberately confuse the files. At San Donato di Val Comino and at

49. Telegram from Police Chief Tamburini to the Capi delle Provincie and the Questori, October 12, 1943. In ACS, Ministero dell'Interno Direzione Generale Pubblica Sicurezza, Divisione Affari Generali e Riservati (1920–45), Cat. A5G, b.63, fasc. 230, Ebrei-Sequestro beni.

50. *Testimonianza di Felice Sena rilasciata il 1 ottobre 1971*, in ACDEC, testimony from the Bosshammer trial.

51. *Letter from the Jewish Community of Modena to the prefect, April 25, 1945*, in AdS Modena, Fondo Prefettura, Gabinetto, b. 1944, Serie 1, fasc. 3—Ministero Interni—Funzionari di P.S.

52. *Letter from the Jewish Community of Modena to Col. Vitale, February 11, 1948*, in ACDEC, Fondo Vitale, Vicissitudini delle singole comunità, 13 B—Modena.

Lanciano in the province of Chieti, municipal employees did the same thing with the register of births, marriages, and deaths of resident Jews.[53] In Cotignola, in the province of Faenza, a "hospitality network" was established which helped and protected not only Jews but also ex-prisoners of war, anti-Fascists, and partisans. Dozens of families and even the *commissario prefettizio* (representative of the prefect) of the town formed part of the network. In Pitigliano in a single night, the drivers in the SIAT transportation system rendered all the buses unusable, for they understood that the German request for transport was intended for the transfer of Jews from the provincial concentration camp of Roccatederighi to Fossoli for deportation.[54] We also have part of the testimony left after the war by the lawyer Carlo Rossi from Bologna:

> I was arrested by the German SS in via S. Chiara and taken to the prison of S. Giovanni in Monte, where, after three weeks, I was transferred to the concentration camp of Carpi (Modena). I was taken to the prison by public security agent Gervasi, in uniform, who although he was a public security agent, showed much understanding of my situation, so much so that he went to my home several times to convey my news. Also during my several SS interrogations, Gervasi, while bringing me from the SS office to the prison of S. Giovanni in Monte, allowed me to meet with my wife in a church, jeopardizing his own existence, since the German SS would not compromise in these matters. Gervasi also offered me financial aid, which I did not accept. The same Gervasi, when I was transferred to the concentration camp at Carpi, volunteered to accompany me to Carpi even though it was not his turn, and on his return to Bologna he carried the news to my wife. In August of the same year I succeeded in escaping from the train carrying me to Germany. And when in October the SS of Bologna began an investigation into my escape, Gervasi—who continued to serve the SS—informed my family and saw to it that they found a safe place in the event of reprisals.[55]

53. Letter from the Mayor of S. Donato di Val Comino to Mr. Gianfranco Moscati of December 25, 1977; copy at ACDEC.

54. Cfr. M. Bassi, "Cotignola: un approdo di salvezza per gli ebrei e per i perseguitati politici durante la guerra (1943–1945)" in *Testimonianze di fede e di carità nel tempo di guerra (1943–1945)* (Faenza, 1985), dossier with pages not numbered.

55. *Testimony of lawyer Carlo Rossi to the Questura of Bologna May 4, 1945*, in AdS Bologna, Fondo Questura—Ebrei.

Meanwhile in Livorno (Leghorn), the *carabinieri* Pilade Barsotti and Rolando Calamai, ordered by the German command to accompany seventeen Jewish children to Fossoli, found a way not to arrive at the destination.[56]

Three types of German authority presided over the occupation of Italy: the political, headed by Ambassador and Plenipotentiary of the Reich Rudolph Rahn; the police, headed by SS-*Obergruppenführer* and General Karl Wolff, chief of the SS in Italy; and the military, headed by General Albert Kesselring. The first two were the authorities most directly interested in the structure of the anti-Jewish persecution. The ambassador had the role of politically negotiating, at the state level, the delivery of the Jews in the various occupied countries or in those under German influence. The police, and more specifically, the Security Police (SIPO-SD), had the responsibility of organizing and executing arrests, detentions, and deportations.

On December 4, 1943, high officials of the two administrations met in Berlin to examine the Italian situation.[57] Eberhard von Thadden represented the Foreign Ministry. For the Security Police, Eichmann's special envoy Dannecker was present, as well as SS-*Sturmbannführer* Friedrich Bosshammer, who would replace him

---

56. Cf. Giuseppe Funaro, "Vicende dell'orfanotrofio israelitico di Livorno dopo l'otto settembre 1943," in *Gli ebrei in Italia durante il fascismo, Quaderno del CDEC* n. 3, cit., pp. 72–77. It is not possible to list here the countless episodes of selfless solidarity. The phenomenon, which has justifiably attracted the interest of many historians, unfortunately escapes, by its very nature, any possibility of comprehensive analysis. An interesting effort at systematic analysis founded upon an hypothesis is the "Altruistic Personality Project" directed by Professor Samuel P. Oliner of Humboldt State University in Arcata, California. The project, begun in 1985, includes studies of rescuers in Poland, Germany, France, and Italy. In any case, any bibliography on this subject must include the following two works which report numerous episodes but without analysis: M. Uffreduzzi, *Il viale dei Giusti* (Rome, 1985), and *Cuore 1944*, ed. C. Gabrielli Rosi and S. Mariani (Lucca, 1975). For the assistance and rescue activities of Catholic laymen and all orders and levels of clergy, at least the following works must be seen: P. Lapide, *Roma e gli ebrei* (Milano, 1967); I. Vaccari, *Villa Emma* (Modena, 1960); I. Vaccari, *Il tempo di decidere* (Modena, 1968); P. Zovatto, *Il vescovo Santin e il razzismo nazifascista a Trieste, 1938–1945* (Quarto d'Altino, Venezia, 1979); G. Garnieri, *Tra rischi e pericoli* (Pinerolo, 1981); and A. Ramati, *Assisi clandestina* (Assisi, 1981). An article by Davide Nissim, "La campagna razziale. L'aiuto agli israeliti nel Biellese," in *Il movimento di Liberazione nel Biellese* (Biella, 1957), pp. 89–94, should also be added to this brief bibliography. Incidents of assistance and rescue are also related in pages scattered throughout volumes of memoirs or personal testimony, but are too numerous to list here.

57. *Report of the meeting of Von Thadden, Bosshammer, Dannecker*, signed Wagner, Berlin, April 12, 1943. In International Military Tribunal of Nuremberg, doc. NG.—5026 and in Indictment, op. cit.

in February. Bosshammer had dealt with Italian affairs within the
Gestapo office in Berlin until the preceding March. At the meeting,
Dannecker reported on how many Jews had been arrested and deported under his direction. The next item of discussion was the
new situation created by the Italian government's decree ordering
the internment of all Jews and the possibility of tighter collaboration in the future. It was proposed to delegate Ambassador Rahn
to express to the Fascist government the satisfaction of the Reich
with this law and to call attention to the necessity of proceeding
rapidly toward the establishment of a concentration camp in
northern Italy. In the meantime, the police in Italy proceeded with
the search and arrest of Jews who were then assembled in the
concentration camp of Fossoli without direct German intervention. This procedure conformed with the Nazi technique already
tested elsewhere of giving free rein to the police of an occupied or
allied country.

On January 4, 1944, the Italian decree requiring the confiscation
of Jewish goods was issued.[58] It is curious that the regulations for
what amounted to robbery followed rather than preceded those for
internment. The suspicion arises that the authorities wanted to
profit fully from the fact that the Jews had abandoned their residences by then to go into hiding. The confiscation included valuable properties, such as industrial and commercial enterprises and
real estate, as well as portable goods of slight value that could be
found in abandoned apartments. Jewish safe deposit boxes and
bank accounts were also to be seized. These operations, entrusted
to officials from the prefectures, were carried out with unusual
zeal. Hundreds of documents contain verbal transcripts of the confiscations of even small items and simple objects of domestic use,
a real disgrace for the bureaucratic apparatus of the state.

To administer and sell the confiscated goods, an agency called
the Ente Gestione e Liquidazione Beni Ebraici (EGELI), in partial
operation since 1938, was reactivated. The Jewish confiscations
provided loot of considerable value for the coffers of the RSI, always in need of new sources of financing and also drained by the

58. L. Picciotto Fargion, *The Anti-Jewish Policy*, p. 28ff.

payment to the Germans of what was called "an occupation indemnity." However, the property did not always pass through EGELI; sometimes it was lost in the maze of a dishonest and rapacious bureaucracy and ended up financing local agencies or Fascist party headquarters.

Jews arrested by the police continued to be crowded into local jails and then interned at Fossoli until the middle of 1944. Early in that year, the terms of the Italian-German collaboration changed radically. The Nazis, whose doubts had by that time disappeared on the appropriateness of opening their own anti-Jewish agency to issue orders to the Italian police, sent Bosshammer to Italy as a substitute for the mobile squad of Dannecker. Bosshammer assumed the role of expert on the Jewish question, with a specialized agency and an established office near the central Gestapo headquarters in Verona.

As soon as he was settled, Bosshammer began to impose his personal orders on the categories of Jews to be arrested or excluded, in continuous contrast to the directives of the Italian Ministry of the Interior. A trying period of executive chaos and conflicts of power between the Fascist and the Nazi police began. At this point, responsibility for arrests, especially the most difficult ones, remained with the Italians, but the initiatives of men in SIPO-SD units were imposed on them. In addition to the less important arrests, the Nazis, alone or with Italian police, conducted a series of large roundups in hospitals, Jewish rest homes, and other public institutions, without regard for age, state of health, citizenship, or the status of those from mixed marriage households.

In February 1944, at the command center attached to the Security Police in Bologna, SS-*Obersturmführer* Herbert Bieber called together the eight police chiefs of Emilia to tell them which Jews to detain.[59] For obvious reasons of length, it is not possible to present here the other numerous documented cases of heavy-handed German meddling and deliberate Italian recalcitrance in matters

---

59. Letter from SS-*Obersturmführer* Bieber of the *BdS in Italien-Aussenkommando Bologna* to the Questori of: Bologna, Forlì, Ravenna, Ferrara, Modena, Reggio, Emilia, Parma, Piacenza, Bologna AdS, Fondo Questura, Ebrei, b. 1, mazzo 2, Ebrei—disposizioni di massima.

of anti-Jewish policy. It is sufficient to say that, as usual, the Fascists had begun a policy over which, at a certain point, they lost control. They could only suggest timid protests at the flagrant violation of Italian race legislation.

In vain, Minister of the Interior Buffarini-Guidi instructed that Jews be left in the concentration camp and not handed over to the Germans. Along the same lines, Police Chief Tullio Tamburini declared on January 23 that "the central German authorities will be interested in directives intended to assure that Jews remain in the Italian concentration camps."[60] Buffarini-Guidi repeated the Italian guidelines again on March 7.[61]

The RSI defended itself as best it could, its range of activity oscillating between the absolute servility of its police agencies and its continual desire to claim autonomy through the only possible channel, the legislative. The dichotomy was demonstrated by the increasingly massive arrests on the one hand, and legislative activity on the other, which scarcely acknowledged the arrests.

The fate of the Jews was no longer in the hands of the RSI. Toward the end of February or the first of March 1944,[62] the concentration camp of Fossoli passed under direct German administration, becoming a transit camp designed to prepare deportation convoys, and not only for Jews. It was classified as a *Polizeiliches Sammel- und Durchgangslager* (holding camp and transit center). This accorded with the classic Nazi system, practiced in every invaded western country, of enclosing the Jews in separated spots, far from the view of the curious, as in national concentration camps (generally one for each country: Drancy in France, Malines in Belgium, Westerbork in Holland), in order to deport them grad-

60. Telegram from Police Chief Tamburini to the Capi della Provincie libere, January 23, 1944, in Modena AdS, Fondo Prefettura 1944, b. 3, cat. 1, fasc. Disposizioni di massima.

61. Telegram from the Ministry of the Interior to the Capi delle Provincie libere, March 7, 1944. See Indictment, op. cit.

62. The Chief of the Security Police in Italy appointed the SS *Untersturmführer* Karl Tithe not later than beginning of March, 1944, as commandant of the Fossoli concentration camp, see Indictment, op. cit. A telegram from the RSI Chief of Police of Modena of February 28, 1944, stated that "the German general, Commander of SS in Italy resident in Verona visiting the concentration camp of internees in Fossoli di Carpi has informed me that next March 15 he will assume charge of the camp itself," published in L. Casali, "La deportazione dall'Italia. Fossoli di Carpi," p. 401.

ually to the extermination camp of Auschwitz-Birkenau in Poland. There, in fact, beginning in the spring of 1942, a program of extermination of the Jews of western Europe began. Victims were jammed into whole convoys of sealed boxcars, and the majority of them were gassed immediately upon arrival.

After participating in depriving Jews of their goods and their freedom, the police headquarters of the RSI took part in handing them over to those who would deprive them of their lives. In the meantime, at the highest levels of the RSI it was deemed necessary to coordinate the entire anti-Jewish policy, which remained partly in the hands of the Ministry of the Interior, partly with the Ministry of Finance (concerned with the confiscation of goods), and partly with the Ministry of Popular Culture (concerned with anti-Jewish propaganda). On April 18, 1944, the Council of Ministers approved a decree establishing a new office to integrate and unify all matters concerning race. The Ispettorato Generale per la Razza, emanating directly from the president of the Council, had as its chief the journalist Giovanni Preziosi, the standard-bearer of Italian anti-Semitism. Preziosi immediately set to work to intensify anti-Jewish propaganda and to propose even more restrictive laws, in a futile persecution of people who, either because they had already been deported or interned or because they had hidden, no longer existed. In the summer of 1944, the camp of Fossoli, threatened by the Allied advance up the peninsula and by probable partisan attacks, was closed. The political prisoners were directed toward a new transit camp at Bolzano in Alto Adige, intended to collect those arrested from then on.[63]

All remaining Jews at Fossoli, even those previously exempt from deportation because they were spouses in, or the children of, mixed marriages, were sent off on one last, overcrowded convoy. The train divided, and some prisoners were sent to Auschwitz while others went to Buchenwald, Ravensbrück, or Bergen-Belsen.[64]

By means of a long research project that I am conducting through

63. *Causa penale, Perizia storica*, op. cit., p. 109.
64. G. Donati, op. cit., pp. 24–26.

my institution, the Centro di Documentazione Ebraica Contemporanea of Milan, I have been able to determine, with full details, the convoys that left Italy. They numbered twenty, with a total of 5,734 people, to which must be added another twenty-three smaller convoys that left from the Italian zone annexed to the Reich as the *Adriatisches Küstenland* with 1,074 people, and the convoy that left from the Italian island of Rhodes in the Aegean on August 3, 1944, with 1,805 people. The total number of deportees determined as of today is 8,613, of whom 7,631 perished. To these should be added 291 who perished in Italy. The victims of the Holocaust identified up to now total 7,922.

III. Jewish Refugees in Italy

Klaus Voigt

6. Jewish Refugees and Immigrants in Italy, 1933–1945

Survivors of the Holocaust who lived in Italy as immigrants and refugees are at one in praising the country for its humanitarian response to their plight and suffering. Italy was subjected to Fascist rule and bonded ideologically to National Socialist Germany from the creation of the Axis in 1937, and yet stands out among the countries of Europe for having extended a helping hand to the desperate Jewish refugees seeking safety within its borders. A comparison with France is instructive. The French attitude on the Jewish question (from the evidence of contemporary diaries and letters, as well as observations by Jewish relief organizations) appears to have been more ambiguous and controversial than the Italian, which was often compassionate.

Following the Nazi accession to power in 1933, a number of persecuted Jews fleeing Germany and Nazi-occupied territories, were able to find a temporary haven in Italy. Many did not stay, however, using Italy only as a stopover on their way to Palestine, the United States, South America, and Shanghai. Roughly speaking, 8,000 Jewish refugees came from Germany (including Poles and other eastern Europeans who had been living in Germany) to stay for some time in Italy; 5,000 came from Austria after the *Anschluss*, 2,000 from Yugoslavia, 1,000 from Poland after the German conquest, and 300 from Czechoslovakia. Following the armistice between Italy and the Allied forces, which was announced by the Badoglio government on September 8, 1943, about 1,500 Jews fled into Italy from the German roundup that followed the withdrawal of the Italian army from occupied zones in France. At the outset of Nazi rule in Germany in 1933, the influx of refugees into Italy was rather slow. According to the statistics of the Italian Ministry of the Interior, about 1,100 had entered the country in October 1934, a further 1,700 in May 1936, and 4,500 in

September 1938, in addition to the 4,500 foreign Jews who had immigrated before 1919.[1]

On September 12, 1938, the Fascist government promulgated a decree that ordered most of the 9,000 Jews who had immigrated after 1919 to leave Italy within six months. The expulsion decree was incorporated with slight modifications in the anti-Jewish racial laws of November 17, 1938. As a result, the number of Jewish refugees and immigrants sank to less than 4,000 prior to Italy's entry into war in June 1940. In the period between the passage of the racial legislation and the war, a total of 10,000 to 11,000 foreign Jews left Italy. To offset this exodus, 6,000 were able to enter the country; most were armed with tourist visas for up to six months, visas issued for the purpose of "tourism, embarkation, medical treatment, study, and business."[2] In an ironic twist, the Italian government introduced these visas after issuance of the expulsion decree for foreign Jews. After the war broke out, most of the Jewish refugees and immigrants, who were still in Italy, were either interned by the Italian authorities in special internment camps, such as Ferramonti-Tarsia in Calabria, or placed under tight police surveillance in remote villages and towns situated mostly in central and southern Italy.[3] At the time of the German occupation, which followed the armistice signed by Badoglio on September 8, 1943, the number of refugees had risen to 9,000, which, added to those who had immigrated before 1919, brings the final reckoning to more than 10,000.[4] This not inconsiderable figure was, however, no higher than that of Switzerland and markedly lower than the

1. See Klaus Voigt, "Refuge and Persecution in Italy, 1933–1945," *Simon Wiesenthal Center Annual*, 4 (1987), pp. 3–64; Klaus Voigt, "Gli emigrati in Italia dai paesi sotto la dominazione nazista: tollerati e perseguitati (1933–1940)," *Storia Contemporanea* 16 (1985) pp. 45–87; Klaus Voigt, "Notizie statistiche sugli immigrati e profughi ebrei in Italia (1938–1945)," *Israel. Un decennio 1974–1984: Saggi sull'ebraismo italiano* (Rome, 1984), pp. 407–20.

2. Ibid., p. 411, for the estimate of 9,000–10,000 foreign Jews who left Italy.

3. See Renzo De Felice, *Storia degli ebrei italiani sotto il fascismo*, 3rd edition (Turin, 1972), pp. 405–8; Carlo Spartaco Capogreco, *Ferramonti. La vita e gli uomini del più grande campo d'internamento fascista (1940–1945)* (Florence, 1987), pp. 35–40; Frantz Hajek, "Appunti sugli ebrei stranieri in Italia durante la guerra," *Gli ebrei in Italia durante il fascismo*, ed. Guido Valabrega (Milan, 1963), pp. 153–57; Settimio Sorani, *L'assistenza ai profughi ebrei in Italia (1933–1947): Contributo alla storia della "Delasem"* (Rome, 1983), pp. 59–82.

4. Voigt, "Notizie statistiche," p. 415.

65,000 and 25,000 Jewish refugees found in the forties in Great Britain and France, respectively.

During the internment period, the number of refugees increased, an inexplicable development were it not for a series of mishaps and unforeseeable events. About 2,000 of the approximately 5,000 Yugoslav Jews who had sought refuge in the Italian-occupied territories on the Dalmatian coast were able to secure passage to the Italian mainland.[5] Then, about 500 shipwrecked passengers of the *Pentcho*, a riverboat from the Danube that had tried unsuccessfully to reach Palestine, were at first interned on the island of Rhodes before being brought to Ferramonti-Tarsia.[6] Next, the aforementioned influx of refugees from the Italian-occupied zone of France (those able to make the perilous journey over the Alps) crowded into the country.[7] Finally, there were those lucky 3,000 interned foreign Jews held in southern Italy whom the Allies were able to liberate before the SS had completed plans for the "Final Solution" there.[8]

Many of these refugees failed to get away. Of the total number of foreign Jews, approximately 2,000 or one-fourth who had fallen under German control north of the Montecassino-Pescara war zone were deported. Because of this roundup, there was a higher proportion of victims among the Jewish refugees and immigrants in Italy than among the Italian Jewish population, of whom approximately fifteen percent were deported.[9]

Now that the basic statistical data has been marshalled, broader questions of responsibility can be addressed: how far and to what extent did the Italians contribute to the rescue of Jewish refugees and immigrants? We can break down the discussion into four distinct periods: 1933–1938, the continuation of tolerated residence; 1938, the new era of racial persecution launched by passage of the

---

5. Ibid., p. 412.

6. See John Bierman, *Odyssey* (New York, 1984), pp. 176–206.

7. See Alberto Cavaglion, *Nella notte straniera: Gli ebrei di S. Martin Vésubie e il campo di Borgo San Dalmazzo* (Cuneo, 1981), pp. 59–69.

8. Voigt, "Notizie statistiche," p. 415.

9. Giuliana Donati, *Ebrei in Italia: deportazione, Resistenza* (Florence, 1974), p. 9.

racial laws until Italy's entry into the war on the side of Nazi Germany in 1940; the period of internment through September 8, 1943; and the onset of deportation to the death camps under the Nazi puppet Fascist regime set up at Salò following the German occupation of the country. How Italy dealt with its Jewish refugees can be analyzed from three perspectives: the policy of government from top to bottom—national ministries, regional prefects, and local municipalities; organized Jewish relief work; and, finally, the attitude of the Italian population taken as a whole.

The early rivalry between Mussolini and Hitler (a rivalry that came close to open conflict after Nazi agents had murdered the Duce's Austrian protégé, Chancellor Engelbert Dollfuss, in July 1934) worked to the advantage of Jewish refugees seeking entry into Italy to escape Nazi oppression—provided that they had not been active in democratic political organizations. True, Mussolini had hailed the Nazi accession to power in Germany as a glowing tribute to the fascist idea. But he was not initially carried away. The Duce still realized that maintenance of good relations with the democratic countries was an unargued imperative of *Realpolitik*, a reality, like it or not, that induced him to cultivate the image of a refined statesman who deserved the trust and goodwill of the western powers for harboring Jewish refugees.[10] A foretaste of worse to come, however, occurred when Italy signed a secret police agreement with Germany in April 1936. Directed against the political opponents of both regimes, it excluded the Jews as a special group—much to the Nazis' discomfort—for Mussolini still eschewed racial politics.[11] Still, the police agreement had a deleterious effect on the Jewish refugees in Italy. The Gestapo, passing on to their Italian counterparts information on individual pre-emigration political activity, was able to stigmatize many of Italy's foreign Jews as "subversive elements." Highlighting Italo-German police cooperation, 500 Germans, Austrians, and Poles, the major-

10. See Jens Petersen, *Hitler-Mussolini: Die Entstehung der Achse Berlin-Rom 1933–1936* (Tübingen, 1973), pp. 339–42, 361–66; Meir Michaelis, *Mussolini and the Jews: German-Italian Relations and the Jewish Question in Italy. 1922–1945* (Oxford, 1978), pp. 65–67, 81–82.

11. De Felice, *Storia*, pp. 244–45, 533–40.

ity of whom were Jews, were arrested for so-called security measures in May 1938 during Hitler's state visit to Italy.[12]

Italy was one of the few countries that kept its borders open for many years and did not create special restrictions against the entry of Jewish refugees, except for those involved in political activities. The refugees found only a few legal restrictions in Italy barring them from gainful employment. Not until passage of the racial laws in 1938, which stripped foreign Jews of the right to work, did their social situation become unmanageable. But one should not take this liberal attitude on the part of the Italian government as humanitarianism. Rome's policy was quite simply pragmatic. As long as the influx of Jews into the country was low, no one need worry. In spite of the absence of racial laws in Italy before 1938, few Jews were tempted to find refuge in Italy. In their minds, Mussolini's regime held out an abiding threat of persecution simply because of its close links to National Socialism.[13] They were anything but mistaken in perceiving an unsympathetic regime in Rome. That the Duce was hardly moved by compassion was given brutal testimony by Italy's closure of the frontier to Jews fleeing Austria after Hitler had consummated the *Anschluss* in March 1938.[14]

Harsh persecution in Italy began in earnest on September 12, 1938, with promulgation of the expulsion decree of September 7. It was rightly reported in the socialist refugee newspaper *Avanti!* that even Hitler had not yet expelled all foreign Jews living in Germany.[15] But who could have foretold that on the actual date of expulsion, March 12, 1939, the actual application of the decree would be suspended? Jews were ready to leave, the prefects wrote to the Interior Ministry, but were unable to do so since they lacked entry visas for other countries. In the logic of Fascist officialdom, Jews who had a proven record of obeying the law should not be punished for obstacles not of their own making.[16] Unquestionably,

12. Voigt, "Refuge and Persecution," pp. 22–25.

13. Ibid., pp. 12–13.

14. Ibid., p. 13.

15. "La cacciata degli ebrei dall'Italia," *Avanti!* 44, n. 37 (Paris, 17 Sept. 1938), p. 2.

16. Voigt, "Refuge and Persecution," p. 27.

too, there was a reluctance to imitate the Nazi mass expulsion from Germany to Poland in October 1938 of Polish Jews, who, since they were not let into Poland, were left to their fate in no man's land. Still, the decree remained on the books, which made deportation an ever-present danger. Mussolini hoped that the Jews, experiencing anxiety from potential deportation, would pack up and leave on their own initiative. At the same time, the Italian government tried a milder and more subtle strategy of deportation: expulsion to the relatively unguarded French frontier, where they could be helped across the border by sympathetic Italian guards. Some of these border gendarmes actually did collect money amongst themselves to provide the women and children with food and provisions. In what other country would one find such consideration, if not kindness? But Mussolini, as if to emphasize his fascist toughness, resolved to remove the foreign Jews from Italian soil in singular disregard of means. No matter how much sympathy the Jewish refugees found among the country's grass-roots officials, the Duce's voice was authoritative. Once having issued the expulsion decree, Mussolini had denied the foreign Jews the right to work. The only way out of impoverishment was for the Jews to find subsistence from the Jewish relief committees.[17]

In spite of the expulsion decree, the Foreign Ministry, with the consent of the Interior Ministry, implemented the aforementioned tourist visa in February 1939, which gave about 5,000 Jews a chance to escape from Nazi-dominated areas at the penultimate hour. But once again, as soon as the Italian government learned that the tourist visa served almost exclusively those Jews of Germany, Austria, and Czechoslovakia who had arrived in Italy without visas for other countries, it suppressed, in August 1939, the tourist visa.[18] Only those refugees who arrived in possession of visas valid elsewhere were given the right of transit. Mussolini had already tightened the noose some weeks before. On learning that many bearers of the tourist visa were trying to cross the French border and thereby profit from what he called "facilitations" on

17. Ibid., pp. 35–37.
18. Ibid., p. 29.

the part of the Italian authorities to hasten the exodus of those who had not left Italy up to the date of the expulsion decree, he ordered the dissolution of the Jewish relief committee in Milan, the major such center, whose existence, in his view, had encouraged the "abuse" of the tourist visa.[19] At the same time, he made clear that all those who did not comply with the tourist visa regulations—those who moved illegally from province to province, who exceeded authorized time limits, or who had no proven means of subsistence—should be returned at once to the German frontier. At least 300 of these unfortunates fell under the Duce's order. But since the prefects dragged their feet in executing it, only 50 to 100 expulsions actually took place.[20] And only in a few cases, when police escort was provided, were the Jews denied the chance to escape. Loopholes abounded. Although the foreign Jews were obliged to report to specified border stations, many ignored such orders and fled to other provinces, where they hoped friendly prefects would grant them a stay. Their hopes were not in vain since some prefects were susceptible to appeals in their behalf by local Jewish communities.

Genoa stands out as a city whose officials lived up to a well-deserved reputation of liberality. The port's big shipping companies were also opposed to expulsion, but for a selfish reason: to avoid loss of their best clients during a time when the traffic in tourism and passenger transport had already fallen into a steep decline. But the prefect of Genoa, to keep on the good side of his superiors in the Interior Ministry, executed haphazardly some of the expulsion orders of the Ministry of Interior. Aware that his edicts were receiving only lukewarm attention, the Duce avoided confrontation with his lax officials and hoped that the pressure created by the permanent menace of expulsion to the German border would suffice in persuading Italy's unwanted Jews to leave the country. Finally, in December 1939, he stopped deportations to the German border altogether.[21] But he was not moved by compassion.

---

19. Massimo Leone, *Le organizzazioni di soccorso ebraiche in età fascista* (Rome, 1983), pp. 161–63.
20. Voigt, "Refuge and Persecution," p. 32.
21. Ibid.

Far from responding to the humanitarian appeals of the American ambassador in Rome, William Phillips, whom the Jewish organizations had enlisted to make appeals in their behalf, the Duce was compelled (by the refusal of the German police to take on any more of Italy's deported Jews) to rescind the deportation decree.[22]

After much hesitation, Mussolini irrevocably threw in his lot with Hitler by attacking an already prostrate France on June 10, 1940. The inevitable internment decrees for Italy's foreign Jews quickly followed. Paradoxically, they welcomed internment—as a less disastrous alternative than expulsion, the worst of all possible worlds. In principle, the internment was a measure to prevent foreign men able to bear arms from returning to their home countries to enroll in an enemy army.[23] Therefore, Jews of the Axis countries should not have been interned. But Mussolini insisted that "concentration camps should also be prepared for the Jews."[24] In this way, internment was linked to the racial policies. The Jewish internees were surprised by the harshness initially meted out. On arrest, they were confined in overcrowded and unhygienic prisons without any knowledge of their ultimate fate. Only weeks later could they breathe more freely when they learned that the trains bearing them to more permanent living quarters in internment camps were headed south rather than toward Germany and certain deportation.[25] The internment decree of September 4, 1940, reads: "The internees are to be treated humanely and protected against offensive and violent behavior."[26] Since Italy's camp guards, with a few notable exceptions, scrupulously respected the September 4 decree, their behavior stands out against the barbarity of the German SS, who systematically humiliated, tortured, and murdered their concentration camp inmates.

22. Ibid., also Michaelis, *Mussolini and the Jews*, p. 277.
23. For France, see Hanna Schramm, Barbara Vormeier, *Vivre à Gurs: Un camp de concentration français 1940–41* (Paris, 1979); for Britain, see Gerhard Hirschfeld ed., *Exil in Grossbritannien: Zur Emigration aus dem nationalsozialistischen Deutschland* (Stuttgart, 1983), pp. 58–61, 155–173.
24. Gina Antoniani Persichilli, "Disposizioni normative e fonti archivistiche per lo studio dell'internamento in Italia (giugno 1940–luglio 1943)" *Rassegna degli Archivi di Stato* 38 (1978): 89.
25. See numerous eyewitness reports in the archives of the Centro di Documentazione Ebraica Contemporanea in Milan, Fondo Israel Kalk, VII/1–2 Testimonianze.
26. "Decreto del Duce del Fascismo, Capo del Governo," September 4, 1940, *Gazzetta Ufficiale*, n. 239, October 11, 1940.

Most of the camps were situated in central and southern Italy, in the valleys of the Abruzzi, in Apulia, and in Calabria. The only camp built specifically for internment of Jews was Ferramonti-Tarsia in Calabria, which provided space for 2,000 inmates, 1,500 of whom were Jews.[27] All other camps were requisitioned or rented military barracks, hospitals, cloisters, country villas, and movie theaters, each one capable of accommodating up to 200 internees. Health and hygienic conditions were generally deplorable. More than 800 cases of malaria were reported in Ferramonti-Tarsia. Nourishment was poor, life monotonous, and intellectual life stagnant.[28] The fate of those women and children who enjoyed "free internment" (forced residence under police control in remote villages and towns) was only slightly better.

Though it is well known that Italy, as long as it was a sovereign state, did not extradite Jews to Germany—except for a few cases that fell under the Italo-German police cooperation—Jewish internees were actually not free of the danger of deportation. During the weeks before Mussolini's dismissal from power on July 25, 1943, there are indications that plans were afoot for a mass extradition to Germany. Daniel Carpi, in a series of essays, has dealt with this question, basing his accounts on Italian Foreign Ministry documents.[29] Since then, files that yield much new information on German-Italian police cooperation have become available. Until July 1942, the Gestapo respected the Italian position that Italy's refugee Jews were not covered by the police agreement of 1936 with the exception of those involved in specified political activity. But after the fall of 1942, the Gestapo changed its mind and, without specific political reasons, demanded extradition of some individuals. When the Italian Foreign Ministry was informed of this measure, it demanded to be heard before any extradition of Jews took place.[30] On May 26, 1943, Raffaele Alianello, director of the

---

27. See Capogreco, *Ferramonti*, and Francesco Folino, *Ferramonti un lager di Mussolini: Gli internati durante la guerra* (Cosenza, 1985), pp. I–XV.

28. See note 25 above.

29. Daniel Carpi, "The Rescue of Jews in the Italian Zone of Occupied Croatia," *Rescue Attempts During the Holocaust: Proceedings of the Second Yad Vashem International Historical Conference April 1974* (Jerusalem, 1977), pp. 465–525.

30. Rome, Archivio Centrale dello Stato (hereafter cited as ACS), Pubblica Sicu-

Office for the Relations with the German Police, sent a letter to the head of the police for foreigners, Giovanni Padellaro, urging him to execute the demands of the Gestapo for extradition. Padellaro immediately composed a letter for his superior, the director of the Division for General and Secret Affairs in the police department:

> The Office for the Relations with the German Police has made known that according to the order of Your Excellency the demands of the German police for extradition shall be executed in the future without interpellation of the Foreign Ministry. I assure you that the order will be followed rigorously. But I feel obliged to remind you that the demands of the German police do not only refer to the extradition of German subjects, but also to Jews chased away from Germany (*ebrei cacciati dalla Germania*) who do not hold German citizenship (such as the stateless, Poles, Dutch, Belgians, and French).[31]

Since the Nazi government in Berlin had in 1941 deprived of their German citizenship all Jews who had emigrated, Padellaro is referring to all Jewish refugees and immigrants in Italy.

The letter ends with the recommendation to abide by the interpellation of the Foreign Ministry, which opposed the extradition of Jews who were not political refugees. In addition, Padellaro urged adherence to the original intention of the police agreement: "For plausible humanitarian reasons it is advisable to weigh each demand of the Gestapo concerning non-Germans and Jews individually." In a draft, the word "humanitarian" was cancelled, as if Padellaro were ashamed to express such a sentiment in an official letter, but it does reveal his true thoughts.

From the evidence presented above, it is not clear whether Fascist Italy was preparing a general extradition of Jews or whether only specific individuals were to be deported. But on May 10, 1943,

---

rezza 1903–44, Ufficio RG, Rapporti con la polizia germanica, Busta 11, RG 28 (1941), Correspondence on Jadwiga Puzyna; Busta 13/Anno 1942, no. 3701–3800, Correspondence on Günter Steinitz; Busta 13/Anno 1942, no. 3801–3900, Correspondence on Julie Brunelikova.

31. Rome, ACS, Pubblica Sicurezza 1930–55, Busta 729, Trattati e convenzioni internazionali, Massima T (1939–43), Appunto per il Signor Capo Divisione, May 28, 1940.

the ambiguity seemed to be cleared up when the police department in the Interior Ministry drafted a memorandum for Mussolini (which was never submitted to Mussolini) in which Jews were described as a distinct group subject to extradition.[32] Only a few hours before Mussolini's fall, the secretary of state in the Ministry of the Interior ordered the police:

> Given the existing war situation, the opportunity exists to trans-fer 2,000 elements (including forty communists) who are now interned in the concentration camps of Ferramonti-Tarsia to the province of Bolzano.[33]

Was the choice of the province of Bolzano, lying in immediate proximity of the German frontier, merely a coincidence? Hardly, because in the spring of 1939 all foreign Jews had been found to have left the province of Bolzano and to have settled in other Italian provinces. Not one Jew had ever been sent there for internment.[34]

During the German occupation of Italy, die-hard Fascists who remained loyal to the Duce and ensconced in public office became willing henchmen of the German police and SS. On November 1, 1943, the decree prescribing internment of foreigners, which had been annulled on September 10 following the armistice with the Allies, was renewed, and on November 30 it was ordered that Italian Jews as well be sent to concentration camps. Shortly afterward, the Italian authorities established a network of about twenty-five local concentration camps to receive Jews rounded up in the provinces. From those collection points, they were brought to the transit camp of Fossoli di Carpi, and from there, shipped to Auschwitz. The Italian police played no inconsiderable part in these arrests and deportations.[35] During the six weeks between the dissolution

32. Rome, ACS, Pubblica Sicurezza 1903–44, Ufficio RG, Rapporti con la polizia germanica, Busta 11, Massime (1942), Appunto per il Duce, May 10, 1943.

33. ACS, Pubblica Sicurezza, Massima M 4 Mobilitazione civile, Busta 24/6 Cosenza. Campi di concentramento. Sgombero campo di concentramento di Ferramonti, Ministry of the Interior, Cabinet of the Minister to Police Direction, July 25, 1943.

34. ACS, Pubblica Sicurezza, A 16 Ebrei stranieri, Busta 9/Bolzano, Ministry of the Interior to Prefect of Bolzano, July 20, 1939, and response, July 26, 1939.

35. ACS, Pubblica Sicurezza, M 4 Mobilitazione civile, Busta 9/25/1/18 Varie, List of concentration camps. See also Giuseppe Mayda, *Ebrei sotto Salò: La persecuzione antisemita 1943–1945* (Milan, 1978), pp. 114–18; Liliana Picciotto Fargion, *L'occupazione tedesca e gli ebrei di Roma* (Rome, 1979), pp. 15–33.

of the former internment camps and the erection of new ones, most of the foreign Jews went into hiding, tried to reach Switzerland, or fled southward where they hoped to meet up with the advancing Allied forces. Many were able to reach Rome, but without means or friends, concealment was next to impossible. Fortunately, collaboration between the Catholic world and Italian Jewry sprang into existence to aid the Jewish refugees. The American Jewish Joint Distribution Committee transferred funds via Switzerland to Pietro Boetto, the archbishop of Genoa, and monasteries and convents, at great risk of SS discovery and reprisal, provided shelter and planned escape routes.[36] Still, as many as one-fourth of Italy's foreign Jews, mainly in central Italy, fell into the Fascist-Nazi dragnet.

In spite of the official persecution following promulgation of the racial laws, the Jews, up to September 8, 1943, received assistance from unexpected quarters in the Italian bureaucracy, thanks to an ongoing tug-of-war between their persecutors and protectors. Help was provided, in the main, by the Foreign Ministry. Apprised by its diplomatic missions of the deportations from German towns to the east, the Foreign Ministry also knew, on the basis of secret service reports, that the deported were being killed by toxic gas.[37] The military, too, were not unsympathetic to the plight of the Jews. But within Italy it could do little in behalf of the foreign Jews, since they were under the jurisdiction of the Interior Ministry and police. Only in the occupied territories of France and Yugoslavia did the military have a free hand, which it put to use by rescuing thousands of people.[38] It must not be forgotten, however, that the Jews had friends in Italy, particularly among the prefects, who frequently side-stepped their directives from above through delay and vacillation. Many low-level officials and police who dealt directly with the refugees and immigrants were gener-

---

36. Mayda, *Ebrei sotto Salò*, pp. 62–64; Michele Sarfatti, "Dopo l'8 settembre: Gli ebrei e la rete confinaria italo-svizzera," *Rassegna Mensile di Israel* (June–July 1981): 150–73.

37. Carpi, "The Rescue of the Jews," p. 520.

38. See Léon Poliakow, Jacques Sabille, *Les conditions des Juifs en France sous l'occupation italienne* (Paris, 1946) (English edition: *Jews Under the Italian Occupation* [Paris, 1959]), which is the basis of all later studies.

ally friendly and sympathetic, too. Ferramonti-Tarsia represents a choice example of their humanitarianism. Ignoring the jaundiced eye of their superiors, the camp's directors, Paolo Salvatore and Mario Fraticelli, permitted the internees a surprising degree of local autonomy exercised through their own elected councils.[39] After Mussolini's fall, Fraticelli took the elected speaker of the inmates, Herbert Landau, a Viennese Jew, to the Interior Ministry in Rome where they both pleaded for the liberation of all internees. On the way back to the camp they stopped at Naples for a short visit with Fraticelli's family in their recently bombed-out house.[40] This quite typical anecdote clearly demonstrates how brave and independent people in Italy sandbagged authoritarian government—a stark contrast with the smooth functioning of the German bureaucratic apparatus.

Open rivalry in Fascist officialdom peaked during the ultimate crisis of Mussolini's rule at the end of 1942. When Hitler's fate was sealed by the German military disaster at the gates of Stalingrad, even some of the Duce's most stalwart minions began to oppose him. The Jewish refugees were once again the unwitting beneficiaries of the spreading disaffection that penetrated to the core of Fascist authority, as the letter of Padellaro clearly shows. When the Germans occupied the country, the fissures cut even deeper. True, fanatic Fascists still eagerly followed orders. But there were officials who, forging ties with the Resistance, helped the Jews by providing them with false identity papers, other valuable documents, and food ration cards. Some of these officials were caught, deported, and ultimately perished in German camps in Mauthausen and Ravensbrück and elsewhere.[41]

We now turn to the attitude of the Italian Jews toward their oppressed refugee co-religionists. On the whole, throughout the era under study, Italian Jewry provided substantial relief work. But

39. Israel Kalk, "I campi di concentramento italiani per ebrei profughi: Ferramonti-Tarsia (Cosenza)," *Gli ebrei in Italia durante il fascismo* (Turin, 1961), pp. 63–71. See also Carlo Spartaco Capogreco, *Ferramonti*, pp. 52–56.

40. Herbert Landau, "Nel turbine della Liberazione," in Centro di Documentazione Ebraica Contemporanea, Fondo Kalk, VII/1 Testimonianze.

41. Sorani, *L'assistenza*, p. 144.

not all were sympathetic or involved. Furthermore, differences arose over how to respond to the rising crescendo of anti-Semitism. The first outbreak of official persecution in Germany—the violent boycott of Jewish shops and free professions in April 1933—did indeed evoke a wave of sympathy in Jewish communities everywhere in Italy. Responding to an appeal of the Union of Italian Israelite Communities, the Italian Jewish communities collected the extraordinary sum of 750,000 lire (150,000 marks), half of which was sent to Chaim Weizmann in London for the German Jewish Palestine Fund, while the rest was held in reserve for relief work in Italy.[42] But in 1934, the central relief committee of the Union of the Italian Israelite Committees closed its doors, and fund-raising efforts elsewhere flagged. A second bid for money in 1935 turned out to be a fiasco, for the Jewish communities were able to come up with only 35,000 lire for the Union, about one-twentieth of the amount collected the first time.[43] The reasons for this doleful result are legion: a slowdown of emigration and flight from Germany, an untoward display of wealth on the part of some refugees, and a return to Germany by some who despaired of finding employment in Italy. Underlying everything was a feeling that the worst was over, a view shared, incidentally, by many German Jews as well. But by 1937, the situation had clearly taken a turn for the worse. A steadily increasing number of refugees arrived in Italy devoid of means and in dire need of help. Into the breach stepped the American Jewish Joint Distribution Committee and, to a lesser extent, the HICEM, an agency composed of three organizations helping Jews—the American Hebrew Immigrant Aid and Sheltering Society (HIAS), the English Jewish Colonization Association (JCA), and Emigdirect, a German-Jewish body assisting east European Jews in Germany.[44] The relief effort after 1934 was centralized by a committee in Milan, the Comitato di Assistenza agli Ebrei profughi dalla Germania, which was directed by a group of active Jews whose humanitarianism was permeated by anti-

42. Leone, *Le organizzazioni di soccorso*, pp. 77, 183.
43. Ibid., pp. 82–85, 114–16, 286.
44. See Yehunda Bauer, *My Brother's Keeper: A History of the American Jewish Joint Distribution Committee 1929–1939* (Philadelphia, 1974), p. 269.

Fascist and Zionist sentiments. The leading figure was Raffaele Cantoni, an inventive man who, to raise money for relief, did not hesitate to sell off part of his own patrimony.[45]

The Italian Jewish relief effort, even in this period of mounting persecution, did not go unopposed. Many feared that assistance to the victims of National Socialism would irritate the Fascist government and trigger anti-Semitic reactions. After the proclamation of the racial laws, voices were raised that urged passivity. The vice-president of the Union of Italian Israelite Communities, Aldo Ascoli, for instance, argued that Italian Jewry was too small and weak to shoulder the burden of relief work.[46] After Mussolini's order to dissolve the committee in Milan had been issued in August 1939— an event that seemed to confirm the apprehensions of the opponents to the relief work—a new group of very active and devoted men, driven by moral and religious convictions, emerged in 1939 to renew and reorganize aid. In December of that year Delasem (Delegation for Assistance to Emigrés) was formed in Genoa under the direction of the lawyer Lelio Vittorio Valobra, a man of high principles and sound organizational skills. Dependent on the Union of Italian Israelite Communities, Delasem secured authorization from the Ministry of Interior, which, in turn, hoped that the organization would be able to accelerate Jewish emigration from Italy.[47] Relief proceeded undisturbed before the German occupation. After the foundation of Delasem, about 2,500 people from all of Italy were under its care. When the Germans arrived, the organization was smashed to pieces. Valobra and most of his collaborators fled to Switzerland, where they continued their work with the support of the Italian resistance movement and the Catholic clergy.[48]

In addition to the work of Jewish agencies, Italian citizens acting on their own took a hand in the rescue of Jews. Although a com-

45. Sergio Minerbi, *Raffaele Cantoni un ebreo anticonformista* (Rome, 1978), pp. 52–64.

46. Rome, Unione delle Comunità Israelitiche Italiane, 44 I Delasem, Rapporti con i comitati locali/Milano, Aldo Ascoli to Mario Falco, September 21, 1939.

47. Leone, *Le organizzazioni di soccorso*, pp. 175–78.

48. Ibid., pp. 179–229, 244–57; Sorani, *L'assistenza*, pp. 117–18.

prehensive study of their historical attitudes toward émigrés and refugees is lacking, we can infer basic impressions by analyzing the use of the word "émigré." In Germany, for instance, émigrés were frowned on as people who have rejected the national community. No surprise, then, that the National Socialist propaganda against émigrés and refugees found sympathy in Germany. In Italy, on the other hand, since millions of Italians were forced by poverty to leave the country to find means of survival elsewhere, "émigré" or "refugee" evoked a much more positive image. Italian history is spotted with many great historical figures and national heroes who had been at one time or another émigrés and refugees: Petrarca, Dante, Garibaldi, and Mazzini. The Italian *Risorgimento*, in fact, had been partly prepared abroad by political exiles. In addition, Italian openness to émigrés derives from emotional identification with their own victims of persecution at the hands of foreign conquerors plundering the peninsula from the Middle Ages onward. Plainly speaking, Italians have not been disposed to anti-Semitism, a fact partially attributable, perhaps, to their tough immunity to xenophobic impulses. Since foreigners have generally been welcomed in Italy, it is no accident that many Italians should treat their Jewish refugees with compassion and understanding.[49]

People acting according to moral precepts in an atmosphere of freedom is one thing; their willingness to show compassion toward a declared enemy of the state under a regime exercising a tight-fisted vigilance against dissent is quite another. Unquestionably, the political reality of the Fascist police state influenced individual behavior by intimidating many Italians into silence. For a while, Fascism did enjoy a broad consensus in Italy, and the popularity of the regime reached new heights on Mussolini's declaration of empire over the ruins of Ethiopia in May 1936. As noted by the great historian-in-exile, Gaetano Salvemini, Fascism was never so esteemed as when it faced down Nazi Germany over the SS-directed assassination of the Austrian Chancellor Engelbert Dollfuss in 1934.[50] This anti-Nazi feature of Italian Fascism expressed

49. No study exists on the historical attitudes of the Italians toward émigrés and refugees. As far as anti-Semitism is concerned, see Michaelis, *Mussolini and the Jews*, pp. 3–9; De Felice, *Storia*, pp. 55–64.
50. Michaelis, *Mussolini and the Jews*, p. 79.

itself in feelings of goodwill toward the refugees and immigrants coming into Italy in their attempt to escape the clutches of Hitler. Small wonder, then, that the bombshell of the Axis should be greeted in Italy with silence. People everywhere were shocked by the slander thus administered to the unique *italianità* of Mussolini's Fascism. The racial laws, if anything, provoked even more national indignation. And no cool Fascist *raison d'état* explanation could conceal the bald fact from the majority of the Italian people that the racial laws violated a historical tradition.[51] When the Italian dictatorship discouraged aid and succor to the refugees, whose pitiable condition was created by the unloved Axis partner, those poor unfortunates had no other choice but to throw themselves on the goodwill of the Italian people.

Working under the severe constraints of an unsympathetic dictatorship, private aid was bound to be haphazard and unevenly administered. Only those refugees with familiarity with the Italian language and the customs of their host country, or who had built up friendships and established neighborhood ties, were in a position to secure help. Those newcomers who arrived without means or personal introductions were rendered dependent on organized Jewish relief. Private care, therefore, was unreliable and insufficient.[52] After the German occupation, the chances of getting help got even worse. Many internees who had been confined to camps or to remote villages and towns, where little contact was permitted with the outside world, were too frightened by their isolation to risk escape. Remote from former friends and relatives, they could, if they got away, turn only to village priests or partisans, should the latter be active in the neighborhood.[53]

Broadly speaking, during the Fascist era, persecution and humanitarianism in Italy went hand-in-hand. Anti-Semitism at the grass-roots, however, was only slight; but that was not always obvious, due to Mussolini's ubiquitous police armed with orders to chase down fugitive Jews. In the absence of democracy, the

51. De Felice, *Storia*, pp. 301–11.
52. Voigt, "Gli emigrati," p. 85; see note 25 above.
53. ACS, Pubblica Sicurezza 1930–55, Busta 741/A Stranieri internati. Affari generali, Ministry of the Interior to the Prefects, July 8 and 25, 1940; Mayda, *Ebrei sotto Salò*, p. 64; Cavaglion, *Nella notte straniera*, pp. 125–138.

Italian people were denied a free press and independent political organizations through which to express their solidarity with the Jews being persecuted under their noses. Where has public opinion ever seriously modified the behavior of an authoritarian regime? Since the widespread humanitarianism was private and informal, therefore, it was able only to hamper and obstruct what was enacted from above. The testimony of survivors is striking: eyewitness reports are practically unanimous in detailing the courageous efforts of numerous Italians from all walks of life who proffered their help. Hardly better evidence can be adduced in proving the relative absence of anti-Semitism in the country. Yet, the Fascist regime did mirror, albeit in a perverted form, popular opinion—but only up to a point. When the Fascists tried to institutionalize anti-Semitism and Mussolini's tilt toward Hitler carried Italy into the war on the side of Germany, the Italian people withdrew into a sullen hostility. If the racial politics and expulsion orders of the Fascist regime were abominable, the courage of countless individual Italians in braving barbarous retaliation as they sheltered Italy's hunted Jews stands out all the more as a telling affirmation of the human spirit. And not only humanitarianism moved them: aid and rescue constituted a refusal to knuckle under to what had become a hated political regime.

Carlo Spartaco Capogreco
(translated by Ruth Feldman)

7. The Internment Camp of Ferramonti-Tarsia

I dedicate this paper to the memory of Israele Kalk who, with great love, intelligence, and generosity, made the material and spiritual life of the internees of the camp of Ferramonti-Tarsia more bearable.

After Hitler's advent to power and the beginning of the anti-Semitic persecutions in Germany, many of the refugees who had fled from the Third Reich found refuge in Italy, where the Fascist government opposed no obstacles to their immigration, on condition that the people involved had not operated actively in political anti-Fascist parties. The wealthiest immigrants were, in fact, permitted various means of facilitating the transfer of their capital to Italian banks.[1]

Starting with the second half of the 1930s, immigration to Italy continued, always increasing in numbers because of the increasing harshness of the Nazi persecution in Germany and the extension of the racial laws to the countries that fell under the German domination. In the summer of 1938—according to the results of an official census—more than 4,000 non-Italian Jews

1. On the problem of Jewish immigration in Fascist Italy, see the article by Klaus Voigt whose comprehensive and exhaustive study of the topic is to be published in the near future. I wish to thank Prof. Voigt for the information and the suggestions he provided for my research on Ferramonti-Tarsia, and I refer the reader to the following essays: "Notizie statistiche sugli immigrati e profughi ebrei in Italia (1938–1945)," in *Israel, un decennio 1974–1984* (Rome, 1984); "Gli emigrati in Italia dai paesi sotto la dominazione nazista: tolerati e perseguitati (1933–1940)," *Storia Contemporanea*, XVI, no. 1, February 1985, "Refuge and Persecution in Italy, 1933–1945" in *Simon Wiesenthal Center Annual*, vol. 4, 1987, pp. 3–64. On the same topic see also: S. Sorani, *L'assistenza ai profughi ebrei in Italia (1933–1947). Contributo alla storia della "Delasem"* (Rome, 1983), and M. Leone, *Le organizzazioni ebraiche in età Fascista* (Rome, 1983). Regarding Fascist policy toward Jews, see R. De Felice, *Storia degli ebrei italiani sotto il fascismo*, Milan 1977 (Turin 1961); M. Michaelis, *Mussolini and the Jews: German-Italian Relations and the Jewish Question in Italy (1922–1945)* (Oxford, 1978), (Italian translation: *Mussolini e la questione ebraica. Le relazioni italo-tedesche e la politica razziale in Italia* (Milan, 1982).

were in Italy, the greater part of them German, Austrian, and Polish. Their situation, which had up to then been fairly favorable (they easily obtained permits to stay and work in Italy), suddenly changed in the autumn of that same year when, with the legal decrees of September 7 and November 17, the Italian government decided to expel, inside of six months, all foreign Jews who had established themselves in Italy after January 1, 1919, and to revoke all Italian citizenships granted to foreign Jews after that same date.

With this provision (which, together with the legislative measures regarding Italian Jews, represented the beginning of Fascist racial politics), hundreds of Italian citizens of Jewish religion or origin became stateless, having lost their original citizenship in the moment in which they had acquired their Italian one.[2]

Since, along with the decree of expulsion of September 7, the Italian government had not yet issued a decree forbidding foreign Jews to enter the country, the flow of refugees toward Italy in the following months actually increased instead of stopping, and the expulsion of the refugees could not really be put into action. Only in May 1940, when the entry of the nation into war was imminent and the Minister of the Interior issued a general prohibition of entry for all foreign Jews, did their arrival cease definitively.[3]

The Fascist regime then decided to intern, in certain towns and villages, as well as concentration camps, all foreign and stateless Jews, over whose heads always hung—like the sword of Damocles—the 1938 expulsion decree. The internment measure was justified officially by reasons of national security. However, from the moment that the majority of the interned Jews (suspected *a priori* of carrying on conspiratorial activities harmful to the national se-

2. The decree n. 1728 of 17 November 1938 (which completed decree n. 1381 of September 7, 1938) translated, in fact, the "Declaration of the Race," approved by the Fascist Grand Council on the night between October 6 and 7, 1938, into law, when, among other things, the decision was taken to expel all foreign Jews from the kingdom.

3. "It is perplexing, but nevertheless true, that despite the expulsion decree, between the beginning of 1939 and Italy's entry into the war, it has been determined that over 4,000 refugees from Germany, Austria, Poland, and Czechoslovakia entered Italy. The principal entry means was the "tourist visa" for foreign Jews, which was granted in February 1939 at the request of the *Direzione Generale per il Turismo. . . .*" (translated from Voigt, "Notizie statistiche," p. 410). On August 19, 1939, the Ministry of the Interior suspended the "residence permit for reasons of tourism," but foreign Jews could still use the "transit visa" for embarkation in Italian ports.

curity) were not citizens of enemy countries, such a provision was, in reality, only for reasons of anti-Jewish persecution.

Two days before Italy entered World War II, on June 8, 1940, the Minister of the Interior issued the "Rules for Concentration Camps and the Localities of Confinement." On subsequent days, numerous circulars gave further instructions, arriving finally at the "Decree of the Duce" of September 4, 1940, which contained the norms for the internment of "enemy subjects."[4]

The concentration camps set up by the Italian government consisted almost entirely of public buildings (schools, barracks, movie theatres, ex-convents, etc.), requisitioned and adapted to receive the internees. Except for the name, they had nothing in common with the terrible German death camps. Only the camp of Ferramonti-Tarsia, built in Calabria, about thirty-five kilometers from the city of Cosenza, was created from scratch, with its barracks-type buildings. With an average population of over 1,000 internees and a maximum of over 2,000—reached in the summer of 1943—Ferramonti was one of the largest of the camps set up in Italy by the Fascist regime.

It consisted of ninety-two barracks, each divided into two dormitories with ninety beds apiece. Near the poorly insulated, wooden barracks, there were cement structures for use as kitchens and sanitary services. The camp stood in the valley of the river Crati, an area of southern Italy that had been for centuries prey to the scourge of malaria. The program for the reclamation of the place, begun by the Fascist regime, had been interrupted many times and the anopheles mosquitoes still reigned there, uncontested. The choice of the location, moreover, was made on recommendation (certainly not disinterested) of the Eugenio Parrini firm, already involved in the reclamation work, and now entrusted with the construction of the barracks and, subsequently, their maintenance, and the handling of the sale of food supplies for the internees.[5]

---

4. Carlo Spartaco Capogreco, *Ferramonti. La vita e gli uomini del più grande campo d'internamento fascista* (Florence, 1987), pp. 35–38.

5. The firm Eugenio Parrini was already involved in construction, in the province of Matera (Comune Pisticci), of an agricultural settlement for persons sent to forced

On June 20, 1940, even before it was completed, the camp of Ferramonti came officially into use. A commissioner of public security was appointed as director, with a group of police officials under him. Fascist militia, composed mostly of local people, served as guards around the perimeter of the camp.[6]

The chief of police, Arturo Bocchini, in a letter written on July 13, 1940, and addressed to the Parrini company, specified that half of the available places in the camp should be occupied by "Aryan internees."[7] But, notwithstanding this proposal, Ferramonti immediately became characterized as a camp for Jews, both refugees and stateless. Only in 1941 did it begin to harbor "Aryans" as well, though in notably smaller numbers.[8]

The extreme unfitness of the location immediately struck and impressed the first arrivals. Dr. Chimenti, a provincial doctor from Cosenza, after undertaking an inspection on behalf of the Ministry of the Interior, testified that the state property of Ferramonti, despite the fact that it was partially reclaimed, was still an endemic malarial zone. And one of the first Jewish arrivals remembers that "the aspect of the countryside gave one such a sensation of a cemetery that the heart flinched, and one wanted only to flee." Even months later, when the camp had been completed, the medical inspector, sent by Rome, admitted with extreme frankness:

> They couldn't have chosen a more unfit place, malarial, in the middle of pools of water. . . . When it rains the whole camp becomes a vast bog. Even on the train I heard extremely unfavorable comments on the site, about which a traveller expressed the suspicion that it had been deliberately selected in order to make the inhabitants sicken and die.[9]

These were the geographic and environmental conditions of the

---

residence. See G. Antoniani Persichilli, "Disposizioni normative e fonti archivistiche per lo studio dell'internamento in Italia (giugno 1940–luglio 1943)," in *Rassegna degli Archivi di Stato*, a. XXXVIII (1987), n. 1–3, pp. 77–96. The same article contains the legal-technical details regarding internment in Italy.

6. Capogreco, *Ferramonti*, pp. 44–46.

7. Rome, Archivio Centrale dello Stato (ACS), Ministero dell'Interno, Direzione generale di Pubblica Sicurezza, Affari Generali e Riservati, Categoria M4–16, Busta 25, Fascicolo Cosenza, Sottofascicolo, P6.

8. Capogreco, *Ferramonti*, pp. 92–93.

9. Ibid., p. 42.

largest Fascist concentration camp for foreign Jews. The social context was that of a marginal and depressed area in the interior of Calabria, a region that, in April 1940, had reached the record figure of 25,000 unemployed.[10]

The inhabitants of the area, from their towns situated on the hills overlooking the camp, still looked with fear and aversion on the Crati valley, a traditionally malarial and inhospitable place. Hence they watched with even more diffidence the growth of the strange barracks "village." The mistrust and suspicion of the Calabrians toward the Jews of Ferramonti was not born, however, from anti-Semitic motivations that the Fascist propaganda took pains to disseminate and nourish. It stemmed, rather, from the ancient sense of territoriality and the traditional isolation of the southern peasant populations.

Gradually, however, as the first contacts took place between the Calabrians and the internees, the initial suspicion and fear gave way to curiosity and solidarity, and the locals realized that the Jews were not the "diabolical" and "dangerous" beings they were declared to be by the hammering propaganda of the regime, but poor, unhappy, persecuted people.

The first months of camp life, during the summer of 1940, were very difficult. The malaria, which the authorities tried to combat with the administration of quinine, constituted a constant and serious menace, and in the 1940–43 period there were 820 certified cases of illness.[11]

Between June and July, over 100 internees from various north-central Italian cities arrived at Ferramonti. Almost always they came handcuffed and accompanied by *carabinieri* or by public safety agents. They got off at the railroad station in Mongrassano and from there were made to proceed to the camp, six kilometers away.[12]

The internees were subjected to three daily roll calls; they could

10. See G. Lingari, *Storia dell Calabria dall'Unità ad oggi* (Bari, 1982). On the attitude of the population of Calabria toward World War II, see G. Conti, *L'opinione pubblica calabrese di fronte alla seconda guerra mondiale (dall'inizio del conflitto alla caduta del Fascismo)* (Reggio Calabria, 1977).

11. See Voigt, "Refuge and Persecution," p. 40.

12. Capogreco, *Ferramonti*, pp. 44–45.

not leave the barracks before seven or after nine, or go beyond the camp confines without a special pass. They could not, obviously, engage in politics, or read foreign publications without authorization. Correspondence with family members was subjected to censorship; that with other people was authorized from time to time. The possession and use of cameras, radios, and playing cards was prohibited. The internees were not, however, obliged to work, and, if they had no income with which to maintain themselves, they received a government subsidy. A mess had been opened, run by the camp builders, and people could have access to it by spending a large portion of their subsidies.

The treatment by the public safety authorities was correct and tolerant, but nonetheless the greater part of the people endured much discomfort and suffering. This was so not only because of the unhealthfulness of the place, the miserable lodgings, and the scarcity of water, but also, above all, from the total uncertainty about their own futures and the preoccupation with the fate of the family members who had, in many cases, remained in the countries of origin, prey to the Nazi persecution.[13]

The camp director of Ferramonti, Commissioner Paolo Salvatore, adopted a policy of respect and tolerance from the very first days of his installation, showing himself to be understanding and willing to consider the demands of the prisoners, provided that no disorders or lack of discipline took place. His policy was, in short, that of *laisser faire*, conceding to the internees the maximum internal authority as long as safeguards and formal respect of the norms were ensured, so that the director could avoid admonitions by higher authorities.[14]

In this context, the Jews of Ferramonti immediately took it upon themselves to improve as far as possible their difficult situation. They created a strong internal organization right away, one with a democratic cast based on direct election of a delegate for each barracks, the *capo-camerata* (dormitory head). In quick succession a whole series of community institutions came into being, such

13. Voigt, "Notizie statistiche," p. 413.
14. The attitude of director Paolo Salvatore toward his internees was described by Israele Kalk as a "gentlemen's agreement." See De Felice, *Storia*, p. 496.

as the cooperative kitchens, the library, the court, the medical clinic, the synagogue, and the assemblies of the *capi-camerate,* a kind of parliament at the head of which was the *capo dei capi* (chief head) of the camp.

To maintain peace and order, the camp director readily supported the organs of self-government created by the internees who preferred to debate and resolve their problems themselves by appealing to their barracks representatives rather than to the camp director, as the official regulations mandated. Gianni Mann, a Jewish ex-industrialist of Austrian origin, was elected the first *capo dei capi* on August 26, 1940.[15]

Suddenly, at the end of September 1940, the camp population climbed to 700 people with the arrival of 300 deportees from Libya. They were Jews (often entire families) from various east-central countries of Europe, who in April had gone from Italy to Bengazi with the intention of proceeding clandestinely to Palestine. With Italy's entry into the war, however, the situation in the colonies also changed. The 300 refugees, arrested in Bengazi, were, after a brief sojourn in the Neapolitan prison of Poggioreale, deported to Calabria. New and urgent problems arose for the camp life with the new arrivals, whom the other internees immediately called *bengasioti,* from the name of the city where they were arrested. The food situation, in particular, drastically worsened, since it took long for the supplies to satisfy the added demand. In addition, it was the first time that women and children had arrived in Ferramonti. The family groups especially found themselves in the worst predicament, since a whole subsidy was given only to the head of the family, while wives received one lira and 10 centesimi and children half a lira.[16]

It cannot be said, however, that outside the camp confines, in the Calabrian towns, things were going better for the common people. The following is the testimony of Emilio Braun, an internee who, having obtained the director's authorization in the first months of camp life, went to Tarsia to buy some supplies.

15. Gianni Mann, the first *capo dei capi* of the Ferramonti camp was born in Vienna in 1896. For his activities as *capo dei capi* see Capogreco, *Ferramonti,* pp. 55–56.

16. Capogreco, *Ferramonti,* pp. 57–70.

We prepared a long list of things that were missing in the camp and finally about fifteen of us, early in the morning and accompanied by two guards, began to walk a country road in the direction of Tarsia. I went immediately to the first grocery store and said to the proprietor that I needed several things for which he would be paid in cash. Finally, I asked, in a very low voice, if he could possibly sell us a little sugar, a commodity which, from the time war broke out, had been rationed, and was sold only with the surrender to the storekeeper of the specific requisite ration cards. The storekeeper then asked how much sugar I would like to have, and I, thinking I was making an exorbitant request, answered: two kilos. He thought it over for a moment and then, without hesitation, said there was no problem. I was interested in knowing the price he wanted for that sweet product, truly precious in wartime. He answered in quite a natural way: "You'll pay the regular price." While weighing out the sugar, looking into my eyes and probably guessing my thoughts, he asked me brusquely: "But would you like to have even more?" "And how!" I answered. "We have a lot of old people, sick people, and children who need sugar." And he replied: "Well, in that case I'll give you all you can use." And he gave us almost fifty kilograms at the list price. I asked him how he could manage to sell us such a quantity of sugar and he replied candidly: "Listen, here in this town the people consume very little or none at all because it's too expensive. We're poor people."[17]

The words of the Tarsia storekeeper that bear witness to the miserable economic conditions of his fellow citizens find ample substantiation in the official statistical data. According to the results of a national inquiry, in the three-year period from 1937 to 1939, Calabria showed the lowest Italian consumption of five products out of the thirteen under consideration, and for the others their record was always close to the very lowest levels. The region consumed 2,555 calories a head as against the national norm of 2,744. Not even the exceptional drop in unemployment, following the emigration to Germany and America of large contingents of

---

17. Testimony of ex-internee Emilio Braun, reported in Capogreco, *Ferramonti*, pp. 177–78.

workers, sufficed to resolve the economic difficulties which, instead of lessening, became even more aggravated.[18]

In the camp, following the arrival of the large number of people from Bengazi and the urgent problems that ensued, the community of internees established two other important institutions: the Committee for Assistance and the school for children. The Committee, directed by the German-Jewish lawyer Max Pereles and created with the intention of furnishing moral and material help to the internees, was to become in a short time an important support center for the inhabitants and for the life of the camp. The school, set up in a barracks made available by the director, was staffed by teachers and intellectuals and initially brought together twenty-five children.[19]

Of greatest help to the material, spiritual, and cultural life of the internees was the work of Israele Kalk, a Latvian Jewish engineer who had lived in Italy for many years and had already in 1939 begun to aid Jewish refugees. He established a free mess for Jewish children refugees and a social service organization with its headquarters in Milan. Endowed with an incredible agility of action that immediately distinguished it from the official Jewish aid bodies, Kalk's organization very quickly succeeded in extending its help to the most remote places where Jews were in difficulty.

After the internment of the refugees in June 1940, Kalk's assistants reached many concentration camps bringing food, clothing, medicine, and, for the children, even milk and toys. The necessary funds were obtained through a very extended network of correspondents, donors, and benefactors. On March 30, 1941, having obtained the permit from the Milan police headquarters, Israele Kalk came in person to Ferramonti. In no time he became the friend of all the internees who, starting with that first visit, learned to gauge time, which passed slowly, by referring to Kalk's visits. He was the bearer not only of material aid, but also of faith and hope.[20]

---

18. G. Cingari, *Storia della Calabria*, p. 306, and G. Conti, *L'opinione pubblica*.
19. Capogreco, *Ferramonti*, pp. 61–62.
20. Israele Kalk was born in 1904 in Piekeln (Latvia). After receiving a degree in engineering in Milan, in addition to his professional activity, he dedicated himself

In the spring of 1941, the Parrini workmen finished erecting barbed wire the length of the camp perimeter, where in the first months there had been only a small ditch, easily crossed. But behind that fence, the extraordinary inventiveness and great adaptability of the Jews created what I would define as the "village" of Ferramonti, a collective structure that drew upon a concentration of intelligence, culture, and professional and lay abilities originating from almost all the east-central European nations. The school kept adding new courses and classes and included a kindergarten. Three synagogues sprang up, one for each rite, and cultural debates and artistic performances became more and more frequent. This was especially true of musical ones, to which the camp director, with pride, often invited the notables of the area. The numerous and well-qualified doctors did everything in their power to look after people's health, also helping, on many occasions, people from the nearby towns. Everyone tried to carry on an activity of some kind, which made the period of internment more bearable. People studied languages, constructed handicraft items, or organized commerce and an exchange (more or less legal) with the local peasants who furnished vegetables, fruit, and oil.[21]

On May 22, 1941, the papal nuncio to the Italian government, Monsignor Borgongini-Duca, visited Ferramonti. In the name of all the internees, the Rumanian doctor Giuseppe Lax, in a brief welcoming speech addressed to the high-ranking prelate, declared, among other things:

> Here in this sad, deserted marsh, one day rows of white barracks sprang up. Under the lovely sun of Calabria, something unusual happened. The war made a little town come into being. The barracks became populated quickly, and in these districts, orig-

---

with great energy to intensive cultural work as writer and translator of the great works in the Yiddish literature which he presented in the monthly *Davar.* When entire families of refugees from Nazism began to arrive in Italy, Israele Kalk started his aid activity in Milan; he founded and directed the "Children's Mess," (Mensa dei Bambini) where the youngest Jewish refugees found food, shelter, and recreation. His passionate and tireless work reached children even in places of forced residence and Italian concentration camps, as well as, at a later time, adults. As part of this activity Israele Kalk visited several times the Ferramonti-Tarsia camp, contributing significantly to a more humane condition of existence in that place of internment. He died in Milan on March 30, 1980.

21. Capogreco, *Ferramonti*, pp. 76–79.

inally destined to hear only the lovely Italian idiom, other and different tongues began to resound. These inhabitants came from far away, forced by the adversities of fate. Everyone carries with him the memory of an abandoned or destroyed hearth, of a scattered family, the dejection due to the ruin of his best hopes, the sorrowful memory of all the dear things that are no more. . . .[22]

The internees of the Catholic faith seized the occasion of the nuncio's visit to ask for appropriate spiritual help. Their request was granted, and two months later the Vatican sent to the camp a sixty-five year old Capuchin, Father Calliste Lopinot, who, thanks to his reasonableness and great accessibility, succeeded very quickly in acquiring the trust and esteem of all the internees.[23]

Another very large group of Jews, mostly Yugoslav, consisting of 127 people, arrived in the camp on July 31, 1941, from Ljubljana (Lubiana). Along with the number of people in the camp, the number of nationalities, political beliefs, and spoken languages grew too (66% German, 10% Yiddish, 10% Polish, etc.).

In October, 187 Jews arrived from Albania and the camp school took in the new little ones, almost all of whom spoke Serbian. In the second school year, a junior and senior high school were established. Jews were no longer the only camp inhabitants. Numerous non-Jews began to be deported from occupied Yugoslavia and, beginning in November, Chinese internees arrived from various Italian cities.[24]

Between February and March of 1942, the largest group ever of internees arrived, the shipwrecked people from the riverboat *Pentcho*. Five hundred young Jews, mostly Czechoslovak, had embarked on May 15, 1940, at Bratislava, hopeful of reaching Palestine by following the course of the Danube, the Black Sea, and the Aegean. It was an almost impossible undertaking for such a ship, completely unsuited to navigating in the open sea. However, con-

22. Greetings of welcome extended to Cardinal Borgongini-Duca by ex-internee Giuseppe Lax, ibid, p. 112.

23. Father Calliste Lopinot was born in Geispolsheim in Alsace. He left ample documentation on the time he spent among the internees of Ferramonti in *Analecta Fratrum Minorum Cappuccinorum*, (Rome (vol. LX, 1944; vol. LXI, 1945), and in an unpublished diary. (See Graham, "Vatican and the Jews" in this volume.)

24. Capogreco, *Ferramonti*, pp. 92–93.

fronted with the Nazi menace, the Jews had decided to attempt this voyage of hope. After months of eventful navigation and incredible hardship, the *Pentcho* ran aground on the rocks near the uninhabited island of Kamila-Nisi in the Aegean. The Italian warship Camoglio, under the command of Lt. Carlo Orlando, rescued the shipwrecked passengers who, after a period spent on the island of Rhodes, were deported to Ferramonti in 1942.[25]

With their arrival, the community had to confront for the first time such a numerous and compact group of refugees, and the problems of getting settled were by no means few. An internee recounts: "The shipwrecked passengers of the *Pentcho* arrived in the camp starved, indigent, and in rags, making a truly pitiful impression." However, the Committee for Assistance immediately occupied itself with this group seeking, within the limits of the possible, to alleviate its misery.[26]

In the same period, the chief rabbi of Genoa, Dr. Riccardo Pacifici, visited the camp and presided over a moving ceremony in one of the synagogues. Pacifici expressed noble words of hope and comfort to his listeners. He was later deported to a Nazi extermination camp from which he was never to return.[27]

In the second half of 1942, 300 Greeks from Greece and Libya were also interned in Ferramonti. Among them was Evangelos Averoff Tossizza, former prefect of Corfu, and, after the war, a government minister several times.[28]

With the passing of the months and the increased number of

25. On the incredible Odyssey of the *Pentcho*, see Y. Halevy, *Habaita* (Tel-Aviv, 1950); J. Bierman, *Odyssey* (New York, 1984); Capogreco, *Ferramonti*, pp. 99–108.

26. Testimony of ex-internee Samuel Avisar in Capogreco, *Ferramonti*, p. 112.

27. Riccardo Pacifici was born in Florence in 1904. A prominent personality of the Italian Jewry, after receiving the title of *rabbino maggiore* he moved to the island of Rhodes to head the local rabbinical college. In 1936 he became chief rabbi of Genoa and stayed there even after the armistice of September 8, 1943, and during the German occupation of Italy he was deported to Auschwitz, where he died on December 12, 1943. Riccardo Pacifici visited the Ferramonti camp three times (March 1942, October 1942, and July 1943).

28. Evangelos Averoff Tossizza was born in Trikkala (Thessaly) in 1910. He became a lawyer and in 1942 (he was the prefect of Corfu) he was arrested and deported to Ferramonti. After the war he was a member of parliament from 1946 to 1967 and Greek Foreign Minister from 1956 to 1963; in 1974, after having opposed the "regime of the colonels," he became Defense Minister in the new government under Caramanlis. He published various literary works in the form of historical novels, in some of which he speaks of his internment in Ferramonti-Tarsia.

internees, the food shortages became more and more acute. Father Calliste recalls:

> For a long time now, many rationed foods were short. With the new restrictions, as of June 1, 1942, the situation worsened in an alarming manner, and hunger made its entry into the camp. From then on, ever more frequently, people came to me saying: "Padre, I'm hungry."[29]

In spite of everything, the Ferramonti community proceeded with its social and cultural development. The painter Michel Fingesten obtained a shed from the camp director, which he equipped as a studio, organizing shows and teaching the art of painting to some of the young people. Musical life was nurtured with passion by Maestro Lav Mirski, formerly director of the Osijek Opera in Yugoslavia. He directed both the synagogue "choir" and that of the Catholic chapel, which gave concerts of the highest artistic level. Even sport had a big impetus, with soccer in first place.[30]

At the beginning of December, the atmosphere in the camp was changed abruptly by the arrival of three unusual internees who had escaped, at great risk, from a work camp in Poland. Pale and malnourished, the new arrivals told of the deportation of 18,000 Jews from their city to the Treblinka death camp. Now the Ferramonti internees could have few doubts left about what was happening to their brothers who had remained in the East, prey to the occupying Nazis.[31]

Consequently, 1943 did not begin under the best auspices. Among other things, on January 22, to the great regret of the camp occupants, the director, Paolo Salvatore, was transferred to another post. He had been the principal originator of the "gentlemen's agreement," the tacit understanding established in the camp be-

---

29. Fr. Callistes in Geispolsheim, D. F. M. Cap., "Ferramonti-Tarsia (Cosenza), die declaratae dimissionis ex publica custodia, 17 septembris, 1943," in *Analecta Fratrum Minorum Cappuccinorum* (Rome, 1944), vol. LX, pp. 70–75.

30. Besides Michel Fingesten, there were among the internees in Ferramonti other important painters such as Eugenio Kron, Siegfried Kuttner, Sebastiano Schechter, and Schoja and Maximilian Hoffmann. Among the interned intellectuals I wish to mention also Ernst Berhard, who introduced the Jungian method of psychoanalysis into Italy. He was released from internment in 1941.

31. The three young Jews from the Polish city of Siedlce were Kawe Herzl, Moshe Liverant, and Zvi Nelkenbaum.

tween custodians and prisoners that had allowed the latter fairly good conditions and broad internal autonomy. The director's conduct had not pleased the more intransigent local Fascists and was the motive behind the pressures that led to the transfer of Salvatore, who was unjustly accused of various inadequacies.[32]

On February 25, during a meeting in Rome with Mussolini, German Foreign Minister Joachim von Ribbentrop demanded the extradition of the Jewish refugees in the Italian occupation zone in France and Yugoslavia. Thanks to Father Calliste's sources of information, the news did not take long to arrive in Calabria, and the specter of deportation to Nazi concentration camps suddenly presented itself to the internees. The understanding shown by the new director, Mario Fraticelli, installed on March 31, and the new visit of the papal nuncio, Monsignor Borgongini-Duca, which took place in May on the pope's instructions, served in some measure to lessen the internees' fears.[33]

In this way the seemingly tranquil summer passed, while the food situation in the camp—and elsewhere in the surrounding towns—became continually more serious and unbearable. Malnutrition was now a habitual reality, and the inexorable malaria struck down a new victim from time to time, but there were no deaths.

In June and July, some groups of anti-Fascist Italians arrived. On July 25, 1943, Mussolini's fall aroused many hopes for the end of the war and rapid liberation, while for the Fascist militia who guarded the camp it was a real blow. Many of them sold their weapons and took to their heels. These arms were acquired by the internees who—foreseeing likely dangers—sought to prepare to defend themselves to the best of their ability.

The climate of uncertainty and chaos created in Italy by the fall of Fascism quickly spread through the camp, involving not only its inhabitants but its very directors. On August 10, General Camillo Mercalli, commander of the army corps for Calabria, made a long on-the-spot inspection, informing the Minister of the Inte-

---

32. Capogreco, *Ferramonti*, pp. 138–39.
33. See Graham, "The Vatican and the Jews" in this volume.

rior afterwards with a full report. On this occasion, the fifty Italian political internees lamented the fact that they had not yet been liberated, as had happened to other internees in different places of detention after the fall of Fascism.[34]

While the political prisoners asked for immediate liberation, the interned Jews and the foreigners of various nationalities, though they too were well aware of the gravity of the moment, did not know with certainty just what they should ask for, or what might await them at the dawning of each new day. Their fears were considerable because they, better than any others in that region, were informed about the developments of the political-military situation by listening to the radio broadcasts of the Allied countries. Consequently, they were in a position to foresee the impending retreat of the German troops from Sicily to the Calabrian territory, with all the possible tragic consequences for the Ferramonti internees, who would find themselves locked behind State Road 19, the principal artery for reaching the north.[35]

On the afternoon of August 27, some Allied fighter planes came close to the camp. Machine-gun fire killed by error four internees and left many others wounded, while an incendiary bomb completely devastated a barracks. Now the war had a direct impact on the camp and claimed its first victims. The tragic happening further aggravated the tension among the prisoners and dramatically presented again to the director Fraticelli the necessity of a rapid evacuation of the camp that might very soon indeed find itself at the center of military operations.[36]

"With the aim of securing the safety of the internees," the director's son recalls, "my father went repeatedly to the prefect of Cosenza and General Mercalli to explain to them the critical nature of the situation."[37] Unfortunately, the authorization from

---

34. Capogreco, *Ferramonti*, pp. 142–44; Simonetta Carolini, *Pericolosi nelle contingenze belliche*, A.N.P.P.I.A. (Rome, 1987), pp. 414–16.

35. "With the overthrow of the Fascist regime Italian racial policy had lost its point. But Marshal Badoglio, having made a public pretense of continuing the war at Germany's side, was understandably reluctant to antagonize his 'ally' by repealing the anti-Jewish laws." (M. Michaelis, *Mussolini and the Jews*, p. 342).

36. Capogreco, *Ferramonti*, pp. 145–46.

37. Testimony of Guido Fraticelli, son of the Ferramonti camp director, in Capogreco, *Ferramonti*, pp. 146–47.

Rome—urgently requested by Cosenza—could not be transmitted because of the Allied bombardments, which had interrupted the communication lines with Calabria. The prefect of Cosenza then decided to send the camp director in person, accompanied by the head of the internees, the lawyer Herbert Landau, to obtain instructions on what to do next.[38]

Meanwhile the British Eighth Army had set foot in Calabria on September 3, 1943, and the news had rapidly reached Ferramonti, where the internees feared that the retreating Germans would be likely to take violent measures against the Jews. Troubled by this fear, before leaving for Rome, director Fraticelli gave precise instructions to vice-director Gaetano Marrari, who stayed behind to supervise the camp in the absence of his superior, that in case the German troops came near, he was to open the gates allowing all the prisoners to get out.

And, in fact, the vehicles of the Herman Göring Panzer Division soon appeared on the horizon, and Marrari had no other choice but to free the internees from the fenced-in area.

Most of the nearly two thousand prisoners then scattered in small groups throughout the hills that overlooked Ferramonti, finding help and solidarity from the local populace, who often sheltered them in their own homes. Only some old and sick people remained inside the camp. To protect them, a group of young people, in order to deceive the Germans and dissuade them from entering the camp, hung on the entrance gate a white and yellow cloth, sign of a cholera epidemic. As a last hope, in case that expedient did not work, those few courageous youths set up a small military post, using the weapons they had acquired from the fleeing Fascist militia.[39]

Dramatic events unfolded in rapid succession that marked the end of an epoch and announced the dawn of liberation. From high on the hills of Santa Sofia d'Epiro, Tarsia, and Bisignano, where they had found safety, the anxious internees could watch the imposing spectacle of the armored Göring Division, pride of the Ger-

---

38. The lawyer Herbert Landau, the last *capo dei capi* of Ferramonti, was born in Cracow, Poland, on December 11, 1891.

39. Bierman, *Odyssey*, p. 203.

man army, rolling along the Crati River, and ascending the peninsula, heading for Salerno. Meanwhile many internees scattered about the countryside continued to search for a secure refuge. Evi Eller, an internee, recalls:

> With a group of friends, we rented a cart from the peasants and carried our few possessions into a school on a nearby hilltop from which you could easily see the road and hear the train that passed through a tunnel. I don't remember very well how many days we stayed up there. In the morning a small American plane flew over our heads and we waved at it frantically, never thinking that it could have machine-gunned us. Because of the many insects, we young people decided to carry our litters out into the open. It was already dark and we were busy talking when we saw fires kindled on all the hills around. The spectacle was very beautiful but we didn't understand its significance. The explanation was given to us by a panting courier who was making the rounds of the various groups of internees. It was September 8, 1943, and the signing of the armistice between Italy and the Allies had been announced.[40]

Down in the valley, on State Highway 19, onto which opened the chief entrance of the camp, the movement of the German forces in retreat went on almost uninterruptedly for three days. On the third day, some vehicles pulled up in front of the camp and a general of the Wehrmacht, accompanied by soldiers, approached the entrance where there was a group of young internees. The general asked for explanations of the camp, the white and yellow cloth, and the small armed post. One of the young men explained that it was a camp for civilian internees, that the few weapons served to defend it from thieves and bandits who were rampaging through the area, and that, unfortunately, inside the camp five cases of cholera had been verified.

The moments that passed while waiting for the German general's reaction were terrible for the youths, who feared that a bluff of this kind could not succeed. But for the men of the Göring Division there was not much time to lose in those September days.

---

40. Testimony of Evi Eller, ex-internee of Ferramonti, in Capogreco, *Ferramonti,* pp. 149–50.

Very urgent tasks awaited them beyond the Pallino, on the Salerno beaches. Therefore, the general made short work of it, giving his men the order not to enter the camp confines and getting quickly back into his car.[41]

Euphoric because of the danger they had escaped, the little group set out toward the south, to meet the advanced elements of the British Eighth Army. On September 14, at around eight in the morning, a tank of the British Eighth Army appeared on the state road and passed through the gates of Ferramonti. The camp seemed deserted. But soon afterward, the few internees who had not followed their companies in flight, ill and malnourished, advanced from the line of barracks toward the big roll-call square, where the British now stationed themselves.

"Friends! We're friends!" the internees shouted, waving a white flag, while the hot sun of a splendid morning lit the first day of liberty for the two thousand prisoners of Ferramonti. And so the liberation of the camp took place, in a totally unexpected manner, the militia and the police having made themselves scarce, the director far away together with the *capo dei capi*, and the greater part of the internees already safe in the hills.

At Ferramonti, with the nightmare of the Germans dispelled and the barbed wire torn down, a new climate of freedom was in the air. The people who had fled left their hiding places and returned to the valley toward the camp from the countryside and the neighboring towns. Meanwhile, a nucleus of the British Eighth Army and a division of the United States Army had established themselves in the offices of the old management, with the intention of reorganizing the old concentration camp to respond to the new necessities.[42]

Once the euphoria of liberation passed, the internees had to face new questions. What to do? Where to go? For many, the anxious

41. "Southern Italy was liberated by the Anglo-Americans before the end of 1943, and while defending it, Kesselring's forces were too fully occupied with military matters to devote much attention to the racial question. Hence the foreign Jews interned . . . were freed after little further suffering," M. Michaelis, *Mussolini and the Jews*, p. 345.

42. Though the Allies had dissolved the old Fascist administration of the camp and abolished the status of "internees" for its inmates, Ferramonti remained active as a transit and collection camp under Allied control until September 1945.

search for family members who might have survived the Nazi persecution began. Some of the Ferramonti men enrolled in the Allied forces to combat the common enemy or put themselves at the disposal of the auxiliary services. Others left for Palestine. A group of 240 Jews reached the United States at the invitation of President Roosevelt. Some Yugoslav Jews were temporarily transferred to Egypt, while many Czechs joined their national army, which was being reorganized in England and Canada.

"When the Allies reached the camp," recounts one of the Czechs, "I weighed barely 87 pounds and even though I was 5 feet 10 inches tall. I was very ill with malaria and was taken care of in the Canadian quarantine station. Nevertheless, I wanted at all costs to go and fight against Hitler, since I had already known at Ferramonti that my parents had been murdered by the Nazis in Auschwitz. The English military doctor did not want to accept me for the army because of my precarious health, but I succeeded in convincing him. We landed in France and fought the Germans at Dunkirk, where many companions who had previously been interned in Italy, fell. When peace was proclaimed, I returned to Czechoslovakia, my Fatherland, to begin a new life. I found not a single one of my relatives. . . . They had all been massacred by the Germans."[43]

The desire to leave those malarial places where one had suffered for so long, the anxiety involved in the search for one's dear ones and one's own home, the wish to reach Palestine, ancient dream of many internees, grew constantly stronger. But how and where to go at the end of 1943, when the hurricane of the war still raged throughout Europe and the world?

The destiny of the ex-camp of Ferramonti remained bound to the march of the broad events of the war. The gradual abandonment of the place by the ex-internees in large and small groups for the most diverse destinations was to continue for another two years, concluding with the end of the war, when all Europe was liberated from the Nazi-Fascist yoke.

43. Testimony of Stefan Strelecky, ex-internee of Ferramonti, in Capogreco, *Ferramonti*, p. 154.

Josef Ithai
(translated by Ivo Herzer)

8. The Children of Villa Emma: Rescue of the Last Youth Aliyah Before the Second World War

The Jews of Yugoslavia rendered much help to the Jewish refugees from Germany and other Nazi-occupied countries. Nothing has ever been written on the subject with special emphasis on the aid, because it was a self-evident matter: Jewish communities are supposed to serve all Jewish needs, including, of course, our co-religionists seeking refuge. But we did not know at the time that we too would find ourselves in the position of refugees seeking help.

We received that help from the Italian people—help extended to us by a nation formally allied with our enemies, our persecutors! The humanitarianism that we found in many circles of Italian people, the army, and even Fascist officials, was comforting next to all that was brutal, merciless, and utterly savage.

After so many years, I remember again those words I was told by our dear friend, Monsignor Don Arrigo Beccari, a priest from Nonantola, who together with Dr. Giuseppe Moreali was awarded the title of "Righteous Among the Nations" and who planted two trees in the alley of the Righteous at Yad Vashem, Jerusalem. When we used to sit in the Abbey of Nonantola, Don Beccari would say: "It is not important what we think, but above all to be *gentile* (humane)." We discussed these principles many times during the dark nights of the Nazi occupation, behind the walls of the monastery of the seminary of Nonantola.

But let us now turn to the story of how our group, unique in the countries under the Nazis, came into being, and how it was saved thanks both to luck and to the many Gentiles who helped us and strengthened our thoroughly shaken faith in mankind.

Toward the end of 1940, Mrs. Recha Freier, who initiated the concept and implemented the idea of the Youth Aliyah (an educational institution in Palestine which gave Israel so many good people), arrived illegally in Zagreb, Yugoslavia. Recha Freier created the idea of the *Aliyah Noar* (Youth Aliyah) in 1933 in Berlin, and she began to send the first youth groups to Palestine. When this experiment succeeded, an office was established in Jerusalem under the direction of Mrs. Henriette Szold. Recha Freier remained in Berlin and contributed a great deal to the rescue of Jews originally from Poland, as well as their children. She organized groups who were to go first to Yugoslavia and then, as children of the Youth Aliyah, proceed to Palestine. After the plan was set up, Recha came to Zagreb (where I lived) to present it to the Zionist organization of Yugoslavia.[1] The Jews of Yugoslavia already lived in fear of the Nazi aggression that was eventually to come, but they nevertheless took upon themselves the responsibility for implementing Recha's plan. I was asked by the Hashomer Hatzair (youth organization of the Zionist Labor wing) and Recha Freier to be the *madrich* (educator, teacher) for those children during their stay in Zagreb. It was to last but a short time, because we did not think we would be able to protect them, as "illegals," for a longer period.

The children came in groups, and I would go to a certain location in the suburbs of Zagreb to receive them from the German guides. It proved to be a deeply moving experience for me, a twenty-three-year old, who knew only the reality of the Zionist youth movement, but had not yet come into contact with the hardships of life and the reality of Nazi persecution. Still, I was able to overcome my diffidence and help the children so that soon we became friends.

Our First Righteous Gentile—Police Commissioner Uroš Žun in Maribor

Toward the end of January 1940, a group of sixteen girls, mostly from Berlin, was scheduled to arrive. When they did not arrive, we

1. Zagreb (the capital of Croatia) was the main center of Yugoslav Zionism and also the starting point of this initiative.

feared that something had happened to them. And indeed, the entire group had been arrested by the Yugoslavs: I found them in a hotel in Maribor (a small Slovenian town on the Yugoslav border with German-annexed Austria), being taken care of by Commissioner of the Border Police Uroš Žun. Žun became involved in the rescue of those children despite the threat of the local Nazis. He refused to carry out the orders of the higher authorities in Belgrade to hand over the children to the Germans. The whole town of Maribor was stirred up; the newspapers wrote, "we will not give up our little girls," and so they were saved.

Žun was our first Righteous Gentile. He ultimately obtained approval for the children to stay on Yugoslav territory. Events that followed were so overpowering and stormy that for a time we even forgot his name. Only recently have we managed to get recognition for him, even though he died in Ljubljana (the capital of Slovenia) in 1977.[2] We had the good fortune, however, to come across other Righteous Gentiles as we were buffeted by our destiny. There were many more who sympathized with us and gave us help on our long journey. It was important for our children to see that not only Nazis existed in this world, but also good people who had not lost the faith and courage to be humane.[3]

In the meantime, more refugees kept arriving in Zagreb. Children came with parents who asked us to take their children; somehow, they believed that it would be better for the children to be in a group together—and the group kept growing. At the last moment, we succeeded in sending Recha Freier to Palestine, as well as ninety children soon thereafter, when they finally obtained the "certificate."[4]

I left Zagreb with them on March 27, 1941, on the day of the Serbian coup that overthrew the pro-German government. We did not know whether I could get to Belgrade, since telephone com-

2. Only while writing my book did I remember that we owe Uroš our acknowledgment. We could not even remember his name and it took several years to learn his name. I take this opportunity to thank the State Archive of the Republic of Slovenia for their cordial cooperation in answering all my questions.

3. On Commissioner Žun's rescue activity, see *Yaldey Villa Emma* (Tel-Aviv: Moreshet, Sifriyat Hapoalim, 1983) (in Hebrew), pp. 22–26.

4. The "certificate" was the confirmation that the Mandatory Power in Palestine (Great Britain) had approved entry of the individual into Palestine.

munications with the capital were cut. The Croatian political leadership fell completely silent; we all knew that the Croatians were not on the side of the new government in Belgrade and its anti-Hitler coup. The situation was potentially quite dangerous. Under orders from the Jewish community to "go anywhere as long as it is closer to Palestine. Do not stay in Zagreb," I took these children with the certificates. We left with considerable monies to tide us over for a few days and heavy hearts, not knowing what the next hour would bring.

We reached Belgrade without difficulty. Belgrade was quiet the night after the coup. We walked in twos; Serbian officers kept stopping us and, obviously moved, were enthusiastic in wanting to help us. An apparently important general shouted obscenely at the custodian of the office of the Union of the Jewish Communities of Yugoslavia to let us in so we could take a rest.

The next day, after the children had somehow managed to board the last train for Greece, I returned via Osijek, where my parents and my brother lived, to Zagreb. The remaining children were waiting for me there. One of them, sixteen-year-old Ehud, asked me, "Did you really come back? We are not used to people keeping faith."

On April 6, 1941, Germany and Italy attacked Yugoslavia and totally defeated the army in a few days. The Jewish community now stood as the main defense of the Jews. The 2,000-year tradition of Jewish self-help, which was always effective during the Diaspora, turned out, however, to be ill-fated.

The Axis partners dismembered Yugoslavia and set up the so-called Independent State of Croatia (NDH) under the *Ustaša*; they were Croatian nationalists who had operated as terrorists before 1941. Their political program was based on a fanatical hatred of Orthodox Serbs (a sizeable minority in Croatia) and a virulent anti-Semitism. The *Ustaša* state was a puppet of Nazi Germany. The Italians occupied the Croatian Adriatic littoral. Slovenia, the westernmost part of Yugoslavia, was subdivided into an Italian and German zone; Serbia was under German occupation.[5]

5. The *Ustaša* were an ultra-nationalist Croatian party founded during the Austro-

The Role of the Jewish Community
During the Occupation

The leaders of the Zagreb Community were undoubtedly good
people with the best intentions and the conviction that the Jewish
population must be "organized," because that way we would be
more able to withstand the assault by the Nazis, as in all other
occupied lands. However, among all of our Zionist leaders, only
Dr. Hans Hochsinger knew the reality we were facing. He kept
insisting (without anyone willing to listen), "Close the Community offices, do not collaborate, the *Ustaša* are deceiving you, they
will kill all of us. Don't give them gold or anything else. If they
threaten to kill the hostages, let them! They intend to kill us
anyway.... Gold is the only thing a Jew needs when fleeing."
Unfortunately, no one listened to Hans, and as a noted business-
man with international contacts, he was among the first ones to
be murdered.

The Zagreb Community office was forced by the *Ustaša* to issue
yellow cloth badges that every Jew had to wear in front and back.
Our people were defiant and took the badges proudly. I, too,
proudly distributed those badges, in the name of the Community,
and entered all the personal data in the files.

Ehud told me, "Don't give us the badge. We don't need it to be
proud Jews, and you don't know what you're doing. You are creating a file for the Gestapo; we went through this in Vienna—don't
give us the badge." Fortunately I took his advice, in the midst of
that initial atmosphere of yielding.

First Contact with the Italians

I was thus left with approximately forty children who were illegally in Zagreb when the Nazis established the Independent State
of Croatia. The *Ustaša* state proved to be the most savage and
ferocious ally of Hitler against our people. All the children were

Hungarian monarchy by a converted Jew, Joseph Frank. In the 1920s, the party program became anti-Semitic and Fascist. The *Ustaša* were among the most bloodthirsty
collaborators of the Nazis.

dejected and the older ones kept saying, "You see, Hitler is pursuing us. One day he'll catch us."

At that time, we came upon the only possible way out: to take the children to Italian-occupied Slovenia in northern Yugoslavia. Ljubljana (Lubiana), the capital, was the seat of Italian High Commissioner Emilio Grazioli. I took the train to Ljubljana, with a regular travel permit and certainly without the yellow badge, for Jews were already forbidden to travel by train.

Eugenio Bolaffio, the representative in Ljubljana of Delasem (Delasem was the great and distinguished organization created by Italian Jewry to aid refugees), informed Grazioli. Grazioli at first would not even consider the idea of issuing an official entry permit for the children;[6] after a lengthy discussion, he exclaimed in exasperation, "Why you idiots, scoundrels, just bring them!" I rushed back to Zagreb.

I should mention here the great opportunity that Ljubljana offered at the time (May 1941): I was able to spread the news of what was happening in Croatia to neutral countries of Europe, Switzerland and Portugal. I phoned Natan Schwalb in Geneva who was the representative of the Histadrut (Jewish Labor Federation) and the kibbutz movement in Europe. He stayed in Geneva during the war and was the only support of the various *halutz* (Jewish pioneers) movements in Europe. For us, Natan was both a symbol and a helping hand. I also phoned Joseph Schwartz of the American Jewish Joint Distribution Committee (the "Joint") in Lisbon. I told them what was happening. Today, we know that Yugoslavia was the site of the first attempt at exterminating Jews using all means; the infamous Jasenovac camp was already in operation.

In Ljubljana I spoke for the first time with the functionaries of Delasem. At first, they did not understand why I should bring the children to Ljubljana. However, when I told Dr. Enrico Luzzato,

---

6. Delasem (Delegazione di Assistenza agli Emigranti Ebrei) was the Italian Jewish aid organization for refugees, founded on December 1, 1939, following a reorganization of the Union of the Italian Jewish Communities. The President of Delasem was the lawyer Lelio Vittorio Valobra; the main office was in Genoa. Delasem did very much to help refugees in every way. It was certainly one of the most important creations of Italian Jewry. Enrico Luzzato was the first Secretary, and Bernardo Grosser was the second.

the secretary of Delasem, that *mavet* (Hebrew for "death") was threatening the children, he understood and pledged to take care of us.

In contacts with Italians in Ljubljana I got to know their mentality. They hated the Germans; they made an effort to admit all the Jewish refugees who were fleeing Croatia; they always let us know that their feelings were on our side. We were yet to see how much the Italian people would do for us: more than anyone else in Europe. Yet the Fascist regime was Hitler's ally—something the Italians themselves did not understand.

Lesno Brdo—Our Second Stage

I returned to Zagreb to pick up the children. But what about the Germans and their Croatian collaborators? How would I be able to take almost fifty children and adults across a border that was becoming more and more sealed? There were rumors that the Italians were turning back our people, that the *Ustaša* were shooting everyone who was fleeing.

The Zagreb Jewish Community, with the help of a policeman, prepared an official-looking document, showing the names of the children and the adults traveling with us and bearing a seal of the "Kingdom of Yugoslavia," which, of course, had no significance or importance anymore. The Community still had a few connections left, and some money.

So it was that one Sunday morning in June I took my poor children, when the streets were calm, and we proceeded on foot toward the main railroad station. By that time Jews were already forbidden to walk without the badge, and to travel by train was clearly punishable by death. Nevertheless, I somehow chose the most audacious option: I was going to do the very thing they thought we would not dare to do. It was not heroism or outstanding cleverness; it was simply the only option available to me on that day. I bought the tickets, and we occupied an entire car. The children understood the situation very well. They had already crossed one border illegally. They knew and felt with all their senses that they must be quiet, they must be good actors, and they must not cry.

The train started to move, and when a policeman came to check the documents, I held the paper carrying the seal of former Yugoslavia with our names at some distance from him. Luckily, he did not come near to check the paper, but said, "All right."

Thus we came to the border between the Independent State of Croatia and Italian-occupied Slovenia, which the Italians had annexed under the name of *Provincia di Lubiana.* What would happen now? All I had was a picture of Lesno Brdo, a town with an old castle where we would be staying, and High Commissioner Grazioli's verbal invitation shouted at Bolaffio and me, to "bring the children for God's sake," even cursing at Bolaffio's expense.

We waited quite nervously for the Italian border police to show up. What a pleasant surprise it turned out to be for the children—for all of us. Two young, stern officers entered the car and demanded entry permits. In poor Italian, I explained that we had no papers, but that we were running from the Germans, and that High Commissioner Grazioli knew about us. "Here is the picture of the castle I leased." At that point the two officers left abruptly without a word. All of a sudden we saw a commotion and heard shouting at the station. Then a group of soldiers started running toward our car, carrying something in their hands. "My God," I thought, "what now? Is this the end of our idyl?" But the Italians began to throw candies and other sweets into the car. This kindness was almost beyond the endurance of our tense nerves. I saw the children with happy tears in their eyes, and the Italians shouted, "But why are they persecuting children? Why?"

The train moved into Italian-occupied territory and came to a brief halt at a small station. Again, Italian soldiers were running in our direction, shouting greetings. "Have no fear. . . . Everything is alright." And it was the same from station to station. At each station there was a festive reception for us. We were celebrating the triumph of Jewish children. Then we understood, especially the children, that the Italians are a sensitive, humane people, and that Fascism could not corrupt them.

In this way, with tears and joy at having been saved, we arrived at the main station of Ljubljana, the seat of the high commissioner. In the middle of the track stood an Italian general, heavy set, decorated with numerous ribbons and medals memorializing Abyssinia and all the glorious wars of Mussolini. The general looked into the car, tears in his eyes, and barked the order, "Clear the waiting room for the children."

He asked me, "Why? What on earth did you do?" Meanwhile, the children were already in the waiting room where Red Cross nurses and soldiers were offering them tea and cookies. I remember how stunned we all were, especially the children from Germany, toward whom, for the first time, men in uniform were acting with kindness. For the boys from Vienna, who had already experienced the concentration camps under Eichmann's rule, this was also a great surprise. Since that time, "Italian" has been for all of us synonymous with humaneness.

A car in the train for Drenov Grič, the station of Lesno Brdo, was already waiting for us. As we were getting off the train, I felt happy, thinking, now I shall take these orphans along the serpentine way to the top of the mountain, to the old Hapsburg castle. Beautiful nature, everywhere the sweet fragrance from the beauty and richness of flowers and vegetation. And so we were on our way up the hill, surrounded by the forest, the lovely Slovene landscape, and distant mountains. Lesno Brdo itself was built on the top with a view of the Horjulska Dolina, a magnificent valley amid mountains with the Alps in the distance. I exclaimed, "Look children, how beautiful everything is!" Ehud glanced at me crossly and half angrily said: "What is so beautiful—the SS will get us here too." I tried a little more to influence them but without success: they had already forgotten the attitude of the Italians and sunk again into despair—refugees without hope.

Lesno Brdo—Youth in a Distorted Reality

We arrived at Lesno Brdo, where we would remain from July 1941 until July 1942. It was 400 years old and had once been a royal Hapsburg hunting castle. The water supply came from the cistern on the roof. We had no provisions. Bolaffio had done all he could to provide what we needed, but it was difficult and slow. Understandably, our children, who had suffered so much, found it hard to calm down. It was also difficult to find the right psychological approach to restore their trust. After some time, however, we got organized. The adults lived on the top floor, which was the center from which we conducted all the important talks with the various "committees" of our community. On the ground floor were the dining room, kitchen, and parlor, where we were fortunate to have a piano.

Without the piano, Lesno Brdo cannot be comprehended, because the late Dr. Boris Jochvedson played the piano whenever he was not suffering from a headache. He was an excellent pianist, a pupil of Glazunov's in Leningrad. In 1920 he escaped as a Social Revolutionary (or at least he believed he was one) and taught piano in Berlin.

Who helped me care for these children? This had been a problem as far back as Zagreb. I did not dare to take care of everything myself. (It later became evident that I could rely upon the sixteen- and seventeen-year-old boys and girls.) And so I enlisted Jochvedson, although he was rather depressed, because I felt cultural support was very important for the children. I also needed someone to take care of our economic affairs; I engaged Marko Schoki (Silberschatz), who knew how to procure supplies under black market conditions. From Zagreb I brought Dr. Helene Barkić, a graduate pharmacist who took over the health care; the late Moritz Awin claimed to know how to cook, and so he cooked.

We attempted to teach the children something; this proved to be a challenge because of the differences in the ages of the children (seven to seventeen years), the sexes, and the religious backgrounds (some came from Orthodox families and others from a secular Jewish Viennese background). Only a few had been in the youth movement, which was quite essential for the evolving atmosphere.

Italian officers who used to visit us brought a radio, and together we listened to BBC broadcasts from London. The Fascists among them could not comprehend. One said to me: "Explain to me: we are friends with Hitler. He is persecuting you while we receive you gladly and defend you. How does this fit all together, where is the consistency?" I did not clarify it for him.

Soon, however, Tito's partisans began to appear. I became fearful that they might clash with our boys, who would naturally shout in German all over the woods. The partisans would then immediately open fire. Therefore, we arranged a meeting with them. We told them who and what we were. Their young *politruk* (political commissar) showed good understanding for my "Marxist theory of Zionism" and we became friends. Lesno Brdo became the night shelter for the partisans. I received from Natan Schwalb in Switzerland many medicines that I turned over to the "sick red uncle," i.e., the partisans.

But when the Italians decided to fight the partisans, things became more difficult: the Italians saw that the partisans came to visit us. Their flag was flying outside the house during each visit, and below in Horjul that flag could be seen by the Italians. I explained to the Italians that I did not know what to do: the partisans come and threaten us with weapons. The Italians told us, "In God's name do not resist, the children might be killed."

An Italian general decided that "war cannot be waged amid children." We were to leave next day for Nonantola, Italy, to stay at Villa Emma. Meanwhile, the partisans had blocked all the roads with trees and no one dared to remove them. We had to obtain a letter from the partisan commander, our good friend Josip Černi, ordering all villagers to give us horses and wagons to carry our belongings to the station in the morning.[7] There was a discussion among us whether we should really leave the ideal Lesno Brdo, but I made the decision to go. With a heavy heart, we took leave of Lesno Brdo. The proprietress of the castle shouted and cursed us, because she knew that the Italians would remove her from that strategic location.

The train was taking us toward Italy, and the children became gradually used to the new situation. Only Berta, our poor Berta, was again sad and apathetic. Ever since the small parcel that the Joint had mailed from Lisbon to her mother in a concentration camp was returned with the ominous stamp "address unknown," Berta had been constantly in tears from pain. Her mother was no more.

---

7. Josip Černi was of Croat origin. This was his alias and we never learned his real name. The Archives of the Republic of Slovenia list him as killed in the fall of 1942.

We arrived in Mestre, a suburb of Venice. Our car was detached
from the train and then reattached. A few long hours passed while
the small children kept pestering me: "You are really impossible;
why, we are almost in Venice. Are we to miss seeing the city? Why
can't you allow us to see it?" I did not know what was happening
during our delay in Mestre. We thought: "It is wartime, the trains
are crowded, one must wait." We learned the truth, however, after
the war: during our stay in Mestre, there was a heated dispute
between the Italians and the Nazis regarding our fate. The Germans demanded that our car be directed to Verona and from there
"east" (it seems that this had been agreed upon way back), but a
general of the *carabinieri*, Giuseppe Pièche, having been informed
by Delasem of our plight, stepped in resolutely opposed to this and
ordered the car to be taken to Modena and Nonantola.[8] After the
war, Pièche received the gold medal of recognition from the Union
of the Jewish Communities of Italy for this action and for other
help to Jews in Italy. General Pièche, together with other high
officers and senior officials of the Foreign Ministry, did everything
possible to thwart the German intentions. These noble and courageous men intelligently and resolutely sabotaged all demands to

8. Ilva Vaccari, *Villa Emma* (Modena: Istituto della Resistenza Modena e Provincia, 1960), pp. 19–20. This book, the first publication about our story, is full of
inaccurate details. Chasja Pincus, *Come from the Four Winds, the Story of Youth
Aliya* (New York: Herzl Press, 1970), ch. III, "The Doctor and the Priest," pp. 90–
108. This is a discussion with a few of the children and adults about the group's
formation and development. Josef Ithai-Indig, "Djeca bježe," Almanah Saveza Jevrejskih Opština, 1963–64, p. 120. This is a brief summary of the rescue story. Comune
di Nonantola, *Ventennale della Resistenza* (Nonantola, 1965), with Joseph Ithai's
article about the group of children and its relations with the resistance in Nonantola,
including the picture of the presentation of the Yad Vashem award to two Righteous
Gentiles in Nonantola. Sergio Minerbi, *Raffaele Cantoni. Un ebreo anticonformista*
(Rome: Carucci, 1978). Minerbi mentions Lesno Brdo and Villa Emma on pp. 113–14.
I giorni di Villa Emma (Modena, 1978). This book is the result of an educational
project of Don Gilli, a young priest and teacher in Nonantola. In order to explain the
Fascist era to his pupils, he sent them to inquire in the village what happened to the
children of Villa Emma. The book contains reports of the inhabitants of Nonantola
who helped us during the German occupation. Daniel Carpi, "The Rescue of Jews in
the Italian Zone of Occupied Croatia," in *Rescue Attempts During the Holocaust*
(Jerusalem: Yad Vashem, 1977), pp. 465–525. Also, this was the first time that the
letter of the General of the *carabinieri*, Giuseppe Pièche, to the Ministry of Foreign
Affairs was published, stating that all the Jews who had been sent from Croatia to
the "East" were gassed. This was the general who saved our group when we were on
the train near Venice. Josef Ithai, *Yaldey Villa Emma* (Tel-Aviv: Moreshet and Sifriyat Hapoalim, 1983). Detailed history of the group from their arrival in Yugoslavia
till their entry into Switzerland, with many photographs.

hand over Jews, using all kinds of excuses for non-compliance with orders. These facts came to be known recently from Italian archives.[9] Not only did the Italian population help Jewish refugees, but the highest-ranking bureaucrats made possible the rescue of tens of thousands of Jews, particularly from Croatia, who kept coming in waves to the Italian border, and most of whom were admitted.

There were, however, problems. Villa Emma did not yet belong to us. The president of the Jewish Community in Modena, Gino Friedmann, had made all the arrangements with the authorities, but we still had to wait to enter the villa in Nonantola. We liked and respected Gino Friedmann very much. He was an unusually cultured and deserving man, widely honored, who was awarded the honorific title of *commendatore* (knight of an Italian order of chivalry) by the government. He strived to show an understanding for all kinds of problems, big and small. As we were sitting outside the building, sad and tired, the local commander of the *carabinieri* ordered all the locks smashed so that we could go in. All the necessary permits and orders would come later. Thus began our life in Nonantola.

We were quite startled when all of a sudden the local inhabitants began to gather and stand waiting in the vicinity of the villa. I summoned my courage to ask: "Eh, good people, what are you waiting for?" "Well, is it really true?," said an old woman, "Is it true that you boil rice in milk for these poor children as a sweet dish?"

When I confirmed it, not knowing the significance of such a way to prepare a dish, they began to wail: "*O Dio mio, poveri bambini,*" (Oh my God, poor children). The whole group, mostly older women, children, and old men, then left in a hurry. We had hardly regained our composure when they returned, each woman with a small flask of oil: "So that the poor children may eat well. Who would boil rice, which should be fried in oil?" Then we understood.

---

9. Menachem Shelach, *Cheshbon Damim, Hatzalah yehudei Kroatia al-yedei ha-italkim 1941–1943 (Blood Account. The Rescue of Croatian Jews by the Italians 1941–1943)* (Tel Aviv: Sifriat Poalim, 1986). Many of his sources were also used by Daniel Carpi, "The Rescue of Jews."

To eat rice boiled in milk was bad enough, but to sweeten it was, from the Italian point of view, truly the lowest level to which a person could sink. In their fashion the good people of Nonantola showed us from the very start that they identified with us as equals, without any trace of the racist theories that they despised.

Lesno Brdo, with all of its romantic surroundings, was for us ancient history. And Lombardy, flat, without mountains, without rapid and noisy streams, what did it hold for us? Would we be able to adjust?

The Year in Villa Emma (Nonantola), July 1942–September 1943

Our life became regular while we constantly tried to improve it. Thus we were able to realize a dream: to give the children vocational training in workshops provided by ORT, an international Jewish organization.[10] In time, a carpentry workshop with a master carpenter was set up, where a few of our young people learned their future trade. For our older children, it was important that the Delasem office had moved to Villa Emma. A few youngsters found useful work in that office, especially in the warehouse of Delasem, which was also transferred to the villa. Villa Emma thus became a center for assistance to Jewish emigrants where we ourselves could also render help. I found among lists of Jewish emigrants our Zionists and other youths, and I began to organize aid from Istanbul and Switzerland. I distributed the funds we received according to my best ability. Hehalutz (the Zionist organization supporting settlements of pioneers in Palestine) in Geneva, through Natan Schwalb, stood by me, insisting that my educational philosophy, based on *halutz* principles, be respected. Hehalutz also sent funds to Villa Emma through the Delasem office so that we could continue to preserve the specific social and Zionist ideals in the educational process of the children.

Despite the fears of the director of the villa, Dr. Umberto Jacchia

10. ORT, an international Jewish organization for vocational education, founded in 1880 in St. Petersburg (now Leningrad). Its main offices are in Geneva. ORT was active during World War II.

and his wife Laura, who stayed permanently at the Villa, the relations between our children and the population of Nonantola became ever closer. The local police tolerated these relations, and there were no incidents.

My friendship with the priests of the local abbey and with Dr. Giuseppe Moreali grew ever closer, so we naturally took them to represent the people of Nonantola. My talks with Don Arrigo Beccari and the late priest from Modena, Don Rossi, only strengthened my hope for a better future.

One of the most beautiful events of our year in Nonantola was our friendship with the Jewish youth of Florence. The group was led by Matilde Cassin, who was raising the youngsters in the spirit of the progressive Italian Judaism, a mixture of leftist ideas, messianic metaphysics, and progressive socialism. It had a little of everything, but it was unusually beautiful and idealistic. Those young Italians saw the children of Villa Emma as their brothers and sisters. Friendships were formed that meant perhaps more for our orphans than personal material salvation. Whoever saw how they were striving to make friends and how they kept in touch by means of letters that were continuously on their way between Nonantola and Florence could easily imagine how much we could have done had the circumstances and fear not hampered us.

For us adults it was an indescribable pleasure to meet with Raffaele Cantoni, who was very much liked. He lived in Florence under police surveillance, but he had the courage to come to us to talk and dream together about everything: the working people of the new Judaism in Zion; his messianic ardor; the synthesis of Zionism, socialism, and religion in the best sense—religion without clericalism. Once I visited Raffaele in Florence and stayed overnight at his home, under which, in the Loggia dei Lanzi, stood the statue of Perseus by Cellini. Again we had discussions that opened my eyes to an interesting epoch of Italian Judaism, of which he was the highest embodiment till his death.

All of these moving events could not, however, soothe our youths: the war went on and the year 1942–43 did not bring them tranquility. The news was bad; there was no calm in Villa Emma, and laughter was rare until the Germans began to retreat. Still, children are children, and we also put on happy shows. The children and the adolescents already felt that some form of freedom was on the horizon.

Spring came and at the beginning of April 1943, a group of Yugoslav children, led by Jakob Altaras, a member of the Hashomer Hatzair, arrived in Villa Emma from Split (Spalato). At that time the *Ustaša* were ferociously persecuting the Jews with the help of the Germans. The Jewish Community of Split had succeeded in sending thirty-three Jewish children from various places in Yugoslavia to Split, and the Italians had agreed to let the children join our group in Nonantola.

The Chief of Police Understands Our Intentions

One day Gino Friedmann, our Delasem representative to the Fascist authorities in Modena, told me he was very worried because I was summoned to the *questura* (police headquarters) in Modena, where I was to answer all sorts of questions. I had no idea what to expect, and he was going with me.

As we sat down in the office of the chief of the Modena police, I went limp at the sight of a stack of my letters to foreign countries—their censorship was quite efficient. I corresponded widely with all Europe, especially with the Committee for Aid in Istanbul, with Natan Schwalb (Hehalutz) in Geneva, with the Joint in Lisbon, and with Richard Lichtheim of the Jewish Agency office in Switzerland. I had a continuous correspondence with Joseph Kaplan in Warsaw (a leader of Hashomer Hatzair) until he was murdered in the fall of 1942; with Hendeles in Bratislava; with Zvi Földi in Budapest; and with friends interned in Korčula (Curzola), an Italian-occupied island in the southern Adriatic. All of these letters lay before me. The chief asked me, "What do these words mean: '*Eretz*,' '*kessef*,' '*moledet*,' '*havilot*'?" It was my principle always to tell the truth to everyone, and it turned out that this was the best policy even under those circumstances. I replied, "'Palestine,' 'money,' 'homeland,' 'packages.'" He then said: "Why in the world don't you write it in German? But we all know that you wish to go to Palestine, may it come true with God's will.

You need money, there is nothing wrong with that. Just write so that we can understand you." Again, we saw the extraordinary way in which the Italians looked at the Jews in general. This police chief was undoubtedly a Fascist, but he was surely not an anti-Semite.

At that time we began to correspond a great deal on the possibility of a direct voyage from Italy to Palestine. The Italian government agreed with the idea, but the problem was the availability of shipping, even more than the question of immigration certificates from the British. Apart from the danger from mines, there was no ship captain who would agree to take us across the turbulent Mediterranean. But we did not lose hope, and I continued working in the Delasem office on the documents for the children.

The Fall of Mussolini

Mussolini fell from power on July 25, 1943. Sonja wrote as follows in her diary (July 26, 1943):

I have to mention first of all that a lot changed politically. Mussolini has been overthrown! It is not possible to go to Modena. All roads are blocked by tanks. I hope all this will end well for us.

The older boys understood the significance of the events. Boris was still a bit skeptical, and all of us wanted to know details. The new conditions soon engulfed Nonantola also; the settling of old accounts with the Fascists was about to erupt. Dr. Moreali ran to us:

Dear Indig, I have been waiting twenty years for this day and here it is! It is easier to breathe, the air is clean. You will feel better in Italy which is not dark any longer. Now you will get to know the real, true Italy. Look how happy our people are. The Fascists will have to hide behind their lists.

Don Beccari said:

I hope all this will end well. And how are the children now? Excuse me, I must hurry to the church to pray. We must seek

God and thank Him that one tyrant has been overthrown, and pray so that He should topple the other one too.

Large posters cropped up: "Long live democracy! Death to all Fascists!" Fascist emblems, as well as slogans and all the reminders of that oppressive regime, began to disappear. The first few days were peaceful in Nonatola, but one day as we were coming home from a trip to Modena we saw a crowd of bitter opponents of Fascism thrashing one of the local Fascist leaders. "He got what he deserved, the Fascist swine," remarked one of those present. "This secretary, this nobody—finally Pietro could revenge himself for the suffering he had to go through." The man was lying on the road, wounded and bleeding, when Moreali, a physician and anti-Fascist—but above all a humanist—asked the people: "Friends, I am a doctor, you know me, help me get him home." But no one made a move to help. And so he, a prominent victim of Fascism, stayed to watch over the wounded man. Not until his son came along were they able to take care of the man. Someone shouted from afar: "Let him get up by himself. Let him ask for help from Mussolini."

Preparations for the Hard Times

Days rushed by. Despite friendships between a few Germans and Croatians among our children, mutual antagonism was strong. My worries deepened regarding the future of the group. On August 17, we received identity cards from the authorities in case we needed them. Everyone worked on these documents—Don Beccari, Dr. Moreali, and the local municipal employees in Nonantola; they all understood it was necessary. After the war, it was reported that they had issued us cards of a fictitious town "Larino" in the south and that Dr. Moreali had signed them. Larino exists and it seems such cards were issued to Jews who came to Nonantola after our flight. We went with "real" cards, except that the town was not supposed to issue them to us. Yet since they simply wrote in our true nationality, they were stating the truth.

We surely needed to look after our safety. Soon after September 8, when we were already hiding, German soldiers arrived and set up a military hospital in the school across the way. The swastika flag was waving across from Villa Emma.

During August, everybody expected the Allies to appear. Our director, Jacchia, disappeared on August 7, and did not come back. Long after the war, I met him in Israel. Jacchia had been a partisan for the remainder of the war, a socialist.

The Armistice and Mussolini's Social Republic

Marshal Badoglio signed Italy's surrender to the Allies on September 8. Italy ended her ill-fated war. We were all glad, but somehow in our hearts we knew that we were facing new trials. All of the Delasem functionaries had disappeared, with the exception of our good friend Goffredo Pacifici. It was known that the Germans would react sharply to Italy's exit from the war. In fact, we heard German tanks that very evening across from Villa Emma. It was decided to abandon Villa Emma: There were almost one hundred Jewish children and adults at the meeting! I went to speak with our friends at the seminary. I knocked on the ancient door of the abbey: "It's me, Indig. May I speak with Monsignor Pelati?" Old Pelati, a good man, the abbot[11] of Nonantola, came quickly. "What is it Indig, what worries you?" "Monsignor, we must hide the children. The older ones we can hide in the countryside and I would like to come to you with the little ones, to the seminary, please!" "Well, of course, actually our archbishop forbids us to help you, but we are Christians so let the boys come." "Monsignor, our little girls, they too want to live!" "Indig, this is difficult, for almost one thousand years there were no girls here; but, so be it . . . in the name of God, the Son and the Holy Spirit." Our old Pelati crossed himself. "Let the children come."

Some minutes later, I came with a procession of the children to be hidden within the shelter of the ancient monastery of the old Nonantola Abbey. There, letters by Charlemagne are kept, and in the consecration by King Louis the Pious this very abbey is mentioned—the abbey that gave shelter to Jewish victims of Nazism.

11. Monsignor Pelati was actually only vicarius (a deputy abbot), because the abbot was either the pope or the Archbishop of Modena.

For the time being, we settled down on benches. The next day, the pasta machine of the abbey began to turn out spaghetti for the children, while our older boys carried bags of wheat that we had from the villa. There were a few nuns in the seminary, and the good souls kept praying for the salvation of our children.

At night we talked, Don Beccari, Monsignor Pelati, Don Tardini, and others, about Zionism, socialism, faith in God, honesty, fascism. The thick walls guarded our free words. It was unusually good and pleasant to talk about everything in an atmosphere of complete freedom and mutual respect. Don Beccari kept stressing, "It is not so much what our outlook on the world is. It is only important whether we are *gentiluomini* (honest people, gentlemen)."

What should we do next?

Don Beccari had the idea that I should take the children south, as a Catholic priest with orphans, and cross the battle line to the Allies. To this end, he took a picture of me dressed as a priest, but it soon became apparent that this could not be carried out with so many children.

Several older boys requested that they be allowed to go south. When I could not persuade them to stay with us, we bade our farewells. I gave them some money; it was not until 1945 that we met in Palestine.

Then my torments began. We tried to get in touch with the Italian partisans in our region and on the Swiss border. Pacifici, the last Delasem employee who had stayed with us, helped us in this endeavor. It seems that in this too our friends in Nonantola made it possible for us to establish contact. But how were we to pay for the passage to Switzerland? Nobody would take us without charge, which was 1,000 lire per child. That was then equivalent to 1 Swiss franc. How could I get in touch with Natan in Switzerland, since phone lines were cut? I made up my mind to go to the border to try to make contact. Since this was our only chance, it was not actually difficult to make that decision. At the border in Como, I simply waited to spot someone coming from Switzerland who looked like a nice person. I thought I would then give him Natan's number and ask him to call Natan the next day, asking him to bring us the 120,000 lire. And so I did. I saw someone coming from the Swiss side, who looked like a trustworthy person. I started talking to him, and he said, "Come with me." "My God, where?" I thought.

It was all right, however; we entered a café where everything was quietly discussed. The next day he came a bit later than he promised—those were difficult minutes for me—and brought all the money and some change plus small Swiss cheeses to give to the children. I cannot forgive myself that in my excitement I failed to write down his name and address: all I know is that he was from Zürich.

I returned to Nonantola without problems. Everyone was agitated, faces white from fear. Our Italian friends who had contacts at the German headquarters informed us that the manhunt for Jews was to begin in approximately ten days. The Germans had freed Mussolini, who proclaimed his "Italian Social Republic." It was now only a question of time. Mussolini bowed completely to his German masters. Anti-Jewish decrees were issued, and we were seized with terror at what the future would bring for us and the Jews of Italy.

In the meantime, we sent a small advance group to try to cross into Switzerland. Despite the fact that they came back, I took half of the children and adults, and we were on our way. We all had identity cards from Nonantola. Before Milan, the train suddenly stopped. What did it mean? "Well, this is the Social Republic," someone said. Through the window we saw SS troopers boarding the train. I thought, "Is this the end?" I told the children to show their identity cards as soon as any inspectors appeared, and to be quiet. It went all right, but at the last moment a young Italian barged into the car telling us he was a partisan and asked us to hide him. Of course, the children put him under a bench, sat on it, and saved him. After the inspection, which went without a hitch, we gave him money and an identity card without a picture, so that he could take care of his situation.

We arrived in Milan, but the train for Varese, where we had to change to a local train to Ponte Tresa near the border, was due to depart the next day. How were we to pass the night during the curfew?

The Public Restroom in Front of
the Railroad Station of Milan

We had Pacifici with us. This man set himself the task of working for the rescue of Italian and foreign Jews and, as a result, he
himself paid with his life. We mourn him as a prototype of the
positive Italian Jew, without any vanity whatever, a proletarian of
Italian Jewry. With his assistance, we entered the underground
public restroom in front of the main Milan railroad terminal. Our
poor children huddled up like sardines and sat quietly, very quietly,
or lay waiting for dawn. That huddled mass was symbolic of our
situation. How they endured their martyrdom, squeezed and cramped
as they were, without any disturbance, conscious of the fact that
we all shared the same fate!

Early the next day, the owner of the restroom came and opened
the doors. We left slowly, not all at the same time, went into the
station and waited for the train to Varese. O restroom in front of
the Milan rail terminal—we will remember you!

On to Free Switzerland!

We left the small train at its last stop, where our guide was
waiting. Who was he? Could we trust him? Did we have even the
luxury of not trusting him? He gave the password, started to walk,
and we followed him. We took leave of good Pacifici, never to see
him again.

Behind us walked a Jewish family from Bengasi. The father was
deaf and kept shouting so that I was afraid he would alert the
Germans. I ordered the children not to let the family follow us,
but without success. They went wherever we did.

After a few hours of walking in the mountain, we came to the
very border and to the spot where we were to cross the Tresa, a
rapid Alpine stream. There, a tiny window near the bottom of the
high border screen was left open, as pre-arranged, and we were
supposed to go through that window, the stout ones and the thin
ones. Our guide, despite the danger, finally agreed to help the family from Bengasi, too. We were all sitting on the uphill path waiting
for the moment when we could begin to cross. How hard it was,

that anxious wait, that fear of Germans at the border! What if someone gave us away?

We began to slip through the small window; it was amazing how the corpulent among us got through, but all made it. And then it started: We held hands in a chain as we were crossing the stream. The guide actually shouted that we should turn left, not right, but we turned right till we realized our mistake. Suddenly our former perceptions about particular individuals turned out to be wrong. That apathetic pianist, Professor Boris, became a courageous helper of children; but some of the adults who normally appeared calm and daring broke down, seeking death in the middle of the small river. The alarm bells attached to the border screen started ringing, and the Germans fired a few shots. The son had to slap his father who wanted to bid him farewell and float away down the river. I gave my hand to little Moritz, who had fallen, and I was forced to drop my bag with all my correspondence in order to lift him. This lasted a few minutes, but it seemed an eternity to us! Suddenly, my God, there stood German soldiers on the other bank where our safety was in sight. Well, there was nothing for us to do but proceed—then it became clear that they were Swiss soldiers!

They received us correctly; they dried our clothes and saw to it that we recuperated from stress. But when we started to talk about staying in Switzerland, they told us, "You should know that Switzerland is in a difficult situation; our food supplies are limited, and we are completely surrounded by the German armed forces. We are a small country and cannot admit people without limits. Why don't you wish to return to Italy? If you didn't do anything wrong, there is no reason why you shouldn't go back." They had no idea that the Germans were exterminating Jews. They simply could not grasp this, or perhaps they did not want to. For them it was quite clear: we had crossed the border by mistake and after a few days they would, of course, help us go back.

During those few days, Natan Schwalb and comrades from Hashomer Hatzair in Switzerland were looking for us. We could not inform them about our presence from the Swiss camp where we were temporarily staying. Nothing could be done; no telephone calls were allowed from the camp, while the telephone sat there on a table near us.

Meanwhile, the Yugoslav embassy in Bern requested that we be allowed to stay in Switzerland. The Jewish Agency joined them in this plea, guaranteeing firmly that we would leave for Palestine immediately after the war ended. And thus, after three days of waiting and excitement, the commandant of the camp assembled us and talked about all sorts of things until finally—only at the end—he said: "Taking all the foregoing into consideration, the federal government in Bern has decided that you may stay in Switzerland till the end of the war."

My strength gave out, and I fainted.

In a few days, the second half of our group arrived unharmed, and so began our stay in Switzerland under normal conditions.

I was often astonished at how little mental damage resulted from our wanderings and suffering. Only our poor Bertha sank into final darkness and found her home later in Palestine in a mental institution, where she died after some years. I visited her there, and I felt pained: was her illness the consequence of our wanderings and the murder of her mother, or did it begin much earlier?

In Switzerland, we finally met Natan Schwalb. Among all the *shlichim* (emissaries), he was the only one who stayed in Europe, trying to help the *halutz* movement in the ghettos under Nazism. He certainly helped us to an unusual degree. The children of Villa Emma now passed under his tutelage, and he established a real Youth Aliyah home in Bex-Les-Bains, a small town south of Montreux. The old former hotel received the children after their lengthy stays in army camps and transit stations of Swiss institutions. Our life assumed normal forms. Since there is no tale to be told about normal life, I am closing the story with thanks to all those who helped us. There were many Gentiles—Slovenes and especially Italians—who not only helped us, but also gave us spiritual strength to await the final day of the war, May 8, 1945. And then we got ready to go to Barcelona through France, to board the ship *Non Plus Ultra*—the first ship after the war, which was to take us to Eretz Israel.

Recha Freier welcomed us on the shore, her face joyous, waving to us: "You really kept your word and brought the children!" And I thought, "How did we actually succeed? Did it really depend on us?"

After 1945 Villa Emma became a center for the Jewish soldiers (Palestine brigade) serving in the British army during the Second World War. One of the soldiers, Chayim Sorek, discovered accidentally a child's diary in German in the attic. He kept it in memory of his little girl, whom he had lost in Poland. In the meantime, the story of the children of Villa Emma became known in Israel, and in 1985, when his friends read his memoirs, they realized that the diary belonged to one of the rescued children. It was as if Villa Emma had sent us its last greeting.

IV. Jewish Refugees Under Italian Occupation

Menachem Shelah

9. The Italian Rescue of Yugoslav Jews, 1941–1943

Italy's behavior toward the Yugoslav Jews represents something unique in the annals of the Holocaust, for it consists of protection and rescue rather than persecution and slaughter. And there is paradox added to uniqueness. The Fascist state, which was hardly a humanitarian mecca, included many high government officials and army officers who went out of their way to rescue Jews at the risk of unpleasant and even dangerous confrontations with the sinister Axis partner, Nazi Germany. More surprising still, these rescue efforts were undertaken on behalf of a few thousand Jewish refugees not even of Italian origin. An astonishing conclusion, which confounds the contemporary world of cynical and pragmatic historians, is inescapable: the whole Italian rescue operation was generated by a powerful moral imperative.

To be sure, in singling out those heroic Italians working under Mussolini, one must be careful not to whitewash Fascism, which, as is well known, wrought destruction and misery in Italy and in many other parts of Europe. Nor should the ideology's corrosion of moral values and the human spirit be overlooked. But in spite of Fascism's dubious legacy, no justification exists for ignoring the positive action of the Italian government on behalf of the country's refugee Jews during World War II. As historians, Jews, and humanists, we have a historical and moral obligation to illuminate those noble and humane deeds that shone through a political firmament blackened by savagery and death camps. The ringing Talmudic phrase comes to mind: "Whoever saves a single life saves all mankind."

At the beginning of April 1941, after an anti-German coup d'état in Belgrade, Hitler decided to invade Yugoslavia, "to put an end to Yugoslavia as a political entity."[1] The weak and crumbling

---

1. *Akten zur Deutschen Auswärtigen Politik, Serie D: 1937–1945, XII-XIII* (Göttingen: 1969), pp. 307–9; Franz Halder, *Kriegstagebuch. Tägliche Aufzeichnun-*

Yugoslav army collapsed in a fortnight. The unfortunate conquered country was divided among Germany and those allies of Germany who had joined in the invasion. Germany grabbed Serbia and parts of Slovenia in the north for itself; Bulgaria took Macedonia in the south; Hungary, the Vojvodina province near the Hungarian border; and Italy, most of the Adriatic coast of Dalmatia, including Montenegro and part of Slovenia. A so-called Independent State of Croatia under Ante Pavelić was set up by Germany and Italy. It consisted of the former territories of Croatia, Bosnia, and Herzegovina. An artificial creation, "Croatia" was a servile Nazi puppet governed by a gang of fanatical nationalists who formed the backbone of the prewar terrorist organization called the *Ustaša*. Their uncomplicated ideology can be summed up: an independent Croatian state based on "knife, bullet, and rifle."[2]

The aggressors had every reason to be satisfied with their Yugoslav spoils. The Germans had crushed the hated, unruly Serbs; the Croats had secured their independence; and the Italians had at last, if belatedly, practically fulfilled the nationalist yearning of turning the Adriatic into an Italian *mare nostro*. But in fact nobody was satisfied, least of all the *Ustaša*, who were humiliated by having to cede the Dalmatian coast to Italy. And the fanatical Italian nationalists, who dreamt of a Balkan Empire, were chagrined at having been denied the whole of Croatia. From these overlapping claims, friction between Italy and Croatia was inevitable, a friction that happened to have a favorable effect on the Jewish refugees in the Italian zone.

Of seminal importance in the formulation of Italy's policy toward its captive Jews were the gruesome massacres perpetrated by the *Ustaša* bands during the first months of their rule. The *Ustaša* hatred of everything and everyone connected with former Serbian rule was translated into barbaric practice by a campaign to "cleanse" Croatia of all "foreign elements." First and foremost on their hate list were Serbs, of whom thousands were killed, expelled, or forc-

---

gen des Chefs des Generalstabes des Heeres 1938–1944, ed. Hans-Adolf Jacobsen (Stuttgart, 1962–64), 2, pp. 330–31.

2. The best book on the *Ustaša* movement is by Bogdan Krizman, *Ante Pavelić i Ustaše* (Zagreb, 1978).

ibly converted to the Roman Catholic faith. The Croatian Jews, who decidedly comprised a "foreign element," were also top priority for the purge. Thanks to German pressure, this meant outright murder.[3]

The French historian, Jacques Sabille, describes the ensuing orgy of murder and carnage:

> The *Ustaša* bands spread terror throughout the country, a terror directed against Serb Orthodox Catholics and Jews. Whole families were murdered, towns completely gutted, and terrible acts of sadistic cruelty perpetrated. . . . The *Ustaša* chapter written in the summer of 1941 was one of the most gruesome in the history of World War II—which is saying a lot."[4]

Italian army garrisons were spotted in Croatian towns and villages. Shocked by *Ustaša* atrocities, they reacted spontaneously by giving help to the persecuted Serbs and Jews—a humane and compassionate reaction that later received the formal approval of high military authority. A political payoff was not long in coming. Many fugitive Serbs eagerly joined the Italians in their twin struggle against the enemy partisans and "friendly" Croatians.

As a consequence of *Ustaša* violence, total anarchy prevailed in the vicinity of the Dalmatian coast, which gave the Italians an opening. By invoking a former agreement reached between Pavelić and Mussolini on May 18, 1941, they occupied the Dalmatian hinterland fifty kilometers from the coast. In the meantime, the *Ustaša* were goaded (not that they needed any such persuasion) by their German advisors in Zagreb to implement the "Final Solution" of the Jewish problem in Croatia. More than two-thirds of about 45,000 Croatian Jews were driven into concentration camps during the summer and autumn of 1941. The majority were instantly killed, while others perished slowly from hunger, epidem-

---

3. There are a few Yugoslav books that deal with *Ustaša* atrocities. In English there is an exaggerated and biased account in Edmond Paris, *Genocide in Satellite Croatia* (Chicago, 1961). The best primary sources can be found in the war diaries of the Italian army units that were stationed in Croatia: Rome, Archives of the Stato maggiore dell'Esercito—Ufficio Storico (hereinafter cited as SME), Diari Storici, Quinto and Sesto Corpo d'armata e Divisioni Bergamo, Re and Sassari.

4. Léon Poliakov and Jacques Sabille, *Jews under Italian Occupation* (Paris, 1955).

ics, and torture.[5] Most of those who managed to escape made it to
the Italian-occupied zone. The local Italian authorities had no immediate policy for dealing with this wave of refugees and were
caught in a dilemma. Having a real food and housing shortage of
their own, the Italians did not want to set a precedent of favorable
treatment that would encourage a further influx of refugees into
their zone. But neither were they ready to ignore the terrible
rumors that abounded about the fate of the Jews in Croatia. Doubtless, the report by a commission of inquiry, established in September 1941 by the commander of the Italian army in Yugoslavia
weighed heavily in the final refusal to send Jews back to Croatia.
Ordered to find out the truth about the alleged *Ustaša* atrocities
against inmates of the concentration camp on the isle of Pag,
which had been recently re-occupied by the Italians, the commission was truly shocked by its findings. Corpses of men, women,
and small children, who had been brutally executed, were found
hacked to pieces, and interviewed witnesses told of barbarous *Ustaša* behavior and torture.

The Italian High Command sent the commission's report, as
well as many photographs, both to the highest government offices
in Rome and to the Royal Court.[6] This action clearly shows that
during the autumn of 1941 Italy had made the firm decision not
to send Jewish refugees back to Croatia. True, German reaction
was not yet clear, but the Italians knew that their leniency spelt
trouble with the Croatians.

As the curtain rose on 1942, the Axis armies stood triumphant
over territories ranging from Norway in the north to Egypt in the
south. In Asia, the Japanese had humiliated the Americans and
were poised for an attack on India. The spring of that year ushered
in even worse news: the construction of a vast network of death
camps with gas chambers in German-occupied eastern Europe,

5. On the "Final Solution" in Croatia, see Menachem Shelah, *The Murder of
Croatian Jews by the Germans and their Helpers during the Second World War*
(Ph.D. thesis, Tel-Aviv University, 1980).

6. On the Pag investigation, see Menachem Shelah, *Blood Account: The Rescue
of Croatian Jews by Italians 1941–1943*, (in Hebrew with English resume) (Tel-Aviv,
1986). On the Italian Court, see Stevan K. Pavlowitch, "The King Who Never Was:
An Instance of Italian Involvement in Croatia, 1941–3," *European Studies Review* 8
(1978), p. 465–87.

which quickly reached peak efficiency in their ghastly mission of mass slaughter. Jews from all over Europe—from France, Holland, Belgium and Slovakia—were deported to the East and liquidated in Treblinka, Auschwitz, Belzec, and Sobibor. The turn of the remaining Croatian Jews arrived in August 1942, when the *Ustaša* leadership and the Nazis signed a grisly agreement whereby Croatia would pay thirty German marks per Jewish head transported to the East (in the words of an Italian official, "thirty devalued pieces of silver"). As a *quid pro quo*, the Germans agreed to leave all Jewish property in Croatian hands. Ominously, the Jews in the Italian zone were thrown in as part of the arrangement without informing Rome. But all was revealed, accidentally, when a mission of the Todt organization, sent from Berlin to accelerate the mining of bauxite in the vicinity of the Italian zone town of Mostar, was invited to lunch at the headquarters of the "Murge" Division. During the meal, the head of the German mission, General Schnell, while discussing the accommodations for German personnel, disclosed that no one need worry about space since the local Jews were ticketed for deportation. The Italian response was spontaneous and swift. The commander, General Paride Negri, heatedly replied: "Oh, no, that is totally impossible, because the deportation of Jews goes against the honor of the Italian army."[7] Both sides reported this exchange to their superiors, and the battle for the lives of the Croatian Jews between Germany and Italy was joined. The main protagonists on the Italian side were high Foreign Ministry officials including Ciano's bureau chief, Count Blasco Lanza d'Ajeta; the head of the Occupied Territories Department, Count Luca Pietromarchi; and the liaison officer of the Italian Second Army to the Foreign Ministry in Rome, Vittorio Castellani. Among the army officers, special mention is due to Generals Mario Roatta, Mario Robotti, and Vittorio Ambrosio, commanders of the Second Army; General of the *carabinieri* Giuseppe Pièche, head of the Intelligence Service in the Balkans; and General Giuseppe Amico, commander of the "Marche" Division. Amico was a par-

---

7. SME, Diario Storico Divisione Murge, Box 735, (19.6.1942); Belgrade, Archives of the Vojno Istorijski Institut (hereinafter quoted as VII), Potsdam 3/41–42.

ticularly devoted friend of the Jews and was eventually killed by the Germans for his efforts. It is a matter of historical record that army initiative and army determination saved the lives of many Jews.

Most zealous on the German side in getting the Italians to release the Croatian Jews to the *Ustaša* were the notorious German foreign minister Joachim von Ribbentrop, the head of the Department "Deutschland" Martin Luther, and the German ambassador in Croatia, Siegfried Kasche. The staff of the German embassy in Rome, headed by Hans-Georg von Mackensen and his deputy, Otto von Bismarck (grandson of the Iron Chancellor), did most of the dirty work. The *Reichssicherheitshauptamt* (RSHA) was involved in the matter through the Gestapo chief Heinrich Müller and Adolf Eichmann.

On August 17, 1942, the first secretary of the German Embassy in Rome, von Bismarck, personally delivered to Foreign Minister Count Galeazzo Ciano's secretary, d'Ajeta, a peremptory demand that all Jews who had taken refuge in Italian territories be immediately handed over to Croatian authorities. After d'Ajeta had consulted with his colleague, Pietromarchi, the two composed a memorandum that underlined the obvious consequences of agreeing to the German demand and urged Ciano to reject it. But Ciano, not yet ready to shoulder such a responsibility, directed Pietromarchi to prepare a new memorandum addressed to Mussolini that would stress the relevant facts but would not make any recommendations. A new memorandum was drafted. To influence the Duce, they hammered away at the real German purpose by employing three different expressions for killing: *dispersione, eliminazione, liquidazione*. To their consternation, Mussolini replied with an answer that was short and decisive. In the margin the Duce wrote: *"Nulla osta,"* meaning "No objection," to the surrender of thousands of helpless Jews.[8]

8. On Bismarck's presentation, see Verax (Roberto Ducci), "Italiani ed Ebrei in Jugoslavia," *Politica Estera*, No. 1 (Rome, 1944). On Mussolini's "Nulla osta," see Shelah, *Blood Account*, ch. 8; Daniel Carpi, "The Rescue of Jews in the Italian Zone of Occupied Croatia," *Rescue Attempts During the Holocaust. Proceedings of the Second Yad Vashem International Historical Conference* (Jerusalem, 1977) pp. 465–525.

The moment of truth had arrived. In secret consultation with the army commanders stationed in Croatia, the Foreign Ministry officials decided to sabotage Mussolini's directive in a way that would not arouse suspicion. They resolved to slow down any actual delivery of Jews.

A secret committee in the Foreign Ministry, created to oversee the Jewish question, managed to build an impenetrable wall around the Jewish refugees through a variety of bureaucratic ruses. A complicated screening process, ostensibly to screen refugees who were somehow entitled to Italian citizenship and protection from those earmarked for deportation, was set up. The Legal Department in Rome was swamped with hundreds of inquiries asking the question in various guises: "Who is a Jew?"[9]

But the Germans were not fooled. At the end of September 1942, the head of the Croatian state, Ante Pavelić, met Hitler. During their talk, Pavelić brought up the indisputable fact of systematic Italian resistance to the delivery of Jews quartered in their territory. The Führer was furious over what he saw to be a general sabotage of Mussolini's orders. Singling out the Italian army commanders in Croatia as most culpable, he reserved his greatest wrath for their commander, General Roatta, whom he contemptuously dismissed as a "half politician." The outraged Hitler ordered his ambassador in Zagreb to prepare a memorandum on the subject and to bring it up at his next meeting with Mussolini. Von Ribbentrop, who took part in the discussion, ordered von Mackensen in Rome to track down the cause of delay immediately.[10] The vehement representations at the Palazzo Chigi by von Mackensen and von Bismarck convinced the Italians that something drastic had to be done to pacify the Germans. Following a consultation between Foreign Ministry officials and General Roatta, it was decided to place the whole problem before the Italian dictator, in the hope that he could be prevailed upon to cancel his previous decision. Roatta met Mussolini in the middle of November 1942.

9. Shelah, *Blood Account,* ch. 9; SME, Box 5283/c: Luca Pietromarchi's private diary entry, 13.9.1942.

10. Andreas Hillgruber, ed., *Staatsmänner und Diplomaten bei Hitler* (Frankfurt am Main, 1972) 2: pp. 118–19, 126, N.G. 3165.

In the endeavor to exploit Mussolini's vanity and megalomania, Roatta argued that handing over Jews would damage Italian prestige in the occupied territories. If the Duce should give in, the *Ustaša* would be provided an opportunity to portray Italy as a German lackey and the Fascists would become the laughingstock of their Serbian cohorts. Finally the Duce was swayed; he agreed to a postponement. But to protect himself, he insisted that some kind of credible excuse be given to hold the Germans at bay. Roatta had a ready answer, one prepared for him by the Foreign Ministry: "Let us put all our Jews in a few camps and present it to the Germans as a preliminary stage in the handing-over process." The Duce agreed.[11]

Thus, more time was bought. During the following weeks all the Jewish refugees scattered about the Dalmatian coast were concentrated in one large internment camp in Kraljevica (Porto Re) and in a number of hotels, and put under very superficial and lenient Italian supervision.[12] In spite of this, the move frightened the refugees and provoked sharp criticism on the part of Italian military personnel in Yugoslavia. Small wonder, since only a few were privy to the real purpose of the move. The widespread negative reaction that swept through the Italian military in Yugoslavia clearly shows the unpopularity of any harassment of the Jews. The letters addressed to the Italian Supreme Command are at once moving and blunt. One *carabinieri* officer wrote:

> As an Italian patriot, I beg you to cancel the new steps taken against the Jews. We have a moral duty to save those people. They sought protection under the Italian flag, and we are obliged to save them and give them freedom at the end of the war. . . . In these terrible times in which justice is everywhere trampled . . . Italy must obey the moral law. . . . What a tragedy if our proud tradition shall be trodden upon.[13]

Another letter, addressed by an army colonel to Foreign Minister Ciano, declared that Italian soldiers and officers should reject

---

11. VII, T82/R405/856; Carpi, "The Rescue of Jews," p. 492.
12. See eyewitness account in Ivo Herzer, "How Italians Rescued Jews," *Midstream*, June/July 1983, pp. 35–38.
13. VII, T82/R405/829–30.

orders to hand over Jews: "We refuse to be pimps to such an ignoble enterprise. . . . Even standing by and allowing such things to happen would soil the honor of the Italian Army."[14]

Indubitably, the turning of the tide in favor of the Allies at the beginning of 1943—the Soviet victory at Stalingrad and the Axis defeat at El-Alamein, which crushed the Fascist imperial dream—strengthened anti-German feeling in the Italian establishment. The prospect of a separate peace added new impetus, if any was needed, to the rescuing of the Jews. Superimposed on moral imperatives, the Jews became a precious asset for future negotiations, a *Realpolitik* consideration that further strengthened Italian resolve to keep them out of the clutches of the Germans.

At the end of summer 1942, reliable sources apprised the head of the Italian Secret Service in the Balkans, General Pièche, of the gassing of Jews in the East. Unlike the Allies, who discounted such reports, the Italians were convinced of their veracity. A special memorandum was dispatched immediately to the Duce.[15]

As for the Germans, the more victory turned into defeat, the more zeal they displayed in the killing of Jews—a telling proof that the Nazis placed the annihilation of world Jewry as their highest and most urgent priority. Given this obsession, it should come as no surprise that the German foreign minister, von Ribbentrop, in his talks with Mussolini in Rome during February 1943, squandered so much precious time and energy on the Jews and their deportation to the death camps at the expense of more pressing war matters. Axis armies were fighting for their lives in Tunisia, Mussolini's regime was on the brink of collapse, and the Germans in Russia were in retreat, but that did not matter. Nothing was more important to von Ribbentrop and Hitler than a few thousand helpless Jews.[16] Subjected to relentless German pressure, Mussolini once again buckled by promising von Ribbentrop to deliver Jews. "It is all the fault of my generals," he explained to von

14. SME, Box 5283/C.
15. For the photograph of the document with the remark: "Visto dal Duce" see in Carpi, "The Rescue of Jews," p. 491; Shelah, *Blood Account*, p. 105.
16. Frederick W. Deakin discusses the meeting without any mention of the Jewish aspect. *The Brutal Friendship. Mussolini, Hitler, and the Fall of Italian Fascism* (London, 1962), pp. 205–23.

Mackensen. "Their attitude to the Jewish question is a consequence of their totally false humanitarian conceptions."[17] And once again, on hearing of Mussolini's capitulation, the Italian officials and officers refused to give in. The counterattack was two-pronged, both military and civilian, against a backdrop of a desperate government reshuffle undertaken by Mussolini to save his regime. General Roatta, in spring 1943, received a command in Italy proper, while Ciano was unceremoniously cashiered as foreign minister. General Robotti, appointed as Roatta's successor, protested sharply against Mussolini's surrender to the German demands by repeating his predecessor's arguments. Exhausted, the Duce replied: "I had no alternative but to yield to von Ribbentrop's nagging. Now it is your turn to find a way to circumvent it. Say that because of partisan activity there are transport difficulties, or something like that." Robotti went away mollified.[18] Giuseppe Bastianini, the undersecretary of state at the Foreign Ministry, also tried his hand with the Duce by spelling out the real repercussions of his surrender to von Ribbentrop: "All of us know the fate of Jews deported by the Germans. They are gassed. All of them—women, old men, and children. We must have no part in it, nor assist in such atrocities. Are you, Duce, prepared to take such a responsibility on yourself?" Shocked by Bastianini's bluntness, Mussolini stammered: "But I promised the Germans to stop the generals' obstructions." Bastianini was able to convince him, finally, that he would figure out a way to pacify the Germans.[19]

Holding off the Nazis was still the perennial problem. Once again, a solution was found in sham organization. When von Mackensen returned to the Palazzo Chigi to ensure that Mussolini's promise to von Ribbentrop was being honored, he was assured: "Oh, yes, there is considerable progress. We are on our way to fulfilling Mussolini's commitment. All the Jews are going to be concentrated in one central camp, where at last the final screening will take place. It is only a matter of time and patience." It was

17. Poliakov and Sabille, *Jews Under Italian Occupation*, pp. 68–69.
18. Ibid., pp. 147–48; Carpi, "The Rescue of Jews," p. 459.
19. SME: Pietromarchi's diary entry, March 31, 1943.

an old Italian stratagem: doubletalk and procrastination, well described as "You know us Italians—*dolce far niente.*"

Fresh news from North Africa hastened Italian decision. Axis
defeats in the deserts convinced the Italians that sooner or later
their army would have to be withdrawn from the occupied territories in Yugoslavia. But not the soldiers alone. Refusing to abandon the Jews under their care, the Italians resolved to evacuate
them too. That decided, it became imperative to move the camps
nearer the Italian mainland. The island of Rab (Arbe) in the north
Adriatic was chosen, and all Jews in the Italian zone were transferred there in May and July 1943. During their short stay in the
camp, the 3,000-odd Jews enjoyed decent conditions. Food was
sufficient, and they were allowed to organize a wide variety of
cultural, sports, and educational activities.[20]

Just as the Jews were being settled in Rab—and the last Croatian
Jews sent to Auschwitz—the ultimate crisis of the Fascist regime
erupted in Italy. Tunisia had fallen in May 1943, and the Axis
armies in North Africa had ignominiously laid down their arms.
When the Allies invaded Sicily at the beginning of July, the final
blow occurred that brought Mussolini down. On July 25, the Fascist Grand Council voted against him. On the same day, he was
deposed by King Victor Emmanuel III and arrested. The entire Fascist edifice collapsed like a house of cards, to the delirious cheering
of crowds thronging the streets of Rome.

The king appointed Marshal Pietro Badoglio as head of the government. Anxious to end Italy's participation in the war, Badoglio
desperately tried to reach an agreement with the Allies behind the
backs of the Germans. Suspicious and aware of the Italian double-
cross, the Germans stood poised on the Alps ready to invade Italy.
On September 8, without any warning, the Allies suddenly announced the armistice with Italy. The Germans were ready to act.
Pouring over the Alps, the *Wehrmacht* swarmed unopposed into
northern and central Italy.

Luckily for the Jews of Rab, the island was temporarily liberated
by Tito's partisans. Most of the camp's inmates were evacuated to

20. On the Rab transfer and the camp, see Shelah, *Blood Account,* ch. 16.

safer places inside Yugoslavia. The young and able-bodied joined the fighters, while the older people and children found shelter in small towns and villages in the liberated territories until the end of the war.

All told, eighty percent of the Yugoslav Jews who fled to the Italian-occupied zone were saved. A similar story of rescue can be told about Jews who had found shelter in Italian-occupied France and Greece.

Countless Italians employed in the Fascist establishment, known and anonymous, took part in the rescue of Italy's refugee Jews. What prompted these highly placed, loyal, and obedient servants of the Fascist state to act in a way that seems to have defied every principle of *raison d'état*? Doubtless, they were perfectly aware that the so-called "Final Solution" comprised Nazi Germany's most urgent war aim. Why should they risk their very lives in challenging the Teutonic colossus over a few thousand Jews who were not even of Italian origin?

To say that every human enterprise and historical event is an outcome of circumstances, change, and the mix of many disparate components and unfathomable imponderables is at once banal and true. In this vein, many historians have detailed the special attitude of the Italian people toward Jews and anti-Semitism in general, the nature of Italian Fascism, and the ideological contrasts between Fascism and Nazism on the Jewish question. We know, too, about the friction and antagonism between the *Ustaša* and both Germany and Italy following the partition of Yugoslavia. And not to be discounted was the growing opposition to the pro-German policy of Mussolini among army and high government officials, let alone the growing awareness, when the Axis faced military defeat, that the rescue of Jews would serve as a useful Italian trump card in future dealings with the Allies. But apart from all the logical and pragmatic reasons, the dominating impulses governing the Italian decision to save Jews were moral and humanitarian. When Count Pietromarchi, one of the protagonists, records in his diary, "Thanks to a small amount of moral courage thousands of Jews were saved," he understates the case. In those days, supreme courage was needed to save the life of a single Jew.

Daniel Carpi, an eminent historian, writes: "The logical and natural question is not why did so-and-so refuse to participate in cold-blooded murder or even try to stop it, but how was it that so many people and even nations directly or indirectly sanctioned such deeds."[21]

Notwithstanding the rightness and nobility of Professor Carpi's lines, one cannot deny that the wholesale murder of Jews and the delivery of Jews to their murderers was in those days the rule rather than the exception. Against that background of perverted normality we can categorically assert that the humanitarian Italian attitude was most unusual. And not only when compared to Nazi Germany and its satellite minions in Vichy France, Slovakia, Rumania, Croatia, and Hungary; the Italian attitude also contrasts favorably with the Allies, whose callous indifference to the plight of the Jews was notorious. One need not delve into mysterious or transcendent explanations. History is made by men who possess free will and the potential for making moral decisions. Indeed, beyond objective circumstances ranges moral choice. Those countless Italian officials, bureaucrats, and army officers, who were informed by different backgrounds and political perspectives, were at one in choosing the moral and humane alternative. That may be the optimistic answer to the terrible question Primo Levi poses in one of his books: "Is this a man?" One is proud to conclude, yes, those brave Italians were men.

21. Carpi, "The Rescue of Jews," p. 507.

John Bierman

10. How Italy Protected the Jews in the Occupied South of France, 1942–1943

In the winter of 1942–43, the French Riviera presented an extraordinary spectacle. All along the Côte d'Azur—in Nice, Cannes, Monte Carlo, Menton, and Cap d'Antibes, those prewar playgrounds of a sybaritic international elite—thousands of Jewish refugees, rich and poor, religious and secular, from all parts of Hitler's Europe, were living openly and in relative security. The Italians were in charge.[1]

In November 1942, Italian troops marched into the Riviera after strategic setbacks in North Africa impelled the Axis to seize military control of the nationally independent Vichy republic, so that the south coast of France could be adequately defended against a possible Allied invasion. The Germans assigned the two south coast departments of Alpes-Maritimes and Var—and six other departments, stretching north to the Swiss border—to their Italian allies, leaving the civil administration in the hands of the collaborationist Vichy regime, headed by Marshal Pétain and Pierre Laval.[2]

When they first took refuge along the Côte d'Azur, after the fall of France in June 1940, the Jews had felt relatively secure under Vichy. But by the spring of 1942, the writing was on the wall. Without prodding from the Germans, the Pétain-Laval regime prepared plans to start rounding up the Jews for deportation, beginning with foreign Jews. The Vichyites were already executing those plans when the Italians marched in.[3] Neither the Germans nor the

1. For the situation of the Jews in the Italian-occupied zone of France, see above all Léon Poliakov and Jacques Sabille, *Jews Under the Italian Occupation* (Paris, 1955); Serge Klarsfeld, *Vichy-Auschwitz: Le rôle de Vichy dans la solution finale de la question juive en France, 1943–1944* (Paris, 1985) where most of the documents published by Poliakov and Sabille are reproduced in French; Michael R. Marrus and Robert O. Paxton, *Vichy France and the Jews* (New York, 1981); Susan Zuccotti, *The Italians and the Holocaust; Persecution, Rescue, Survival* (New York, 1987).
2. Marrus and Paxton, *Vichy France and the Jews*, p. 283ff.
3. Ibid., pp. 232–34.

leaders of Vichy had anticipated any interference from the Italians, so one may imagine their surprise and outrage when their plans for the Jews ran into a stubborn wall of resistance. This began when the Italian consul-general in Nice, Alberto Calisse, learned that the Vichy prefect of Alpes-Maritimes, an enthusiastic anti-Semite named Marcel Ribière, was about to round up all the Jews of his department and send them to forced labor in the German-occupied zone. Calisse immediately contacted his foreign ministry in Rome with an urgent plea for instructions. Within days he got his answer.[4]

"It is not possible to permit the forcible transfer of the Jews," said the Foreign Ministry. "The measures to protect the Jews, both foreign and Italian, must be taken exclusively by our organs." Calisse and his military colleagues immediately informed the Vichy authorities that they were "to annul every order of an anti-Jewish nature." These instructions, in all probability, came all the way down from Count Ciano, the Italian foreign minister, who was also Mussolini's son-in-law.[5] Laval and the Nazis both believed this, as documentary evidence indicates. Laval was so incensed at this Italian interference that he called in the Italian ambassador to complain. But the result was the opposite of what Laval had intended: the Italians promptly extended their protection of the Jews to include those in all the departments occupied by their forces—not just the Alpes Maritimes—and the Italian Foreign Ministry notified Vichy in very plain language indeed that only the Italians were entitled to arrest or intern Jews, irrespective of nationality, in the departments they controlled. A message from the ministry to Italian missions in both Vichy and occupied France made it clear that this was no token opposition. I quote from the ministry's circular: "This is not a matter of negotiation, or of an approach, but of a definite declaration to the French authorities."[6]

Nor was Italian protection merely a matter of preventing arrests and deportations. Everyday human rights were to be safeguarded, too, as a letter from Calisse to Ribière made quite clear: "I have

4. Poliakov and Sabille, *Jews Under Italian Occupation*, p. 22f.
5. Ibid., pp. 24, 54 (Document 2); Klarsfeld, *Vichy-Auschwitz*, pp. 15f, 199.
6. Poliakov and Sabille, p. 26; Klarsfeld, p. 212.

the honor to confirm to you what I told you verbally that the fixing of the stamp 'Jew' should not be applied to [the documents of] Jews living in the zones where Italian troops are quartered." Calisse also warned the Vichy prefect that Italy would not permit the setting up of forced labor units in its zone. Only "humane legislation" would be applied in the Italian sector, he said.[7] What was more, the Italians were quite prepared to put up a show of force to underline their determination not to allow the Jews to be interfered with. For example, Colonel Mario Bodo, commandant of the *carabinieri* in Nice, posted his men outside the Jewish reception center and synagogue on the Boulevard Dubouchage to prevent Vichy police from going inside to make arrests.[8]

If Vichy was outraged, the Nazis were aghast. On January 12, 1943, the Gestapo chief in Paris, SS-*Standartenführer* Helmut Knochen, appealed to his boss, SS-*Standartenführer* Heinrich Müller, in Berlin to inform the *Reichsführer* SS [that is, Himmler] as quickly as possible of the methods employed by the Italians and to get this special treatment of the Jews by the Italians stopped. Knochen added, almost plaintively: "It is impossible to understand how our Axis partner should fail to adhere to our policy in regard to the Jewish question."[9]

A month later, after consulting in Paris with his colleague Eichmann, Knochen was complaining to Müller in tones of even greater agitation: "The best of harmony prevails between the Italian troops and the Jewish population," he lamented. "The Italians live in the homes of the Jews. The Jews invite them out and pay for them. The German and Italian conceptions here seem to be completely at odds." The zealous Knochen saw in the Italian attitude a serious threat to the successful application of the Nazi extermination plan not just in Vichy territory but throughout France. If the anti-Jewish measures were not applied to the Italian zone, he warned, the influx of Jews into it—an influx that was only beginning—would assume "formidable dimensions and the result will be only half measures."[10]

---

7. Poliakov and Sabille, p. 53 (Doc. 2).
8. Ibid., p. 28.
9. Ibid., p. 50 (Doc. 1); Klarsfeld, p. 196.
10. Poliakov and Sabille, p. 62 (Doc. 5); Klarsfeld, p. 219.

Ten days later, the intervention of Italian troops forced Vichy police to release a number of foreign Jews whom they had arrested in Grenoble and Annecy, and General Carlo Avarna di Gualtieri, representative of the Italian Supreme Command at Vichy, sent a stiff note to Pétain's chief-of-staff telling him such arrests could not be allowed "whether they are Jews of Italian, French, or foreign nationality." Avarna di Gualtieri added: "These measures belong exclusively to the competence of the Italian military occupation authorities. For this reason, the Italian Supreme Commander requires the French Government to annul all arrests and internments which have been ordered up to now."[11]

The Nazis were so incensed that Himmler called on German Foreign Minister Joachim von Ribbentrop, who was about to leave for Rome for a meeting with Mussolini, and pressed him to raise the matter. Hitler himself also briefed von Ribbentrop on this issue before his meeting with the Duce. When Mussolini and von Ribbentrop met at the Palazzo Venezia, the Duce appeared to agree entirely that his people's protection of the Jews must cease immediately. If the German ambassador, Hans-Georg von Mackensen, is to be believed, the Duce's attitude was "far from ambiguous." He said that it was a matter in which his generals must not meddle and that their attitude was due "not only to a lack of understanding, but also to a sentimental humanitarianism, which is not appropriate in these hard times." The necessary instructions would therefore be issued that very day to General Vittorio Ambrosio, the Italian commander in Vichy France, telling him he must allow the French authorities a completely free hand in this matter. When von Mackensen suggested that Ambrosio might object, the Duce "laughingly shrugged his shoulders as if to say 'I am the one who gives the orders around here!'" Von Mackensen's interpretation, however, was very soon to be proved wrong. Mussolini sent for Ambrosio, apparently to give him the promised instructions in person, but Ambrosio somehow persuaded him to relent.[12]

11. Poliakov and Sabille, p. 86 (Doc. 18); Klarsfeld, p. 229.
12. Poliakov and Sabille, pp. 32, 68–70 (Doc. 8); Klarsfeld, p. 243.

Now a new and intriguing figure appears on the scene—one who might have stepped out of the libretto of an opera buffa, an inspector-general of police named Guido Lospinoso. To make it appear to the Germans that he meant to keep his promise about the Jews of the Riviera, Mussolini had his Foreign Ministry notify Berlin that he was appointing Lospinoso—at the time an inspector-general of police whom he called "a most energetic man"—to be his commissioner for Jewish affairs in the Italian occupation zone. He would leave for Nice immediately to start work independently of the Italian military authorities. The Germans were told that the Duce's orders were "unambiguous and emphatic" and that military officers who continued to protect Jews "and other undesirable elements" in any way would be punished. The Germans appear to have been convinced that the Italians meant business, but they had not reckoned on the stubborn humanitarianism of Inspector-General Lospinoso and the genius he was to demonstrate in the art of *"far niente"* (doing nothing).[13]

His strategy was simply to lie low, do nothing, and make himself totally unavailable to either the Nazis or their Vichy collaborators. A series of telegrams between Gestapo officers in France and their chiefs in Berlin convey the flavor of Lospinoso's elusive modus operandi.

On April 5, Knochen, having been advised by Müller that Lospinoso had been in Nice "for some days," reported to Berlin that he had tried to get details from the Italian embassy but had been told that "nothing is so far known" about Lospinoso's mission. On April 7, Müller cabled Knochen, asking him to "make sure whether Lospinoso is really in France." On April 8, Knochen cabled back, saying he had just learned that Lospinoso had been in France, but had returned to Rome after only three days on the Riviera. On April 9, Müller told Knochen he had asked the German embassy in Rome to persuade the Italians to send Lospinoso to Berlin for talks with the Gestapo there, or else "get into direct and personal contact with you as soon as possible."[14]

13. Poliakov and Sabille, pp. 70–72 (Doc. 8); Klarsfeld, pp. 245–46.
14. Poliakov and Sabille, pp. 74–79 (Doc. 10–14); Klarsfeld, pp. 265–66.

But Lospinoso neither went to Berlin nor got in touch with Knochen, and by May 24 Knochen was reporting to Müller with obvious exasperation that "Inspector-General Lospinoso of the Italian police still has not come to see me and we know nothing of his possible presence in the Italian zone." Said Knochen: "These facts only confirm my suspicion that certain Italian authorities are not at all interested in the solution of the Jewish question in France and that they are employing in this regard, as far as possible, delaying tactics."[15]

An internal report to Knochen at this time from one of his subordinates, SS-*Obersturmführer* Heinz Röthke, was very specific about Lospinoso's activities. It stated that Lospinoso was in league with a prominent Italian Jew named Angelo Donati, a longtime resident of France, and that together they were working to make sure that the Jews of the Riviera would continue to enjoy Italian protection. In fact, Röthke reported, it was Donati who was calling the tune and telling Lospinoso how to run his department:

> Donati has daily contact with Lospinoso and also conversations on the telephone with Lospinoso's collaborators in the course of which he gives them their orders. They, for their part, give him an account of the measures taken and of the difficulties they encounter. . . . We may therefore conclude that the handling of the Jewish question in the Italian zone is in practice under the direction of a Jew, with all the consequences that must be drawn from that fact.[16]

On June 22, Knochen learned to his obvious chagrin that the elusive Lospinoso, who had so far avoided meeting him, had recently met with the Vichy police chief, René Bousquet. Knochen shot off a telegram to SS-*Obergruppenführer* Ernst Kaltenbrunner, second only to Himmler in the police hierarchy. "It seems desirable to me," said Knochen, "that we should express to the Italian government our surprise at seeing Inspector-General Lospinoso evading a visit to the supreme chief of the SS and police and the commandant of the security police, yet at the same time estab-

15. Poliakov and Sabille, p. 84 (Doc. 18); Klarsfeld, pp. 280–1.
16. Poliakov, Sabille, pp. 95–96 (Doc. 21).

lishing contact with the chief of the French police about the application of anti-Jewish measures. . . . I consider that the procedure of the Italians is an extremely serious matter, which endangers the application of the new measures against the Jews."[17]

On July 21, Röthke, in the Paris headquarters of the Gestapo, submitted another internal memo on the situation in the Italian zone, where he estimated that 50,000 Jews were present. The attitude of the Italians, he wrote, was "incomprehensible." They were protecting the Jews "by every means in their power." He added with unconcealed indignation: "The Italian zone of influence, particularly the Côte d'Azur, has become the Promised Land for the Jews in France. In the last few months there has been a mass exodus of Jews from our occupation zone into the Italian zone." Röthke would no doubt have been even more indignant had he been aware that the grateful Jews of the Côte d'Azur had raised relief funds for the victims of Allied air raids on Italian towns.[18]

On the day that Röthke submitted that report, Lospinoso was meeting a second Vichy official, while still avoiding contact with the Germans. His conversation this time was with one Louis Antignac, director of the Enquiry and Control Section of the Commissariat-General for Jewish Affairs, the Vichy Jew-hunting bureau. Antignac was to report on that meeting to his chief, the notorious Louis Darquier de Pellepoix, in a note marked "very secret." From this note one gets an almost hilarious impression of the wily Lospinoso tying Antignac in knots with a masterly display of false naïveté. First, Lospinoso told Antignac of his meeting with police chief Bousquet the previous month, pretending not to know that Jewish policy was not properly a matter for the police but for Antignac's Commissariat. He artfully showed Antignac a piece of paper on which he said Bousquet had jotted down some suggestions for cooperation on the Jewish question. Antignac, eager to obtain evidence of Bousquet's poaching on Pellepoix's territory, asked for a copy, but Lospinoso—full of apologies—refused, saying he was unable to pass on an official document of which only one copy

17. Ibid., pp. 97–98 (Doc. 22); Klarsfeld, p. 296.
18. Poliakov and Sabille, p. 106 (Doc. 25); Klarsfeld, pp. 309–11.

existed and which, anyway, had no signature. Antignac's secret report shows how Lospinoso continued to stoke the fires of jealousy between the police and Pellepoix's department:

> Seeing my astonishment that the Commissariat-General had not been informed of the contacts between the French police and the Italian racial police, M. Lospinoso explained to me that during his conversation with M. Bousquet the question had never been raised of the existence of a commissariat charged especially with the handling of the Jewish question. I then pointed out that this body had been in existence for nearly three years.[19]

There can be little doubt that Lospinoso was baiting Antignac. No policeman of his rank could possibly have been as naïve as he pretended to be, and no functionary of a Fascist state could fail to be aware of the jealous guarding of turf that was inevitable between two rival bureaucracies, such as the Vichy police and the Commissariat-General for Jewish Affairs. But the humorless Antignac seems to have taken it all at face value, including Lospinoso's deadpan master stroke. "He put a question to me," Antignac told his chief, "which needs no comment: he asked if the minister and I were Jews."

Amazingly, Antignac seems to have believed that, however stupid, Lospinoso was sincere. So when Lospinoso asked for a list of the names of those Jews Vichy considered most dangerous—obviously so that he could take extra care of them—Antignac let him have it. "I believe this functionary is animated with a spirit of understanding of which we ought to make use without delay," he told Pellepoix. "I have in consequence given instructions to [a subordinate] to give M. Lospinoso a list of undesirable aliens."[20]

At about the time this farcical encounter occurred, the Gestapo in Marseille, glowering across the demarcation line between the German and Italian occupation zones, were reporting to Knochen in Paris that "the Jews continue to appear in the best hotels and restaurants of the Côte d'Azur and to conduct themselves as provocatively as before. The Italian officers show themselves openly

---

19. Poliakov and Sabille, p. 108 (Doc. 26); Klarsfeld, pp. 311–13.
20. Poliakov and Sabille, p. 111 (Doc. 26); Klarsfeld, p. 313.

in the company of Jewesses."[21] Goaded by such shameless behavior and still unable to make contact with Lospinoso, the Gestapo made a desperate attempt at least to lay their hands on his collaborator, Donati, sending a kidnap team from Marseille to abduct him. But, as Röthke reported to SS headquarters later, the would-be kidnappers were fatally hampered because, "having regard to the [delicate state of] German-Italian relations at that time, they were ordered to proceed with extreme care."[22]

Finally, on August 18—almost five months after his arrival in Nice—Lospinoso had his first and only known meeting with any Nazi official when he went to Gestapo headquarters in Marseille to see an SS-*Hauptsturmführer* named Mühler. He told Mühler that he was shortly going to Rome to receive fresh instructions. Mühler cabled Knochen in Paris to say that on return from Rome, Lospinoso would let him know the result of his discussions: "I shall inform you immediately." But if Mühler thought Knochen would be pleased to hear of his meeting with Lospinoso he was brutally disappointed. "I have received your telegram and I am surprised that you had a discussion with the official Italian representative without first getting in touch with us," Knochen cabled back. "I ask you to send us a detailed report and also your opinions about L." The icy note of barely contained fury seems unmistakable in Knochen's message. Mühler hastened to assure Knochen that his conversation with Lospinoso was at the latter's request and that it had "no official character whatever." Lospinoso "only wanted to be informed about certain matters of principle before going to Rome."[23]

This is the last piece of documentary evidence I have been able to find about the way Lospinoso discharged his function as Mussolini's special commissioner for Jewish affairs. The record surely provides a prime example of how Italians at all levels and by a variety of means sabotaged the murderous racial policies of the Nazis and their surrogates.

Tragically, on September 8, all Lospinoso's efforts, and those of

21. Poliakov and Sabille, p. 112 (Doc. 27); Klarsfeld, pp. 314–15.
22. Poliakov and Sabille, p. 126 (Doc. 36); Klarsfeld, p. 350.
23. Poliakov and Sabille, p. 114–16 (Doc. 28–30); Klarsfeld, pp. 330, 335, 339–40.

his compatriots, were undone by the sudden announcement that the Badoglio government had signed an armistice with the Allies. Immediately, Italian troops moved out of the Côte d'Azur in total disarray, German troops moved in, and all but a few hundred Jews were trapped and fell into Nazi hands.

V. The Vatican and the Jews in Italy

Robert A. Graham, S.J.

11. Relations of Pius XII and the Catholic Community with Jewish Organizations

In World War II, the Jewish community, both national and international, was in close, continuous, and fruitful contact with the Vatican and the Catholic population as never before in history. Repeatedly, the world Jewish organizations dedicated to rescue work received a sympathetic hearing and substantial help from Pius XII, the then-reigning pontiff. Often enough, the Jewish organizations themselves came late on the scene, after the Vatican, unsolicited, had already intervened at crucial moments. Is it exaggerated to see in this opening, and in the mutual sentiments aroused on both sides in the midst of tragedy, the roots of the epoch-making decrees of the Vatican Council II on Jewish-Christian relations? A common ground had perhaps been found.

This paper, limited perforce to the case of Italy, is concerned principally with these relationships in the Italian framework. We can set the stage for our review by citing for the record how Jewish representatives and individuals regarded the action of the Holy See and the Catholic world at the moment of their liberation from the deadly threat that had hung over them for so long. These voices began to be raised in public with the arrival of Allied troops in Rome on June 5, 1944. On June 22, the Jewish chaplain of the French forces, Rabbi André Zaoui, wrote to the pope. He records that on June 6 he had been received by the pope:

> I could express to the head of the Church the sentiments of profound gratitude and respectful admiration of my Israelite brethren of the French Expeditionary Forces for the immense good and the incomparable charity that your Holiness extended generously to the Jews of Italy and especially the children, women and elderly of the community of Rome.[1]

1. Copy in possession of present writer. Other citations following can also be

On this occasion, the rabbi wished to repeat his sentiments. Subsequently, he had been able to visit the Salesian Pius XI Institute where he learned that for six months sixty Jewish children, including some from France, had been sheltered.

On July 21, a letter from the National Jewish Welfare Board, signed by Frank L. Weil and David de Sola Pool, conveyed to the pope the same message of recognition and gratitude:

> Word comes to us from our army chaplains in Italy of the aid and protection given to so many Italian Jews by the Vatican and by priests and institutions of the Church during the Nazi occupation of the land.

The executive director of the War Refugee Board, John W. Pehle, in his final report wrote:

> The Holy See and the Vatican hierarchy throughout Europe were solicited time and again for special assistance both as a channel of communication to the leaders and people of enemy territory and as a means of rendering direct aid to the suffering victims of Hitler. The Catholic clergy saved and protected many thousands and the Vatican rendered invaluable assistance to the Board and to the persecuted in Nazi hands.[2]

On October 29, 1944, a French Capuchin priest, Calliste Lopinot, led a group of Jews recently liberated from the Italian internment camp at Ferramonti-Tarsia to an audience with the pope. In a long presentation to the pope, which included signatures, Dr. Max Pereles, the leader of the group, reviewed the experiences of the several thousand inmates since 1941.

The above-mentioned audience and the accompanying documents were, not surprisingly, not published at the time in the Vatican daily newspaper, *L'Osservatore Romano*, for the war was not over. All northern Italy, two-thirds of the entire peninsula, remained in German hands and much was already developing there that boded ill for Jews. It was not until after the war that the story

---

found in Pinchas Lapide's *The Last Three Popes and the Jews* (New York, 1967), also, *The Jerusalem Post*, October 19, 1958.

2. "Final Summary Report of the Executive Director, War Refugee Board, Sept. 15, 1945."

finally came out. Notable was the visit paid on September 21, 1945, to the Vatican by Dr. Leo A. Kubowitzki (Kubovy), secretary general of the World Jewish Congress. He came not only in the name of the Congress, but also in the name of the Union of Italian Israelite Communities, to thank the pope for what had been done for the Jews during the war. After the audience, Kubowitzki visited Monsignor Giovanni Battista Montini, the pope's chief aide for relief work, to whom he presented a check for $20,000 as a token of the thanks of the world Jewish community.[3] He was followed on November 7 by Rabbi Reuben Resnik, director in Italy of the American Jewish Joint Distribution Committee. Not to be outdone, on November 29, a group of about eighty delegates representing 15,000 refugees from many European countries—Poland, Germany, Hungary, Rumania, Austria, the Soviet Union, Switzerland, France, Italy, and others—who were meeting at the Lido of Rome were received at their own request by the pope. They came, they said, "to thank the Supreme Pontiff personally for the generosity he had shown them when they were persecuted during the terrible period of Nazi-Fascism." When the Union of Italian Israelite Communities held their first postwar Congress in Rome in March 1946, the Union's president, Raffaele Cantoni, wrote in their name to the pope to express their thanks "for the work of assistance and charity carried on by the Holy See throughout all Europe during the war in favor of Jews."

The above testimony should suffice to make the point. At the death of Pope Pius XII in 1956, the same expressions of acknowledgment and gratitude were heard on all sides, e.g., from Israeli Foreign Minister Golda Meir, as if to confirm anew the earlier testimony of survivors. However, more important than these verbal witnesses are the events that called them forth. The long years of World War II created a myriad of different situations in a dozen and more countries of Europe. Our interest here is the interaction between the Jewish communities and Catholic organizations in the face of a common problem, especially in Italy.

---

3. Aryeh L. Kubovy (Kubowitzsky), "The Silence of Pope Pius XII and the beginnings of the 'Jewish document,'" *Yad Vashem Studies*, VI, 1967.

The situation of Jews in Italy, whether Italian citizens or the thousands of Jews from other countries who fled into the country when they could, can be studied in terms of time and place. The German seizure of Italy from Rome northward in September 1943, following the Italian surrender to the Allies, certainly marked a tragic turn. Up to that point, under Mussolini's Fascism, Italy was still a sovereign state, and although there were grave problems before the Jewish community, they could be negotiated "within the family" to some degree of satisfaction, often with the help of the Holy See. After September 1943 geography played a crucial role, and the tragic results left an indelible trace in history.[4] We can therefore consider the course of events according to this partition:

(1) Foreign Jews in Italy, from the outbreak of World War II until the fall of Mussolini (1939–1943):

   (a) The internment camp at Ferramonti-Tarsia

   (b) Foreign Jews in the Italian-occupied parts of Yugoslavia (Croatia, Slovenia)

   (c) Foreign Jews in Italian-occupied parts of southern France (Nice, the Riviera, Haute Savoie)

(2) The Jews in Italy under German occupation (1943–1945)

   (a) Rome

   (b) The northern cities

   (c) The Adriatic littoral

The discussion will focus on the role played by Jewish organizations and the Holy See in the rescue of Jews, against the background of the Jewish-Catholic dialogue occasioned by the tragic state of affairs.

Foreign Jews in Italy

Ferramonti-Tarsia

The problem of foreign Jews in Italy antedates World War II, when Hitler's persecution drove many thousands across the Ger-

---

4. *Relazione sull'opera svolta dal Ministero degli Affari Esteri per la tutela delle comunità ebraiche (1938–1943).* (Undated [Rome, 1946]).

man border. One of the main tasks of the Delasem (the Italian Jewish organization for aid to immigrants) was to expedite the transit of these foreign Jews to safe harbors outside of Italy. In 1940, when Italy entered the war, the government set up internment camps where foreign Jews were concentrated to await a destination that remained agonizingly uncertain. One of the best known of these internment camps was at Ferramonti-Tarsia in the province of Cosenza in Calabria, where several thousand Jews from many nations passed through.[5]

The Vatican's involvement in the fortunes of the inmates of Ferramonti-Tarsia arose from the visit on May 22, 1941, that the papal nuncio to Italy, Archbishop Francesco Borgongini-Duca, paid to the camp during a round of visits to the various camps for foreigners, including prisoners of war.[6] Some of the internees were Catholics who took the opportunity of asking to have a chaplain and a chapel for their religious consolation. As a result, a French Capuchin, Father Calliste Lopinot, took up his duties, which he fulfilled with great energy and to the high satisfaction not only of the Catholics, to whom he was officially assigned, but also to the whole camp. With his easy access to Rome, he managed to raise money from the Polish and Czech embassies to the Holy See. Of course, he did not neglect the concerns of inmates, regardless of religious affiliation.[7] One service of inestimable value of Father Calliste, perhaps difficult to appreciate for normal times, was to enable his protégés to get in touch with their families in their home countries through the Vatican Information Service. The communications were passed from the Vatican to the local nuncios (except for the one in Berlin), who, in turn, sent them to the local bishops for delivery. It is symptomatic of the atmosphere of the times that in one country, Rumania, anti-Semites took offense at the use by Jews of the Catholic facilities. They pretended to be

---

5. Carlo Spartaco Capogreco, *Ferramonti*, (Florence: La Giuntina, 1987).

6. *Actes et documents du Saint Siège relatifs à la Seconde Guerre Mondiale, Secrétairerie d'Etat de Sa Sainteté, édités par Pierre Blet et al.* Vatican City, 11 vols, 1965–1981. Vol. 8 p. 217f, 264. Volumes 6,8,9 and 10 are dedicated to papal interventions in the humanitarian sphere, hereinafter cited as *Actes.*

7. "De Apostolatu inter Hebraeos in publicae custodiae loco cui nomen Campo di concentramento Ferramonti-Tarsia (Cosenza)," *Analecta ordinis Fratrum Minorum Capuccinorum,* 60 (1944) pp. 70–75; 61 (1945) pp. 40–47 Accounts by Fr. Calliste dated respectively September 17, 1943 and October 9, 1943. *Actes* 8, p. 532.

scandalized at the preference the Vatican gave to the Jews. Cardinal Secretary of State Luigi Maglione had to explain to the Nuncio Andrea Casullo, in Bucharest, in a letter of August 20, 1943, that the Holy See made no distinctions, and if most of these letters were from Jews to their own families, this meant only that there were indeed many Jews who wanted to communicate with their families, separated as they were by the troubles of the times.[8]

But the grave moment for the Jews of Ferramonti-Tarsia came when rumors arose that they would be turned over to the Germans. From their above-mentioned correspondence with relatives at home, they had gotten some inkling of the forced deportations in Poland. At first, it was thought that their relatives in Poland could (with German and Italian permission) come to Italy—an unrealistic hope. The danger loomed that they themselves might be destined for deportation.

On September 10, 1942, Father Calliste reported to Nuncio Borgongini-Duca that camp morale was very low. They had learned that foreign Jews in France had been deported to Poland. Even though the details were lacking, he said, they understood enough to be profoundly disturbed. Were they to be next? Wrote the priest:

> It is at this time that the internees feel that the Holy See is their sole support. They turn with full confidence to your Excellency, through me, and they are certain their destiny is in good hands.[9]

In the spring of 1943, international concern was dramatically heightened. On March 5, Jewish circles in London asked the intervention of the Holy See, through the archbishop of Westminster, for 400 Czechs interned in Italy and reportedly in danger of deportation to Germany. The Vatican was able to reply that the nuncio Borgongini-Duca had received assurances from the Italian government that these reports were "completely without foundation."[10] This turned out to be correct, but rumors of this kind were inevitable. Next day on March 6, the apostolic delegate in Wash-

8. *Actes* 9, p. 410f, 436.
9. *Actes* 8, p. 642.
10. *Actes* 9, pp. 168f.

ington, Archbishop Amleto Cicognani, reported to Cardinal Maglione that Stephen S. Wise, president of the American Jewish
Congress, had asked the Vatican's intervention on behalf of Yugoslavs of Jewish origin in Italy and in countries occupied by Italy
who were in danger of being handed over to the Germans. This,
said Wise, would be their condemnation to death. The appeal went
by way of Myron C. Taylor, who was the personal representative
of President Roosevelt to Pius XII.[11] A similar appeal came directly
from Jewish sources in London, transmitted by the British minister, Sir d'Arcy Osborne, on March 20.[12] This time, the Jews in
question were more precisely identified as Poles and Yugoslavs in
the Ferramonti-Tarsia camp. The internees at Ferramonti-Tarsia
were luckier than they thought. Located far to the south, at the
heel of Italy, they were all liberated in September 1943 by Allied
troops coming from Sicily.

Foreign Jews in the Italian-Occupied Parts of Yugoslavia

In these crucial years, 1942–1943, the Italian Fascist government
never turned over to the Germans (or to their cooperating allies)
any foreign Jews in Italian hands, much less Italian Jews. This fact,
perhaps not widely known, was not because Berlin had never tried
to lay hands on them. On the contrary, the German leadership
became quite irritated with the Italians and with Mussolini at the
conspicuous lack of acquiescence. Other regimes—in France,
Croatia, and Slovakia—surrendered their foreign Jews. But not the
Reich's principal Axis partner, Fascist Italy. At the end of February
1943, Foreign Minister Joachim von Ribbentrop came to Rome
where he pressured Mussolini to deliver foreign Jews in the Italian-
occupied territories. The Duce gave assurances, but nothing happened. However, as late as June 24, a few weeks before his removal
from power, he called in a public speech for the "repatriation of
foreigners in Italy." It was taken abroad as foreshadowing the long-
delayed deportations, and it was certainly enough for Rabbi Ste-

---

11. Actes 9, p. 171. Also, Ennio Di Nolfo *Vaticano e Stati Uniti, 1939–1952*
(Milan, 1978), p. 240. Letter of Myron C. Taylor of March 1, 1943, to Archbishop
Amleto Cicognani.
12. *Actes* 9, pp. 197f.

phen E. Wise, through Myron Taylor, to urge the Vatican to intervene on June 29.[13] Wise, in turn, reacted to a telegram from the
London section of the World Jewish Congress urging such an appeal to the United States and to the papal representative, Archbishop Cicognani, in Washington.[14]

Naturally, the Holy See did all that it could to encourage Mussolini, or whoever else in the government was deciding these
things, to stand up to the Germans. In an inter-office memo of
March 13, 1943, Cardinal Maglione recalled that already on January 1, 1943, he had noted that Mussolini had "suspended" the
dispatch of Jews from Croatia. He went on:

> I learn now that the Germans have insisted anew to get a firmer
> attitude towards the Jews on the part of Italy. We can therefore
> instruct the Nuncio Borgongini-Duca to have Father Tacchi-
> Venturi intervene once again, without alluding to the above. And
> meanwhile we can telegraph Cicognani that we will take up the
> question again.[15]

This last was in reference to Rabbi Wise's appeal through Myron
Taylor. Accordingly, the papal secretary of state asked a Jesuit,
Father Pietro Tacchi-Venturi, on March 17, to intervene with the
"competent Italian authorities," on behalf of Jews in Croatia
whose deportation was threatened. Tacchi-Venturi, as is known,
had direct access to Mussolini himself, as well as to several ministries, and was used by the Vatican to obtain concessions for various individual Jewish cases. On March 30, the Vatican learned
from the Nunciature that the question of Jews living in territory
controlled by Italian troops had been resolved "favorably."[16] Tacchi-Venturi's reply, dated April 14, was more detailed.[17] He applied
first, he said, to the Ministry of the Interior which referred him
instead to the Foreign Ministry. Under-Secretary of State for Foreign Affairs Giuseppe Bastianini received him and discussed the
policy. The Italian government, said Bastianini, did not intend to

13. *Di Nolfo, Vaticano*, p. 260.
14. *Actes* 9, p. 413.
15. Ibid., 183.
16. Ibid., 213.
17. *Actes* 9, pp. 254f.

imitate its German ally and had emphatically refused to adopt the same procedures. Mussolini, he went on, set this rule: for the Jews, separation, but not persecution. Recorded Tacchi-Venturi: "We don't want (he used this strong term with me) to be *carnefici* (butchers)." Hence the 3,000 to 4,000 Croatians who had fled into the Italian zone would not be sent back where they came from to save them from the hard lot awaiting them 'in some inhospitable corner of Poland.'" Rather, they were to be sent to Dalmatian towns for internment. According to Bastianini, Italy still resisted demands from Vichy, probably under German instigation, to surrender Jews in southern France.

Of course, the definitive test of Fascist policy was not to be found in the words of some official, but in the actual development of the situation. As late as June 14, 1943, the Italian Foreign Ministry could assure the Vatican once again: "No delivery of Jews to Germany will be carried out."[18]

The situation of Jews in the Italian-occupied part of Yugoslavia on the eve of Mussolini's fall was described by A. L. Easterman of the World Jewish Congress in a letter to the papal delegate in London dated July 19. He reported that about 20,000 Jewish refugees were on the Italian mainland and in Italian-occupied territories. Of these, 2,500 Jews were at Kraljevica (Porto Re), Split (Spalato), Korčula (Curzola), Kupari (Cupari), and Dubrovnik (Ragusa). Easterman pointed out that, should Italy capitulate to the Allies at this moment, these Jewish refugees would be in danger. Hence the urgency of removing these thousands to a safer zone in the south. Easterman repeated this information and appeal in a telegram addressed directly to Pope Pius XII, dated August 2, 1943, again in the name of the World Jewish Congress.[19] On August 12, the Cardinal Secretary of State was informed by the chargé d'affaires of the newly installed Badoglio regime that there were no concentration (internment) camps in northern Italy, and for Jews in such places as Trieste, the government had given them all assurances and possibilities of moving to wherever would cause

18. *Actes* 9, p. 338, note.
19. *Actes* 9, pp. 417f.

them the least preoccupation.[20] Within a few weeks, however, with the armistice in force, such promises could no longer be maintained. There remained one ray of light. Even after the German takeover, Easterman could report to the papal delegate in London on September 24, 1943, in these terms:

> I have been informed that approximately 4,000 Jewish refugees, as well as Yugoslav nationals, who were in internment camps and generally resident along the Dalmatian coast in formerly occupied Croatia, have been removed to the Island of Rab [Arbe] in the Adriatic. As this island has been captured by Yugoslav partisans, the Jews can therefore be regarded as removed from immediate danger.[21]

The letter of the World Jewish Congress official concluded with "warmest thanks" for the efforts of the Holy See to help bring this about.

Foreign Jews in Italian-Occupied Parts of Southern France

In October 1942, Italian troops occupied eight *départements* (French administrative subdivision) in southern France. Italian policy toward the Jews already there, not to speak of thousands of others streaming there from the German zone, was so much in contrast with the treatment of Jews in German-occupied France as to arouse Nazi irritation and protest. But instructions to the military commanders from Rome were peremptory: "It is necessary to make it plain that in the zone occupied by Italian troops the French authorities cannot be permitted to force foreign Jews, Italian Jews included, to move to areas occupied by German troops."[22] Officially, it was the Vichy government that demanded that these Jews be handed over, but in reality, the Germans were behind the pressure. On February 3, 1943, the German embassy in Rome ex-

---

20. *Actes 9*, p. 427.
21. *Actes 9*, pp. 488f. Most of the camp joined the partisans, but several hundred aged and infirm staying behind were seized by the SS and deported.
22. A telegram of December 29, 1942, cited in *Relazione sull'opera svolta*, p. 25. Angelo Donati, banker of Nice, credited himself and the Italian consul general Calisse with provoking this stand. He also said he had reasons to believe that the answer was written by Mussolini. ("J'eus toutes les raisons de croire que la réponse fut rédigé par Mussolini.") Source: Paris, Centre de documentation juive contemporaine, CCXVIII-66. "Exposé de M. Donati." No date.

postulated with the Foreign Ministry, only to get the usual evasive reply. A few days later, on February 10, the Foreign Ministry official responsible for this area, Count Giovanni Vidau, said frankly to his German interlocutor that to hand over these foreign Jews to the French meant "their consignment to the German police for deportation to Poland."

But how much longer could this policy of resisting extradition be maintained? After von Ribbentrop's February visit to Rome the problem came to a head. It was probably a tip from the Italian Foreign Ministry itself that led to a hurried order from the Vatican Secretariat of State of March 18. The moment of truth was clearly approaching. It was necessary for the papal nuncio to Italy, Borgongini-Duca, to arrange that very night for an audience on the next day with the Italian under-secretary of state Giuseppe Bastianini "to ask him to intervene in the question of the Jews in France."[23] On the day before, March 17, Mussolini assured German Ambassador von Mackensen that he would issue orders that the Vichy police be given a "free hand." In reality, Mussolini never issued such orders.[24]

Bastianini, an intimate of Mussolini, was certainly glad to be able to add the Pope's exhortations to his arsenal of arguments in favor of maintaining resistance to German demands. We learn from the account of Carmine Senise, the head of the Italian police:

> In a meeting at the Foreign Ministry, Bastianini, myself, General Castellano of the Supreme Command, Count Vidau of the Foreign Ministry and I don't remember who else, were entirely in agreement that we would never lend ourselves to the brutal steps called for by the Germans and we also agreed on very reasonable and humane steps to take. Bastianini and I then talked to Mussolini, who approved and who also decided to send our Inspector General to put it into execution.[25]

23. *Actes* 9, p. 196.
24. Telegram of Ambassador von Mackensen to the German Foreign Ministry, March 18, 1943. Nuremberg document NG 2242. Mackensen told Berlin that the Duce has assured him he would that very day order General Ambrosio, commander in South France, to give the French police a "fully free hand" (völlig freie Hand). If that is what Mussolini told the diplomat he was lying. He had just sent Lospinoso to the scene with quite contrary instructions.
25. Carmine Senise, *Quando ero capo della polizia. 1940–1943* (Rome, 1946), p. 103.

The inspector general was Guido Lospinoso, a police official. He was ordered to report at midnight to see Mussolini, who told him to depart at once for France.[26] Having arrived at his post, Lospinoso did not tip his hand. The German police actually thought he was sent to hand the Jews over to them. In reality his mission was to sabotage French and German aims. His first step, after consulting with Jewish leaders, was to move some of the Jewish refugees in the Italian-occupied zone of France to Haute Savoie for internment, lodging them in resort hotels long unused because of the war. These were at Vence, Barcelonette, Saint-Martin de Vésubie, Saint-Gervais, Mégève, and other places. Here, for the moment, they were certainly out of the reach of the Vichy police and the SS. Was it intended eventually to move them all to Italy?

What next? A close observer and participant in the Jewish struggle on the Riviera, a French Capuchin, Marie-Benoît du Bourg d'Iré, went to Rome on the urging of Angelo Donati (an Italian Jew, active in refugee relief work, who played a considerable role throughout the period of Italian occupation in southern France). On July 16, he had an audience with Pope Pius XII. He reported on the condition of French Jews and the gratitude of French Jewish leaders for the charity and devotion shown them by the Catholic Church. He also brought information about camps in eastern Europe and a report on Spanish Jews who were prevented from leaving France. Finally, Father Marie-Benoît gave a summary of his own personal immediate concerns:

> I have spoken already of the humane and benevolent attitude of Italy towards the Jews. But fears persist. What will become of these 8,000 to 10,000 Israelites now grouped together in a certain number of controlled residences, in the event that Germany, for one reason or another, should occupy the zone presently held by the Italians? Their situation would immediately become catastrophic. Since they are only a few kilometers from the Italian frontier, would it not be possible to have them cross into Italy, where they could be put to some useful works? Would a recommendation in this sense to Italy be possible?[27]

---

26. Lospinoso's own account. Interview in *La Stampa* (Turin), April 5, 1961.
27. *Actes* 9, pp. 393–97.

The French priest concluded his presentation with the words:

> I promised the Jews of France, French or foreign, to make these needs known to the Holy See, as well as other needs they might let me know of later.[28]

Cardinal Maglione, Vatican secretary of state, did not need urging. He issued corresponding orders and, among other steps we know of, he moved to get the doors of Spain opened for Jews destined for that country.[29] On July 25, Mussolini fell. The new Badoglio government, which proclaimed its intention to continue the war, had to contemplate the long-feared withdrawal of troops from France. In a document of August 11, the director of general affairs in the Foreign Ministry sent to the new minister of foreign affairs, Raffaele Guariglia, a joint memo on the problem of the Jewish refugees, which concluded that Italy should simply close its eyes to the clandestine entry into the country of all Jews who could get there. They would be considered political refugees. At an interministerial meeting of August 28, it was decided that these Jews could be brought to a zone between Nice and Menton where 25,000 Italian soldiers were to be stationed. The premature announcement of the armistice on September 8 made this rescue impossible.[30]

The Vichy-German-Italian controversy of the first half of 1943 hardly came to the attention of the world press; nor was there any mention of Rome's resistance to Berlin's pressure. The world Jewish organizations were themselves tardy in sending out alarm signals. It was not until August 20 that the apostolic delegate in Washington, Archbishop Cicognani, telegraphed the Vatican. Some representatives of the World Jewish Congress, he stated, had implored the intervention of the Holy See "to save Jews residing in countries from which the Italian government is withdrawing its troops."[31] It was desired, said Cicognani, that the Jews in France and northern Italy be enabled to take refuge in central and southern Italy.

---

28. *Actes* 9, p. 397.
29. *Actes* 9, pp. 417, 442.
30. *Relazione*, p. 35.
31. *Actes* 9, pp. 437f. The two officials of the World Jewish Congress who called on the Apostolic Delegate in Washington were Dr. Stephen S. Wise and Dr. Nahum Goldmann.

There was talk of a plan by which the Italian government would provide four ships for the transport of these Jews across the Mediterranean, to Spain, Tunis, Algeria, or Morocco. Angelo Donati actually went through the motions of making all the necessary démarches for what was easily seen as unrealizable in time of war. Donati's first objective, one must conclude, was to get these Jews into Italy by any means. If they could later be transferred out of Italy, so much the better. To accomplish this, Father Marie-Benoît was to persuade the pope to put pressure on Badoglio. The project of the four ships was, however, not presented to the Vatican before the armistice—too late for any Vatican intervention.[32]

The Jews in Italy Under German Occupation

Rome

Father Marie-Benoît installed himself in Rome, where he had once held a position as professor of theology. A new challenge suddenly developed. Foreign Jews from France and elsewhere seemed to pour into the Eternal City, and they had to be taken care of. Since the Jewish leaders had to go into hiding, Marie-Benoît took over the actual direction of Delasem's activities.

In the early weeks following Mussolini's dismissal, the foreign Jews arriving in Rome were lodged in the orphanage of the Jewish community. Since this could not possibly continue after September 8, they were placed with false papers in different boarding houses, private apartments, and convents in the city. There followed an intense, delicate, and dangerous activity. The French Capuchin, who could move about openly, was aided by helpers, many of whom were Jews. Needed were false documents, forged or legitimate, clothes, and medicines. It is estimated that the number of Italian and foreign Jews in need of aid was 4,000, of whom 1,500 were non-Italian. These fell into five categories, each requiring particular attention: foreign Jews from France, foreign Jews who had arrived in Italy prior to 1940, Yugoslav Jews, Italian Jews who came from other parts of Italy to Rome, and finally, Roman

---

32. *Actes* 9, p. 401f, pp. 465–67.

Jews. In behalf of their protégés, the priest and his numerous allies had contact with Roman officials: the *questura* (the central police office), the city government, food rationing offices, the Vatican's own Secretariat of State, the papal nunciature to Italy, and the Vatican's Vicariate (diocese of Rome). In addition, Father Marie-Benoît dealt with various diplomatic missions and consulates. He very skillfully maneuvered within the complex world of the wartime bureaucracy, which was totally dependent on documents, authentic or not. The Marie-Benoît operation was also in contact with the representative of the international Red Cross in Rome, and with the ambassadors of Poland, Belgium, Spain, and Portugal accredited by the Holy See. The Swiss Legation in Rome, as well as the Hungarian, French, and Swiss consulates, not to speak of the clandestine resistance parties, were also contacted.

Father Marie-Benoît even thought of appealing to the German embassy to the Vatican for some form of intervention in behalf of the Jews. All told, these nine months present a paradoxical, incredible situation. The French priest set up his headquarters at the generalate of the Capuchins and daily received Jews who came to him. Why did the German SS in Rome not simply eliminate this open defiance to their power and arrest the priest or trail his clients to uncover where they lived? That this danger existed was, of course, evident to the priest, but he obviously decided to defy all the risks.

As is well known, Pius XII made tremendous efforts to spare Rome from devastation by having it declared an open city, doubtless an unrealistic ambition, but one not without significance. Believing themselves secure in the shadow of the Basilica of San Pietro, thousands of refugees seeking safety from the war crowded into the city. The Jews were only a small percentage of these refugees living by their wits, under constant danger of discovery and arrest. After the October 16, 1943, raid in which more than 1,000 Roman Jews, mostly living near the synagogue on the Tiber, were seized and deported to Auschwitz, the surviving Jews fled to the protection of non-Jews and, in particular, to the numerous religious convents in Rome. Pius XII had opened these convents (even those of strict cloister) to the persecuted, and he threw around them papal protection. The convents became off-limits to the SS and the neo-Fascist police.

Father Calliste Lopinot, a confrère of Marie-Benoît, writing from his own close experiences and knowledge, quoted the report of an unidentified apostolic visitor charged with 200 convents in Rome:

> I began by recommending strongly to the superiors of houses engaged in the active ministry to receive in all charity and to hide all persons in danger of being arrested by the Germans. Very soon I found that I myself needed to do the same thing and to hide, as ecclesiastical superior, these persons, even in monasteries of strict cloister (contemplative nuns). I came to this decision after reading this text of *Proverbs*, 25, 11–12: "Rescue those who are being taken away to death. Hold back those who are stumbling to the slaughter. If you say, behold we did not know this, does not he who weighs the heart perceive it? Does not he who keeps watch over your soul know it, and will he not requite a man according to his work?"[33]

But the safety and security of the Roman, Italian, and non-Italian Jews did not depend solely on the Open City, on the sheltering canopy of Pius XII and St. Peter's, or on the goodwill (or connivance) of the civil and diplomatic officials. For an operation such as that conducted by Delasem and by Father Marie-Benoît, money was necessary, and in large quantities.

The financing of Jewish rescue work in World War II is mostly shrouded in the discretion of the responsible agencies involved. Early on, funds were available in generous proportions from the American Jewish Joint Distribution Committee, popularly referred to as the "Joint." But later, even the Joint could not legally send money to the Axis countries because of the U.S. and British economic blockade. Not even Secretary of the U.S. Treasury Henry Morgenthau could get around this until the later years of the war. At the end of 1943, however, the Joint managed to replenish Delasem's relief fund, particularly for its work in Rome.

---

33. "La protection des Juifs par l'Eglise Catholique pendant l'occupation de Rome par les Nazis. 8 Sept. 1943—Juin 1944," mimeographed presentation of Fr. Calliste Lopinot, Capuchin priest, at the International Conference to combat anti-Semitism, Seelisberg, August 1947. The Vatican prelate mentioned is not further identified.

Delasem, since 1937, had received financial help from this American organization. As an Italian agency duly recognized by the Fascist government, Delasem could receive money through the official office of exchange. In September 1943, Lelio Vittorio Valobra, the president of Delasem and his assistants, learned from an indiscreet official in the Genoa *questura* that Delasem's days were numbered. Taking the hint at face value they returned immediately to their office before the police could act. They took away the indexes, correspondence, and money, which was to be put in the safekeeping of the archbishop of Genoa, Cardinal Pietro Boetto.[34] Up until December 1943, Marie-Benoît and his friends received money from the cardinal in the name of Delasem. But then this source became unavailable because communication between northern Italy and Rome was cut off. According to the testimony of Marie-Benoît, the effort was made to get Joint money by way of the American and the British diplomatic representatives at the Vatican. The Joint would deposit American dollars in a London bank while Sir Francis Osborne, the British minister, would sign a statement certifying that some unidentified person or institution—a merchant, industrialist, or banker—would provide the necessary funds in lire against the dollar guarantee. The plan worked to perfection. Harold H. Tittman, the U.S. chargé d'affaires at the Holy See, sent a cipher telegram to Washington. Within twenty days, the Joint had deposited $20,000 in a London bank for Delasem. Marie-Benoît concluded:

> After a certain time, still in need of funds, the same procedure was repeated, through the same channels, this time for the sum of $100,000, deposited for us in London by the "Joint." Evidently there were people or institutions in Rome that counted on an Allied victory soon, and were willing to put their money on the line.[35]

34. Carlo Brizzolari, *Gli Ebrei nella storia di Genova*, (Genoa, 1971), pp. 286–95, also *Actes* 8, pp. 513f.

35. Letter of Fr. Marie-Benoît of June 24, 1961 to Lelio Vittorio Valobra on the finances of Delasem in Rome. Copy communicated to present writer by the French priest. There is a fleeting allusion to this operation in the files of the British Foreign Office, "remittance to the Vatican for work amongst the Jews" (London, Public Record Office, FO 371/36673). This is a note of the Treasury of December 28, 1943. A remark on the margin explains, "probably for non-Italian Jews."

The Northern Cities

During the long German occupation of northern Italy, there was time for the SS to organize their operations systematically. There were fewer restraining influences in the north than in the Eternal City to hamper their operations. On November 30, 1943, a German-inspired ordinance of the chief of police, Tullio Tamburini, called for the arrest of all Jews, regardless of nationality, even those enjoying exemptions from the old Fascist regime. In December, all Jews were declared to be *ipso facto* an enemy nationality. Soon a concentration camp for Jews was set up at Fossoli di Carpi, in the province of Modena. It became a staging center for Jews to be deported to Auschwitz. On April 17, 1944, in reply to a query, the bishop of Carpi wrote to Monsignor Montini, in the Vatican Secretariat of State, that his priests had been able to see non-Jewish internees in this camp and to provide religious and material consolation. But access to the Jews was "more difficult," and their destiny was unknown: "When the internees leave it cannot be known where they went to, at least not to any degree of certainty." Some of them remained only a few days. He said he had done and would continue to do all he could for the Jews.[36] From the cardinal archbishop of Milan, Ildefonso Schuster, the Vatican learned via the nuncio Filippo Bernardini in Switzerland on July 30, 1944:

> Situation getting worse. Ferocious repressions, shooting of persons, priests and sisters arrested for having helped Jews. In this connection, have sent the Republican [neo-Fascist] and German authorities a *promemoria*, showing that help given Jews in grave danger is simply evangelic charity and was not assistance. Meanwhile am informed that in concentration camp of Fossoli, fifty Jews have been executed, after having been forced to dig their own grave.[37]

Since the Vatican never recognized, or had any direct contact with, the Italian Social Republic at Salò, it was obliged to make its appeals through the German embassy to the Holy See. At the

---

36. *Actes* 10, pp. 219f.
37. *Actes* 10, pp. 366f. This telegram crossed another on the same subject from the Vatican, cfr, p. 368, note.

end of October 1944, an internal memo of the Secretariat of State recorded:

> All our requests to the German embassy in favor of Jews arrested have had no results. Even the nuncio to Italy had no better success, as concerned Jews arrested by the Italians. We are appealing for Jews still detained in Italy, for example in the concentration camp of Fossoli di Carpi, and in the judicial prison of Verona, to receive at least some milder treatment and the possibility for priests to have access to them. The Secretariat of State heard, directly, that both leave much to be desired.[38]

We are dealing here with twenty months of German Nazi ferocity in northern Italy. Individual acts of sacrifice during this time were innumerable and were generously recognized by grateful Jewish beneficiaries after the war. For example, a young priest from Lucca, Don Aldo Mei, was executed on August 4, 1944, for having sheltered a Jewish boy. The bishops of northern Italy were in contact with each other in giving Jews food and money. Genoa first felt the impact of Jews coming across the French border clandestinely after September 1943. The leader of Delasem in Genoa, Valobra, managed to get to Switzerland, where he could continue to help his fellow Jews. In Genoa, Delasem affairs passed into the hands of Cardinal Boetto's secretary, Don Francesco Repetto.[39] A similar situation arose in Milan, where Don Giuseppe Bicchierai was active as Cardinal Schuster's right hand man. For the archdiocese of Florence, headed by Cardinal Elia Dalla Costa, we have a testimony of Raffaele Cantoni, one of the early organizers of Jewish relief work in Italy. Traveling on a train from Pisa to Florence, he heard fellow passengers commenting with satisfaction on the "end of the war." But was there just reason for their enthusiasm? With Italy at war with Germany, thought Cantoni, what would be the condition of the Jews? The only hope was the Catholic Church. He continues in the third person:

> The next morning he went to the archiepiscopal seat in Florence. He was received by the Cardinal's secretary Monsignor Mene-

---

38. *Actes* 10, p. 463.
39. Brizzolari, *Gli ebrei nella storia di Genova*, p. 302.

ghelio, who assured him that the Church was at the disposition of the persecuted and that everything possible would certainly be done for the Jews hunted by the Nazis and the Fascists. And so it turned out.

Concludes Cantoni: "We were certain that we could count on the Church in the hour of danger and we were not disappointed."[40] Genoa, Milan, Turin, Florence, and Bologna swarmed with neo-Fascists and Germans. Informers and traitors were at work. Traps were sprung. The hunted could not simply disappear. Assisi, the city of St. Francis, had better fortune. The bishop, Giuseppe Nicolini, a Benedictine, did not have a moment of hesitation. The venerable city, full of convents and churches, had already become, after Mussolini's fall, an asylum for evacuees fleeing the wartime bombardments. In September, a new wave of refugees, many of whom were non-Italian Jewish refugees from France, descended on the city. Don Aldo Brunacci recalled later:

> One Thursday in September, 1943, after the usual monthly clergy meeting in the seminary, the bishop called me aside in the alcove next to the chapter room and, showing me a letter of the Secretariat of State of his Holiness, said to me: We must organize to give aid to the persecuted and particularly to the Jews. This is the will of the Holy Father Pius XII. It has to be with the maximum of secrecy and prudence. No one even among the priests should know about it.[41]

The Adriatic Littoral

In October, 1943, Hitler created what was called the Operational Zone Adriatic Littoral (Adriatisches Küstenland). It included the Italian and Yugoslav provinces of Udine, Gorizia, Trieste, Pola, Fiume, and Ljubljana. Here, especially in Trieste and Udine, were ancient centers of Jewish culture. The succeeding months witnessed a veritable martyrdom for all the inhabitants. It was a border zone, with partisan activities and repression conducted by Cossack SS units recruited from Russia. Little became known dur-

---

40. *Osservatore della Domenica, (Rome)* June 28, 1964.
41. Don Aldo Brunacci, *Ebrei in Assisi durante la guerra. Ricordi di un protagonista.* (Assisi, 1985), p. 9.

ing the war of the tragic events occurring in this area. Adminis-
tratively, the area was separated from the Republic of Salò and
indeed was a law unto itself, cut off from Italy and not integrated
into Germany. What makes it significant is that here were concentrated, in a group, the chief perpetrators of the Jewish exterminations in eastern Europe. These were the very men who in
1940 first engaged in the killing of 100,000 of their fellow Germans—the feeble-minded, the aged, the insane, those with hered-
itary diseases. After mid-1941, these now experienced and heart-
less "mercy squads" were moved to Belzec, Treblinka, and other
extermination camps to carry out the same work on a much larger
scale.

After the war it was stated in a report that at Trieste, in a former
rice-processing plant called La Risiera di San Sabba, an extermination camp had been established, equipped with gas chambers. It
appears, however, that San Sabba was, in fact, not eventually employed for this purpose, whatever other sinister role it played.[42] But
the report was anything but unfounded. Among these specialists
were none other than Christian Wirth, the commandant of the
camp, Odilo Globocnik, Franz Stangl, Otto Wächter, and other
smaller cogs in Hitler's euthanasia team.

It appears that the Jews rounded up in this German-controlled
area were mostly elderly people and children. The adults in good
health, much to the regret of the German police, had already escaped. A large group from Trieste had reached Assisi.

The bishop of Trieste, Antonio Santin, was close to the Jewish
community in those tragic months. After his retirement at the
solemn rite in the Cathedral of San Giusto, he said: "The president
of the Jewish community, Mario Stock, at the end of the ceremony,
embraced me, thanking me anew for all that I had done." Behind
the gesture of Stock was a long story of the intimate and effective
concern of Bishop Santin for the Jewish community of Trieste and
for refugees from Yugoslavia. The city was a veritable crossroads
of European Jewry, especially in the prewar years of emigration.

---

42. Pier Arrigo Carnier, Lo sterminio mancato. La dominazione nazista nel Veneto Orientale. 1943–1945. (Milan, 1982), p. 166.

Already before the war, Santin had taken a strong stand on the Italian racist laws, even confronting Mussolini when the latter came to his city. During the war he was in regular contact with the Jewish relief committee of Trieste and its president, Giuseppe Fano. He had particularly close relations with Carlo Morpurgo, secretary of the local Jewish community, who, in spite of Santin's warnings, preferred to stay with his people, tragically, to the end.[43]

Santin had recourse to the Italian military authorities for Croatian Jews in Italian hands. He went further. At the urging of Delasem in 1942, he prevailed on the Vatican to protest also in behalf of the Jews in Croatian hands.[44] He was instrumental in securing safety for some hundred Jews (Croats, Czechs, Slovaks, Poles, Hungarians, Germans, and Austrians) fleeing from Ljubljana (Lubiana) in 1942. In March, 1944, Jews were dragged out of various hospitals in Trieste and dispatched to Auschwitz. Santin raised a violent protest to the Italian prefect of the province. The entire city, he said, was offended by this event. He also intervened for various individual cases, sometimes successfully, sometimes not.[45]

Bishop Santin's own thinking was displayed in no uncertain terms at the very beginning of the German occupation, though at that moment he could only surmise grimly what was in store for the population. In a sermon on the feast of the patron saint, San Giusto, on November 3, 1943, he urged his faithful to extend the helping hand to all in need and, in particular, to the Jews.[46] Not content with a formal sermon, the archbishop wrote at this time to the German commander of the city, Baron Wolsegger: "They are not my faithful but the charity of Christ and the sense of humanity knows no limits."[47]

---

43. *Actes* 8, p. 712

44. *Actes* 8, p. 675. Pietro Zavatto, *Il vescovo Antonio Santin e il razzismo nazifascista a Trieste (1938–1945)*, (Trieste, 1979), pp. 42f.

45. *Actes* 10, pp. 239f.

46. Zavatto, *Il vescovo Antonio Santin*, pp. 51f.

47. On November 11, 1943, Santin wrote to Pope Pius XII, urging him to intervene with the German authorities in defense of Trieste Jews. Giuseppe Mayda, *Ebrei sotto Salò: La persecuzione antisemita 1943–1945* (Milan, 1978), asks (p. 139) petulantly what the pontiff did about this. The author evidently did not read the *Actes* very carefully, if at all. We find in *Actes*, volume 9, at page 578, the written protests that Cardinal Secretary of State Maglione sent to the German ambassador on November 26, in Santin's sense. The bishop was himself received in audience by Pius XII at this

How was it possible for the Jews to have survived in Italy under Fascism? The fact remains that no Jews (Italian or foreign) were handed over to the Germans for deportation before September 8, 1943—as long as Italy was a sovereign state.

The world Jewish organizations used every means of action to save the Jews in Italy from the fate that was befalling their fellow Jews elsewhere in the Axis world. From experience they had learned that they could count on the understanding and effective action of Pius XII—effective to the extent that the Vatican had any influence at all on nations at war. One can speak of a "synchronization" of action between these organizations and the Holy See. The two parties thought alike, and their forces were coordinated in the same direction.

---

time and probably handed over his letter in person. On his return Santin wrote to his clergy, on December 2, of his encouraging support from the pope (cited by Guido Botteri, *Antonio Santin, Trieste 1943–1945* [Udine, 1963], p. 32f).

Susan Zuccotti

12. Pope Pius XII and the Holocaust: The Case in Italy

At 5:30 A.M. on the rainy morning of Saturday, October 16, 1943, German SS police in Rome launched what would be the greatest single roundup of Jews in occupied Italy. In thousands of moldering apartment buildings in Rome's former ghetto and in hundreds of others scattered throughout the Holy City, police pounded on doors and roused sleeping people from their beds. Waiting trucks sped victims, often still in their night clothes, to a temporary detention center at the Italian Military College, only six hundred feet from Vatican City. Within nine hours, 1,259 Jews from a community of about 12,000 had been arrested and confined. These included 896 women and children.[1]

Two days later, before dawn on Monday, October 18, trucks again gathered up the arrested Jews and carried them to the cargo-loading platform of Rome's Tiburtina Station. As the prisoners arrived, guards quickly packed them into about twenty freight cars and bolted the doors from outside. Fifty to sixty people in each car waited in darkness, stifling heat, and terror until the loading process was completed. At about 2:00 P.M., the dreadful journey north began.

The trip, with no toilet facilities, almost no food or water, and barely enough space to sit down, took five days. At 11:00 P.M. on the Sabbath, Friday night, October 22, the death train arrived at Auschwitz, too late for unloading. Early the next morning, the Jews of Rome experienced the infamous selection process that had already destroyed millions of their co-religionists from all corners

---

1. For excellent accounts of the Rome roundup, see Michael Tagliacozzo, "La Comunità di Roma sotto l'incubo della svastica: La grande razzia dell 16 ottobre 1943," *Gli ebrei in Italia durante il fascismo: Quaderni del Centro di Documentazione Ebraica Contemporanea*, III, November 1963, pp. 8–37, and same author, "La persecuzione degli ebrei a Roma," *L'occupazione tedesca e gli ebrei di Roma*, ed. Liliana Picciotto Fargion (Rome: Carucci, 1979), pp. 149–71; and Robert Katz, *Black Sabbath: A Journey Through a Crime Against Humanity* (Toronto: Macmillan, 1969).

of Europe. With a flick of his hand, Dr. Josef Mengele himself directed the sick, elderly, weak, and all mothers and children into one line, and those "fit for labor" into another. An entry in the Auschwitz log for October 23, 1943, one week after the initial Rome roundup, stated subsequent developments succinctly:

> RSHA—Transport, Jews from Rome. After the selection 149 men registered with numbers 158451–158639 and 47 women registered with numbers 66172–66218 have been admitted to the detention camp. The rest have been gassed.[2]

"The rest" included more than 800 people. They were soon followed by 181 of the 196 young men and women selected to be slaves for the Third Reich, who died from starvation, exhaustion, and disease within a few months. Fifteen returned to Italy in 1945 to bear witness to the destruction of the "pope's Jews."[3]

During the roughly forty-eight hours from October 16 to 18, when the more than one thousand arrested Roman Jews lay waiting for the departure of the death train, not a single public word of protest was issued from the Vatican. During the five days when the train wound its agonizingly slow way north, no public protest occurred. Finally, in the Vatican newspaper *L'Osservatore Romano* on October 25–26, 1943, after most deportees were dead, Pope Pius XII's only public comment on the events of October 16 appeared. The article said in part:

> As is well-known, the August Pontiff, after having vainly tried to prevent the outbreak of the war ... has not desisted for one moment from employing all the means in His power to alleviate the suffering which, whatever form it may take, is the consequence of this cruel conflagration. With the augmentation of so much evil, the universal and paternal charity of the Supreme Pontiff has become, it might be said, ever more active; it knows neither boundaries nor nationality, neither religion nor race.[4]

---

2. Quoted by Tagliacozzo in *L'occupazione tedesca*, pp. 163–64.

3. Katz, p. 341. Like most Holocaust statistics, this figure varies slightly. Tagliacozzo in *L'occupazione tedesca*, p. 164, states that eighteen returned, while the Centro di Documentazione Ebraica Contemporanea, Milan, *Ebrei in Italia: Deportazione, resistenza* (Florence: Tipografia Giuntina, 1975), 13, places the number at sixteen.

4. Quoted in Meir Michaelis, *Mussolini and the Jews: German-Italian Relations*

Baron Ernst von Weizsäcker, German ambassador to the Holy See, assessed the article in a report to his Foreign Ministry on October 28. He wrote, in part, "There is no reason whatever to object to the terms of this message . . . as only a very few people will recognize in it a special allusion to the Jewish question."[5]

During the dreadful week following the October 16 roundup, Pope Pius XII had been somewhat more active behind the scenes. On the evening following the raid, the pope permitted Bishop Alois Hudal, rector of the German Catholic Church in Rome, to write a mild letter to General Rainer Stahel, German army commander of the city. The letter said in part:

> A high Vatican dignitary in the immediate circle of the Holy Father has just informed me that this morning a series of arrests of Jews of Italian nationality has been initiated. In the interests of the good relations which have existed until now between the Vatican and the German High Command . . . I earnestly request that you order the immediate suspension of these arrests both in Rome and its vicinity. Otherwise I fear that the pope will take a public stand against this action which would undoubtedly be used by the anti-German propagandists as a weapon against us.[6]

Ambassador von Weizsäcker was convinced that the threat of a "public stand" was very real. After all, he wrote in a message to the German Foreign Ministry on October 17, "People say that when similar incidents took place in French cities, the bishops there took a firm stand. The pope, as supreme head of the Church and bishop of Rome, cannot be more reticent than they."[7] But despite Bishop Hudal's letter and Ambassador von Weizsäcker's well-grounded fears, the Roman Jews were not released. On the contrary, at least 835 more were arrested and deported from Rome before the city was liberated in June, 1944.[8] But the pope never took the public stand that he had threatened.

---

and the Jewish Question in Italy, 1922–1945 (Oxford: Clarendon Press, 1978), p. 370.

5. Ibid., p. 371.
6. Ibid., p. 366. For background of the letter, see Katz, pp. 198–203, and Michaelis, pp. 365–66.
7. Tagliacozzo in Gli ebrei in Italia, p. 30.
8. L'occupazione tedesca, p. 41.

Exactly what "firm stand" had French bishops taken, that the pope might have been expected to duplicate? In the summer of 1942, as foreign Jews in unoccupied France were being rounded up and delivered to the German occupiers of northern France and ultimately to Auschwitz, Monsignor Jules-Geraud Saliège, archbishop of Toulouse, prepared a letter that was read in all the churches of his diocese on Sunday, August 22. The letter said, among other things:

> That children, women, fathers and mothers should be treated like animals, that family members should be separated and sent off to an unknown destination, it has been reserved for our time to witness this sad spectacle. . . . Jews are men. Jewesses are women. They are part of the human race. They are our brothers like so many others. A Christian cannot forget it.[9]

A week later, Monsignor Pierre-Marie Théas, bishop of Montauban, informed Catholics in all the churches in his diocese of the vicious roundup in Paris on July 16, 1942, in which 12,884 foreign Jewish men, women, and children had been arrested and held for deportation. He added:

> I proclaim that all men . . . are brothers for they are created by God. . . . The present anti-Semitic measures are a contemptible attack on human dignity, a violation of the most sacred rights of the individual and the family. May God grant consolation and strength to the persecuted.[10]

That same Sunday, Cardinal Gerlier of Lyon published an equally frank letter of condemnation throughout his diocese. Then on September 20, Monsignor Moussaron, archbishop of Albi, did the same.

Ambassador von Weizsäcker was correct in his report to his ministry. While Pope Pius XII might have decided, for his own reasons, not to condemn the Holocaust in general, he could have been expected, in his capacity as bishop of Rome, to protest the deporta-

---

9. Georges Wellers, *L'étoile jaune à l'heure de Vichy: De Drancy à Auschwitz* (Paris, Fayard, 1973) p. 417.
10. Ibid.

tions of Jews in his own diocese, as French bishops had done. Yet the pope did not do so.

It is possible to argue that a specific public Vatican protest of the October 16 roundup, while placing the pope on sounder moral ground, would nevertheless have helped the Jews of Rome very little. The Nazis would never have released Jews already caught or ceased future arrests, just as they did not in France. Furthermore, Roman Jews, and indeed the Jews throughout Italy, needed no warning from the pope after the roundup to convince them to go into hiding. Within a few weeks after October 16, a day that also saw large roundups in Milan and Turin, almost no Jews remained in their homes. Many more would be arrested in the remaining months of the German occupation. Total figures exceed 6,800 for the Italian peninsula.[11] But the vast majority of the later victims were caught in hiding, not at home.

In addition, while many historians believe, as one put it, that "public opinion (in France) was struck by the protests of the bishops,"[12] Italian non-Jews did not need the pope to tell them that arrests and deportations were an abomination. They willingly opened their homes to Jewish fugitives. The Italian rescue operation was unique in Europe because its success rate (eighty-five percent of Italy's 45,200 Jews in 1943 survived—a statistic equalled only in Denmark) was achieved contrary to established government policy.[13] In December 1943, Mussolini ordered that all Jews in Italy be interned, and again the pope was silent, but Italian non-Jews simply ignored the law.

More damaging to the papal record in Italy than the silence after October 16, however, is the speculation about what might have occurred if Pope Pius XII had spoken publicly about what he knew before October 16. The evidence strongly suggests that he was aware of plans for a roundup in Rome at least a week before it

---

11. *Ebrei in Italia*, 9, and Liliana Picciotto Fargion, "Die Deportation der Juden aus Italien. Statistische Untersuchung," unpublished but intended for publication by the Institut für Zeitgeschichte in Munich, is a statistical study, country by country, of victims of the Holocaust. In addition, the 1,805 Jews deported from the Italian colonies of Rhodes and Cos were also Italian citizens.

12. Jacques Duquesne, *Les catholiques français sous l'occupation* (Paris: Grasset, 1966), p. 254.

13. *Ebrei in Italia*, 9, and Picciotto Fargion, "Die Deportation . . ."

actually took place. Eitel Friedrich Moellhausen, acting German ambassador to Italy during the temporary incapacity of Ambassador Rudolf Rahn, learned in September of Nazi plans to arrest and deport the Roman Jews. He also knew that the orders for deportation referred to the "liquidation" of victims. Moellhausen was horrified, in part because he abhorred mass murder and in part because he believed that deportations from the Holy City would bring about a public papal condemnation harmful to the German war effort.

In an effort to avert the roundup, Moellhausen informed German Foreign Minister Joachim von Ribbentrop of the plan on October 6, and suggested that Roman Jews instead be used to build fortifications in Italy.[14] Told in effect to mind his own business, on October 9, Moellhausen then, if not before, informed the German ambassador to the Holy See, von Weizsäcker.[15] According to Moellhausen, von Weizsäcker, hoping that behind-the-scenes papal objections would deter Nazi plans, in turn informed Vatican officials. Those officials would most certainly have informed the pope.[16]

Von Weizsäcker's secretary Albert von Kessel stated after the war that he was not certain whether von Weizsäcker actually told the pope, and von Weizsäcker himself never mentions the Rome roundup in his memoirs.[17] But even if Moellhausen were wrong and the pope did not hear about the plan from von Weizsäcker, it is highly unlikely that he did not learn of it from other sources. Too many people knew. German diplomats attached to the embassy and to the Holy See, many of whom were Catholics and acquainted with priests, knew. Some Italian police knew. Many Italian bureaucrats responsible for census data and ordered to provide the names and addresses of Roman Jews during the week before October 16 knew. It is inconceivable that the pope himself, with his vast information network of priests and active Catholic laymen throughout Rome, did not know.

14. Tagliacozzo, in *Gli ebrei in Italia*, pp. 15–16.
15. Ibid., pp. 16–17, and Michaelis, p. 364.
16. Katz, pp. 134–39, from a personal interview with Moellhausen.
17. Silvio Bertoldi, *I tedeschi in Italia* (Milan: Rizzoli, 1964), pp. 35–7, and Ernst von Weizsäcker, *Memoirs*, trans. John Andrews (Chicago: Henry Regnery Company, 1951).

In addition, it is clear that Pope Pius XII knew, long before October 16, that "resettlement in the east" meant gassing for the majority and slave labor until death for those remaining. Reports from diplomats from Allied nations and from several international Jewish organizations reached him as early as September 1942. While he may have dismissed information from these sources as Allied propaganda, similar reports from Catholic churchmen were harder to ignore. There were, after all, thousands of Catholic witnesses to the Holocaust in the German army and bureaucracy, and in parishes in the vicinity of the death camps. At least some of those witnesses had consciences, and spoke to their priests. At least some of those priests passed the word along to their superiors and, ultimately, to the Vatican.

The case of SS-*Standartenführer* Kurt Gerstein is the most dramatic and best-documented example of this referral system. In the summer of 1942, Gerstein, a disinfection officer, personally witnessed a horrifying mass gassing at Belzec. Three thousand men, women, and children were packed into four adjacent gas chambers, only to wait for two hours and forty-nine minutes, in full knowledge of their fate, until the primitive Diesel engine which was to asphyxiate them could be made to work. The killing process then took thirty-two minutes. In August 1942, Gerstein went to the office of Monsignor Cesare Orsenigo, the papal nuncio to Berlin, to describe what he had seen, but he was not received. He claimed in 1945 that "I then reported all of this to hundreds of persons, among them, Dr. Winter, the syndic to the Catholic bishop of Berlin, with the request that the information be forwarded to the pope."[18] The Vatican has never denied receiving the report.

It is difficult to disagree with the conclusion of Walter Lacqueur that "the Vatican ... had direct or indirect channels of communication with every European country but Russia," and that it "was either the first, or among the first, to learn about the fate of the deported Jews."[19] With this knowledge and with his awareness

---

18. Quoted in Saul Friedländer, *Pius XII and the Third Reich: A Documentation,* trans. Charles Fullman (New York: Knopf, 1966), p. 129.

19. Walter Lacqueur, *The Terrible Secret: Suppression of the Truth about Hitler's 'Final Solution'* (Boston: Little, Brown, 1980), p. 56.

of Nazi plans for the roundup and deportation of Roman Jews, Pope Pius XII might have sent the same threat of a "public stand" that he sent after the roundup via Bishop Hudal. There is no evidence that he did so. At the very least, he might have sent a secret warning to leaders of the Jewish community. They in turn could have quietly advised their members to hide. Yet again, there is no evidence that the pope ever took such a step, and more than 1,000 Jews were caught in their homes. Since any indication of a Vatican effort to avert a roundup or render it less effective would have strengthened the Church's case in the face of bitter attacks on the pope's silence during the Holocaust, it is reasonable to assume that if it had occurred, it would have been mentioned after the war.

How can the pope's behavior in October 1943 be explained? Certainly churchmen in Vatican City, totally surrounded by the German army, felt vulnerable to Nazi incursions and determined to protect their institution. Hitler had indeed threatened many times to invade the Vatican, imprison the pope, and install a puppet as head of the Church. Yet a secret warning to Jewish leaders would have remained just that—a secret—while saving hundreds of lives. Furthermore, while the public reminders of several French bishops to their flock to respect Jewish lives had led to rebukes and to the arrests of some priests, they had not resulted in large-scale Nazi attacks on Church institutions. In Italy, where the strongly Catholic population was largely free from anti-Semitism, opposed to Nazis and Fascists alike, and prepared to help both political and Jewish fugitives from the SS, a public papal protest against the persecutions might well have strengthened the Church in the eyes of the people and made the Germans even more reluctant to attack it. But the pope and his advisors were not inclined to take such a risk.

More to the point, perhaps, historians have pointed out that the pope was unwilling to offend the Germans or denounce the Holocaust because he did not wish to jeopardize the lives of hundreds of Jews hiding in Vatican institutions and thousands of others in churches and monasteries. Statistics of individuals in hiding are elusive by definition, but most experts agree that about 450 Jews eventually hid in enclaves of the Vatican, while more than 4,000 others found shelter in churches, monasteries, and convents in Rome alone.[20] Many thousands more hid in religious institutions throughout the country. These holy places were not immune from attack; on the contrary, they were frequent targets. Among the best-known raids were the coordinated Nazi-Fascist attacks on several Vatican properties in Rome on December 22, 1943, in which at least eleven Jews and many anti-Fascists were caught; a purely Italian Fascist assault on the Basilica of Saint Paul Outside the Walls on February 3, 1944, when at least six Jews were arrested; and the Nazi-Fascist attack on the Convent of the Franciscan Sisters of Mary in the Piazza del Carmine in Florence on November 27, 1943, which resulted in the arrest, deportation, and death of about thirty Jewish women and children.[21] These are only three of many such incidents, but perhaps, if the pope had spoken out, there would have been more. At least the pope seems to have thought this to be the case.

While the pope's concern for Jews hiding in Italy may have been a major factor in his long-term silence about the Holocaust, it does not explain his specific behavior with regard to the October 1943 roundup, for two reasons. First, as stated earlier, a warning to the Jewish community would have remained a secret and endangered no one. Second, most of the hundreds or thousands of Jews who hid in Church institutions were not yet there in October. Like most Jews throughout occupied Europe, those in Italy did not immediately recognize the danger.

There were several reasons for this phenomenon. First, like their co-religionists elsewhere, Italian Jews could not believe that deportations "would ever happen here," in a civilized country where anti-Semitism had been rare and where they themselves had been accepted and integrated at all levels of society. Furthermore, they reasoned, Italian Jews had always been fervent patriots and good citizens, and had done nothing to deserve persecution. Second,

---

20. Michaelis, p. 365.
21. Amedeo Strazzera-Perniciani, *Umanità ed eroismo nella vita segreta di Regina Coeli: Roma 1943–1944* (Rome: Tipo-Litografia V. Ferri, 1959), pp. 111–13; Michaelis, p. 390; and Milan, Centro di Documentazione Ebraica Contemporanea (hereinafter quoted as CDEC), 5-H-b: *Vicissitudini dei singoli/particolare*, Ravenna Falco Gabriella di Ferrara and Abenaim Pacifici Vanda di Firenze.

with the prompt reinstatement (by the Germans) of Mussolini as prime minister of the new Italian Social Republic (the Republic of Salò) and the return of Fascist Italy to the war effort on the side of the Third Reich, it was easy to overlook the real nature of Italian independence and assume that the status of Italian Jews would not change from the earlier war years.

Third and most ironically, Jews in Rome felt safe in the shadow of the Vatican. Since the abolition of the ghetto with the entry into Rome of the troops of King Victor Emmanuel II in 1870, their relations with the Vatican had been amicable. While Catholic publications like *L'Osservatore Romano* occasionally took anti-Semitic positions, and while the then-pope, Pius XI, never opposed Italy's racial laws when they appeared in 1938 or later, Vatican officials extended some assistance to individual Jews in distress. Fabio Della Seta, a Jewish student in Rome unable to attend a state university because of the racial laws, has written of Vatican institutions of higher learning that opened their doors to Jewish applicants.[22] Other Jews remember employment offers and assistance with emigration.

Even more reassuring and immediate was the reaction of Pope Pius XII to the Nazis' infamous gold extortion scheme in September 1943. At 6:00 P.M. on September 25, Jewish Community leaders were informed that they had to deliver fifty kilograms of gold to SS *Obersturmbannführer* Herbert Kappler, chief of the German security police in Rome, within thirty-six hours, or witness the deportation of two hundred Roman Jews. The horrified leaders began collecting gold the following morning, but contributions arrived slowly at first. Eventually the deadline was extended somewhat, and at 4:00 P.M. on September 28, the gold was delivered to Gestapo headquarters in Via Tasso, carefully weighed, and accepted.[23]

Accounts of the Vatican role in the crisis vary. Some historians allege that Pope Pius XII was so outraged by the affair that he immediately offered a gift of gold. A few even maintain that the

---

22. Fabio Della Seta, *L'Incendio del Tevere* (Trapani: Editore Celebes, 1969), p. 129.

23. For full accounts of the gold extortion scheme, see Tagliacozzo and Katz.

gift was accepted. The facts as related by Ugo Foà, president of the Jewish Community of Rome, are somewhat different. Foà, who was nothing if not respectful and deferential to all authority, wrote after the war:

> The Holy See, learning immediately of the fact [of the extortion], spontaneously made it known to the president of the Community [Foà himself] through official channels that if it was not possible to collect all the fifty kilograms of gold within the specified thirty-six hours he would place at his disposal the balance, which could be paid back later without hurry when the Community was in a condition to do so.[24]

This "noble gesture of the Vatican," Foà went on to say, was not needed, for he was able to collect the fifty kilograms of gold from other sources.

According to Foà, then, the Vatican offered not a gift, but a loan contingent on the failure to collect gold from others. But other witnesses even question Foà's claim that the offer was spontaneous. Renzo Levi, another Jewish Community leader, later reported that he had requested the gold in the early hours of the collection period when contributions were coming in slowly. The pope had agreed to the loan, but it was not needed.[25]

Whatever the precise details, the papal gesture was commendable, for it relieved Jewish Community leaders of their terrible fear of failure. It also reassured Roman Jews and made them feel less alone. Unfortunately, however, as news of the "offer" spread and was exaggerated, the Vatican gesture began to appear as a firm indication of support and solidarity.[26] The pope was on their side, many Roman Jews came to believe, and there was no need to hide. He would warn them of pending trouble, and in addition, the Nazis would never dare defy him. All this was wishful thinking, of

24. Foà report, quoted in full in Luciano Morpurgo, *Caccia all'uomo!* (Rome: Casa Editrice Dalmatia S.A., 1946), p. 115.
25. Katz, p. 87, from his interview with Renzo Levi.
26. Even from as far away as Florence, Bernard Berenson heard that Roman Jews could raise only ten of the fifty kilograms of gold, and that the pope had offered twenty and the Roman aristocracy, ten. He added in his memoirs, "It is hard to believe such a tale." See Bernard Berenson, *Rumor and Reflection* (New York: Simon and Schuster, 1952), p. 143.

course, strongly reinforced by the intentional good behavior of the occupying forces in Rome in September and early October.[27] Jewish shopkeepers, for example, noted with obvious relief and pleasure that German soldiers readily paid the full price for cameras and souvenirs while touring the Holy City.

Most Italian Jews seemed not to have heard about less benign behavior elsewhere. For example, on September 16, in Merano, a beautiful mountain resort town near Bolzano, Nazis arrested and deported twenty-five Jews, including a six-year-old child and a sick seventy-four-year-old woman.[28] On September 18, in small Italian villages along the French frontier, the German SS arrested and imprisoned 349 Jewish refugees from France.[29] Then for several days in September, other SS troops near Lago Maggiore murdered forty-nine Jewish men, women, and children on the spot and threw their bodies into the lake.[30]

Gradually, anti-Jewish incidents began to occur south of the frontier. On September 28, Fascist militia and *carabinieri* arrested Jews in Cuneo, near Turin, while German soldiers destroyed a synagogue in Vercelli, between Turin and Milan. At about the same time, Nazis arrested several Jews in Novara, near Vercelli.[31] Many more arrests occurred in the northeast of the country, and on Yom Kippur, Saturday, October 9, a deportation train left Trieste with at least 100 Jews. None ever returned.[32] Yet the majority of the Italian Jews, still unaware of events, remained at home. And still, it might be noted, Pope Pius XII, certainly informed of the atrocities in the north, remained silent.

27. SS-*Obersturmbannführer* Herbert Kappler's orders from SS Chief Heinrich Himmler to prepare the Rome roundup included the admonition on September 25, "The success of this undertaking will have to be ensured by a surprise action and for that reason it is strictly necessary to suspend the application of any anti-Jewish measures of an individual nature, likely to stir up among the population suspicion of an imminent action." See Tagliacozzo, in *L'occupazione tedesca*, p. 152.

28. *Ebrei in Italia*, page insert. One of the twenty-five survived.

29. Of the 349, 330 were deported, and only nine returned after the war. For a full account, see Alberto Cavaglion, *Nella notte straniera: Gli ebrei di S. Martin Vésubie e il campo di Borgo S. Dalmazzo, 8 settembre–21 novembre 1943* (Cuneo: Edizioni L'Arciere, 1981).

30. Giuseppe Mayda, *Ebrei sotto Salò: La persecuzione antisemita 1943–1945* (Milan: Feltrinelli, 1978), pp. 79–90; *Ebrei in Italia*, p. 31; and CDEC, Fatti di Meina.

31. Mayda, pp. 68–9.

32. Ibid., p. 139; *Ebrei in Italia*, p. 29; and Silva Gherardi Bon, *La persecuzione antiebraica a Trieste (1938–1945)* (Udine: Del Bianco, 1972).

As seen above, perceptions changed totally after the roundups in Rome, Turin, and Milan on October 16, 1943. The facts of the arrests and deportations were often garbled, but enough was known to convince Jews in Italy that it was essential to hide. Most did so. At that time, churches, monasteries, convents, and other religious houses opened their doors to thousands of Jews, and Italian men and women of the Church stood nobly and courageously in the forefront of a rescue effort that, with the exception of Denmark, saw no equal in occupied Europe.[33] The pope's inclination to silence might well have been influenced by a concern for Jews in hiding and for their Catholic protectors. But that development followed, rather than preceded, the Rome roundup.

In the last analysis, the failure of Pope Pius XII to warn Roman Jews of a probable roundup, to threaten the Germans with a public condemnation before that roundup occurred, and to denounce the persecution of Italian Jews strongly and publicly defies specific explanation and blends with the broader question of the papal silence about the Holocaust throughout the war. The factors determining that silence have been analyzed elsewhere and need only be mentioned briefly here.[34] The pope undoubtedly envisioned as his primary role the defense of the Church as an institution and the protection of Catholics, including converted Jews, throughout occupied Europe. He was also concerned not to alienate German Catholics by publicly condemning atrocities or by appearing to hasten the defeat of the Third Reich. To achieve these ends, he chose a policy of strict neutrality and adhered to it firmly until the end.

Also with these objectives in mind, the pope granted his bishops considerable latitude to act in their own dioceses as they thought best. He was anxious to avoid the aggravation of atrocities in reprisal for a public condemnation by Church officials, as had oc-

---

33. For a fuller treatment of the Italian rescue movement and the participation of men and women of the church, see Susan Zuccotti, *The Italians and the Holocaust: Persecution, Rescue, and Survival* (New York: Basic Books, 1987).

34. See, for example, Guenther Lewy, *The Catholic Church and Nazi Germany* (New York: McGraw-Hill, 1964); Carlo Falconi, *The Silence of Pius XII*, trans. Bernard Wall (Boston: Little, Brown, 1970); Alberto Giovannetti, *Il Vaticano e la guerra (1939–1940)* (Vatican City: Libreria Editrice Vaticana, 1960) and *Roma città aperta* (Milan: Editrice Ancora, 1962); and Friedländer.

curred in the Netherlands when a public protest by the archbishop of Utrecht against the persecution of Jews had led to the deportation of Catholic converts.[35] He might have reflected that atrocities could hardly be more horrifying than they already were and that Jews who converted to Catholicism were regularly deported in any case from all occupied nations, including Italy.[36] He might also have acknowledged that his perhaps justifiable grant of regional autonomy in this field did not exempt him from local responsibility in his capacity as bishop of Rome. It was all very well to allow bishops in anti-Semitic Germany and Poland to remain prudently silent, but in Italy a condemnation of the Holocaust would scarcely have alienated Catholics.

Pope Pius XII's passionate anti-bolshevism and reluctance to see the defeat of Europe's "bulwark against Stalin" played an additional role in his decision to remain silent. After October 1943, he was also undoubtedly influenced by a concern for the safety of Jews in religious institutions in Italy. To these factors, he brought certain characteristics of his own personality—an inclination not to take risks, a firm insistence on the possibilities of discreet diplomacy, and a strong preference for avoiding confrontation.[37] His decision to remain silent in the face of the greatest evil of our time—an evil perpetrated by Christians against the people of the Old Testament and the countrymen of Jesus—might well have been painful to him. It was almost certainly a decision with which a different pope might have disagreed.

The public silence of Pope Pius XII does not mean, however, that he did nothing to help Jews in Italy. The presence of several hundred Jews in enclaves of the Vatican and of several thousand in other religious institutions in Rome and throughout the country has been noted. Italian priests were in the forefront of the rescue movement, and many acted on the suggestions of their bishops. In Florence, for example, Cardinal Elia Dalla Costa asked Dominican Father Cipriano Ricotti and parish priest Don Leti Casini to co-

35. One of the Catholic converts deported from a convent and gassed at Auschwitz was Edith Stein, beatified in 1987.
36. While the Nazis usually respected the Christian children of mixed marriages, they rarely spared the baptized children of two Jewish parents.
37. Falconi, pp. 85–93, mentions these personal characteristics.

ordinate the placing of Jews in religious institutions, and supplied them with letters in his name asking that doors be opened. At least twenty-one institutions cooperated, and at least 220 Jews, but perhaps double that number, were sheltered.[38]

This pattern was repeated in several other Italian cities. In Genoa, a priest named Don Francesco Repetto recruited scores of Catholic men and women to help him, and established a rescue network that sheltered and supplied hundreds of Jews and escorted many others to Switzerland. Don Repetto was secretary to the archbishop, Cardinal Pietro Boetto, and carried a letter of support from him.[39] In Turin, Monsignor Vincenzo Barale, secretary to the archbishop, coordinated a similar rescue operation.[40] At the palace of the archbishop of Milan, Cardinal Ildefonso Schuster, a secretary referred at least one Jewish supplicant to Don Paolo Liggeri, a priest who ran yet a third network.[41] In Perugia, at least 100 Jews found shelter with the help of sixty-year-old Don Federico Vincenti of the Church of San Andrea, who enjoyed the support of Archbishop Mario Vianello.[42] And in Assisi, Bishop Giuseppe Nicolini recruited Don Aldo Brunacci, canon of the Cathedral of San Rufino; Father Rufino Niccacci, head of the seminary of Saint Damiano; Luigi Brizi, a local printer; and several others. Members of this network sheltered hundreds of Jews, produced false papers, and personally escorted fugitives on the first leg of their dangerous journeys to Switzerland or to Allied territory in southern Italy.[43]

One astute researcher of Italian rescue operations has observed

---

38. Paola Pandolfi, *Ebrei a Firenze nel 1943: Persecuzione e deportazione* (Florence: Tesi di laurea, Università di Firenze, Facoltà di Magistero, 1989), pp. 36–40.

39. E: CDEC, 9/2: *Medaglie d'oro: Risconoscimento ai benemeriti* Benemeriti (medaglie d'oro) Repetto Don Francesco; and Carlo Brizzolari, *Gli ebrei nella storia di Genova* (Genoa: Sabatelli, 1971), pp. 303–11 and 321–28.

40. CDEC, 9/2, Benemeriti (medaglie d'oro) Don Vincenzo Barale; and A. Cauvin and G. Grasso, *Nacht und Nebel (notte e nebbia)* (Turin: Casa Editrice Marietti, n.d., but after 1980), p. 20.

41. CDEC, 5-H-b, Vittorio Luzzati, Savona, "L'odissea di un Ebreo," personal testimony of Luzzati. Don Liggeri was caught and deported for his assistance to Jews. For an account of his experiences in concentration camps, see his *Triangolo rosso: Dalle carceri di S. Vittore ai campi di concentramento e di eliminazione di Fossoli, Bolzano, Mauthausen, Gusen, Dachau, marzo 1940-maggio 1945* (Milan: La Casa, 1946).

42. Alexander Ramati, *The Assisi Underground: The Priests Who Rescued Jews* (New York: Stein and Day, 1978).

43. Ibid.

that priests in every occupied European country tended to act toward Jews just as their countrymen did.[44] Italians in general were inclined to help Jews, and Italian priests were no exception. Furthermore, bishops who were compassionate, as many in Italy apparently were, had a natural rescue network at their fingertips in the form of the priests in their dioceses, and may have resorted to it quite spontaneously. On the other hand, the many ties between priest-rescuers and their hierarchical superiors suggest the tantalizing possibility of a further link to the pope himself.

Evidence of such a link is elusive, for written documents do not seem to exist. Because of the danger involved, the pope would naturally have been careful about committing to paper any instructions to his bishops to aid Jews. Nevertheless, at least one priest, Don Aldo Brunacci of Assisi, remembers seeing such a letter. Of a meeting with Bishop Nicolini in 1943, he told American interviewer Mae Briskin, "He had in his hand a letter from the Secretary of State at the Vatican that said the situation of the Jews was becoming increasingly perilous, and called upon all bishops to help them."[45] In the Holy City itself, of course, the pope in his capacity as bishop of Rome should have taken local initiative, and the eminent historian Meir Michaelis believes that he did just that. Michaelis has concluded that Pope Pius XII personally ordered that extraterritorial Vatican sanctuaries in Rome be opened to fugitive Jews.[46]

The evidence is slight and occasionally contradictory. Not all bishops, for example, were well inclined toward Jews in hiding. The best-known case is that of the cardinal patriarch of Venice, who complained that Italian Fascists were arresting poor, old, and sick Jews while the wealthy continued to move about freely.[47] The patriarch expressed the wish, in the words of German Consul Koes-

---

44. Mae Briskin, "Rescue Italian Style," *The B'nai B'rith International Jewish Monthly*, May 1986, vol. 100, n. 9, p. 21.

45. Ibid., p. 22. See also Don Aldo Brunacci, *Ebrei in Assisi durante la guerra. Ricordi di un protagonista* (Assisi, 1985), p. 9.

46. Michaelis, p. 364.

47. The patriarch expressed his attitude to a friend of the German Consul in Venice, Koester, and the latter reported the matter to his superiors at the German Foreign Ministry on December 3, 1943. Koester added that he believed that "the patriarch spoke with the intention of having the information passed on by me to a higher level." The report is quoted in full in Friedländer, pp. 209–10.

ter in a report to his ministry on December 7, 1943, that "the measures against the Jews ... be carried out by German authorities, because then justice would at least be guaranteed for all." According to Koester, "It is well-known that the patriarch's chief wish is to have all Jews and half-Jews shut up in a ghetto." The German consul added that the patriarch had also said that "during the forty-five days of Badoglio's traitorous regime ... the Church had taken careful note that the real wirepullers were Masonic and Jewish circles, with the result that the situation was one of extreme jeopardy for the Church."[48]

Less flagrant but perhaps more typical was the case of a bishop in the Valle d'Aosta who strongly reprimanded one of his parish priests, Don Giuseppe Péaquin, because he was sheltering Jews. During the winter of 1943–44, Don Péaquin protected two Italian Jews, Davide Nissim and his wife, and an entire family of Yugoslav Jews who did not speak Italian. Don Péaquin's village was one of those where everyone knew what everyone else was doing, and many of his parishioners protested the danger he was bringing upon the entire population. Yet the priest ignored both his parishioners and his bishop, continued to help others, and eventually had to seek refuge with the partisans.[49]

The record in Italy would suggest that the cardinal patriarch of Venice and the above-mentioned bishop from the Valle d'Aosta were in a distinct minority within the Church, and that numerous archbishops, bishops, priests, monks, and nuns were deeply involved in Jewish rescue. Pope Pius XII certainly knew what was being done to save Jews. Whether he initiated, encouraged, or even approved of that behavior is less clear. The question will undoubtedly receive more attention from historians in the future, and one may hope for affirmative answers. For only acting thus could the pope begin to address his terrifying failure in October 1943.

48. Ibid., p. 210.
49. CDEC, 9/1: *Riconoscimento benemeriti dell'opera di soccorso* Biella, statement of Davide Nissim, December 13, 1954.

Michele Sarfatti
(translated by Ivo Herzer)

Selected Bibliography of Anti-Jewish Persecution in Italy

The first studies of anti-Jewish persecutions in Italy between 1938 and 1945 were published just a few months after the liberation of Rome (June, 1944), Tuscany (summer of 1944) and northern Italy (April 25, 1945). This initial effort, consisting mostly of incomplete studies (with some exceptions such as the one by Momigliano), slowed down quite soon and the 1950s saw a limited number of publications. Then came the blossoming of the publications and projects that appeared in the first years of the following decade (between 1960 and 1963 there were the publications by De Felice, the collected works edited by Valabrega for the Jewish Youth Federation of Italy and by the Center for Contemporary Jewish Documentation).

This brief phase was succeeded by a new period of almost fifteen years, marked by important publications that were, however, quite disconnected from each other. Starting with 1978 the overall picture began to change again. The special edition by *Il Ponte* and the works of Michaelis and Mayda, among others, were published, followed one year later by those of Happacher, Fölkel, and Picciotto Fargion; a new, contemporary phase opens up, characterized by an increased interest in the history of persecutions in Italy and by an intertwining of the various studies.

These chronological considerations, no doubt only roughly outlined above in quantitative rather than qualitative or substantive terms, are based on the dates of publication of the works surveyed rather than on the period when the studies had been conducted. They indicate that by now the historical research on anti-Jewish persecution in Italy has exhausted its initial phase and has entered its mature state where the methodology itself can and must be subjected to analysis.

At the same time, an examination of the works published in the last phase shows that, either because of the uneven development of the historiography, or because of its dispersion across different countries (and therefore a multiplicity of different languages and publishing sites), even some important studies conducted in the early phases are in danger of remaining unutilized.

These two assessments point to the need to begin a systematic bibliographic research, whose purpose would be to serve both as a tool for the researcher and as a stimulus for analyses of the very research itself.

The bibliography that has been developed and presented here is certainly partial, since, as the first systematic attempt in this field, it suffers from the limitations of the author, as well as the impossibility of cataloging all the different types of written documents in existence. While it is obviously not possible to justify the author's limitations, the incompleteness due to the variety of bibliographic material is the result of very deliberate choices that can and must be clarified. Thus it should be pointed out that for a variety of causes in each instance, not all the listed works correspond to all the criteria described below.

1. Thematic Criteria

The following are listed: works devoted exclusively or principally to anti-Jewish persecutions in Italy; works devoted to events or questions of importance to this topic (for example, the camp of Fossoli di Carpi) even though not concerning only Jews; some works of wider range containing chapters judged important for the above topic, such as, for example, the most important general histories of anti-Jewish persecutions in Europe containing chapters dealing with Italy (it was not possible to do likewise for the general histories of modern Italy, because most of them do not devote much attention to anti-Jewish persecutions); autobiographies of Italian Jews containing chapters on the above theme.

2. Linguistic Criteria

The bibliography cites works published in Italy or in Italian, the most interesting and notable works in English, and some publications in other languages.

3. Chronological Criteria

Listed are works published after the liberation (1944 or 1945, depending on the particular cities) until early 1988.

4. Topical Criteria

Listed are works that qualify as historical studies or results of research expressly dealing with events and episodes of anti-Jewish persecutions; diaries and autobiographies of Jews published as self-contained volumes.

It should be noted that autobiographies and testimonies published in journals or as part of collections of articles by various authors, diaries of partisans without actual references to the persecutions, and all works of biographical character have been excluded. In fact, some of these works are very relevant to the topic, but the vast amount of material to be examined and its enormous dispersion have made it advisable not to conduct a selection at this site (which would at any rate be incomplete and erroneous), but rather to fill this gap by an appropriate bibliographic research project.

5. Bibliographic Criteria

Listed are: all the studies and autobiographies published as independent works that have been found; the most interesting (i.e. the major part) contained in collections of studies by various authors, or in the major historical and cultural journals.

Scope of Research

The publications listed have been identified by examining existing bibliographies (cited in section A3) and catalogs of the library of the *Centro di Documentazione Ebraica Contemporanea* (CDEC, Center for Contemporary Jewish Documentation)—by author and by subject. I wish to thank the librarians and other members of CDEC for their numerous suggestions. Also cited are bibliographic references in the particular publications.

Note Regarding the Index of the Bibliography

The specific theme of the bibliography is developed in sections A2, A3, B2, B3, B4, B5, B6, B9, B10; section A1 is deliberately a summary one; sections B1, B7, B8 are incomplete, inasmuch as they deal with collateral topics.

The individual works were listed under the various sections on the basis of their contents. In a limited number of cases a criterion of prevalence had to be applied (giving first priority to the nine main sections, followed by the most developed topic of the author). The individual sections, however, (and in particular sections B3, B4, and B5) must be considered to be interdependent.

Note on Individual Entries

In cases of new editions or translations into Italian, the original edition appears first if the catalog information is complete, followed by entries of successive editions. If the new editions or Italian translations are significantly revised, then the original edition, if its complete catalog description is available, is indicated in parentheses.

Note on Section A2

As a result of the decision to list only the individual works of various authors, the collections of studies (of one or more authors) have not been cited as independent entries in this bibliography. It should, however, be noted that some of these would deserve to be listed in section A2: the three collections of essays *Gli Ebrei in Italia durante il Fascismo* of 1961–1963; the publications *Ebrei, sionismo, Fascismo* by Valabrega and *Ebrei in Italia: deportazione, Resistenza* of 1974; the special number of *Il Ponte* of 1978; the volume *Spostamenti di popolazione e deportazioni in Europa 1939–1945* of 1987.

Abbreviations

ADEI	Associazione Donne Ebree D'Italia
ANED	Associazione Nazionale Ex Deportati Politici nei Campi Nazisti
ANEI	Associazione Nazionale Ex Internati
ANPI	Associazione Nazionale Partigiani d'Italia
ANPPIA	Associazione Nazionale Perseguitati Politici Italiani Antifascisti
CDEC	Centro di Documentazione Ebraica Contemporanea
CDJC	Centre de Documentation Juive Contemporaine
DECENNIO (1984)	Israel 'Un decennio' 1974–1984. Numero unico dell'Israel. Saggi sull'Ebraismo italiano, Francesco Del Canuto, ed. (Rome: Carucci, 1984), 420p.
DIFESA (1978)	Il Ponte, XXIV, 11–12 (novembre–dicembre 1978) (special number under the title La Difesa della Razza), pp. 1303–1532.

EBR/IT (1974)   *Ebrei in Italia: deportazione, Resistenza*, ed-
                         ited by CDEC (Florence, 1974), 59p. (also Flor-
                         ence, 1975, 61p.).
FGEI   Federazione Giovanile Ebraica d'Italia
MEMOIRE (1987)   *Mémoire du Génocide. Un recueil de 80 arti-
                         cles du "Mond Juif,"* revue du Centre de Doc-
                         umentation Juive Contemporaine, directeur
                         et rédacteur en chef: Georges Wellers, Serge
                         Klarsfeld et al., eds, 1987, 702p.
QUAD/EBR (1961)   "Gli Ebrei in Italia durante il fascismo," *Quad-
                         erni della FGEI* (Turin, 1961), 123p. (also Bo-
                         logna: Forni, 1981), 123p.
QUAD/EBR (1962)   "Gli Ebrei in Italia durante il fascismo," n. 2,
                         Guido Valabrega, ed., *Quaderni del CDEC*
                         (Milan, 1962), 177p.
QUAD/EBR (1963)   "Gli Ebrei in Italia durante il fascismo," n. 3,
                         Guido Valabrega, ed., *Quaderni del CDEC*
                         (Milan, 1963), 230p.
QUAD/INT   *Quaderni del Centro di Studi sulla deporta-
                         zione e l'internamento* (published by ANEI,
                         Rome).
RMI   *La Rassegna Mensile di Israel* (published by
                         UCII, Rome)
SPOSTAMENTI (1987)   *Spostamenti di popolazione e deportazioni in
                         Europa 1939–1945* (Bologna: Cappelli, 1987),
                         xiv + 506p.
UCII   Unione delle Comunità Israelitiche Italiane
VAL/EBR (1974)   Valabrega, Guido, *Ebrei, sionismo, fascismo*
                         (Urbino: Argalia, 1974), 531p.

Bibliography of the Anti-Jewish Persecutions in Italy, 1938–1945

A. General Works

(1) The Jews in Italy from the Unification to the Liberation, 1861–1945
(Selected General References)
(2) History of the Anti-Jewish Persecutions in Italy, 1938–1945
(3) Bibliographies

B. Specific Studies

(1) The Period Before 1938
(2) Fascist Anti-Semitism
(3) The Period of the Fascist Regime and the Italian Monarchy: Anti-
Jewish Legislation and Its Implementation, 1938–1943
(4) Internment of Foreign Jews and Anti-Fascist Italian Jews, 1940–
1943
(5) The Period of the Italian Social Republic and German Occupation:
Deportations, September 1943–April 1945
(6) The Fate of Individual Jewish Communities, 1938–1945
(7) Italian Authorities and Jews Outside Italy (Colonies, Occupied Zones,
Diplomacy, etc.), 1938–1943

(8) Italian Jews Outside Italy
(9) Jewish Participation in Anti-Fascism and the Resistance; Aid Organizations
(10) Jewish Testimonies of the Persecutions

A1. The Jews in Italy from the Unification to the Liberation, 1861–1945 (Selected General References)

Bedarida, Guido. *Ebrei d'Italia* (Livorno: Tirrena, 1950), 324p.

Canepa, Andrew M. "Cattolici ed ebrei nell'Italia liberale (1870–1915)," in *Comunità*, XXXII, 179, aprile 1978, pp. 43–110 (brief synopsis: "Reflections on Antisemitism in Liberal Italy," in *The Wiener Library Bulletin*, XXXI (n.s.), pp. 47–48, 1978, pp. 104–11.

Della Pergola, Sergio. *Anatomia dell'ebraismo italiano. Caratteristiche demografiche, economiche, sociali, religiose e politiche di una minoranza*, (Assisi-Rome: Carucci, 1976), xvi+358p.

Finzi, Roberto. *Gli Ebrei nella società italiana dall'unità al fascismo*, in *DIFESA (1978)*, pp. 1372–1411.

Fubini, Guido. *La condizione giuridica dell'ebraismo italiano. Dal periodo napoleonico alla Repubblica* (Florence: Nuova Italia, 1974), xxvii+129p. Revised edition of articles published under the same title in *RMI*, XXXVI, 12, dicembre 1970, pp. 472–90; XXXVII (1971): 1, gennaio, pp. 19–32; 3, marzo, pp. 169–85; 7, luglio, pp. 426–39; XXXVIII (1972): 2, febbraio, pp. 77–91; 6, giugno, pp. 363–82; XXXIX, 1, gennaio 1973, pp. 34–45.

Hughes, H. Stuart. *Prisoners of Hope. The Silver Age of the Italian Jews 1924–1974* (Cambridge: Harvard University Press, 1983), 188p. See also *Prigionieri della speranza. Alla ricerca dell'identità ebraica nella letteratura italiana contemporanea* (Bologna: Mulino, 1983), 189p.

Milano, Attilio. *Storia degli ebrei in Italia* (Turin: Einaudi, 1963), xxii+727p.

Minerbi, Sergio. *Raffaele Cantoni. Un ebreo anticonformista* (Assisi-Rome: Carucci, 1978), 278p.

Momigliano, Arnaldo. "The Jews of Italy," in *The New York Review*, 24 October 1985, pp. 22–26. See also "Gli ebrei d'Italia," in Momigliano, Arnaldo, *Pagine ebraiche* (Turin: Einaudi, 1987), pp. 129–42.

Roth, Cecil. *The History of the Jews of Italy* (Philadelphia: Jewish Publication Society of America, 1946), xiv+575p. Roth wrote the last chapter in collaboration with Gino Luzzatto "Gino Luzzatto and Jewish History," in *Nuova Rivista Storica*, XLIX, 1–2, gennaio–aprile 1965, pp. 166–69.

A2. History of the Anti-Jewish Persecutions in Italy, 1938–1945

(a) General Histories of the Persecution in Italy

Carpi, Daniel. "The Origins and Development of Fascist Anti-Semitism in Italy (1922–1945)," *The Catastrophe of European Jewry. Antecedents, History, Reflections*, Yisrael Gutman, Livia Rothkirchen, eds. (Jerusalem: Yad Vashem, 1976), pp. 283–98 (revised translation of "Hitpathutah u-Mahalakheha shel ha-Antishemiyut ha-Fashistit be-Italya (1922–1945)," *Yalkut Moreshet*, X, April 1969, pp. 79–88. Also "Italy. Holocaust Period," *Encyclopaedia Judaica* IX (Jerusalem, 1971), col. 1132–37.

De Felice, Renzo. *Storia degli ebrei italiani sotto il fascismo*, third revised and expanded edition (Turin: Einaudi, 1972), xxxvi + 628p. See also (Milan: Mondadori, 1977), 2 vol., xxxii + 768p. First edition (Turin: Einaudi, 1961), xxxix + 697p.

Della Pergola, Sergio. "Appunti sulla demografia della persecuzione anti-ebraica in italia," *RMI*, XLVII, 1–6, gennaio–giugno 1981, pp. 120–37.

Mayda, Giuseppe. *Ebrei sotto Salò. La persecuzione antisemita 1943– 1945* (Milan: Feltrinelli, 1978), 274p. Brief synopsis, "La persecuzione antisemita 1943–1945," *DIFESA (1978)*, pp. 1428–39.

Michaelis, Meir. *Mussolini and the Jews. German-Italian Relations and the Jewish Question in Italy 1922–1945* (London: The Institute of Jewish Affairs, 1978), xii + 472p. See also slightly revised edition with a documented appendix, *Mussolini e la questione ebraica* (Milan: Comunità, 1982), 572p. Earlier, Michaelis treated the topic in "The Attitude of the Fascist Regime to the Jews in Italy. Part One: Up to the Enactment of the Racial Laws (1938)," *Yad Vashem Studies* IV, 1960, pp. 7–41; see also translated and expanded "I rapporti italo-tedeschi e il problema degli ebrei in Italia (1922–38)," *Rivista di Studi Politici Internazionali*, XXVIII, 2, aprile–giugno 1961, pp. 238–82.

Momigliano, Eucardio. *40.000 fuori legge*, in *40.000 fuori legge* (Documenti, n. 2) (Rome: Carboni, 1945), pp. 1–24, Momigliano, Eucardio, *Storia tragica e grottesca del razzismo fascista* (Milan: Mondadori, 1946), 142p.

Picciotto Fargion, Liliana. "The Anti-Jewish Policy of the Italian Social Republic (1943–1945)," *Yad Vashem Studies*, XVII (1986), pp. 17–49; see also "La politique antisémite de la République Sociale Italienne," *Le Monde Juif*, XLIV, 1988; also published in *MEMORIE (1987)*, pp. 133– 58.

Valabrega, Guido. "Il fascismo e gli ebrei: appunti per un consuntivo storiografico," *Il fascismo e le autonomie locali* S. Fontana ed., (Bologna: 1973), pp. 401–26; see also "Il fascismo e gli ebrei: un esperimento di consuntivo storiografico," *VLA/EBR (1974)*, pp. 11–40.

Voigt, Klaus. "Refuge and Persecution in Italy, 1933–1945," *Simon Wiesenthal Center Annual*, IV, 1987, pp. 3–64. The first part is an expanded and revised version of "Gli emigrati in Italia dai paesi sotto la dominazione nazista: tollerati e perseguitati (1933–1940)," *Storia Contemporanea*, XVI, 1, febbraio 1985, pp. 45–87.

Zuccotti, Susan. *The Italians and the Holocaust. Persecution, Rescue and Survival* (New York: Basic Books, 1987), xviii + 334p. The Italian translation will be published in 1988.

(b) Italy in the General Histories of Anti-Jewish Persecutions in Europe

Dawidowicz, Lucy S. *The War Against the Jews. 1933–1945* (New York: Holt, Rinehart and Winston) also (London: Weidenfeld and Nicolson, 1975), xviii + 460p. ("Italy": pp. 368–71 and *passim*).

Hilberg, Raul. *The Destruction of the European Jews*, revised and definitive edition (New York-London: Holmes and Meier, 1985), 3 vol., xii + 1273p. ("Italy," pp. 660–79 and *passim)*. First edition (Chicago: Quadrangle, 1961), x + 788p.

Levin, Nora. *The Holocaust. The Destruction of European Jewry 1933– 1945* (New York: Crowell, 1968), xvi + 768p. ("Italy": pp. 459–68 and *passim*).

Poliakov, Léon. *Bréviaire de la Haine (Le III Reich et les Juifs* (Paris: Calmann-Lévy, 1951), xv + 385p. ("Italy": pp. 188–93 and *passim)*. See also *Harvest of Hate. The Nazi Program for the Destruction of the Jews of Europe* (New York: Syracuse University Press, 1954), 388p.; *Il nazismo e lo sterminio degli Ebrei* (Turin: Einaudi, 1955) 400p.; ("Italy": pp. 219–24 and *passim*).

Reitlinger, Gerald. *La soluzione finale. Il tentativo di sterminio degli Ebrei d'Europa 1939–1945* (Milano: Saggiatore, 1962), 702p. ("Italy": pp. 425–31 and *passim*). Translation, with the parts on Italy and the occupied territories revised by Massimo Adolfo Vitale: *The Final Solution. The Attempt to Exterminate the Jews of Europe 1939–1945* (London: Vallentine and Mitchell, 1953), xii + 622p. Also, revised and expanded edition (London: Vallentine and Mitchell, 1968), xii + 668p. ("Italy": pp. 378–84 and *passim*).

A3. Bibliographies

(a) General Bibliographies of Jews in Italy

Luzzatto, Aldo, and Moldavi, Moshe. *Bibliotheca italo-ebraica. Bibliografia per la storia degli Ebrei in Italia. 1964–1973*, Daniel Carpi, ed. (Rome: Carucci, 1982), 251p. Continuation of the volume by Attilio Milano of 1964.

Milano, Attilio. *Bibliotheca historica italo-judaica* (Firenze: Sansoni Antiquariato, 1954), 209p. Books and articles published in Italy and abroad from 1800 to the beginning of 1954 on the history of Jews in Italy.

———. *Bibliotheca historica italo-judaica. Supplemento 1954–1963* (Florence: Sansoni Antiquariato, 1964), 82p. Continuation of the preceding volume.

———. "Bibliografia degli studi sulla storia degli ebrei in Italia (1964–1966)," *RMI*, XXXII, 11, novembre 1966 (appendix), 19p. Continuation of the preceding volume.

Romano, Giorgio. *Bibliografia italo-ebraica (1848–1977)* (Florence: Olschki, 1979), 208p. Books published in Italian from 1848 to 1977 on all Jewish topics.

(b) General Bibliographies of Anti-Jewish Persecutions in Europe

Bibliografia della deportazione (Milan: ANED-Mondadori, 1982), 94p.

Devoto, Andrea. *Bibliografia dell'oppressione nazista fino al 1962* (Florence: Olschki, 1964), ix + 149p.

———. *L'oppressione nazista. Considerazioni e bibliografia 1963–1981* (Florence: Olschki, 1983), xv + 396p. Continuation of the preceding book.

Friedman, Philip and Robinson, Jacob. *Guide to Jewish History under Nazi Impact* (New York: Yad Vashem Martyrs' and Heroes' Memorial Authority and YIVO Institute for Jewish Research, 1960), xxxi + 425p.

Persecution and Resistance under the Nazis, The Weiner Library, part I edited by Ilse R. Wolff, part II compiled and edited by Helen Kehr (London: Institute of Contemporary History, 1978), 500p.

Szonyi, David M. *The Holocaust: an Annotated Bibliography and Resource Guide* (New York: Ktav, 1985), xiv + 396p.

(c) General Bibliographies of Anti-Jewish Persecutions in Italy

Mayda, Guiseppe. *Bibliografia*, in Mayda, Giuseppe, *Ebrei sotto Salò. La persecuzione antisemita 1943–1945* (Milan: Feltrinelli, 1978), pp. 255–66.

Michaelis, Meir. *Bibliography*, in Michaelis, Meir, *Mussolini and the*

Jews. German-Italian Relations and the Jewish Question in Italy 1922–1945 (London: The Institute of Jewish Affairs, 1978), pp. 432–62. See also *Bibliografia*, in *Mussolini e la questione ebraica*, pp. 521–59.

(d) Bibliographic and Archival Reviews of Anti-Jewish Persecutions in Italy

Antoniani Persichilli, Gina. "Disposizioni normative e fonti archivistiche per lo studio dell'internamento in Italia (giugno 1940–luglio 1943)," *Rassegna degli Archivi di Stato*, a. XXXVIII, n. 1–3, 1978, pp. 77–96.

Canepa, Andrew M. "Half-hearted Cynicism. Mussolini's Racial Politics," *Patterns of Prejudice*, XIII, 6, November–December 1979, pp. 18–27.

Cereja, Federico. "La deportazione italiana nei campi di sterminio: lettura storiografica e prospettive di ricerca," *La deportazione nei campi di sterminio nazisti. Studi e testimonianze*, Federico Cereja and Brunello Mantelli, eds. (Milan: Angeli, 1986), pp. 17–37. The first part of the essay appears slightly modified as "La deportazione italiana nei campi di sterminio," in *Italia Contemporanea*, 160, settembre 1985, pp. 95–103.

Michaelis, Meir. "The 'Duce' and the Jews. An Assessment of the Literature on Italian Jewry under Fascism (1922–1945)," *Yad Vashem Studies* XI, 1976, pp. 7–32.

Picciotto Fargion, Liliana. "La persecuzione antiebraica in Italia," *L'Italia nella seconda guerra mondiale e nella Resistenza*, Francesca Ferratini Tosi et al., eds. (Milan: Istituto Nazionale per la Storia del Movimento di Liberazione in Italia-Angeli, 1988), pp. 197–213.

Pusceddu, Fausto. "Archivi italiani e fonti documentarie relative alla storia degli ebrei in Italia," in *Italia Judaica. Atti del 1 Convegno internazionale. Bari, 18–22 maggio 1981* (Rome: Ministero per i Beni Culturali ed Ambientali, 1983), pp. 229–38.

Romano, Giorgio. "La persecuzione e le deportazioni degli ebrei di Roma e d'Italia nelle opere di scrittori ebrei," *Scritti in memoria di Enzo Sereni. Saggi sull'Ebraismo Romano*, Daniel Carpi, Attilio Milano, Umberto Nahon, eds. (Jerusalem: Fondazione Sally Mayer, 1970), pp. 314–39. See also slightly expanded under the title "La persecuzione antiebraica nell'opera di scrittori ebrei italiani," in Romano, Giorgio, *Ebrei nella letteratura* (Rome: Carucci, 1979), 67–99.

Sarfatti, Michele. *L'internamento nei campi degli ebrei italiani antifascisti e degli ebrei stranieri (1940–1943). Rassegna bibliografica e spunti di ricerca.* To be published in 1988.

Toscano, Mario. "Gli ebrei in Italia dall'emancipazione alle persecuzioni," *Storia Contemporanea* XVII, 5, ottobre 1986, pp. 905–954.

B1. The Period Before 1938

Calo', Anselmo. "La genesi della legge del 1930," *RMI*, LI, 3, settembre–dicembre 1985, pp. 334–439.

Carpi, Daniel. "The Catholic Church and the Italian Jewry Under the Fascists (To the Death of Pius XI)," *Yad Vashem Studies*, IV, 1960, pp. 43–56.

———. "P'iluto ha-medinit shel Weizmann b'Italia ba-shanim 1923–1934" ("The Political Activity of Chaim Weizmann in Italy during the Years 1923–1934"), *Ha-Zionut*, II, 1971, pp. 169–207.

———. "Il problema ebraico nella politica italiana fra le due guerre mondiali," *Rivista di Studi Politici Internazionali*, XXVIII, 1, gennaio–marzo 1961, pp. 35–56.

Carpi, Leone. *Come e dove rinacque la marina d'Israele. La Scuola Marittima del 'Bethar' a Civitavecchia* (Rome: NEMI, 1967), 160p.

Del Canuto, Francesco. "Come si giunse alla missione in Etiopia presso i Falascia," *DECENNIO (1984)*, pp. 23–45.

———. *Il movimento sionistico in Italia dalle origini al 1924* (Milan: Federazione Sionistica Italiana, 1972), 154p.

Della Seta, Simonetta. "Gli ebrei del Mediterraneo nella strategia politica fascista sino al 1938: il caso di Rodi," *Storia Contemporanea*, XVII, 6, dicembre 1986, pp. 997–1032.

Di Porto, Bruno. "La questione ebraica in 'Echi e Commenti,'" *DECENNIO (1984)*, pp. 185–213.

Eckert, Tamar. *Il movimento sionistico-chalutzistico in Italia fra le due guerre mondiali* (Tel Aviv: Kevuzat Yavne, 1970), 136p. (Also in Hebrew: *Ha-tenu'à ha-tzionìth chalutzìth be-Italia ben shetè milchamòth ha-'olàm*, Tel-Aviv, 1970).

Levi, Elio. "Episodi di vita ebraica milanese fra le due guerre mondiali," *Scritti in memoria di Leone Carpi. Saggi sull'Ebraismo italiano*, Daniel Carpi, Attilio Milano e Alexander Rofè, eds. (Jerusalem: Fondazione Sally Mayer, 1967), pp. 229–40.

Luzzatto, Amos. "La Comunità in Italia durante il fascismo," *QUAD/EBR (1961)*, pp. 14–20.

Michaelis, Meir. "Gli ebrei italiani sotto il regime fascista dalla marcia su Roma alla caduta del fascismo (1922–1945). 1: Dall'affermarsi del fascismo alla legislazione razziale ('19-'38)," *RMI*, XXVIII, 1962: 5, maggio, pp. 211–29; 8, agosto, pp. 350–68; 10, ottobre, pp. 451–65; XXIX, 1963: 1–2, gennaio–febbraio, pp. 18–41; 7–8, luglio–agosto, pp. 291–308; XXX, 1964: 1, gennaio, pp. 3–23; 6–7, giugno–luglio, pp. 247–60; XXXII, 1, gennaio 1966, pp. 15–37.

Milano, Attilio. "Gli enti culturali ebraici in Italia nell'ultimo trentennio (1907–1937)," *RMI*, XII, 6, febbraio–marzo 1938, pp. 253–69.

Minerbi, Sergio. "L'azione diplomatica italiana nei confronti degli ebrei sefarditi durante e dopo la I guerra mondiale (1915–1929)," *RMI*, XLVII, 7–12, luglio–dicembre 1981, pp. 86–119.

———. "Gli ultimi due incontri Weizmann-Mussolini (1933–1934)," *Storia Contemporanea*, V, 3, settembre 1974, pp. 431–44.

Nahon, Umberto. "La polemica antisionista del 'Popolo di Roma' nel 1929," *Scritti in memoria di Enzo Sereni. Saggi sull'Ebraismo Romano*, Daniel Carpi, Attilio Milano, Umberto Nahon, eds. (Jerusalem: Fondazione Sally Mayer, 1970), pp. 216–53.

Ottino, Carlo Leopoldo. "Jabotinsky e l'Italia," *QUAD/EBR (1963)*, pp. 51–81.

Pavoncello Piperno, Celeste. " 'La Nostra Bandiera': l'adesione agli 'ideali' fascisti di un gruppo di ebrei italiani," *RMI*, XLVIII, 7–12, luglio–dicembre 1982, pp. 15–22.

Pellegrini, Ernestina. "Ebraismo ed europeismo nella Toscana degli anni trenta," *Il Ponte*, XXXVIII, 10, ottobre 1982, pp. 1017–51.

Polacco, Evelina. "La fondazione e l'attività nel primo quinquennio" and "La progressiva espansione fino alla persecuzione razziale e alla seconda guerra mondiale (1933–1939)," *Dalla nascita ai giorni nostri. Breve storia della Federazione Italiana della WIZO* (Venice: ADEI, 1971), pp. 21–35, 41–47.

Romano, Giorgio. "Il Sionismo in Italia fino alla seconda guerra mondiale," *RMI*, XLII, 7–8, luglio–agosto 1976, pp. 341–54.

Toscano, Mario. "Fermenti culturali ed esperienze organizzative della gioventù ebraica italiana (1911–1925)," *Storia Contemporanea*, XIII, 6, dicembre 1982, pp. 915–61. Significantly expanded version of "Prime note sui fermenti culturali e le esperienze organizzative dei giovani ebrei italiani tra il 1911 ed il 1926," *RMI*, XLVII, 7–12, luglio–dicembre 1981, pp. 136–42.

Valabrega, Guido. "Prime notizie su 'La Nostra Bandiera' (1934–1938)," *QUAD/EBR (1961)*, pp. 21–33. See also *VAL/EBR (1974)*, pp. 41–57.

———. "Per la storia degli ebrei sotto il fascismo: prime notizie su 'Davar' (1934–1938)," *Il Movimento di Liberazione in Italia*, 107, aprile–giugno 1972, pp. 101–20. See also under the title "Prime notizie su 'Davar,'" *VAL/EBR (1974)*, pp. 58–88.

———. "Rileggendo 'Sionismo bifronte,'" *DIFESA (1978)*, pp. 1464–77.

B2. Fascist Anti-Semitism

Benedetti, Luciano. "Brevi note sulla questione ebraica e la politica estera fascista (1922–1939)," *Studi Senesi*, XCVII, 2, 1985, pp. 353–68.

Benini, Aroldo. "Il contributo italiano alla storia del razzismo," *Il Paradosso*, V, 21, gennaio–marzo 1960, pp. 50–57.

Bernardini, Gene. "The Origins and Development of Racial Antisemitism in Fascist Italy," *The Journal of Modern History*, XLIX, 3, September 1977, pp. 431–53.

Caffaz, Ugo. *L'antisemitismo italiano sotto il fascismo* (Florence: Nuova Italia, 1975), 131p.

Calo', Anselmo. "Stampa e propaganda antisemita del regime fascista prima delle leggi razziali," *DECENNIO (1984)*, pp. 115–63.

Ledeen, Michael A. "Italian Jews and Fascism," in *Judaism*, XVIII, 3, summer 1969, pp. 277–98. "The Evolution of Italian Fascist Antisemitism," *Jewish Social Studies*, XXXVII, 1, January 1975, pp. 3–17. See also "La 'questione ebraica' nell'Italia fascista," *Nuova Antologia*, CIX, 2086, 1974, pp. 185–201.

Michaelis, Meir. "La politica razziale fascista vista da Berlino. L'antisemitismo italiano alla luce di documenti inediti tedeschi (1938–1943)," *Storia Contemporanea*, XI, 6, dicembre 1980, pp. 1003–45. "Riflessioni sulla recente storia dell'Ebraismo italiano," *RMI*, XLII, 5–6, maggio–giugno 1977, pp. 191–211; XLV, 1–3, gennaio–marzo 1979, pp. 22–42; XLVIII, 1–6, gennaio–giugno 1982, pp. 167–78. "Ancora sulla 'questione ebraica' nell'Italia fascista," *Nuova Antologia*, CXVI, 2138, aprile–giugno 1981, pp. 230–49.

Pichetto, Maria Teresa. *Alle radici dell'odio. Preziosi e Benigni antisemiti* (Milan: Angeli, 1983), 148p.

Preti, Luigi. *Impero fascista, africani ed ebrei* (Milan: Mursia, 1968), 375p. The author has already developed this topic in *I miti dell'impero e della razza nell'Italia degli anni '30* (Rome: Opere Nuove, 1965), 140p.

Robertson, Esmonde M. "Race as a Factor in Mussolini's Policy in Africa and Europe," *Journal of Contemporary History*, XXIII, 1, January 1988, pp. 37–58.

B3. The Period of the Fascist Regime and the Italian Monarchy: Anti-Jewish Legislation and Its Implementation, 1938–1943

(a) Studies

Colombo, Yoseph. "Il probleme scolastico per gli ebrei d'Italia nel '38. La scuola di Milano," *RMI*, XXXI, 6, giugno 1965, pp. 259–72.

De Felice, Renzo. "La Chiesa cattolica e il problema ebraico durante gli anni dell'antisemitismo fascista," *RMI*, XXIII, 1, gennaio 1957, pp. 23–35.

Del Canuto, Francesco. "Ebraismo e Sionismo: un risveglio di coscienze negli anni difficili (1938–1944)," *RMI*, XLVIII, 7–12, luglio–dicembre 1982, pp. 29–59.

Fubini, Guido. "La legislazione razziale. Orientamenti giurisprudenziali e dottrina giuridica," *DIFESA (1978)*, pp. 1412–27.

Judenverfolgung in Italien, den italienisch bestzten Gebieten und in Nordafrika (Frankfurt am Main: United Restitution Organization, 1962), xxvii + 229p.

Lattes, Dante. "Coloro che son partiti," *RMI*, XXVI, 8–9, agosto–settembre 1960, pp. 347–50.

La scuola media ebraica di Trieste durante il periodo razziale, Bruna Schreiber, ed. (Trieste: Comunità Israelitica di Trieste, 1982), 29p.

Levi, Fausto. "Le leggi razziali e la scuola," *Scuola e Resistenza. Atti del convegno promosso dalla Regione Emilia-Romagna per il XXX della Resistenza (Parma 19–21 maggio 1977)*, Nicola Raponi, ed. (Parma: Pilotta, 1978), pp. 87–95.

Lo Giudice, Maria Rosaria. "Razza e giustizia nell'Italia fascista," *Rivista di Storia Contemporanea*, XII, 1, gennaio 1983, pp. 70–90.

Marazzi, Lorenzo. *La repressione politica e razziale all'Azienda Tranviaria di Milano nel periodo fascista* (Milan: Comitato Unitario Antifascista dell'Azienda Trasporti Municipali di Milan, 1987), 75p.

Ottolenghi, Achille. "La legislazione antisemita in Italia," *Fascismo e antifascismo. Lezioni e testimonianze* (Milan: Feltrinelli, 1962), vol. I (*1918–1936*), pp. 202–9.

Passolunghi, Pier Angelo and Zovatto, Piero. "La reazione cattolica al razzismo fascista (1938)," *La Scuola Cattolica*, CIV, 1, 1976, pp. 47–82.

Pedatella, Anthony R. "Italian Attitudes Toward Jewry in the Twentieth Century," *Jewish Social Studies*, XLVII, 1, Winter 1985, pp. 51–62.

Pellicani, Antonio. *Il Papa di tutti. La Chiesa cattolica, il fascismo e il razzismo 1929–1945* (Milan: Sugar, 1964), xiv + 145p.; see ch. VI, pp. 101–15: "La questione della razza."

Sabatello, Franco. "Il censimento degli ebrei del 1938 (note metodologiche sulla sua preparazione, la sua realizzazione ed i suoi risulati," *RMI*, XLII, 1–2, gennaio–febbraio 1976, pp. 25–55.

Sabatello, Eitan Franco. "Aspetti economici ed ecologici dell'Ebraismo romano prima, durante e dopo le leggi razziali (1928–1965)," *Scritti in memoria di Enzo Sereni. Saggi sull'Ebraismo Romano*, Daniel Carpi et al., eds. (Jerusalem: Fondazione Sally Mayer, 1970), pp. 254–92.

Schwarzenberg, Claudio. *Diritto e giustizia nell'Italia fascista* (Milan: Mursia, 1977), 310 p.; see ch. X, pp. 143–61, "Antisemitismo e legislazione razziale."

Segre, Augusto. "Sionismo e sionisti in Italia (1933–1943)," *Scritti in memoria di Nathan Cassuto*, Daniel Carpi et al., eds. (Jerusalem: Kedem-Yad Leyakkirenu, 1986), pp. 176–208.

———. "Movimenti giovanili ebraici in Italia durante il periodo razziale," *RMI*, XXXI, 8–9, agosto–settembre 1965, pp. 382–93.

Spinosa, Antonio. "Le persecuzioni razziali in Italia," *Il Ponte*, VIII, 1952: 7, luglio, pp. 964–78; 8, agosto, pp. 1078–96; 11, novembre, pp. 1604–22; IX, 7, luglio 1953, pp. 950–68.

Stigliani, Nicholas A. and Marzotto, Antonette. "Fascist Antisemitism and the Italian Jews," *The Wiener Library Bulletin*, XXVIII (n.s.), 35–36, 1975, pp. 41–49.

Treves, Piero, "Formiggini e il problema dell'ebreo in Italia," *Angelo Fortunato Formiggini un editore del Novecento*, Luigi Balsamo e Renzo Cremante, eds. (Bologna: Mulino, 1981), pp. 55–72.

Valabrega, Guido. "Reazione sociale, razzismo, antifascismo: spunti di ricerca e discussione," *QUAD/EBR (1963)*, pp. 97–119. See also *VAL/EBR (1974)*, pp. 156–89.

Ventura, Carlo. "Il centro fascista di Trieste per lo studio del problema ebraico," *Trieste*, VIII, 43, maggio–giugno 1961, pp. 20–23.

Voghera, Bruna. "Gli anni difficili (1939–1945)," *Dalla nascita ai giorni nostri. Breve storia della Federazione Italiana della WIZO* (Venice: ADEI, 1971), pp. 49–55.

Voigt, Klaus. "Notizie statistiche sugli immigrati e profughi ebrei in Italia (1938–1945)," *DECENNIO (1984)*, pp. 407–20.

(b) Collections of Anti-Jewish Laws

"Alcuni esempi di legislazione razziale fascista," in *QUAD/EBR (1961)*, pp. 101–23.

"Le leggi razziali italiane (legislazione e documentazione)," with an introduction by Renzo Sertoli Salis (special number of *Dottrina fascista*, febbraio 1939) (Milan: Varese, 1939), 135p.

Provvedimenti per la difesa della razza italiana, second edition (Milan: Pirola, 1939) (August?), 70p.

Staderini, Tito. *Norme legislative riguardanti gli appartenenti alla razza ebraica. Raccolta dei provvedimenti legislativi e ministeriali coordinati ed annotati*, updated edition (Rome: Colombo, 1939), 183p. Preceding editions: *Difesa della razza* (Rome: Colombo, 1939), 99p.; *Legislazione per la difesa della razza* (Rome: Colombo, 1939), 135p.

"Una selezione: Legislazione razziale fascista (1938–1944), *DIFESA (1978)*, pp. 1510–32.

B4. Internment of Foreign Jews and Anti-Fascist Italian Jews, 1940–1943

Bierman, John. *Odyssey: The Last Great Escape from Nazi-Dominated Europe* (New York: Simon and Schuster, 1984), 255p.

Capogreco, Carlo Spartaco. *Ferramonti. La vita e gli uomini del più grande campo d'internamento fascista (1940–1945)* (Florence: Giuntina, 1987), 194p.

Carolini, Simonetta, ed. *'Pericolosi nelle contingenze belliche.' Gli internati dal 1940 al 1943* (Rome: ANPPIA, 1987), 422p.

Ferrari, Liliana. "L'attività della Santa Sede per i prigionieri nei campi di internamento italiani," *Qualestoria*, XII, 3, dicembre 1984, pp. 64–71.

Folino, Francesco. *Ferramonti. Un lager di Mussolini. Gli internati durante la guerra* (Cosenza: Brenner, 1985), xv + 373p.

Hajek, Frantz. "Appunti sugli ebrei stranieri in Italia durante la guerra," *QUAD/EBR (1963)*, pp. 153–57.

Iacoponi, Italia. "Campi di concentramento in Abruzzo durante il secondo conflitto mondiale: 1940–1945." *Rivista Abruzzese di Studi Storici dal Fascismo alla Resistenza: Nereto*, IV, 2–3, 1983, pp. 325–35; *Notaresco*, V, 1, 1984, pp. 131–51; *Civitella del Tronto*, V, 2, 1984, pp. 213–25; *Tossicia*, VI, 1, 1985, pp. 199–210; *Badia di Corropoli*, VI, 2–3, 1985, pp. 351–64; and *Teramo*, VII, 1–2, 1986, pp. 213–70.

Kalk, Israel. "I campi di concentramento italiani per ebrei profughi: Ferramonti Tarsia (Calabria)," *QUAD/EBR (1961)*, pp. 63–71.

Minardi, Marco. *Tra chiuse mura. Deportazione e campi di concentramento nella provincia di Parma 1940–1945* (Montechiarugolo: Comune di Montechiarugolo, 1987), 131p.

Pacifici, Riccardo. "Due giorni a Ferramonti," *A perpetua ricordanza di Riccardo Pacifici* (Turin: Comunità Israelitica di Genova, 1967), pp. 61–66. See also Pacifici, Riccardo, "Il 'campo' di Ferramonti negli ultimi tempi del regime fascista," *QUAD/INT*, 6, 1969–71, pp. 89–91.

Vaccari, Ilva, *Villa Emma. Un episodio agli albori della Resistenza modenese nel quadro delle persecuzioni razziali* (Modena: Istituto Storico della Resistenza in Modena e Provincia, 1960), 45p.

Vizio, Sergio. "Gli ebrei croati in Alba 1942–1945," *Notiziario dell'Istituto Storico della Resistenza in Cuneo e Provincia*, n. 28, 2nd semester 1985, pp. 117–27.

B5. The Period of the Italian Social Republic and German Occupation; Deportations, September 1943–April 1945

Apih, Elio. "Il 'Polizeihaftlager' della Risiera di San Sabba," *Qualestoria*, XII, 3, dicembre 1984, pp. 51–59.

Ascarelli, Attilio. *Le fosse Ardeatine* (Rome: Palombi, 1945), 95p. See also, with the addition of an appendix (Bologna: Canesi, 1965), 204p.; also (Rome: Silva e Ciarrapico, 1974), 204p.

Aufstehen! (In piedi) Friulani deceduti nei campi di sterminio nazisti 1943–1945, (Udine: ANED, 1978), 92p.

Basilotta, Lucia. "I nati nella provincia di Cuneo morti nei campi di sterminio," *Notiziario dell'Istituto Storico della Resistenza in Cuneo e Provincia*, 11, giugno 1977, pp. 39–51.

Bassi, Michele. *Cotignola: un approdo di salvezza per gli ebrei e per i perseguitati politici durante la guerra (1943–1945)*, estratto da *Testimonianze di fede e di carità nel tempo di guerra (1943–1945)*. Diocesi di Faenza e Modigliana (Faenza: 1985), 23p.

Bon Gherardi, Silva. "Un campo di sterminio in Italia," *DIFESA (1978)*, pp. 1440–53.

Buffarini Guidi, Glauco. *La vera verità. I documenti dell'archivio segreto del ministro degli Interni Guido Buffarini Guidi dal 1938 al 1945* (Milan: Sugar, 1970), 247p.

Cardosi, Giuliana. "Olga e Theodor Fritz Bergmann, supposti ebrei, arrestati e deportati nei Lager nazisti," *Libri e Documenti*, 1985, 1, pp. 1–22.

Cardosi, Giuliani, Cardosi, Marisa, Cardosi, Gabriella. "La questione dei 'matrimoni misti' durante la persecuzione razziale in Italia 1938–1945," *Libri e Documenti*, VI, 1980, 3, pp. 6–21; VII, 1981, 1, pp. 1–28; also published as an extract (Milan, 1981), 48p.

Carpi, Daniel. "Batei kelleh u-mahanot rikuz b'Italia b'tekufat ha-shoah" (Prisons and concentration camps in Italy during the Holocaust), *Dappim l'hekker hashoah v'ha mered*, I, 1969, pp. 178–204.

Casali, Luciano. "La deportazione dall'Italia. Fossoli di Carpi," *SPOSTAMENTI (1987)*, pp. 382–406.

Cavaglion, Alberto. "La deportazione dall'Italia. Borgo San Dalmazzo," *SPOSTAMENTI (1987)*, pp. 356–81.

———. *Nella notte straniera. Gli ebrei di S. Martin de Vésubie e il campo di Borgo San Dalmazzo 8 settembre–21 novembre 1943* (Cuneo: Arciere, 1981), 179p. Previously Cavaglion wrote on this topic in: "Gli Ebrei di St. Martin de Vésubie e lo sbandamento della 4a armata," in *8 settembre. Lo sfacelo della quarta armata* (Turin: Book Store, 1979), pp. 205–27. Also a brief synopsis: "St. Martin Vésubie. Un refuge des Juifs: fin 1942–8 septembre 1943," *Archives Juives*, XIX, 1–2, 1983, pp. 29–34.

―――. "La deportazione degli ebrei piemontesi: appunti per una storia," *La deportazione nei campi di sterminio nazisti. Studi e testimonianze*, Federico Cereja e Brunello Mantelli, eds. (Milan: Angeli, 1986), pp. 107–25.

CDEC, "Il processo Bosshammer," *QUAD/INT*, 7, 1973–1974, pp. 105–7.

Comaschi nei Lager per la libertà, edited by Istituto Comasco per la Storia del Movimento di Liberazione (Como: Amministrazione provinciale di Como, 1980), 79p.

Comitato Onoranze Ai XII Martiri Del 1 agosto 1944, *Relazione morale e finanziaria* (Pisa: 1945), 79 p.

Conti, Laura. "Primi risultati di una ricerca sul Polizeilichesdurchgangslager di Bolzano, *Il Cristallo*, VI, 2, dicembre 1964, pp. 27–41.

Dallo squadrismo fascista alle stragi della Risiera (Con il resoconto del processo) Trieste, Istria, Friuli 1919–1945 (Trieste: ANED, 1978), 182p.

Debenedetti, Giacomo. "16 ottobre 1943," *Mercurio*, I, 4, dicembre 1944, pp. 75–97. See also (Rome: OET, 1945), 82p.; also (Milan: Saggiatore, 1959), 64p.

Di Vita, Dorina. "Gli Ebrei di Milano sotto l'occupazione nazista," *QUAD/INT*, 6, 1969–1971, pp. 16–72.

Donata, Briante, et al. *I deportati pavesi nei lager nazisti* (Pavia: Amministrazione provinciale di Pavia, 1981) 174p.

Donati, Giuliana. "Persecuzione e deportazione degli ebrei dall'Italia durante la dominazione nazifascista," *EBR/I (1974)*, pp. 5–32.

Dordoni, Annarosa. *'Crociata italica.' Fascismo e religione nella repubblica di Salò (gennaio 1944-aprile 1945)* (Milan: Sugar Co., 1976), 201p. (pp. 85–99: *La componente antisemitica di 'Crociata italica'*).

Fabbroni, Flavio. *La deportazione dal Friuli nei campi di sterminio nazisti* (Udine: Istituto Friulano per la Storia del Movimento di Liberazione, 1984), 129p.

Fogar, Galliano. "La Risiera di San Sabba a Trieste," *SPOSTAMENTI (1987)*, pp. 407–44.

Fölkel, Ferruccio. *La Risiera di San Sabba. Trieste e il litorale Adriatico durante l'occupazione nazista* (Milan: Mondadori, 1979), 198p.

Fortuna, Piero. "Gorizia. 23 novembre 1943," *Trieste*, VI, 31, maggio-giugno 1959, pp. 17–18.

Friedländer, Saul. *Pie XII et le IIIè Reich. Documents* (Paris: Seuil, 1964), 235p., ch. VIII, pp. 185–200: "La déportation des juifs de Rome et d'Italie (octobre-décembre 1943)." See also *Pio XII e il Terzo Reich. Documenti* (Milan: Feltrinelli, 1965), 214p.; *Pius XII and the Third Reich. A documentation* (New York: Knopf, [also London: Chatto and Windus], 1966), 238p.

Fucile, Saro and Liana Millu, eds. *Dalla Liguria ai campi di sterminio*, ANED-Regione Liguria, (1980), 126p. See also (Genoa: ANED-Regione Liguria, 1985), 136p.

Funaro, Giuseppe. "Vicende dell'orfanotrofio israelitico di Livorno dopo l'otto settembre 1943," *QUAD/EBR (1961)*, pp. 72–77.

Garneri, Giuseppe. *Tra rischi e pericoli. Fatti e testimonianze nel periodo della Resistenza, della Liberazione e della persecuzione contro gli Ebrei* (Pinerolo: Alzani, 1981), 174p.

Happacher, Luciano. *Il lager di Bolzano. Con appendice documentari* (Trento: Comitato provinciale per il 30mo. anniversario della Resistenza e della Liberazione, 1979), 258p.

Iscritti alla Comunità Israelitica di Trieste deportati negli anni 1943–1945 e che non hanno fatto ritorno, n.d., 6p.

Izcor Eloim Le-Tovah. I deportati della Comunità di Roma durante l'occupazione nazista, n.d., 8p.

Jona, Ugo and Servi, Gino. "I cittadini ebrei di Pitigliano." *Monumento al Fascismo,* edited by Associazione Toscana Volontari della Libertà, Sezione di Grosseto (Grossetto: 1984), pp. 57–68.

Katz, Robert. *Black Sabbath. A Journey Through a Crime Against Humanity* (New York: Macmillan, 1969), xvii + 398p. See also, but without the chapter: *A conclusion: Sabato nero* (Milan: Rizzoli, 1973), 357p.

Keren Kayemeth-Le-Israel, ed. *In memoria degli ebrei di Firenze deportati e caduti,* Commissione de Firenze (Florence: 1952), 19p.

———. *Death in Rome* (New York: Macmillan, 1967), xvii + 334p. See also *Morte a Roma. Il massacro delle Fosse Ardeatine* (Rome: Editori Riuniti, 1968), 273p.

Kostoris, Sergio. *La risiera di Trieste. Un crimine comune non militare* (Rome: Barulli, 1974), 72p.

La Comunità Israelitica di Ferrara in memoria dei propri martiri (1943–1945) (Ferrara: Comunità Israelitica di Ferrara, 1949), 18p.

La Tragedia degli Ebrei sotto il terrore tedesco. Nove mesi di martirio (Rome: Ciack, 1945), 16p.

Leiber, Roberto S.I. "Pio XII e gli ebrei di Roma 1943–1944," *La Civiltà Cattolica,* CXII, 5 (4 marzo 1961), pp. 449–58.

Libro del ricordo dei martiri (Milan: Comunità Israelitica di Milan, 1960), 31p.

Lops, Carmine. "Gli Ebrei romani dispersi nei Lager nazisti," *QUAD/INT,* 6, 1969–1971, pp. 16–72.

Luksich Jamini, Antonio. "Il salvattagio degli ebrei a Fiume durante la persecuzione nazifascista," *Il Movimento di Liberazione in Italia,* 37, luglio 1955, pp. 44–47.

Martini, Massimo. *Il trauma della deportazione. Ricerca psicologica sui sopravvissuti italiani ai campi di concentramento nazisti* (Milan: ANED-Mondadori, 1983), 203p.

Mayda, Giuseppe. "La deportazione degli ebrei italiani," *Il dovere di testimoniare. Perché non vada perduta la memoria dei campi di annientamento della criminale dottrina nazista* (Turin: Consiglio regionale del Piemonte-ANED, 1984), pp. 38–50.

Miccoli, Giovanni. *Fra mito della cristianità e secolarizzazione. Studi sul rapporto chiesa-società nell'età contemporanea,* (Casale Monferrato: Marietti, 1985), vi + 510p., ch. IV, pp. 131–337: "La Santa Sede nella II guerra mondiale: il problema dei 'silenzi' di Pio XII."

Michaelis, Meir. "La persecuzione degli ebrei," *Annali della Fondazione Luigi Micheletti,* II, 1986, pp. 367–85.

Morelli, Dario, ed. "La persecuzione degli ebrei," *Annali della Fondazione Luigi Micheletti,* II, 1986, pp. 367–85.

Morelli, Valeria. *I deportati italiani nei campi di sterminio 1943–45* (Milan: Artigianelli, 1965), 494p.

Morley, John F. *Vatican Diplomacy and the Jews during the Holocaust 1939–1943* (New York: Ktav, 1980), xvii + 327p. (ch. X, pp. 166–94: "Italy").

Nissim, Davide. "La campagna razziale. L'aiuto agli israeliti nel Biellese," *Il Movimento di liberazione nel Biellese. Studi e documenti*, edited by Centro Studi per la Storia della Resistenza nel Biellese (Biella: 1957), pp. 89–94.

Novitch, Miriam. "Nuovi documenti sulla deportazione degli ebrei italiani," *QUAD/INT*, 2, 1965, pp. 85–90.

Pacifici, Emanuele, ed. "L'Ospedale e la casa di riposo israelitici di Roma durante l'occupazione tedesca," *QUAD/INT*, 10, 1978–1982, pp. 65–70.

Perrone Capano, Renato. *Delitti di fascisti pseudorepubblicani (Roma 1943–1945)* (Naples: Berisio, 1972), 153p. Ch. V, pp. 95–112, "Delazione o consegna di ebrei ai tedeschi per i campi di concentramento."

Picciotto Fargion, Liliana. "La deportazione degli ebrei dall'Italia," *SPOSTAMENTI (1987)*, pp. 297–313.

————. "Eli ebrei in Italia tra persecuzione e sterminio. 1943–1945," *Notiziario dell'Istituto Storico della Resistenza in Cuneo e Provicia*, n. 28, 2nd semester 1985, pp. 25–42.

————. *L'occupazione tedesca e gli ebrei di Roma. Documenti e fatti* (Rome-Milan: Carucci-CDEC, 1979), 207p.

————. "Polizia tedesca ed ebrei nell'Italia occupata," *Rivista di Storia Contemporanea*, XIII, 3, luglio 1984, pp. 456–73.

Presidenza Del Consiglio Dei Ministri. *Elenchi nominativi delle domande accolte per gli indennizzi a cittadini italiani colpiti a misure di persecuzione nazionalsocialiste di cui alla legge 6 febbraio 1963, n. 404*, supplemento ordinario alla "Gazzetta Ufficiale" n. 130 del 22 maggio 1968, 766p.

Romano, Giorgio. "Una testimonianza sul 'capitolo' italiano al processo Eichmann," *RMI*, XXVIII, 3–4, marzo–aprile 1962, pp. 238–47.

Sala, Dante. *Oltre l'Olocausto. 105 ebrei strappati alla deportazione* (Milan: Movimento per la Vita, 1979), 135p.

Scalpelli, Adolfo. "L'Ente di Gestione e Liquidazione Immobiliare: note sulle conseguenze economiche della persecuzione razziale," *QUAD/EBR (1962)*, pp. 92–104.

Schiffrer, Carlo. *La Risiera* (Trieste: Associazione Nazionale Famiglie Caduti e Dispersi in Guerra—Sezione provinciale di Trieste, 1961), 20p. Slightly expanded version of the article published in *Trieste*, VIII, 44, luglio–agosto 1961, pp. 21–24.

Schwarzenberg, Claudio. *Kappler e le fosse Ardeatine* (Palermo: Celebes, 1977), 139p.

Segre, Renata. "Appunti sulle persecuzioni antisemite e sulla vita delle Comunità israelitiche nell'Italia occupata," *Rassegna del Lazio*, XII, 1965 (fascicolo speciale), pp. 100–106.

Steurer, Leopold. "La deportazione dall'Italia. Bolzano," *SPOSTAMENTI (1987)*, pp. 407–44.

Succi, Terenzio. "Un campo di sterminio in Italia," *DIFESA (1978)*, pp. 1440–53.

Tagliacozzo, Michael. "La Comunità di Roma sotto l'incubo della svastica. La grande razzia del 16 ottobre 1943," *QUAD/EBR (1963)*, pp. 8–37 (see also with modifications: "La razzia degli ebrei di Roma il 16 ottobre 1943" (in Hebrew), *Scritti in memoria di Enzo Sereni. Saggi sull'Ebraismo Romano*, Daniel Carpi, Attilio Milano, Umberto Nahon, eds. (Jerusalem: Fondazione Sally Mayer, 1970), pp. 252–80 of the Hebrew segment; see also updated and summarized "La persecuzione degli ebrei a Roma," in Picciotto Fargion, Liliana, *L'occupazione tedesca e gli ebrei di Roma. Documenti e fatti,* (Rome-Milan: Carucci-CDEC, 1979), pp. 149–71.

———. "Le responsabilità di Kappler nella tragedia degli ebrei di Roma," *RMI*, XXXVI, 7–9, luglio–settembre 1970, pp. 389–414.

Uffreduzzi, Marcella. *Il viale dei giusti. Solidarietà verso gli ebrei e persecuzione nazista* (Rome: Città Nuova, 1985), 164p.

Un mondo fuori dal mondo. Indagine DOXA fra i reduci dai campi nazisti (Florence: Nuova Italia, 1971), xix + 366p.

Vaccari, Ilva. *Il tempo di decidere. Documenti e testimonianze sui rapporti tra il clero e la Resistenza* (Modena: CIRSEC, 1968), 555p. Ch. V, pp. 75–99: "Gli ebrei."

Valabrega, Guido. "Ultime lettere di deportati ebrei," *QUAD/INT*, 1, 1964, pp. 61–73; see also *VAL/EBR (1974)*, pp. 123–138.

———. "Appunti sulla persecuzione antisemita in Italia durante l'occupazione nazista," *Il Movimento di Liberazione in Italia*, 74, gennaio–marzo 1964, pp. 20–46. See also *VAL/EBR (1974)*, pp. 89–122.

B6. The Fate of Individual Jewish Communities, 1938–1945

Bonfiglioli, Renzo. "Gli ebrei a Ferrara dal fascismo alla liberazione," *Competizione democratica*, I, 2, aprile 1955, pp. 13–23.

Brizzolari, Carlo. *Gli ebrei nella storia di Genova* (Genoa: Sabatelli, 1971), 379p.

Burmeister, Karl Heinz and Steinhaus, Federico. *Contributo per una storia della Comunità israelitica di Merano. Beiträge zu einer Geschichte der Jüdischen Kultusgemeinde von Meran* (Trento: centro culturale 'Anna Frank,' 1987), 100p.

Cavaglion, Alberto. "Memorie ebraiche a Cuneo," *Notiziario dell'Istituto Storico della Resistenza in Cuneo e Provincia*, n. 28, 2nd semestre 1985, pp. 139–45.

Gherardi Bon, Silva. *La persecuzione antiebraica a Trieste (1938–1945)* (Udine: Del Bianco, 1972), 269p.

Giannantoni, Franco. *Fascismo, guerra e società nella Repubblica Sociale Italiana (Varese 1943–1945)* (Milano: Angeli, 1984), xxix + 874p. (ch. X, pp. 233–83: "Gli ebrei").

Irico, Nicoletta and Muncinelli, Adriana. "Vittime della speranza. Gli ebrei a Saluzzo dal 1938 al 1945," *Notiziario dell'Istituto Storico della Resistenza in Cuneo e Provincia*, n. 28, 2nd semestre 1985, pp. 59–116.

Jona, Salvatore. "La persecuzione degli ebrei a Genova," *Genova*, XLV, aprile 1965, pp. 54–67. Also published as an extract: (Genoa, 1965), 15p.

Lorenzetti, Marcella. "La Comunità israelitica di Livorno durante il fascismo," *QUAD/INT*, 7, 1973–74, pp. 15–32.

Morgani, Teodoro. *Ebrei di Fiume e di Abbazia 1441–1945* (Rome: Carucci, 1979), 158p.

Norsa, Ugo. "La persecuzione nazifascista degli ebrei mantovani, La Resistenza mantovana 1919–1945," (Mantova: Comitato per il monumento alla Resistenza, 1968), pp. 119–21.

Pandolfi, Paola. *Ebrei a Firenze nel 1943, persecuzione e deportazione* (Florence: Edizioni Sea Dupliart, 1980), 88p.

Pardo, Lucio. "Lontano da qui, chissà dove, chissà quando . . . Vicende di Ebrei a Bologna quarant'anni fa . . . ," *Strenna Storica Bolognese*, XXXV, 1985, pp. 243–54.

Pavoncello, Nello. *Gli ebrei in Verona (dalle origini al secolo XX)* (Verona: Vita Veronese, 1960), 108p.

Peano, Elena. "Gli ebrei di Mondovì 1938–1945: alcune vicende," *Notizia-rio dell'Istituto Storico della Resistenza in Cuneo e Provincia*, n. 28, 2nd semestre 1985, pp. 129–38.

Perrone Capano, Renato. *La Resistenza in Roma* (Napoli: Macchiaroli, 1963), 2 vol., 514+581p. (ch. IX, vol. II, pp. 85–155: "La lotta contro gli ebrei in Roma occupata."

Picciotto, Liliana. "Vicende di donne ebree in Emilia Romagna sotto il fascismo e il nazismo," *La donna nel ventennio fascista (1919–1943)*, Ilva Vaccari, ed. (*Donne e Resistenza in Emilia Romagna*, 1) (Milan: Vangelista, 1978), pp. 255–76.

Reitano, Angela. "La persecuzione razziale," *Il coraggio del no. Figure e fatti della Resistenza nella provincia di Pavia*, Ugoberto Alfassio Gri-maldi, ed. (Pavia: Amministrazione provinciale di Pavia, 1976), pp. 105–36.

Roccia, Domenico. *Il giellismo vercellese* (Vercelli: Sesia, 1949), 280p. (Pp. 135–58: "Persecuzioni contro gli Ebrei.")

Sarasso, Terenzio. *Storia degli ebrei a Vercelli* (Vercelli: Comunità israe-litica di Vercelli, 1974), 151p.

Sereni, Paolo. "Gli anni della persecuzione razziale a Venezia: Appunti per una storia," *Venezia Ebraica. Atti delle prime giornate di studio sull'ebraismo veneziano (Venice, 1976–80)*, Umberto Fortis, ed. (Rome: Carucci, 1982), pp. 129–51.

———. "Della Comunità ebraica a Venezia durante il fascismo," *La Re-sistenza nel veneziano*, Giannantonio Paladini e Maurizio Reberschak, eds. (Venice: Università di Venezia, Comune di Venezia e Istituto veneto per la storia della Resistenza, 1984), pp. 503–40.

Volli, Gemma. "Trieste 1938–1945," *QUAD/EBR (1963)*, pp. 38–50.

Waagenaar, Sam. *Il Ghetto sul Trevere* (Milano: Mondadori, 1972), 395p. See also *The Pope's Jews* (La Salle: Library Press Book, 1974), xiv+487p.

Zamorani, Germana. "Gli ebrei a Ferrara dalle leggi razziali alle deporta-zioni," *Partiti politici e CLN*, Pietro Alberghi, ed. *Atti del Convegno sull'Emilia Romagna nella Guerra di Liberazione, vol. II* (Bari: De Donato, 1976), pp. 631–48.

Zavatto, Pietro. *Il vescovo Antonio Santin e il razzismo nazifascista a Trieste (1938–1945)* (Quarto d'Altino: Rebellato, 1977), 91p.

B7. Italian Authorities and Jews Outside Italy (Colonies, Occupied Zones, Diplomacy, etc.), 1938–1943

Abitbol, Michel. *Les Juifs d'Afrique du Nord sous Vichy* (Paris: Maison-neuve et Larose, 1983), 220p.

Brand, E. "The Attitude of the Italians Towards the Jews in the Occupied Territories," in *Yad Vashem Bulletin*, 6–7, June 1960, pp. 17–18.

Carpi, Daniel. "Notes on the History of the Jews in Greece during the Holocaust Period. The Attitude of the Italians (1941–1943)," *Festschrift in Honor of Dr. George S. Wise* (Tel Aviv: Tel Aviv University, 1981), pp. 25–62. Also, with a documented appendix: "Nuovi documenti per la storia dell'Olocausto in Grecia. L'atteggiamento degli italiani (1941–1943)," *Michael: On the History of the Jews in the Diaspora*, VII, 1981, pp. 119–200.

———. "Ma'asseh ha-hatzalah shel yehudim b'ezor ha-kibbush ha-italki b'Kroatia," in *Nissiyonot u-f'ulot hatzalah b'tekufat ha-shoah*, Yisrael Gutman, ed. (Jerusalem, 1976), pp. 382–432. See also "The Rescue of

Jews in the Italian Zone of Occupied Croatia," *Rescue Attempts During the Holocaust. Proceedings of the Second Yad Vashem International Historical Conference, April 1974*, Yisrael Gutman and Efraim Zuroff, eds. (Jerusalem, 1977), pp. 465–525.

De Felice, Renzo. *Ebrei in un paese arabo. Gli ebrei nella Libia contemporanea tra colonialismo, nazionalismo arabo e sionismo (1835–1970)* (Bologna: Il Mulino, 1978), 464p. See also: *Jews in an Arab Land. Libya, 1835–1970* (Austin: University of Texas Press, 1985), x + 406p.).

Diamant, Zanvel. "Jewish Refugees on the French Riviera," *YIVO Annual of Jewish Social Science*, VIII, 1953, pp. 264–80.

Franco, Hizkia M. *Les Martyrs Juifs de Rhodes et de Cos* (Elisabethville: Congrégation Israélite du Katanga, 1952), 173p.

Herzer, Ivo. "How Italians Rescued Jews," *Midstream* (June/July 1983), 35–38.

Jezernik, Božidar. "La vita quotidiana nei campi d'internamento," *Qualestoria*, XII, 3, dicembre 1984, pp. 34–50.

Klarsfeld, Serge. *Vichy-Auschwitz. Le rôle de Vichy dans la solution finale de la question juive en France. 1943–1944* (Paris: Fayard, 1985), 408p.

Kovačić, Ivo. *Koncentracioni logor Kampor na Rabu 1942–1943* (Rijeka: Centar za Historiju Radničkog Pokreta i NOR-a Istre, Hrvatskog Primorja i Gorskog Kotara i Općinska Konferencija SSRN Rab, 1983), 126p.

Loi, Salvatore. "L'esercito italiano di fronte alle persecuzioni razziali," *Revue Internationale d'Histoire Militaire*, 1978, pp. 276–87.

Mazor, Michel. "Les Juifs dans la clandestinité sous l'occupation italienne en France," *Le Monde Juif*, XXVI, 59, juillet–september 1970, pp. 21–31.

Minerbi, Sergio I. "Il progetto di un insediamento ebraico in Etiopia (1936–1943)," *Storia Contemporanea*, XVII, 6, dicembre 1986, pp. 1083–1137.

Molho, Michael, ed. *In Memoriam. Hommage aux Victimes Juives des Nazis en Gréce*. See also second edition revised and expanded by Joseph Nehama (Salonica: Communauté Israélite de Thessalonique, 1973), 469p.

Morelli, Anne. "Les diplomates italiens en Belgique et la 'question juive,' 1938–1943," *Bulletin de l'Institut Historique Belge de Rome*, 53–54, 1983–84, pp. 357–407.

Panicacci, Jean-Louis. "Les Juifs et la question juive dans les Alpes-Maritimes de 1939 à 1945," *Récherches Regionales. Côte d'Azur et contrées limitrophes*, 1983, 4, pp. 239–331.

Picciotto Fargion, Liliana. "Il problema internazionale dei profughi negli anni trenta e la soluzione etiopica di Mussolini," *DECENNIO (1984)*, pp. 287–302.

Poliakov, Léon and Sabille, Jacques. *Yidden under der Italienischer Okkupatzie* (in Yiddish) (Paris: CDJC, 1952), 201p. See also *Jews under the Italian Occupation* (Paris: Editions du Centre, 1955), 207p.; see also *Gli ebrei sotto l'occupazione italiana* (Milan: Comunità, 1956), xvii + 187p. The book contains reprints of Poliakov, Léon, *La condition des Juifs en France sous l'occupation italienne* (Paris: Editions du Centre, 1946), 174p.; and of Sabille, Jacques, *L'attitude des Italiens . . .* , three articles in *Le Monde Juif*, V, 1951, later reprinted in *MEMOIRE (1987)*, pp. 120–32; the essay by the first author is slightly revised in the text and documentation; the three articles have been substantially modified.

Pommerin, Reiner. "Le controversie di politica razziale nei rapporti dell'Asse Roma-Berlino (1938–1943)," *Storia Contemporanea*, X, 4–5, ottobre 1979, pp. 925–40.

Potočnik, Franc. *Il campo di sterminio fascista: l'isola di Rab* (Turin: ANPI, 1979), 185p. (translation).

Romano, Jaša. *Jevreji Jugoslavije 1941–1945. Žrtve Genocida i Učesnici NOR* (Jews of Yugoslavia 1941–1945. Victims of Genocide and Participants in the War of National Liberation) (Belgrade: Savez Jevrejskih Opština Jugoslavije, 1980), 590p.

Sabille, Jacques. *Les Juifs de Tunisie sous Vichy et l'Occupation* (Paris: Editions du Centre, 1954), 188p.

Shelah, Menachem. *Heshbon Damim. Hatzalah yehudei Kroatia al-iedei ha-italkim 1941–1943 (Blood Account. The Rescue of Croatian Jews by the Italians 1941–1943)* (Tel Aviv: Sifriat Poalim, 1986), 188p.

Steinberg, Lucien. *Les autorités allemandes en France Occupée* (Paris: CDJC, 1966), 355p. (III, pp. 193–223: "Les autorités italiennes en France occupée face à l'action antijuive").

———. "Le batallion juif de l'Ile de Rab," *Le Monde Juif*, XXV, 54, avril–juin 1969, pp. 43–47. See also *MEMOIRE (1987)*, pp. 319–23.

Trevisan Semi, Emanuela. *Allo specchio dei Falascià. Ebrei ed etnologi durante il colonialismo fascista* (Florence: Giuntina, 1987), xii + 166p.

Verax (pseudonym for Roberto Ducci). "Italiani ed ebrei in Jugoslavia," in *Politica Estera*, I, 9, settembre 1944, pp. 21–29.

B8. Italian Jews Outside Italy

Fano, Angelo. "L'Alijàh dall'Italia dal 1928 al 1955," *RMI*, XXI, 7, luglio 1955, pp. 263–76.

Garosci, Aldo. *Storia dei fuorusciti* (Bari: Laterza, 1953), 308p.

Levi, Alessandro. "I campi universitari italiani in Svizzera (1944–1945)," *Svizzera Italiana*, VII, 62, marzo–aprile 1947, pp. 93–101.

Levi, Leo. "Cenni sull' 'Aliàth Hanòar' dall'Italia," *Aliàth Hanòar' presente e futuro d'Israele*, (Milan: Bollettino della Comunità Israelitica di Milano e Comitato italiano per l'"Aliàth Hanòar," 1953), pp. 61–69.

Milano, Attilio. *Storia degli ebrei italiani nel Levante* (Florence: Israel, 1949), 226p. (ch. XI, pp. 201–11: "L'ultima 'ascesa' in Palestina").

Montagnana, Marcello. "I rifugiati ebrei italiani in Australia e il movimento antifascista 'Italia Libera' (1942–1946)," *Notiziario dell'Istituto Storico della Resistenza in Cuneo e Provincia*, 31, giugno 1987, pp. 5–114.

Prezzolini, Giuseppe. *America in pantofole. Un impero senza imperialisti. Ragguagli intorno alla transformazione degli Stati Uniti dopo le guerre mondiali* (Florence: Vallecchi, 1950), 447p. (Pp. 341–375: "L'immigrazione degli ebrei italiani dopo il 1938.")

Roth, Cecil. "Reminiscenze sugli ebrei italiani durante le loro traversie," *RMI*, XXXI, 5, maggio 1965, pp. 204–08.

Sarfatti, Michele. "Il 'Comitato di soccorso per i deportati politici e razziali' di Losanna (1944–1945)," *Ricerche Storiche*, IX, n. 2–3, maggio–dicembre 1979, pp. 463–483.

———. "Dopo l'8 settembre: gli ebrei e la rete confinaria italo-svizzera," *RMI*, XLVII, 1–6, gennaio–giugno 1981, pp. 150–73.

Scarantino, Anna. "La comunità ebraica in Egitto fra le due guerre mondiali," *Storia Contemporanea*, XVII, 6, dicembre 1986, pp. 1033–82.

B9. Jewish Participation in Anti-Fascism and the Resistance; Aid Organizations

(a) Jewish Participation in Anti-Fascism and the Resistance

Formiggini, Gina. *Stella d'Italia Stella di David. Gli ebrei dal Risorgimento alla Resistenza* (Milan: Mursia, 1970), 470p.

Luzzatto, Guido Ludovico. "La partecipazione all'antifascismo in Italia e all'estero dal 1918 al 1938," *QUAD/EBR (1962)*, pp. 32–44.

———. "Gli ebrei e l'opposizione al fascismo," *RMI*, XXXI, 4, aprile 1965, pp. 151–59.

Picciotto Fargion, Liliana. "Sul contributo di ebrei alla Resistenza italiana," *RMI*, XLVI, 3–4, marzo–aprile 1980, pp. 132–46.

———. "La partecipazione ebraica alla Resistenza," *EBR/IT (1974)*, pp. 47–51.

Ravenna, Eloisa. "Relazione sulla partecipazione degli ebrei alla Resistenza in Itala," *Jewish Resistance during the Holocaust. Proceedings of the Conference on Manifestations of Jewish Resistance. Jerusalem, April 7–11, 1968* (Jerusalem: Yad Vashem, 1971), pp. 485–88.

Sarfatti, Michele. "Ebrei nella Resistenza ligure," *Atti del Convegno La Resistenza in Liguria e gli Alleati. Genova, marzo 1985* (Genoa: 1988, to be published).

Sorani, Settimio. *La partecipazione ebraica alla Resistenza in Toscana e il contributo ebraico nella Seconda Guerra Mondiale* (Florence: Giuntina, 1981), 31p.

Steinberg, Lucien. *La Révolte des Justes. Les Juifs contre Hitler. 1933–1945* (Paris: Fayard, 1970), 605p. Ch. III, pp. 97–135: "Dans l'Italie fasciste." See also *The Jews against Hitler. Not as a Lamb* (London: Gordon and Cremonesi, 1978), ix + 358p.

Treves, Piero. "Antifascisti ebrei od antifascismo ebraico?" *RMI*, XLVII, 1–6, gennaio–giugno 1981, pp. 138–49.

Valabrega, Guido. "Aspetti della partecipazione di ebrei italiani alla seconda guerra mondiala," *VAL/EBR (1974)*, pp. 139–55.

Vitale Massimo, Adolfo. *The Destruction and Resistance of the Jews in Italy* (in Yiddish), *YIVO Bletter*, New York, XXXVII, 1953, pp. 198–204. Also in English, Suhl, Yuri, *They Fought Back. The Story of the Jewish Resistance in Nazi Europe* (New York: Crown, 1967), pp. 298–303; in Italian, with the title "Persecuzione e Resistenza degli ebrei in Italia," in: Suhl, Yuri, *Ed essi si ribellarono. Storia della resistenza ebraica contro il nazismo* (Milan: Mursia, 1969), pp. 323–28.

Volli, Gemma. "Gli ebrei nella lotta antifascista," *Emilia*, VII, 8–9, agosto–settembre 1955, pp. 226–30.

(b) Aid Organizations

Fano, Giuseppe. "Cenni sulla Constituzione del Comitato Italiano di Assistenza agli Emigranti Ebrei. Riassunto aggiornato sull'attività del Comitato negli anni 1938–1943," *RMI*, XXI, n. 10–11, ottobre–novembre 1965, pp. 494–530.

Leone, Massimo. *Le organizzazioni di soccorso ebraiche in età fascista (1918–1945)* (Rome: Carucci, 1983), xv + 295p.

Sorani, Settimio. *L'Assistenza ai profughi ebrei in Italia (1933–1947). Contributo alla storia della Delasem*, Amedeo Tagliacozzo, ed. (Rome: Carucci, 1983), 328p.

B10. Jewish Testimonies of the Persecutions

(a) Collections of Testimonies

Bellak, Giorgina and Giovanni Melodia, eds. *Donne e bambini nei lager nazisti. Testimonianze dirette* (Milan: ANED, 1960), 126p.

Bravo, Anna and Daniele Jalla, eds. *La vita offesa. Storia e memoria dei Lager nazisti nei racconti di duecento sopravvissuti* (Milan: Angeli, 1987), 438p.

Caracciolo, Nicola. *Gli ebrei e l'Italia durante la guerra 1940–1945* (Rome: Bonacci, 1986), 226p.

Morgani, Tedoro. *. . . Quarant'anni dopo* (Rome: Carucci, 1986) 188p.

Ottani, Giancarlo. *Un popolo piange. La tragedia degli ebrei italiani* (Milan: Giovene, 1945) 186p.

(b) Autobiographies

Artom, Emanuele. *Diari. Gennaio 1940–febbraio 1944*, Paola De Benedetti and Eloisa Ravenna, eds. (Milan: CDEC, 1966), 182p.

Basilea, Sandra. *Sei viva Anne?* (Bologna: Cappelli, 1956), 157p.

Bemporad, Memo. *Le macine. Storia di una famiglia israelita negli ultimi 60 anni di vita italiana* (Rome: Carucci, 1984), 294p.

Benby, D. *'Je reviens du camp de Bergenbelsen.' Récit d'un rescapé* (Istanbul: Kâgit ve Basim Isleri, 1945), 35p.

Berenson, Bernard. *Rumour and Reflection* (New York: Simon and Schuster, 1952), xi + 461p. See also *Echi e riflessioni (Diario 1941–1944)* (Milan: Mondadori, 1950), 476p.

Campagnano, Hulda. "Ladòr ashèr lo iadà. Corotèa shel em zeirà beshanà poralìt begolàt Italia" (Jerusalem: Ben-Zvi, 1981), 70p. See also "E ne parlerai ai tuoi figli . . . Storia di una madre ebrea a Firenze negli anni 1943–1944," *Scritti in memoria di Nathan Cassuto*, Daniel Carpi et al., eds. (Jerusalem: Kedem-Yad Leyakkirenu, 1986), pp. 101–75.

Cavaliere, Alberto. *I campi della morte in Germania nel racconto di una sopravvissuta* (Milan: Sonzogno, 1945), 92p.

Della Seta, Fabio. *L'incendio del Tevere* (Trapani: Celebes, 1969), 221p.

Eisenstein, Maria. *L'internata numero 6. Donne fra i reticolati del campo di concentramento* (Rome: De Luigi, 1944), 165p.

Fargion, Maria Luisa. *Lungo le acque tranquille* (Milan: Pan, 1979), 352p.

Fermi, Laura. *Atoms in the Family. My Life with Enrico Fermi* (Chicago: University of Chicago Press, 1954), ix + 267p. Also *Atomi in famiglia* (Milan: Mondadori, 1954), 336p.

Halpern, Bronka. *Keren or ba-chashekha* (Jerusalem: Rubin Nass, 1967), 178p.

Herman, Marco. *Da Leopoli a Torino. Diario di un ragazzo ebreo nella seconda guerra mondiale* (Cuneo: Arciere, 1984), 92p.

Jani, Emilio. *Mi ha salvato la voce. Auschwitz 180046* (Milan: Ceschina, 1960), 163p.

Jona, Salvatore. *Resistenza disarmata. Cadibrocco (Liguria) 1943–45,* (Genoa: ERGA, 1975), 155p.

Levi, Enzo. *Memorie di una vita (1889–1947)* (Modena: STEM Mucchi, 1972), 238p.

Levi, Montalcini Rita. *Elogio dell'imperfezione* (Milan: Garzanti, 1987), 228p.

Levi, Primo. *La tregua* (Torino: Einaudi: 1963), 255p. See also *The Truce* (London: Bodley Head); also, *The Reawakening* (Boston: Little Brown, 1965), 222p.

————. *Se questo è un uomo* (Turin: De Silva, 1947), 197p. Also (Turin: Einaudi, 1958), 204p. See also *If this is a Man* (London and New York: Orion, 1959), 206p.

————. *Il sistema periodico* (Turin: Einaudi, 1975), 242p. Also *The Periodic Table* (New York: Schocken, 1984), 233p.

Lombroso, Silvia. *Si può stampare. Pagine vissute 1938–1945* (Rome: Dalmatia, 1945), 231p.

Lopez, Guido. *I verdi, i viola e gli arancioni* (Milan: Mondadori, 1972), 282p.

Milano, Aldo. *Diario* (Sao Paulo: Livraria Nobel, 1917), 52p.

Millu, Liana. *Il fumo di Birkenau* (Milan: Mondadori, 1957), 179p. Also (Florence: Giuntina, 1979), 179p.

————. *I ponti di Schwerin* (Poggibonsi: Lalli, 1978), 260p.

Modigliani, Carlo. *Una croce e una stella. Dal mio diario* (Milan: Gastaldi, 1959), 141p.

Modigliani, Piero. *I nazisti a Roma. Dal diario di un ebreo* (Rome: Città Nuova, 1984), 103p.

Morpurgo, Fano Letizia. *Diario. Ricordi di prigionia* (Trieste: Comunità Israelitica di Venezia, 1966), 85p.

Morpurgo, Luciano. *Caccia all'uomo! Vita, sofferenze e beffe. Pagine di diario 1938–1944* (Rome: Dalmatia, 1946), 359p.

Morpurgo, Marcello. *Valdirose. Memorie della comunità ebraica di Gorizia* (Udine: Del Bianco, 1986), 221p. Several passages of the book were published under the title "Lavoro obbligatorio" and "Difesa territoriale" in "Ricordi di un goriziano," *QUAD/EBR (1963)*, pp. 158–64.

Nahon, Umberto, ed. *Per non morire. Enzo Sereni: vita, scritti, testimonianze* (Milan: Fedreazione Sionistica Italiana, 1973), 279p.

Nissim, Luciana. "Ricordi della casa dei morti," Luciana Nissim and Pelagina Lewinska, eds., *Donne contro il mostro* (Turin: Ramella, 1946), pp. 17–58.

Ottolenghi, Minerbi Marta. *La colpa di essere nati. Romanzo* (Milan: Gastaldi, 1954), 399p.

Piazza, Bruno. *Perchè gli altri dimenticano* (Milan: Feltrinelli, 1956), 201p.

Roberta, Di Camerino. *R, come Roberta*, Marco Mascardi, ed. (Milan: Mondadori, 1981), 186p.

Rocca, Enrico. La distanza dai fatti (Milan: Giordano, 1964), 256p.

Sacerdoti, Giancarlo. *Ricordi di un ebreo bolognese. Illusioni e delusioni 1929–1945* (Rome: Bonacci, 1983), 169p.

Saralvo, Corrado. *Più morti più spazio* (Milan: Baldini e Castoldi, 1969), 324p.

Segre, Augusto. *Memorie di vita ebraica. Casale Monferrato-Roma-Gerusalemme 1918–1960* (Rome: Bonacci, 1979), 464p.

Segre, Vittorio. *Storia di un ebreo fortunato* (Milan: Bompiani, 1985), 237p. Also, *Memoirs of a Fortunate Jew. An Italian Story* (Bethesda: Adler, 1987), 273p.

Tedeschi, Giuliana. *Questo povero corpo* (Milan: EDIT, 1946), 125p.; a new edition is planned for 1988.

Toaff, Elio. *Perfidi giudei, fratelli maggiori* (Milan: Mondadori, 1987), 249p.

Treves, Benvenuta, ed. *Tre vite dall'ultimo '800 alla metà del '900. Studi e memorie di Emilio, Emanuele, Ennio Artom* (Florence: Israel, 1954), 254p.

Valech Capozzi, Alba. *A.24029* (Siena: Soc. Ans Poligrafica, 1946), 101p.

Glossary

Adriatisches Küstenland
Adriatic Littoral, a region including Udine, Gorizia, Trieste, Pola, Fiume, and Ljubljana, annexed to Germany after the armistice of September 8, 1943

Aliyah emigration to Palestine/Israel, (literally, "ascent" in Hebrew)

American Jewish Joint Distribution Committee popularly referred to as "Joint," American philanthropic organization aiding Jews abroad

Anschluss the annexation of Austria by Hitler in 1938

Axis coalition of states headed by Germany, Italy, and Japan, 1936–1945

Delasem *Delegazione Assistenza Emigranti Ebrei* (Delegation for assistance to émigrés [refugees]), Italian Jewish aid organization founded in December 1939

Einsatzgruppen special Nazi squads whose mission was to kill Jews

Halutz Zionist pioneer/settler

Hashomer Hatzair Socialist Zionist youth movement

Hehalutz federation of Zionist pioneering (halutz) organizations

Histadrut Zionist labor federation

italianità Italian national character, spirit, or feelings

Judenaktion roundup of Jews, in Nazi parlance

Kehillah Jewish community (leadership)

Lager From the German *Lager* (camp), implying concentration camp; Italians use the word to distinguish between Nazi concentration (extermination) camps and the Fascist internment camps, most of which had tolerable conditions

Mittelstand elements of German society consisting of small farmers, artisans, small businessmen, lower levels of officialdom and professionals supporting the conservative and anti-Semitic political cause in the final years of the nineteenth century

Ostjuden Jews from eastern Europe

Pentcho riverboat carrying young, mostly Czech Jews bound for Palestine. It ran aground in the Aegean, the passengers were saved by an Italian warship and the refugees were transferred to the Ferramonti camp

Podestà appointed mayor/head of local administration under Fascism

Prefetto (prefect) representative of the government in each province

Questura police office, police headquarters

Reichssicherheitshauptamt (RSHA) Reich Security Main Office in which the SS police (SD) was merged with the state police (SIPO). Gestapo was part of the SIPO

SIPO-SD see RSHA

Repubblica Sociale Italiana (RSI),
also known as *Repubblica di
Salò* Fascist government
headed by Mussolini under German control, following the Italian surrender
Risorgimento the movement for
the unification of Italy (1848–
1870)
Todt Organization German engineering and construction organization serving the military
Ustaša Croatian extremists who
governed the Nazi puppet "Independent State of Croatia" (NDH)
after the dismemberment of Yugoslavia by the Axis powers in
1941
Wannsee Conference the "Final
Solution of the Jewish Question" was decided at that meeting on January 20, 1942
Wilhelmine Germany the period
under Kaiser Wilhelm II

The SS ranks corresponded to the
military ranks as follows:
Gruppenführer General com-
manding a division
Brigadeführer General com-
manding a brigade
Standartenführer Colonel
Sturmbannführer Major
Hauptsturmführer Captain
Obersturmführer First Lieuten-
ant
Sturmführer Second Lieutenant

Contributors

John Bierman's career as a newspaper and television correspondent has taken him to almost every corner of the world. He is the author of *Righteous Gentile: The Story of Raoul Wallenberg, Missing Hero of the Holocaust* and *Odyssey*.

Paul Bookbinder is Associate Professor of History at the University of Massachusetts in Boston. His most recent publications are "The Holocaust as a Phenomenon in Germany Today," in Sanford Piuske (ed.), *Holocaust Studies Annual*, vol. 3, and "Carl Schmitt vs. Hermann Heller: Totalitarian Dictatorship vs. Parliamentary Democracy," *International Journal of Social Science*. Prof. Bookbinder is an active participant in "Facing History and Ourselves."

Andrew Canepa is a principal in Foreign Trade Associates, an international marketing firm, San Francisco; curator, Italian-American Collection, San Francisco Public Library; author of numerous articles on Jewish emancipation, assimilation, and anti-Semitism in modern Italy.

Carlo Spartaco Capogreco is a pediatrician by profession. He has been active as a historian in researching the story of the internment camp of Ferramonti and has contributed numerous articles, as well as a photographic exhibition. In 1987 he published the book *Ferramonti: La vita e gli uomini del più grande campo d'internamento Fascista*, and in 1988 he founded the Ferramonti Foundation.

Alberto Cavaglion is a graduate of the University of Turin in literature and philosophy. He was awarded a fellowship from the Istituto Italiano per gli Studi Storici "B. Croce" in Naples and a grant from the L. Einaudi Foundation. He published studies on the deportations and survival of Italian Jews, as well as a biography of Italo Svevo. Dr. Cavaglion is a research associate of the Centro di Documentazione Ebraica Contemporanea in Milan.

Liliana Picciotto Fargion is a researcher at the Centro di Documentazione Ebraica Contemporanea in Milan and is completing the *Sepher Hazikaron*, which memorializes the Jewish victims deported from Italy. The book will be published in 1989. She is the author of *L'occupazione tedesca e gli ebrei di Roma* (1979) and has written numerous articles on the Jews under Fascism. Dr. Picciotto Fargion is the editor of the magazine of Jewish culture *La Rassegna Mensile di Israel* and is a contributor to *Italia Contemporanea*.

Robert A. Graham, S.J. is one of the four historians to whom Pope Paul VI assigned the task of editing the wartime papers of the papal secretariat of state. These were published in twelve volumes as *Actes et documents du Saint Siège rélatifs à la Seconde guerre Mondiale*. Dr. Graham also published *Vatican Diplomacy* and since 1966 has contributed diplomatic studies to *La Civiltà Cattolica*.

Josef Ithai lives in the kibbutz Gat, Israel. His detailed memoir, describing the history of the rescue of the youth aliyah group *Yaldey Villa Emma* (*The Children of Villa Emma*), was published in 1983. He also wrote a summary of his book, "Djeca bježe," in *Almanah Saveza Jevrejskih Opština, 1963–1964* (in Serbo-Croatian).

Meir Michaelis is full professor at the Hebrew University of Jerusalem and member of the Institute of Contemporary Jewry. He was lecturer in modern Jewish history, Oranim College (now part of Haifa University) and visiting fellow, St. Anthony's, Oxford. Prof. Michaelis' book *Mussolini and the Jews* and the revised Italian edition (*Mussolini e la questione ebraica*) was awarded Premio Acqui Storia in 1983. Prof. Michaelis has over 70 publications in learned journals and is currently working on two books: *Jews in the Italian Partisan Movement, 1943–1945,* and *Anti-Semitism in Italy, 1900–1945.*

Michele Sarfatti is a researcher at the Archives of the Centro di Documentazione Ebraica Contemporanea in Milan. He published several articles on the Jews during the Nazi-Fascist persecutions and two books on the Resistance in the Valle d'Aosta and on the European pacifist movement.

Menachem Shelah is Senior Lecturer in Contemporary History at Haifa University (Oranim) and Research Fellow at the Yad Vashem Institute in Jerusalem. Most of his publications deal with the Holocaust in Yugoslavia. His book *Blood Account* is about the rescue of the Croatian Jews by the Italians during World War II.

Klaus Voigt is an independent historian affiliated with projects of the Deutsche Forschungsgemeinschaft, Berlin. He was lecturer at the University of Paris III and assistant at the European University Institute in Florence, Italy. He has written extensively on the history of the refugees and émigrés from Nazism. His book *Refuge on Recall: Exile in Italy 1933–1940* was published in February, 1989.

Susan Zuccotti obtained her doctorate in modern European history from Columbia University. Dr. Zuccotti's book *The Italians and the Holocaust: Persecution, Rescue, and Survival* was published in 1987. She is presently doing research on the Holocaust in France.

Index